Africa for Sale?

Afrika-Studiecentrum Series

VOLUME 29

The titles published in this series are listed at brill.com/asc

Africa for Sale?

Positioning the State, Land and Society in Foreign Large-Scale Land Acquisitions in Africa

Edited by

Sandra J.T.M. Evers
Caroline Seagle
Froukje Krijtenburg

BRILL

LEIDEN • BOSTON
2013

Cover illustration: Mountains behind Ampasy Nahampoana, Southeast Madagascar, © C. Seagle.

Library of Congress Cataloging-in-Publication Data

Africa for sale? : positioning the state, land and society in foreign large-scale land acquisitions in Africa / edited by Sandra J.T.M. Evers, Caroline Seagle, Froukje Krijtenburg.
p. cm. — (Afrika-Studiecentrum series ; v. 29)
ISBN 978-90-04-25193-9 (pbk. : alk. paper) — ISBN 978-90-04-25264-6 (e-book) 1. Land use, Rural—Africa. 2. Real property—Foreign ownership—Africa. 3. Farm ownership—Africa. 4. Investments, Foreign—Africa. I. Evers, Sandra. II. Seagle, Caroline. III. Krijtenburg, Froukje, 1956- IV. Series: Afrika-Studiecentrum series ; v. 29.

HD966.A34 2013
333.3096—dc23

2013011078

This publication has been typeset in the multilingual "Brill" typeface. With over 5,100 characters covering Latin, IPA, Greek, and Cyrillic, this typeface is especially suitable for use in the humanities. For more information, please see www.brill.com/brill-typeface.

ISSN 1570-9310
ISBN 978-90-04-25193-9 (paperback)
ISBN 978-90-04-25264-6 (e-book)

This book is printed on acid-free paper.

CONTENTS

LIST OF ILLUSTRATIONS

Andrew et al.

Map

Sapignoli and Hitchcock

Figures

Tables

Adamczewski et al.

Figures

Tables

Map

Buchalik

Map

LIST OF CONTRIBUTORS

AMANDINE ADAMCZEWSKI is an agronomist graduated from INP-ENSAT (*École nationale supérieure d'agronomie de Toulouse*) and specialized in territorial and natural resource management. Currently a Ph.D. student at the CIRAD (*Centre de coopération internationale de recherche agronomique pour le développement*), UR Green (*Gestion des Ressources renouvelables et Environnement*), she is working on the (socio-economic and institutional) impacts of rural land and natural resource regulation policies in Sahelian countries.

NANCY ANDREW is Associate Researcher at the multidisciplinary centre *Les Afriques dans le Monde (CNRS/Sciences-Po-Bordeaux)*. She recently completed research for the NWO-WOTRO project on farm dwellers and private wildlife production in South Africa. Other publications and research areas include land reform and conflict, social and rural development, gender dimensions, food security, smallholder agriculture and globalization.

FEMKE BRANDT is a PhD candidate at VU University Amsterdam. In her dissertation she explores how farm dwellers and commercial farmers reconfigure power and belonging in the Karoo in the context of private farm conversions to wildlife production for trophy hunting. She conducted ethnographic fieldwork in the Karoo during 2009.

LUCJAN BUCHALIK is an ethnologist and specialist in African studies. He was awarded the academic degree of Doctor of Humanities in ethnology in 2008 at Adam Mickiewicz University in Poznań. He is the author of the following books *Niewolnicy kobiet czyli pokrewieństwo żartów Dogonów i Kurumba* ("Women's slaves in other words the affinity of the Dogon and Kurumba jokes") and *Dogon ya gali. Dawny świat* Dogonów ("*Dogon ya gali*. The ancient world of the Dogon").

PERRINE BURNOD is an economist at *UMR Tetis, CIRAD*. She did her PhD thesis on migration and land access in the Comoros islands and completed a post-doc on foreign direct investment in land in Mali and Madagascar in the biofuel sector. She is now working on large-scale land acquisitions in the context of Madagascar in partnership with the Malagasy Land Observatory.

Ruben De Koning (Netherlands) is a freelance consultant specialized in natural resource related conflicts in Africa. He previously worked at the Stockholm International Peace Research Institute (SIPRI) and is a former member of the UN Group of Experts for the DRC.

Robert K. Hitchcock (PhD, Anthropology, University of New Mexico, 1982) is Professor of Geography at Michigan State University, East Lansing, Michigan, USA and a board member of the Kalahari Peoples Fund. Since the 1970s he has worked on issues relating to land use, land rights, development, and resettlement in Africa, the Middle East, and North and South America.

Jean-Yves Jamin, an agronomist at *UMR G-Eau, CIRAD*, did his PhD on land issues in the Office du Niger area in Mali. He works on irrigated land in Maghreb, West-Africa, and South-Asia, and focuses on water and land management.

Dr. Akachi Odoemene is an African Historian trained at the University of Ibadan, Nigeria. Dr. Odoemene is a Research Fellow of both the "South-South Research Grants 2012" (the Africa/Asia/Latin America—APISA/CLACSO/CODESRIA Collaborative Program) and the African Peacebuilding Network (APN) Research Grants (Social Science Research Council [SSRC], New York). He is currently a Senior Lecturer in the Department of History and International Relations, Federal University Otuoke (FUO), Bayelsa State, Nigeria.

Nomalanga Mkhize studied History at Rhodes University. In 2012 she obtained her Ph.D. degree from the University of Cape Town. Her Ph.D. thesis was entitled: "Private game farms and the tenure security of farm workers and dwellers in Cradock—implications for tenure reform in South Africa". She is currently teaching at the Department of History of Rhodes University.

Hermine Papazian is an agronomist who graduated from the Rural Polytechnic Institute of Katibougou , Mali and the National Agronomy Institute of Paris—Grignon, (INA-PG) in France. She specializes in development research, agronomy systems, management of water, operations and agricultural companies. She focuses on the organization and enforcement of abilities of farmers organizations and the valuation of projects.

Gitte Postel has published extensively on South African literature and culture, both as a scholar and a journalist. She obtained her PhD at Leiden University after which she worked as a researcher and lecturer at universities in The Netherlands and South Africa.

Maria Sapignoli (PhD. Essex University, 2012) is an Italian social anthropologist and a research fellow at the Max Planck Institute for Social Anthropology. She has conducted ethnographic work in Botswana and in several international organizations, including the United Nations Permanent Forum on Indigenous Issues. Her current work is on the legal and anthropological aspects of globalization, governance, and development.

Dhoya Snijders is a PhD candidate at the department of Organizational Sciences of VU University Amsterdam. His main research interests are environmental policy, conservation and development, and information infrastructures. He has been engaged in fieldwork in Southern Africa since 2005.

Marja Spierenburg is Associate Professor at the Department of Organization Sciences of VU University Amsterdam. Her research focuses on the role of the private sector in nature conservation and land reforms in Southern Africa. Her publications include 'Sponsoring nature: Environmental philanthropy for nature conservation' (Earthscan 2011, co-authored with Maano Ramutsindela and Harry Wels).

Michael J. Strauss is Professor of International Relations at the *Centre d'Etudes Diplomatiques et Stratégiques (CEDS)* in Paris, where he earned his Ph.D. He focuses on territorial control, notably state leases. His books include 'The Leasing of Guantanamo Bay and The Viability of Territorial Leases in Resolving International Sovereignty Disputes'.

Evelyne Tegomoh holds an MPhil in Visual Anthropology from the University of Tromsoe and has been lecturing at the department of Sociology and Anthropology, University of Buea, Cameroon, since 2004. Before that, she worked with the Norwegian Peace Corps, *Fredskorpset*, attached to the Tromsoe University Museum during which she made the film, 'Let's Share the Beauty'. She is currently a Volkswagen PhD fellow under the research project: 'Human Mobility, Networks and Institutions in the Management of Natural Resources' in Africa at the African Studies Centre, Leiden.

JEAN PHILIPPE TONNEAU, a Geographer at *UMR Tetis, CIRAD*, works on territories and governance, especially in Maghreb, Sahel and Brazil. He studies relations between land tenure, rural activities and societal projects. He has participated in studies about impacts of land reforms in Brazil, focusing on contributions to sustainable development.

BEN WHITE is Emeritus Professor of Rural Sociology at the International Institute of Social Studies in The Hague, and former Professor in Social Sciences at the University of Amsterdam. His main fields of interest are processes of change in agrarian societies, and the anthropology and history of childhood and youth. He is one of the coordinators of the Land Deal Politics Initiative (www.iss.nl/ldpi).

ANNELIES ZOOMERS is Professor of International Development Studies (IDS) at Utrecht University and chair of the IS-academy on land governance for equitable and sustainable development (LANDac). After finishing her PhD, she worked on long and short-term consulting assignments (Worldbank, IFAD, DGIS, ILO, EU, etc.). Since 1995 she was Associate Professor at the CEDLA (Amsterdam), and was Professor of International Migration at the Radboud University (Nijmegen) between 2005 and 2009. She has published extensively on land policies, international migration and sustainable livelihoods.

INTRODUCTION: CONTESTED LANDSCAPES—ANALYSING THE ROLE OF THE STATE, LAND REFORMS AND PRIVATIZATION IN FOREIGN LAND DEALS IN AFRICA[1]

Sandra J.T.M. Evers, Caroline Seagle and Froukje Krijtenburg

The past several decades have witnessed an unprecedented intensification of foreign investments in, and acquisitions of, large swathes of arable land in the global South. Often referred to as 'land grabbing' or 'foreign land acquisitions' (FLAs, herein),[2] millions of hectares are increasingly claimed by and leased out to transnational or domestic entities, governments, multinational private companies, and international organisations (Cotula et al. 2009; Vidal 2010; Smaller and Mann 2009; IIED 2009; Rice 2010). Stemming from broader historical, economic and social trends (Zoomers 2010), FLAs nevertheless reflect a new frontier of land control (Anseeuw et al. 2012, 2; Peluso and Lund 2011). Many financially rich, resource poor countries are now turning to resource rich, financially poor countries to ensure security in food, minerals and energy (Borras and Franco 2012). This is not entirely new; the colonial and pre-colonial period witnessed vast 'grabbing' of territory by outside actors, thus signaling that FLAs may be historically embedded. As part of broader trends in de-territorialization, globalization and market capitalism, the rapid rush to control land stems from multiple converging forces; World Bank and IMF (International Monetary Fund) policies attempting to reverse the impacts of over a decade of SAPs (Structural Adjustment Programmes) through the encouragement of economic liberalization, land privatisation and export-oriented economies have created circumstances favourable to mega-land acquisitions. Within

[1] This volume is the outcome of an international conference held in November 2010 entitled, '*Africa for Sale? Analysing and Theorizing Foreign Land Claims and Acquisitions*' at the University of Groningen. The conference was hosted by the Netherlands Association of African Studies (NVAS). We like to thank the authors of this volume for their feedback on the editorial introduction.

[2] In activist circles but also in academic literature, foreign large-scale land acquisitions are commonly referred to as 'land grabs' as they are often assumed to be illegal and corrupt—colonial hegemony with a new [neoliberal] face. However, this view overlooks the reality that many deals occur through perfectly legal policy structures embedded in positive law. Marx, who first coined the term 'land grabbing' (White et al. 2012: 621) was additionally referring to 'perfectly legal' processes, such as the English and Scottish 'enclosures' and highland clearances.

this context, the rise and embrace of Foreign Direct Investment (FDI) as a means of boosting economic growth has accompanied new regulatory frameworks surrounding land access and reform, and an overall loosening of state policies surrounding private foreign investments (Borras et al. 2011). It is estimated that over 46 million hectares of territory were leased out to or the subject of potential land deals with foreign investors since 2006 (World Bank 2010). Other figures differ, with IFPRI (International Food Policy Research Institute) suggesting that 20 million hectares had been officially transferred to investors by 2009 worldwide (in von Braun and Meinzen-Dick 2009). It is clear, however, that most deals—up to 70%—are occurring in Africa (World Bank 2010), and in total the FAO estimates that 20 million hectares of land have been leased out to private companies, states and businesses in Africa alone (Hallam 2009).

But why the rapid rush for land? While foreign acquisitions of land are nothing new and can be traced back to the colonial period, where control of vast swathes of territory was directly linked to mass production schemes and exports initiated by colonial powers, the past few decades suggest an intensification of foreign direct investment (FDI) in land (Görgen et al. 2009), driven by what Hall (2011b) refers to as the global 'triple-F' dilemma of 'food, fuel and finance'. The 2007/08 financial meltdown, combined with the FAO's 2008 declaration that world food production would have to double by 2050 in order to meet global demand, sparked a worldwide crisis of food security. During this period, the price of food, particularly staple crops such as wheat, rice and maize, skyrocketed, leading foreign investors to speculate that agricultural markets were prime arenas for increased profit-making (Steinberg 2008).[3] Indeed, speculation over the increasing value of arable land is a major driver of FLAs, involving not only private investors but also banks, governments and sovereign wealth funds (Cuffaro and Hallam 2011).[4] Rising food prices, driven by vast investor interests (primarily European private banking and investment firms) in the future of commodity markets, combined with concern of the scarcity of food supplies, led to what the FOE describes as a process of 'excessive speculation' in agricultural markets, fuelling foreign investments in territory that was increasing in value despite nothing happening on the ground (FOE 2012: 13). Many have noted discourses of food scarcity

[3] Much of this price increase related to the growth of biofuels (rather than food) markets.

[4] See Halliday, F. 'Sovereign Wealth Funds: Power vs. Principle' Transnational Institute (10 March 2008). Available from: http://www.tni.org/archives/act/18035, Accessed 31.07.12.

confound the reality that "world food supplies are sufficient to feed the world's population one and a half times over" and obscure a more structural problem of distribution (Weis 2007 in Kay 2012, 6).

Moreover, land is being acquired for various reasons, not just food production. Agricultural markets today include both food and non-food agricultural products, such as sugarcane, palm oil and jatropha plantations: crops eventually processed into biofuels (Borras, McMichael and Scoones 2010). Territorial enclosures for tourism have also led to new enclosures and consolidations of land, as in the case of private game reserves (PGRs) in South Africa (discussed in Andrew et al., this volume). Furthermore, nature conservation initiatives, including REDD (Reducing Emissions from Deforestation and Degradation of Forests), have accelerated land enclosures (Vidal 2008; Corson 2011; De Schutter 2010a), a process which Fairhead, Leach and Scoones (2012) recently coined 'green grabbing'. In turn, large-scale mineral exploitation has intensified in recent years due to the restructuring of mining laws intended to attract foreign investors. Such laws often reflect a shift from nationalization to privatization of the mining industry, and frequently involve joint venture agreements made between foreign companies and host governments (see de Koning, this volume). Linkages between these various land deals are not always evident, though recent scholarship has examined the interdependencies and similarities between multiple types of acquisitions (Borras et al. 2011; Hall 2011a), such as the emerging 'green economy' of large-scale mining, nature conservation and biodiversity offsetting (see Seagle 2012). This suggests that FLAs do not occur discretely but rather as a convergence of trends embedded in broader market liberalization and valuation schemes, globalization and increasing private sector engagement in development (see chapter by Zoomers, this volume).

But while land deals in their current manifestation clearly stem from a neoliberal logic that prioritizes the growth and expansion of free markets, exports and capitalist accumulation, McMichael has observed that FLAs signal a more complex and contradictory process of accumulation embedded in late capitalism: he writes that land deals constitute a

> ... reflex of changing conditions of accumulation: first, as capital's costs of production: (energy) and reproduction (wage-foods) rise in tandem; and second, as finance capital capitalizes offshore agro-food zones as (speculative) substitutes for ecologically exhausted Northern crop lands and as energy crop sites. As such, the land grab provides a lens on the contradictory dynamics of the food regime, which, at one and the same time, situates the land grab as something other than simply a contemporary enclosure of land for capitalist expansion (McMichael 2012, 681–682).

As many FLAs often operate through [renewable] leases (in rare cases full ownership) assigned by the government, what we are seeing is the rapid control—rather than outright 'grab'—of territory by foreign investors (Peluso and Lund 2011). Indeed, this reflects not only rapidly shifting property relations and processes of accumulation, but also an uneven and contradictory food regime (McMichael 2012).

While some projects never come to fruition, others involve not only the transfer of technology, financial capital and employment potential, but also cultural values, very specific ideas about land use and development, and certain labour arrangements. Some states aim to expand national boundaries to create 'enclaves' of development and investment flows in host countries; such has been the case, for instance, with some Chinese investments in Africa and elsewhere (see Nyiri 2009) and the phenomenon of Special Economic Zones (SEZs). Speculative or not, discourses of foreign land control have raised concern among citizens in many host countries. Contrary to widespread accounts, the collapse of the Malagasy government in 2009, spurred by the Daewoo Logistics land deal which would have devoted approximately 1 300 000 hectares to palm oil and maize (Teyssier et al. 2009/2010), was due primarily not to peasant protests but to dissent from civil society organizations and concentrated in Antananarivo, the capital city (Randrianja 2012). Nevertheless, the mediation of the conflict was a symbolic representation of the central government's control over land and natural resources, and assisted Andry Rajoelina in articulating his rationale for ousting incumbent President Marc Ravalomanana (Burnod 2010). It remains uncertain what stage the deal actually was in. (Randrianja 2012). This example suggests that a gap exists in broader discourses of 'land grabs' and actual realities; moreover, the sentiments of the 'local population' are hardly homogeneous and often absent from the debates.

Analysing the Role of the State: Land Reforms and the Restructuring of Rural Landscapes

However, within this vast collection of literature, the role of the state and intermediate actors in triggering, mediating, negotiating, or regulating foreign land deals, while crucial to consider, has surfaced less prominently in the debates (for a recent contribution, see Wolford et al. 2013). Indeed, it is generally agreed that '[a]ny attempt to understand the current dynamics of enclosures would be incomplete without addressing the critical role of the state' (Makki and Geisler 2011, 3). With the impetus of the World Bank, African governments assist foreign investors in engaging in a policy process of titling and commodifying land. Land reforms instigated by the state in compliance with imperatives of Foreign Direct Investment (FDI) policies embraced by the World Bank have created an atmosphere favourable to large-scale land acquisitions. The intensification of reforms has spread, in many cases, across all natural resource sectors—land access and ownership, minerals, water, forests, and various commodities (see Smillie and Létourneau 2009). Some land redistributions take place prior to the large-scale lease of territory, while other reforms occur during or just after the swap of land. Contracts with investors are often negotiated with the central host state, and governments play an important role in paving way for foreign investments.

This volume captures the entire range of state involvement with FLAs and illustrates how these deals reach into every level of interaction that states have, from their relations with other states at one extreme to their relations with local village populations at the other. We focus on how the state, in both historical and contemporary contexts, acts as a crucial actor in creating the fertile ground for foreign investments. Authors in this volume analyze the actors, power structures and regulatory frameworks involved in land deals, and ultimately the consequences for local people—who often face resettlement, livelihood shifts and potential conflicts but who might also find spaces in which to resist foreign control or perhaps benefit from opportunities created. The chapters in this volume make clear that the 'grabbing' of territory has roots in shifting land policy and deeply engrained social, political and economic dynamics and inequalities. In terms of setting the stage (naturally stimulated by international dynamics and institutions), the state plays an important role in negotiating land reforms often geared towards land registration and privatization; these policy shifts often accompany or precede foreign investments in land and facilitate the implementation of large-scale projects. Several chapters, for example, demonstrate the costs and benefits of land reform policies as they affect agricultural land in Botswana (see Sapignoli and Hitchcock, this volume) irrigated land in Mali (Adamczewski et al., this volume) and areas designated as wildlife tourism and hunting sites (see Andrew et al., this volume and Snijders 2012). Contrary to the widespread assumption that foreign actors 'grab' land illegally from weak governments, states often invite outside investments and work in partnership with foreign actors to negotiate the contracts, regulatory measures and implementation phase.[5] FLAs bring up important issues of food sovereignty and the reorganization of rural economics, but also spark issues of state sovereignty, the role of domestic investors in driving enclosures, and state-state bilateral relations (see Strauss, this volume). Authors in this volume present various reflections on and case studies of land deals that specifically accompany state-led land policy shifts, and in doing so, demonstrate how state authority, wealth and control is (re)distributed or (re)concentrated in the event of an acquisition.

Within this context, we are interested in the following questions: While the weakening of the nation-state was a key symptom of neoliberalism, do FLAs signal the resurgence of a new 'neoliberal state' wherein governments play a central role in facilitating enclosures (see Peck and Tickell 2002 and Büscher 2010)? Are we witnessing a new form of state-making and the production of national identity, or an imposition of global forces on domestic modes of production—indeed the 'foreignization of space' (Zoomers 2010)? In other words, do FLAs in fact mask the expansion of state power, as development was once slated to do (see Ferguson 1994), or are we seeing new 'governance states' wherein international actors supersede the state to control social, environmental and political decision-making (Duffy 2006)? While the state plays a crucial role in facilitating, promoting or blocking some mega-land deals, the activities of the state are poorly understood and remain lacking from broader land debates.

The authors in this volume present rich empirical evidence and theoretical reflections on the land grab debate in Africa, revealing varied and complex relations between local communities, foreign entities and various 'faces of the state' (Navaro-Yashin 2011). These state bodies might include local and domestic investors, regional authorities, or civil society groups involved in shifting regulatory frameworks. Authors zoom in on both the global structures and rural transformations taking place as well as the socio-cultural repercussions of land dispossession and resettlement. Many cases show that, contrary to popular media, smallholders and local populations can sometimes resist outside control or even benefit from land deals, often with the help of decentralized state structures. While the state plays an important role as facilitator of large-scale agricultural

[5] A recent special issue of Development and Change (March 2013), edited by Wendy Wolford, Saturnino M. Borras Jr., Ruth Hall, Ian Scoones, and Ben White, provides an important glimpse of the state's role in the global 'land grab' (see Wolford et al. 2013).

investments, both domestic and foreign, it is often a key actor involved in managing local conflicts and social relations. This has not only changed productive relations and land/labour arrangements, but also restructured rural landscapes, lifestyles and social cultural value systems.

The state can be viewed as a broker both prior to and during a land deal in terms of facilitating and implementing land privatization and titling reforms. Land reforms often follow a number of trajectories and are driven by various forces (for detailed typologies, see Borras and Franco [2012], discussed below, and Hall [2011a]). These often result in the redistribution of communal or 'public' land back to the state for lease or sale, and sometimes involve titling or registering land to smallholder groups or individuals (including foreign companies) with claims to land. The central problematic in this regard, however, is the incompatibility between customary land tenure arrangements and those of national law, not to mention the diversity and complexity of land use and access regimes in the countryside. Historically, we are reminded of James Scott's concept of 'legibility' which he used to capture dynamics of land policy change stemming from foreign austerity measures in the 1970s. Legibility refers to a practice wherein states attempt to take "exceptionally complex, illegible, and local social practices, such as land tenure customs or naming customs" and generate a 'standard grid' whereby they could be "centrally recorded and monitored" (Scott 1998, 2). Legibility is thus a process of visibility, of enacting state authority over territory; tensions emerge between customary tenure and legal tenure, privatization and communal rights, cultural value and market valorization.

In this volume, various chapters show how FLAs are embedded in a process of state legibility and control, wherein governments and domestic actors take a leading role in negotiating and facilitating land reforms. But we also see that a historical focus is crucial to consider, as current processes of dispossession and land control are often embedded in deeply rooted in-country inequalities and North-South political economic relations (see chapters by Postel and Andrew, Brandt. et al.). At the crux of this process lie various contestations over land, labour and production, but also synergies and opportunities created for various actors affected by land deals. These dynamics are worthy of exploration, as the consequences of land reforms in terms of rural land access and ownership are often intense and incredibly varied. Grounding themselves on rich empirical material, the authors of this volume address these dynamics and critically examine the impacts of large-scale land projects in Africa.

State engagements in FLAs can be roughly analytically divided into six stages: 1) Creation of a legally favourable environment (land titling and land reforms) to facilitate foreign investments in and access to land; 2) Designation of land, in some cases, as Special Economic Zones suited for foreign investments; 3) Negotiation of contracts with foreign stakeholders interested in such investments; 4) Implementation phase of the contract in the local setting; 5) Mediation and legitimation of the project in the local setting; 6) Dispute regulation in cases when conflicts in the project zone arise.

As the chapters in this volume highlight, the nature of the state intervention is quite different in the various phases of such projects. In phases one and two, the state aims at realising two things at the same time; on the one hand, it restructures its economy at the impetus of the World Bank and debt repayment schemes in order to facilitate land titling and levy taxes, and on the other, it opens up land for foreign investment under the banner of economic development. Despite the strings of the World Bank, host governments are often in a position to adapt their own regulatory and legislative structures to foreign interests; in principle they also determine the investment zones (it should be noted however that some investors bypass the central state and seek their entry directly at the decentralised state level) and negotiate the contracts (which often but not always include social and environmental assessments) in stage three. Once the contract is concluded, the implementation phase usually means a withdrawal of the central state. The de-central state officials at, for example, the district or municipality level mediate the arrival of the project in the local setting through their collaboration with project personnel; these individuals also mediate the message to local villagers that this is a state approved project in which compliance of local populations is required.

Often local authorities (for example at the level of the municipality) take on the role of brokers. They either facilitate the implementation of FLAs or act as mediators when conflicts arise; in some cases, local authorities can help defend local land rights and re-allocate land access despite foreign control of contested territory. De Koning (this volume) describes how struggles over access to mineral wealth in the DRC between artisanal miners and industrial companies resulted in conflict resolution through the state's decentralized structures, to the benefit of the artisanal miners. This case reveals that local level dynamics and social structures can assist vulnerable populations in securing their land rights. This often occurs where the involvement of local authorities in local or regional economies and related land-based social relationships can succeed in creating a buffer from negative impacts. In other cases, however, as the chapter by Sapignoli and Hitchcock demonstrates, state attempts to divide land into specific categories have resulted in lost access to land and, in many cases, dispossession among the San of Botswana. They show how a land policy that bypassed the land boards and led to the cessation of hunting activities, continues to have significant impacts in the country, particularly on the poor; this example underlines the major impact states have on defining rural landscapes and livelihoods. In South Africa, as shown by Andrew et al. (this volume), state-led restitution and land reform programmes designed to improve the black rural population's access to and control of land did not have the desired outcome and failed to benefit the vast majority of those targeted; conversely, liberalisation and land policies reinforced private ownership, creating opportunities for investors, including foreigners, reflecting broader changes occurring within commercial agriculture (see Andrew et al. this volume). In such cases, local authorities often fail to monitor (or are not charged with monitoring) whether an investor is abiding by local rules and sensitivities. Free Prior and Informed Consent (FPIC) is in this regard often a scant process in which villagers can hardly assess what is going to happen on their land, let alone understand the consequences of the project. Scholars of land deals have repeatedly pointed out that meaningful consultation with local populations and appropriate social and environmental impact assessments are almost never effected (Cotula 2011).

It is often only in cases where problems do arise (usually because of contradictory views of what land is and who may access it) and villagers seek remedy to their felt harms, that the central state (or its legal systems) comes back into the limelight. One could call this the 'boomerang principle' in which, after the completion of the contract, the project is launched in the local setting and the central state withdraws, but once a process of conflict and dispute resolution has to be engaged in, the state is forced to position itself again, both legally and in terms of their dealings with the citizens in the project area.

In this book, the various stages of the insertion of foreign investors in local settings are discussed. Andrew et al., Sapignoli and Hitchcock, and Adamcewski et al. discuss the role of the state in the first phase when land reforms paved the way for increased foreign investments in territory. State-state bilateral relations in turn play a key role in shaping policies which open up land for foreign investments. In this regard, it is crucial to consider how foreign entities engage with host governments, how states engage with each other (see Strauss, this volume), and how policies advocating increased privatization and FDI lead to rural transformations (see Postel, this volume). Consequences of such deals for local land-users range from resettlement, land use change or dispossession to new forms of (sometimes adverse) incorporation or exclusion from land based activities (Hall 2011a).

What is clear is that FLAs are imparting vast and complex changes to rural agrarian systems (Lavers 2012). Moreover, states play more varied and important roles in land deals than previously thought. Nevertheless it is crucial to stress that the analytical distinction between foreign, national and local is sometimes difficult to make as these might converge in the same person. But such actors can wear different hats at the same time, like a local chief or mayor who also invests in land while facilitating other investments in a local setting (see World Bank 2010). Foreign investors usually go through national, local business and NGO levels when concluding and eventually implementing the project. Thus, it should be kept in mind that 'foreign' large-scale land acquisitions in reality concern an amalgam of international, national and local stakeholders vying for land and sometimes playing on various sides of the fence, as is the case with smallholders giving up their own plots to perform wage labour for investors, or a mayor mediating the advantages of a project to local groups. Nevertheless, in terms of compensation and ultimate benefits to local populations, the (re)concentration of land resulting from land titling, unequal joint venture agreements or land leases can in many cases lead to elite or corporate capture of benefits at the local level (Hall 2011a; McMichael 2012).

Chapters analyse the role of the state in redefining rural landscapes and livelihoods in several African countries (Botswana, South Africa, the Democratic Republic of Congo, Nigeria, Kenya, Burkina Faso, Cameroon, and Mali). Relating case studies of various land acquisition classifications ranging from foreign food production, mining, conservation and tourism, and sugar-cane production, each chapter contributes to wider debates centred on how FLAs produce new in-country and state-state dynamics, and how land reforms instigated by the state have led to a transformation in rural landscapes. In doing so, authors examine how labour arrangements, property relations and local relationships to land have changed as a result of FLAs. How do state policies concerning land reforms impede or allow the foreign acquisition of arable land? What are the effects of these land laws on people struggling against dispossession? What land tenure or titling arrangements characterize these deals, and how are rural communities affected by such policies?

What new land-labour relations emerge as a result of land enclosures and territorialisation processes, and with what effect on rural agrarian systems of production? Finally, how does the state manage potential conflicts, resettlement procedures and resulting rural social differentiations?

To summarize, authors in this volume point in their contributions to the fact that FLAs are not an entirely new phenomenon that suddenly arose over the past twenty to thirty years. South Africa especially has a long history of FLAs on a large scale, resulting in many changes in titling and tenure arrangements, and in the long run irreversibly undermining first the formal and later the socio-economic position of local communities. The role of the state is crucial in analysing the historical roots of the current land rush in terms of policies aimed at economic liberalization, privatization and land reforms, which indeed facilitated the entry of private investors. Accordingly, in this volume we bring the question of the state back into FLA debates. The following sections will relate our theoretical frame for understanding the implications of FLAs before reflecting more on the role of the state and presenting a chapter overview.

Theorizing Landscape: Land as Material and Intangible Heritage

In this volume, the focus on the state, land reforms, state policies and their complex impacts on local populations is discussed through the analytical angle of 'contested landscapes'; in this we suggest that spatial concepts related to 'place' and 'space' (ontological assessments of geographical place) can help analytically unpack social scientific research on land use, cover and access shifts arising from foreign large-scale land acquisitions. Where place refers to the physical realities of a particular location, space is less stable and rather composed of 'intersections of mobile elements' (Certeau 1984, 117 in Pannell 2006, 163; Svašek 2002, 498). 'Space' is often denoted in relation to *how* people live in and imbue meaning to a particular location or 'place'. It is indeed how people 'navigate' (Vigh 2009) within a given locality, and is thus highly diverse. Particularly in rural parts of Africa, human lives are shaped by location—whether individuals are engaged in smallholder rice production (Adamczewski et al.), artisanal mining (de Koning), wage labour on private game farms (Andrew et al.), or pastoralism (Sapignoli and Hitchcock), to name a few activities.

In many rural areas, where there is a high dependence on land, local needs for natural resources are not purely economic or utilitarian; human-environment interactions are also deeply embedded in cultural practices and social relationships that are not always appropriately considered in valuation schemes emerging from FLAs (Makunike 2009, 87). In this sense, land deals bring up issues not only of food and state sovereignty but also cultural sovereignty (Deng 2011). While many local groups have daily livelihood activities tied to land, historical connections to landscape, such as the presence of places of first settlement, ancestral tombs and accompanying customs, draw parallels between land and local [material and intangible] heritage (Krijtenburg this volume; Evers and Seagle 2012; see also Cormier-Salem and Bassett 2007). There is a constant dialogue between the concepts of place and space; when a place is changed or compromised in some way—for example, through an environmental change or land access shift—new spaces are created by people as a means of re-situating themselves within the changed landscape (see Postel, this volume). In this regard, place is imbued with meaning, interpretation and significance; space represents the ideological and ontological shifts that may occur when the physical location changes.

Together one can think of the place/space conglomerate as constitutive of 'landscape,' which Pannell (2006, 163) describes analogically as both 'map' (place, the physical locality and its features at a given time) and 'itinerary' (space, a chosen route through the place). Tim Ingold also highlights this point in his book, *Lines* (2007) where he discusses how people trace their lines of movement through historical and temporal landscapes. However, landscapes are approached and used differently by different actors. In a rural area, for instance, we might find women, children and men using the landscape differently; similarly, we might find domestic or foreign actors creating new landscapes of extraction, nature tourism or agricultural production—all of which are discussed in this volume. Each landscape is dynamic and perceived, used and navigated differently. Landscapes and representations of landscape can thus tell a great deal about the social, cultural, gendered, economic, and political structures of a given locality.

Drawing upon Samuels (1979), who observed that landscapes are formed in constant dialogue with social, cultural and economic factors and expressions, Roymans et al. (2009, 339) developed the concept of 'landscape biography' in order to consider how landscapes are shaped as an outcome of a long-term ('*longue durée*') and "complex interplay between the history of mentalities and values, institutional and governmental changes, social and economic developments and ecological dynamics". Landscapes are always transformed over time: re-shaped, re-used and re-molded according to changing conditions (Ibid). As landscapes (or features of a landscape) change, the social space changes as well. In turn, memories are embedded within the lived experience of a particular landscape and responsible in some degree for identity construction (Roymans et al. 2009). Many people might have a national, ethnic or personal attachment to place, but attachments to 'space' are more fluid and mobile. This is in part due to the fact that while a physical location (place) may be immovable, changes to the material features of a place may result in shifting perceptions of space; in this sense, foreign large-scale land acquisitions often lead to constantly shifting landscapes as a result of the power relations flowing between the various stakeholders in the local setting.

As described above, chapters show how current developments in foreign large-scale land acquisitions are legally and historically embedded in policies concerning the restructuring of rural landscapes; in this sense, we can see physical relationships with the environment—such as land-labour relations, access to natural resources and conceptions of cultural heritage—changing as a result of land enclosures. Herein we find not only contestations over economic opportunities created by land deals, but also socio-temporal valuations of 'landscape' and differences in land use strategies, livelihood priorities and cultural imperatives. How are human relationships with landscapes compromised in the event of a large-scale land transfer? And how have movement patterns, or 'landscape biographies' (see Roymans et al. 2006) been adjusted due to restrictions of land access? Chapters zoom in on how land reforms, titling policies, privatization, and the arrival of outside stakeholders in local settings have changed ideas concerning the value of land, land use and social-cultural relations (see chapters by Postel, Tegomoh, Andrew et al., and Buchalik in this volume).

The following sections give insight into recent debates on FLAs before analyzing the role of the state, land reforms and privatization in shaping foreign land deals and accompanying agrarian changes.

Accessing Land in Africa: 'Empty', 'Idle' or 'Under-used'?

Africa is often portrayed as the 'lost continent': steeped in tradition, isolated from markets and trapped in the past—a place where vast swathes of land either lie unoccupied or are poorly utilised (Jarosz 1992). As formal land titling is generally absent from most tenure regimes in Africa, governments commonly hold official rights to territory. In fact, untenured, customary land makes up the largest land category in all of Africa (World

Bank 2003, xxiii). Not surprisingly, therefore, the World Bank (2010) suggests that between 445 and 1.7 billion hectares of 'unused' and 'marginal' land lies dormant, ready for investment. Land deemed by host governments to be 'non-private' or 'public' territory is often set aside for foreign investments and acquisitions (Franco 2009).

Echoing the World Bank discourse, land sought by investors is often described as void of human presence altogether or host to unproductive land uses deemed unworthy by, or invisible to, the state (Lavers 2012, 803). Although argued to the contrary by proponents of the 'empty' land discourse, land acquired by foreign companies is often simultaneously claimed or used by rural communities who have economic, social and existential connections to the territory in which they live. Despite the rapid rise in urbanization over the past twenty years, the number of people living in rural areas is growing and reflects an increasing demand for and reliance on land in the countryside (Borras and Franco 2012). While numerous studies have detailed the lack of [local] benefits arising from FLAs, foreign investments in land are promoted as necessary to stimulate economic growth and rural sustainable development in host countries, provided land deals are appropriately 'disciplined' by regulatory mechanisms, referred to by the World Bank (2010) as 'good governance' (Mann 2010). Voluntary guidelines focused on compensation, mitigation and social-environmental regulations are indeed believed by some to transform mega-land deals into development opportunities for poor countries, imparting new technologies, improved agricultural productivity, poverty alleviation, and modernisation (IIED 2009; World Bank 2010; Deininger 2011). Accordingly, land deals are expected to improve rather than hinder rural sustainable development (see Cotula et al. 2009). The 8th Millennium Development Goal on 'global partnerships for development' is a case in point, as it aims commonly to involve foreign investors in poverty alleviation and environmental protection (De Schutter 2009, 13; Cotula et al. 2009, 9; Hamann 2010). In turn, there is a growing assumption that Foreign Direct Investment (FDI) can improve sustainable development in the global South, provided the strength of the host country's ability to absorb positive inflows is high (Lall and Narula 2004).

Conversely, many scholars suggest that projected benefits of such deals are ambiguous at best, and underline the often disastrous repercussions for local land users who face displacement, land dispossession, livelihood loss, environmental degradation, and lost access to land and natural resources upon which they depend (Borras et al. 2011; White et al. 2012;

Hall 2011a; de Schutter 2010b, 2011; Li 2011; GRAIN 2008).[6] In turn, deals are described as lacking in 'free prior informed consent', and thus "violate or disrespect customary land rights" and "fail to deliver on employment and development" (FOE 2012, 7). The long-anticipated and seminal World Bank report (2010), '*The Global Land Rush: Can it yield sustainable and equitable benefits?*' concedes that "investors failed to follow through on their investments plans, in some cases after inflicting serious damage on the 'local resource base'" and that much vaunted sustainable development projects were "rarely if ever" realized in host countries (see Blas 2010). It should be noted, however, that the World Bank's confession belies the institution's own assertion that foreign land deals should be promoted despite the risks involved, provided that voluntary codes of conduct are appropriately adhered to. In addition to numerous empirical studies emerging on the local consequences of large-scale land acquisitions (see LDPI working paper series [2010–2013] and major research initiatives underway at PLAAS, Utrecht University, the University of Amsterdam and the VU University Amsterdam), case studies carried out by FOE (2010, 27) suggest that "while foreign companies pay lip service to the need for 'sustainable development'... demand for land is resulting in the loss of pasture and forests... causing an increase in greenhouse gas emissions".

Against this backdrop, international observers are demanding that local livelihoods, interests and needs be prioritized (Mann 2010, 8; de Schutter 2011). A growing body of activist networks analysing the politics of global land acquisitions have voiced concern over whether foreign land deals can meaningfully address issues of poverty, rural food security and environmental degradation (see GRAIN, the International Land Coalition, and La Via Campesina). Some scholars have promoted a human rights-based approach to protecting local land rights compromised by FLAs (de Schutter 2010a). Much scholarship has focused on how rural landscapes and livelihoods, as well as the agrarian economy more generally, are being rapidly transformed by advents in foreign large-scale land (Bernstein 2010). Hall's (2011a) typology of rural social differentiation, incorporation and exclusion processes has been most recently complemented by Borras and Franco (2012)'s land transfer mechanism model, which describes how

[6] For detailed case studies, see the proceedings from the 2011 'Global Land Grabbing' conference held in Brighton. Available at http://www.future-agricultures.org/papers-and-presentations, Accessed 03.08.12.

land is swapped between states and foreign entities (discussed below). Li (2011) has examined how land-labour arrangements shift following project implementation, noting that in the event capitalism requires both land and labour, poor peasants facing dispossession are sometimes contracted to work on the new concessions. However, in other cases, Li notes that where the land is needed—but local populations are not—evictions and loss of livelihood may occur (see also de Schutter 2011).

It is important to consider that while not all land deals lead to dispossession, many land users encounter everyday "struggles against dispossession" (Borras and Franco 2012, 53), meaning that shifting regimes of land access as well as new labour and property relations can create everyday hardships that may heighten the risk of rural poverty—even when populations are not relocated or dispossessed out-right. This was, for example, the case for farm dwellers in South Africa, when in the 20th century tenant arrangements were gradually abolished by the state (see Postel, this volume), or when in the 21st century white farm owners converting to game farming sometimes use gradual yet coercive tactics to push black farm dwellers off the property (see Andrews et al., this volume). These studies show that land acquisitions do not follow a unilinear or predictable path, and that each acquisition has its own complexity, involving various different social, political, environmental, historical, and economic contexts. Similarly, many authors agree that rural transformations taking place before, after and during land acquisitions are incredibly varied. This echoes Scott (1998)'s call that state governance pay closer attention (and adapt) to contingencies and shifting local realities.

These studies help us to begin to understand and categorize which types of deals are occurring where and with what repercussions and/or opportunities for local communities. Again, the lack of transparency surrounding such deals has impeded a better understanding of precise local repercussions and global stakeholder relations. By focusing on rural agrarian change, chapters re-position the most vulnerable groups at the centre of the land acquisition debate. Amidst the wealth of empirical studies now existing on the land grab debate, in this volume we focus on the need to situate land deals within a specific historical (land policy) context, which is done in nearly all the chapters. Some authors go further to show that not all deals lead to negative impacts among rural populations, and it is important to consider possible benefits that investments in agriculture can have or are claimed to have. Still other chapters accurately show how land privatization and consolidation put pressures on land-based livelihood practices, in many cases preventing smallholders from sustaining themselves and future generations. The following section will go into a deeper analysis of the role of the state in development and FLAs.

State-making and the Role of 'Development' in Foreign Land Investments

Modern states have long relied upon the 'development' apparatus as crucial to the making of the nation-state. Development was an arena in which 'everyday forms of state formation' were thought to occur (Joseph and Nugget 1994), allowing the state to penetrate lower forms of governance through initiatives designed to 'improve' the well-being of populations—such as education, public administration and new land redistribution laws (Li 1999, 296). As a discourse, 'development' mediates interactions between the state and its citizens, but also creates the semblance that the state indeed exists; it is made visible as a 'provider' of services to populations and thus has a care-taker role. While the state is far from homogeneous, it is often imagined as a collective national entity or homogeny (Scott 1998; Navaro-Yashin 2011). Ferguson (1994) suggests that development discourse masks the reality of state expansion and diversification; he notes that, through seemingly 'de-politicized' development projects, the state penetrates deeper corners of national boundaries and exerts control over land, people and production. In this sense, while the discourse of development is strongly anti-political, actual development interventions are highly politicized in nature and assist in maintaining state power and hegemony (Ferguson 1994).

The involvement of foreign investors in 'sustainable development' through the large-scale lease or sale of land demands some analysis of how state power is shifting or re-asserting itself in the context of FLAs. Scholars are beginning to link large-scale land deals with 'everyday processes of state formation' (Sikor and Lund 2009) and some contend that "[l]arge-scale land investment should be seen as an extension of the historical processes" aimed at re-asserting the power and identity of the state (Mosley 2012, 1). In Brazil, similar observations have been made; Oliveira (2011) describes how large-scale land investments represent a crucial form of state formation that not only facilitates primarily international investments in territory—through legal policy mechanisms—but also risks increased social-ecological ruptures. He attests to "the importance of internal dynamics of capital within each country and the way in which governments can harness these international pressures towards domestic efforts at state-making and territorial consolidation" (Oliveira 2011, 3). In the horn of Africa, where distinct historical differences distinguish the region from other parts of the continent, state formation has been linked to the adoption and expansion of foreign land deals (see Lavers 2012; Mosley 2012; Abbink 2011). In Ethiopia, for example, in an attempt to realize development initiatives promoted by organizations such as the World Bank, the state often seeks to make foreign investments beneficial to smallholder agricultural production (Lavers 2012). But the state's promotion of large-scale (often private) land investments on the one hand and smallholder agricultural production on the other (Sikor 2012, 1082) reveals the contradictory nature of the state's underlying role and purpose; in some cases, instances of double allocation have occurred, as demonstrated in Adamczewski et al.'s discussion of land deals in Mali (this volume). In terms of the land allocation procedure, FLAs often involve a recentralization of state power and the brokerage of land deals with a few key members of government.

In short, evidence is beginning to show that one cannot analytically separate 'everyday processes of state formation' from the growth of FLAs. A key indicator of the state's renewed role in land governance and development is the turn towards foreign direct investment (FDI) which, heavily promoted by international institutions such as the World Bank, has led to a wealth of policy changes favourable to foreign interests. The historical underpinnings to this shift can be dated to neoliberal restructuring during the 1970s, when state power decreased substantially due to Structural Adjustment Programmes (SAPs). SAPs "weakened the capacity of the States to design and implement appropriate policies to alter the structure of their economies and accelerate progress towards achieving Africa's social development goals" (CEA 2011, 1). At the same time, liberalization schemes and SAPs signaled the rise of a 'corporate food regime' (as opposed to a previous emphasis on domestic food regimes) and growing dependence on private agribusinesses to supply global food chains (McMichael 2012, 682). Accompanying these changes were World Bank and UN calls on host governments in the South to adopt Foreign Direct Investment (FDI). Today, FDI functions relatively free from policy restrictions (Lall and Narula 2004, 449) and, in the developing world, is often expected to increase technology transfers, job creation and rural economic growth. Nevertheless, it is generally accepted that weak governance and low levels of local human, technological or supplier capabilities will hinder the positive flow of benefits from FDI (if any); interestingly, most states targeted for FLAs (and FDI) are those with 'weak governance' (Deininger 2011).

Foreign land transactions have become a key means in which host governments can adopt FDI to attract investments and offset debt accumulation. In return, foreign actors may promise to improve infrastructure or facilities and offer attractive royalties to host states, and in almost all cases, foreign actors acquire and exploit land in partnership or 'joint ventures' with the state. Many investors work through [often private] enterprises or subsidiaries engaged in land development at the local level. Where it involves the private sector, and particularly multinationals, improvements to host countries also depend on whether and how the subsidiary company operating through foreign actors interacts with the State. Thus, the institutional arrangements within each specific country are important to consider in terms of how beneficial a land project might be (Lall and Narula 2004, 450; see also Cuffaro and Hallam 2011) Moreover, Borras and Franco (2012, 52–53) found that institutional arrangements surrounding land reform actually facilitated the acquisition of land in many country case studies. The following section will explore the role of land reforms in the FLA debate.

Unpacking the Role of the State: Land Reforms

While land deals are almost always carried out in close collaboration with national governments and thus rendered legally valid (Borras and Franco 2012, 37), they are rarely transparent and very little is known about the actual contractual agreements between states and potential investors (for a recent contribution, see Cotula 2011). This lack of transparency surrounding FLAs has, in fact, been one of the major drivers behind case studies explored in the present volume. Issues of transparency resound through the chapters to varying degrees in the consequences that are described—characteristically qualified by the authors in terms of impeding states and communities and other interested parties and drawing lessons that might help local populations alleviate some of the negative consequences. The World Bank (2010) has noted that governments' inability to provide reliable accounting, records of transactions or implementation processes and transparent financial documentation inhibits the ability of states to effectively manage land deals. In turn, neoliberal reforms and World Bank austerity measures encouraging developing countries to advocate export-oriented economies as a means of reducing debt and securing international aid have led a growing Third World dependence on volatile markets. The growing dependence of the rural poor on international markets has made them more vulnerable to stochastic price shifts (de Schutter interview 2009).

Despite this uneasy playing ground, many host governments actively seek out foreign investments. State-administered land reforms favourable to land privatization often assist governments in transferring 'public' or state territory to foreign companies, regardless of customary land entitlements. On a broader level, as a result of such reforms, we can see a shift in agricultural production from smallholder-led production for domestic consumption to private-led production for exports and foreign consumption. One can also see that the state is getting stronger and tightening control over the countryside. This has been seen for example in the case of Rwanda (Huggins 2009).

In turn, within the context of the current land rush, food produced for subsistence or for domestic markets is increasingly being replaced by food produced for energy purposes (biofuels) or foreign markets. De Schutter (2011) has argued that this shift conflicts with what should be the first priority of low-income countries: to feed themselves. The increasing price of food and reliance on imports—combined with the loss of subsistence activities in many cases—arguably makes rural peasants more vulnerable to dispossession (Hall 2011a). In Odoemene's discussion (this volume) the Nigerian reliance on food imports, due to inadequate government agricultural policies, is cited as the main reason for the state's attracting white Zimbabwean farmers to start large-scale farming in Nigeria. This point is further substantiated in Adamczweski et al.'s chapter, where smallholder irrigated rice production in Mali is steadily being replaced by large-scale, foreign or national agricultural investments. This shows how smallholder-led agrarian economies are confronted by both state and international interests.

Conversely, upon the realization that there is "no conflict over the long term between inward FDI and domestic capabilities", many states choose to reduce restrictions on foreign investments in the hope that transfers of technology, skills and finance will improve local development and national economies (Lall and Narula 2004, 448). However, policy restrictions limiting the state's role in large-scale land projects also means that governments are not positioned to respond to local frictions arising from land deals. Similarly, many new mining laws which aim specifically to open up territory to foreign companies contain clauses which withdraw the role of the state in project implementation. Such laws have accompanied major mining contracts over the past 10–15 years (Sarrasin 2006; see de Koning, this volume).

The state's role in regulating FLAs at various levels of governance (national, regional and local) is also poorly understood. As mentioned, 'good governance' models advocated by the World Bank are intended to promote a voluntary 'corporate ethic' and mode of self-regulation, such that the state requires less intervention in the actual project and can act "more efficiently in society" (O'Laughlin 2008, 945 in Borras and Franco 2012, 35). These include global conventions such as Corporate Social Responsibility (CSR) and the Principles of Responsible Agricultural Investment (RAI principles) which are specifically designed to 'regulate' land deals such that 'win-win' scenarios are ensured for all stakeholders involved (local communities, host governments, foreign investors, and environmental advocacy groups such as conservation NGOs) (for a discussion see von Braun and Meinzen-Dick 2009; see also World Bank 2010 and Deininger 2011). Most recently, the FAO released the 'Voluntary Guidelines on Responsible Governance of Tenure of Land, Fisheries and Forests in the Context of National Food Security' (2012) as a means of outlining ways in which host governments can protect local land rights and food security.[7]

However, the voluntary code of conduct written into many land transfer arrangements contains an underlying tone of 'tacit complicity' in sometimes socially and environmentally destructive projects. The codes are non-binding and bolster the World Bank's contradictory assertion that, despite numerous accounts of negative impacts ranging from outright displacement to lost natural resource access for the rural poor, the risks of large-scale land deals "correspond to equally large opportunities" (World Bank 2010, 142). Many scholars have voiced criticism over the regulatory model, insisting that it does not adequately address the underlying causes of (and potential solutions to) rural poverty (Borras and Franco 2010a; White et al. 2012; Li 2011) and worse, rather than improving rural agricultural production systems, FLAs potentially represent a frontal attack on the rural peasantry itself (Olivier de Schutter 2011). These authors have argued for situating the rural poor at the centre rather than periphery of the FLA debate, and urge global institutions backing foreign investments to avoid viewing local populations as collateral damage that must be better 'managed' through voluntary regulations. This would involve re-structuring foreign investments *specifically* such that rural livelihood improvement is treated as a top priority rather than peripheral spin-off. As a result, scholarly and activist networks are calling for alternatives to large-scale investments in agriculture (Kay 2012).

[7] Full report available at: http://www.fao.org/nr/tenure/voluntary-guidelines/en/, Accessed on 31.07.12.

Typologies of Land Transfer: Land Use, Titling and Ownership

Land policies and laws are often formulated in response to changing social, political and economic interactions with—and contestations between—various different actors. These relationships are mediated by class and wealth hierarchies, gender, ethnicity, and power relations. In this sense one cannot draw conclusions on land-based social realities through the formal lens of the state (Scott 1998). Büscher and Dressler (2007), drawing upon the example of community based conservation schemes in South Africa, describe what they call a 'discursive blur'—a process of obfuscation involved in translating local complexities to higher levels of policy organization in the development world. In this process of translation, much information is either over-simplified, misunderstood or lost. Referring to this fuzzy area of mediation between global, national and local, Igoe and Brockington (2007, 435) note that the concept of the "blur has a value of its own", wherein "ideas such as participation, sustainability and win-win solutions are used by competing networks of people to mobilize resources as efficiently and quickly as possible". One can see this in the voluntary guidelines, where discursive representations of 'win-win' scenarios may not correspond to local realities. Similarly, Tsing (2002) has urged scholars to look less at 'things'—such as clear boundary markers, legal papers and titles—as a means of tracking land rights and land transfer arrangements, but instead to analyze how land based social relations are structured within specific contexts (in Borras and Franco 2010b).

As mentioned above, the enforcement of positive law by the state, as it concerns tenure and related legal structures, is something Scott (1998) has described as a process of state-formation, wherein the state attempts to make complex social phenomena (such as land use and ownership) more 'legible'. This process of legibility conceals a state strategy to impose more efficient control of and order over populations (Scott 1998; see also Oliveira 2011). As "land-based social relations vary from one historical institutional setting to the next", so too are they "shaped by specific socio-economic, political, cultural and historical factors" (Borras and Franco 2012, 50). The embeddedness of these relations in certain landscapes over time suggests that clear 'things' (such as land reforms and titling procedures) developed at the national level indeed do not always reflect dynamic land use and access regimes locally—nor do they reflect the embodied value of labour and cultural practices people inscribe in a landscape over time. Here again we come back to the concepts of place and space, as shown in Buchalik's chapter (this volume) who describes how the interaction between traditional landscaping and a major national road network in Burkina Faso gave rise to new 'symbiotic' forms of local landscaping.

The complexity of agrarian landscapes, as described in sections above, and how they are now rapidly changing as a result of the current land rush, is being slowly unpacked by scholars of FLAs. With regard to how land use regimes are shifting, Borras and Franco (2012, 51–52) provide an analytical distinction between four different types of land reform accompanying FLAs: Type A ('distributive') refers to a situation wherein land-based wealth and power held by either the state, a private entity or the community is transferred or distributed to the landless poor by government bodies. Type B ('re-distributive') follows this same framework though focuses on redistributing wealth and power. Both Types involve a process of granting either new rights to land (Type A) or protecting pre-existing or former land rights (Type B).

These above land policies can be aptly contrasted with Types C and D, which is what we are now noting in the context of FLAs. Types C and D ('non [re]-distribution' and 're-concentration') refer to land transactions taking place when bureaucratic state structures maintain the *status quo* of land-based inequalities and processes of exclusion. This process of embedded exclusion is what we see with Type C. When a transfer of rights does occur, but land access and control is captured by the elite dominant classes, corporate interests, the state, or village chiefs, the land transaction is referred to as Type D. Drawing upon this typology, Borras and Franco (2012, 52) suggest that state policies towards land and rural populations have steadily been moving away from Types A and B ('distributive' and 're-distributive') to Types C and D ('non [re]-distribution' and 're-concentration'). Various chapters in this book uphold this typology, where land reforms designed to either uphold or protect local land rights did not have the desired outcome of improving rural food security, but rather created spaces for elite capture, growth of private enterprise and foreign land control. It is thus crucial to analyze how land reforms and policies not only historically underpin but possibly facilitate foreign acquisitions of Africa's arable land.

As mentioned earlier, land titling reforms and privatization often accompany or precede foreign land deals. In this context, ill-defined notions of 'ownership' politicize the negotiation process with local populations and sometimes exacerbate divisions and inequalities within communities (Daniel and Mittal 2009, 10). Evidence has consistently shown that customary tenure systems and local land rights are regularly swept aside or not adequately respected in the context of foreign land deals (Anseeuw et al. 2012). Despite state efforts over the past decades, lack of legal entitlements to land means that many local claims to land fall outside of the legal and regulatory framework agreed upon by States and foreign actors, which is premised upon private ownership (Ibid). Here again we see land transfer mechanisms more resembling of Types C and D (see above), where state attempts to transfer land back to rural populations backfires by creating spaces for elite capture, private enterprise and land consolidation.

While many international organizations strongly advocate land titling as a means of safeguarding the rights of peasants living on proposed concessions (in particular Oxfam Novib), land titling and reforms can sometimes produce intense socio-cultural tensions and conflicts on the ground. Land tenure security via land reforms does not always lead to protection against land dispossession, which has been seen in the case of Mozambique, where community land titles were swept away to make way for mass sugarcane (ethanol) plantations and many were evicted from what they believed was legally titled territory (Borras and Franco 2012, 54). Processes of dispossession occurring within the context of formal 'land rights' (or titling procedures) echo Peluso and Ribot's (2003) theory of access, which broadly states that having (legal) rights to land does not ensure the ability to access it. Individual privatization of land—or the distribution of legally titled plots to smallholders—on previously customarily-owned land can in many cases lead to a situation where peasants may sell assets (i.e. land) as a means of ensuring food security or paying off debts. This is a classic example of what Harvey (2003) calls 'accumulation by dispossession', wherein the privatization and commodification of previously public assets—a key symptom of neoliberal capitalism—has the result of benefiting the wealthy and re-concentrating wealth in the hands of private enterprises or wealthy elite (again reflecting land transfer mechanisms Types C and D). We can see this becoming an increasing concern within the context of large scale investments in food production, where many countries in the global South are becoming key exporters of food and residents rely more heavily on imports for food security.

These complex dynamics of land reform and shifting socio-cultural landscapes are unpacked by the chapters in this volume, which seek to problematize the role of the state in FLAs. The following section will go into more detail by providing an overview of each chapter.

Chapter Overview: Global Drivers, Local Impacts and Contested Landscapes in Africa

The following section traces the anatomy of each chapter, showing how authors speak to above-mentioned debates surrounding the role of the state in transnational, foreign and domestic land acquisitions, land reforms and privatization; they show how new landscapes are being actively produced through dynamic encounters between various actors involved in a land deal, and how these transformations affect smallholders and their families reliant on land in Africa.

Both Ben White and Annelies Zoomers lay the framework for the volume by tracing a genealogy of the converging political, economic and social structures leading to foreign land acquisitions. They also critically examine the 'regulatory model' of the World Bank. Ben White takes a historical perspective to provide a comprehensive overview of—and theoretical reflections on—the transnational character of land deals, global drivers of agrarian change over time and major discourses of legitimacy used in corporate land access strategies. He points out several contradictions to the World Bank's (2010) seminal report on foreign land acquisitions, arguing that negative impacts of land deals cannot be wholly mitigated with the Bank's proposed 'voluntary code of conduct'. Revealing various reports of human displacement, environmental degradation or social upheaval, White draws upon Olivier de Schutter to fundamentally challenge the 'regulatory' model of land investments; rather, he suggests that researchers must find an alternative model of agrarian change, premised upon improving rural livelihoods instead of feeding markets.

In contrast to White, who compares historical processes of land dispossession with the current land rush, Annelies Zoomers focuses primarily on the contemporary era (2009–present) and emphasizes the need to deepen the policy debates surrounding FLAs. She notes that broader food security and climate mitigation policies stimulate the enclosure of Africa's arable land, often superseding formal state structures, and that such debates should be part and parcel of the analysis of FLAs. Additionally, current debates about 'regulating' FLAs fail to consider the deeper political, economic and historical structures underpinning foreign land claims and acquisitions over time. Without situating these claims within the context of broader development debates, current policies aimed at protecting local land rights will inevitably fail. She goes on to state that governments have an important role to play and scholars must look closer at how and why policies of decentralization fail within the context of FLAs.

Echoing Zoomers' call to consider broader causalities of foreign land claims, Michael Strauss argues that we must consider the role of bilateral relations in shaping land deals in Africa. He points out that scholars often neglect the state's role as both an intermediary in the business transactions but also as a key actor in the acquisition of territory itself. South Korea and Saudia Arabia, for example, are leasing thousands of hectares of land in many parts of Africa (Sudan, Ethiopia and Tanzania). Bilateral relations thus play a crucial role in shaping many land deals in Africa; Strauss points out the challenges and benefits posed to inter-state dynamics resulting from foreign land deals.

Flowing from White, Zoomers and Strauss' focus on global drivers, the following four chapters bring the global debates down to the local level and examine how projects are negotiated, implemented and structured with regard to state interventions and land reform policies. Ruben de Koning's discussion of competing claims to land in the Democratic Republic of Congo (DRC) reveals how land access tensions between small-scale artisanal miners and large-scale mining companies play out in practice. It addresses a key point of interest in wider debates about the role of the state in foreign large-scale investments: namely, how mining projects are mediated, structured and legitimized at the national level within the context of national mining reforms which pave the way for foreign investments, and potential consequences for artisanal mining communities vying for access to the same territory. He goes further to demonstrate how the state negotiated between competing interests, noting that regional governance was strong enough to protect many artisanal land rights. He argues that local power complexes emerging around artisanal mining operations have withheld large-scale industrial investment, thereby sometimes preventing displacement of artisanal miners from concessions.

In their chapter, Andrew et al. analyze the impacts of private commercial farm conversions to wildlife tourism ('game farms') on farm dwellers in South Africa's Eastern Cape, where landless peasants live and work on white-owned farms. While some of these farm dwellers are evicted from the farms following conversion, others are contracted by owners to work on the farms as day labourers. Laying out the context for post-1994 land reform based on the already existing privatization of land under colonialism and apartheid, they trace the ways that further land enclosures for the purpose of wildlife-based tourism spread in this liberalizing environment. The authors show how conversions to game farms often involve human displacement, the fracture of social and kin networks, migration and loss of livelihood activities (e.g. subsistence agriculture and livestock-holding). Historical power relations and racial inequalities that have persisted since apartheid have weakened state policies aiming to improve the lives of farm dwellers. Game farms are part of a broader trend of land territorialization and consolidation by the private sector, in which wildlife conservation, hunting and tourism are increasingly legitimized as spurring 'economic growth' and thus beneficial for both farm dwellers and landowners. Local actors (commercial farmers) have in many cases managed to align their interests with those of investors, some foreign, some domestic.

Similar to Andrew et al.'s discussion of land tenure shifts surrounding game farm conversions, Sapignoli and Hitchcock demonstrate how a land reform policy in Botswana, aimed at both reducing land degradation and improving rural incomes, failed to benefit the poorest members of the community. They specifically analyze how shifts from communal to individual (privatized) land tenure led to processes of dispossession among the San and other marginalized groups. In addition to examining the impacts of the land division into specific categories—the authors also analyze how the rural poor have responded to the reforms. Upholding the discussion of both Andrew et al. and White, they note that, since the colonial period, state efforts at land reforms intended to reduce poverty often had the opposite effect and excluded local groups, providing more land access opportunities to extra-locals.

Following upon Sapignoli and Hitchcock's discussion of land reforms and private enclosures, Amandine et al. examine land policies leading to a national shift from smallholder supported, irrigated rice cultivation for domestic markets to foreign (and domestic) large-scale agricultural investments in the heavily irrigated ON (*Office de Nigér*) region of Mali. The authors make the important point that domestic investments in land are also driving the current land rush in Africa; and land allocation procedures often involve the re-centralisation of previously de-centralised government institutions. In some cases, land deals were negotiated with wealthy elites in government without consultation with smallholders or necessary impact assessments this led in some cases to 'double allocation'—where land legally used by smallholders was also handed over to investors. The authors analyze both policies and regulations related to land investments as well as to what extent both small and large-scale farming can co-exist under new state laws. They unravel the various conflicts that have occurred in the ON region, some of which include displacement of smallholder communities, loss of land access and livelihood shifts resulting from land allocations to primarily foreign companies. In doing so, they critically examine the role of smallholder agriculture in shaping Mali's domestic economy.

In a discussion of the role of the Nigerian government in paving the way for white Zimbabwean farmers to take up large-scale farming, Akachi Odoemene traces the implementation phase through an analysis of various manifestations of state and public rhetoric. Highlighting the rhetorical trope of 'New Nigeria' against the backdrop of a historical survey of Nigeria's agricultural development, land reforms and food production policies, the author demonstrates the implicit, unfavourable and historical dimensions of state discursive strategies of legitimization. In the wake of government efforts to improve agricultural practices and production, the Nigerian state drew upon a modernization discourse in pushing through various land reforms targeted at foreign investments. However, while intended to persuade the general public of the benefits of a new land order, the discursive tools used by the state produced a fierce counter rhetoric among populations.

The next four chapters in this volume examine how various actors are situated in 'place' (geographical location) and 'space' (ontological assessments of geographical place) and how this has led to 'contested landscapes' and constantly shifting land access and ownership regimes. Issues of local land use valuations, customary land ownership, land tenure and access, and privatization are examined against the backdrop of rising foreign and domestic interests in large tracts of so-called 'empty' land. These chapters show how new perceptions of 'landscapes' are molded out of dynamic interactions between foreign actors and local stakeholders. They seek to explain what underlying cultural or ideological factors play a role in contestations over territory, examining the value of land from a local perspective.

Lucjan Buchalik's discussion of the construction of a major road connection network in the Kurumba region in Burkina Faso underscores the need for understanding local conceptions and forms of land ownership within the context of foreign land deals. Examining local land tenure systems among the Voltaic peoples of Burkina Faso, he demonstrates how in the interaction between traditional practices of communal land development and state practices of it traditional and modern conceptualizations of land use merge. Two case studies illustrate the different geographical and socio-economic outcomes this merging can effect.

Taking a historical approach to analyzing 20th century South African literature within the context of the state land reforms, Gitte Postel examines historical roots of conflicting white and black discourses surrounding identity, belonging and land ownership in 20th century South Africa. She demonstrates that the influence of the state has been overwhelmingly effective in accommodating foreign land deals and placing the local farmers in the periphery of not only land ownership and land use but also official debates and imaginaries about land. However, conflicting discourses on land did not evaporate; they were—as an undercurrent, transformed into more symbolical forms of expression—still part of political and social/cultural discourse. Gitte Postel shows that these historical dynamics are still having an effect that is felt today.

Drawing upon empirical examples of high level politicians from the Western Highlands of Cameroon, Evelyne Tegomoh shows how internal mobility for investments in land symbolically and discursively turns 'nationals' into 'foreigners'. In doing so, she provides new insights into mobility and the impacts of FLAs on socio-cultural perceptions of belonging. Analyzing the role of elites specifically, she notes that landholders and buyers do not rely on existing land registration systems; rather, their practices are tacitly endorsed by the state in an effort to modernize agriculture. These dynamics are often accompanied by state-led land reforms, wherein the adoption of land laws opening up territory for investment has made more land available to politically and economically powerful individuals and entities.

Finally, Froukje Krijtenburg explores stakeholder conceptualisations of 'land protection' relating to Mijikenda sacred land in Kenya, whose land is potentially targeted by, foreign investors. In a joint effort to prevent foreign acquisitions of sacred Mijikenda places, local actors and a centralized state party submitted Mijikenda sacred places for inscription on the World Heritage list in 2008 and managed to have ten of them designated as World Heritage sites. The discussion explores whether indeed Mijikenda sacred land can now be considered 'protected' from foreign land acquisitions from the local perspective, by exploring the different stakeholder discourses in the context of the World Heritage inscription.

In closing, an important, general observation can be made relating to the authors' contributions described here. Overall, though in different ways, the chapters demonstrate the central role of the state (encouraged by economic policy) in creating the fertile ground for large-scale land deals, in addition to highlighting the importance of detailed empirical studies to distill the rootings and becomings of these processes. Collectively as well as individually, the following chapters enrich the global large-scale foreign land acquisition debate with persuasive statements based on nuanced analyses.

Bibliography

Abbink, A. 2011. 'Land to the foreigners': economic, legal, and sociocultural aspects of new land acquisition schemes in Ethiopia. *Journal of Contemporary African Studies*, 29(4): 513–535.

Anseeuw, W., L. Alden Wily, L. Cotula, and M. Taylor. 2012. 'Land rights and the rush for land: findings of the global commercial pressures on land research project'. Rome: ILC (International Land Coalition).

Bernstein, H., 2010. *Class Dynamics of Agrarian Change*. Halifax, NS: Fernwood/Sterling,VA: Kumarian Press.

Borras, S. Jr. and J.C. Franco. 2010a. From threat to opportunity? Problems with the idea of a 'code of conduct' for land-grabbing. *Yale Human Rights and Development Law Journal*, 13(2): 507–23.

——. 2010b. The 'land sovereignty' alternative: towards a peoples' (counter)- enclosure. A preliminary discussion. ICAS Working Paper Series No. 001.

——. 2012. Global land grabbing and trajectories of agrarian change: a preliminary analysis. *Journal of Agrarian Change*, 12(1): 34–59.

Borras, S. Jr., R. Hall, I. Scoones, B. White, and W. Wolford. 2011. Towards a better understanding of global land grabbing: an editorial introduction. *Journal of Peasant Studies* 38(2): 209–216.

Borras, S. Jr., P. McMichael and I. Scoones. 2010. The politics of biofuels, land and agrarian change: editors' introduction. *Journal of Peasant Studies*, 37(4): 575–592.

Burnod, P. 2011. 'Appropriations foncieres: après l'affaire Daewoo, que se passé-t-il a Madagascar?' CERI, CNRS (Juin 2011). Available at: http://www.ceri-sciencespo.org/archive/2011/juin/dossier/art_pb.pdf, Accessed 08.08.12.

Büscher, B. 2010. Seeking 'telos' in the 'transfrontier'? Neoliberalism and the transcending of community conservation in Southern Africa. *Environment and Planning* A(42): 644–60.

Büscher, B. and W. Dressler. 2007. Linking neoprotectionism and environmental governance: on the rapidly increasing tensions between actors in the environment-development nexus. *Conservation and Society*, 5(4): 586–611.

Commission Économique des Nations Unies pour l'Afrique (CEA) / United Nations Economic Commission for Africa (UNECA); Commission de l'Union Africaine (CUA) / African Union Commission (AUC). 'Governing development in Africa: The role of the State in economic transformation (Issues paper) Ethiopia', (February 14, 2011): pp. 1–15.

Corson, C. 2011. Territorialization, enclosure and neoliberalism: non-state influence in struggles over Madagascar's forests. *The Journal of Peasant Studies*, 38(4), 703–26.

Cotula, L. 2011. Land deals in Africa: What is in the contracts? London: IIED.

Cotula, L., S. Vermeulen, R. Leonard, and J. Keeley. 2009. Land grab or development opportunity? Agricultural investments and international land deals in Africa. London: IIED.

Cuffaro, N. and D. Hallam. 2011. "Land Grabbing' in Developing Countries: Foreign Investors, Regulation and Codes of Conduct'. Paper presented at the International Conference on 'Global Land Grabbing', University of Sussex/LDPI, Brighton (6–8 April 2011).

Daniel, S. and A. Mittal. 2009. *The great land grab. Rush for world's farmland threatens food security for the poor*. The Oakland Institute, Oakland, USA.

De Certeau, M. 1984. *The practice of everyday life*. Berkeley and Los Angeles: University of California Press.

De Schutter, O. 2009. Interview, 'Good governance is the key to managing 'land grabbing'. Available from: http://www.dw-world.de/dw/article/0,,4524232,00.html, Accessed 08.08.2012.

——. 2010a. Report of the Special Rapporteur on the right to food. Report presented at the United National General Assembly, 65th Session, 11 August 2010.

——. 2010b. 'The green rush: the race for farmland and the rights of land users'. Working paper, Louvain: Catholic University of Louvain, Belgium (November 2010). Available at: www.harvardilj.org/wp-content/.../07/HILJ_52-2_De-Schutter.pdf, Accessed 08.08.12.

——. 2011. How not to think land grabbing: three critiques of large-scale investments in farmland'. *Journal of Peasant Studies*, 38 (2): 249–79.

Deininger, K., 2011. Forum on global land grabbing: challenges posed by the new wave of farmland investment. *Journal of Peasant Studies*, 38(2): 217–47.

Deng, D.K. 2011. '"Land belongs to the community": Demystifying the "global land grab" in Southern Sudan'. Paper presented at the International Conference on 'Global Land Grabbing', University of Sussex/LDPI, Brighton (6–8 April 2011).

Duffy, R. 2006. Non-governmental organisations and governance states: the impact of transnational environmental management networks in Madagascar. *Environmental Politics*, 15(5): 731–49.

Fairhead, J., M. Leach and I. Scoones. 2012. Green Grabbing: a new appropriation of nature? *Journal of Peasant Studies*, 39(2): 237–261.

Ferguson, J. 1994. *Anti-Politics Machine: Development, Depoliticization, and Bureaucratic Power in Lesotho*. Minneapolis: University of Minnesota Press.

Franco, J. 2009. 'Land Policies in State/Public Land: A Civil Society Perspective'. *Land Reform Bulletin*. Rome: FAO.

Friends of the Earth (FOE). 2012. 'Farming Money: How European banks and private finance profit from food speculation and land grabs' (January 12 2012). Available from: http://www.foeeurope.org/node/46, Accessed 08.08.12.

Görgen, M., B. Rudloff, J. Simons, A. Üllenberg, S. Väth, and L. Wimmer. 2009. Foreign Direct Investment (FDI) in land in developing countries. GTZ (Deutsche Gesellschaft für Technische Zusammenarbeit). Available from: http://www2.gtz.de/wbf/4tDx9kw63gma/gtz2010–0060en-foreign-direct-investment-dc.pdf, Accessed 31.07.12.

GRAIN. 2008. SEIZED! The 2008 land grab for food and financial security. Briefing (October 2008). Available at: http://www.grain.org/article/entries/93-seized-the-2008-landgrab-for-food-and-financial-security, Accessed 08.08.12.

Hall, R. 2011a. 'The many faces of the investor rush in Southern Africa: towards a typology of commercial land deals'. ICAS Working Paper Series No. 2, The Hague: International Institute of Social Studies (ISS).

——. 'Land Grabbing in Africa and the new politics of food'. Policy Brief no. 041, Brighton: Future Agricultures Consortium.

Hallam, D. 2009. 'Foreign Investment in Developing Country Agriculture—Issues, Policy Implications and International Response'. Paper presented at the Global Forum on International Investment, OECD (7–8 December 2009). Available at: http://www.responsibleagroinvestment.org/rai/sites/responsibleagroinvestment.org/files/OECD_RAI%20Issure_Policy%20Implications.pdf, Accessed 08.08.12.

Hamann, Ralph. 2010. Mining companies' role in sustainable development: The 'why' and 'how' of corporate social responsibility from a business perspective. *Development Southern Africa*, 20(2): 237–254.

Harvey, D. 2003. *The New Imperialism*. Oxford: Oxford University Press.

Huggins, C. 2009. 'Historical and contemporary land laws and their impact on indigenous peoples' land rights in Rwanda'. Rights and Resources Initiative (May 2009), pp. 1–26.

Igoe, J. and D. Brockington. 2007. Neoliberal conservation: a brief introduction. *Conservation & Society*, 5(4): 432–49.

IIED. 2009. 'Land grabs' in Africa: can the deals work for development? (Briefing, September 2009)

Ingold, T. 2007. *Lines: A Brief History*. Abingdon: Routledge.

Jarosz, L. 1992. Constructing the Dark Continent: Metaphor as Geographic Representation of Africa. *Geografiska Annaler Series B, Human Geography*, 74(2): 105–115.

Joseph, G.M. and D. Nugent. 1994. *Everyday Forms of State Formation: Revolution and the Negotiation of Rule in Modern Mexico*. Durham: Duke University Press.

Kay, Sylvia. 2012. 'Positive Investment Alternatives to Large-Scale Land Acquisitions or Leases'. Transnational Institute (TNI).

Lall, S. and R. Narula. 2004. Foreign Direct Investment and its role in economic development: do we need a new agenda? *The European Journal of Development Research*, 16(3): 447–464.

Lavers, T. 2012. 'Land grab' as development strategy? The political economy of agricultural investment in Ethiopia. *Journal of Peasant Studies*, 39(1): 105–132.

Li, T.M. 1999. Compromising Power: Development, Culture and Rule in Indonesia. *Cultural Anthropology*, 40(3): 277–309.

——. 2011. Centering Labor in the land grab debate. *The Journal of Peasant Studies*, 38(2): 281–99.

Makki, F. and C. Geisler. 2011. Development by dispossession: land grabbing as new enclosures in contemporary Ethiopia. Paper presented at the International Conference on 'Global Land Grabbing', University of Sussex/LDPI, Brighton (6–8 April 2011).

Makunike, C. 2009. 'Large-scale agricultural investment in Africa: 85 points to ponder' *in* Kugelman, M. and S.L. Levenstein, *Land Grab? The Race for the World's Farmland*. Washington D.C.: Woodrow Wilson International Center for Scholars.

Mann, Howard. 2010. Foreign land purchases for agriculture: what impact on sustainable development? United Nations Sustainable Development Innovation Brief, Issue 8 (January 2010).

McMichael, P. 2012. The land grab and corporate food regime restructuring. *Journal of Peasant Studies*, 39(3–4): 681–701.

Mosley, J. 2012. Peace, bread and land: agricultural investments in Ethiopia and the Sudans. Africa Programme AFP BP, Chatham House Briefing Paper (January 2012).

Navaro-Yashin, Y. 2002. *Faces of the State: Secularism and Public Life in Turkey*. Princeton: Princeton University Press.

Nyiri, Pál. 2009. 'Foreign Concessions: Past and Future of a Form of Shared Sovereignty'. Inaugural Lecture, VU University Amsterdam.

O'Laughlin, B. 2008. Governing Capital? Corporate Social Responsibility and the Limits of Regulation. *Development and Change*, 39 (6): 945–57.

Oliveira, G. de L.T. 2011. 'Land Regularization in Brazil and the Global Land Grab: A State-making Framework for Analysis'. Paper presented at the International Conference on 'Global Land Grabbing', University of Sussex/LDPI, Brighton (6–8 April 2011).

Pannell, S. 2006. 'From the poetics of place to the politics of space: redefining cultural landscapes on Damer, Maluku Tenggara,' *in* Fox, J.J. (ed.), *The Poetic Power of Place: Comparative Perspectives on Austronesian Ideas of Locality*. Canberra: ANU E Press.

Peck J, and Tickell A. 2002. Neoliberalizing space. *Antipode* 34: 380–404.

Peluso, N.L. and C. Lund, guest editors. 2011. What difference does land control make? Shifting agrarian environments and the reorientation of land governance practices. *Journal of Peasant Studies*, 38(4).

Randrianja, S. 2012. *Madagascar, le coup d'État de mars 2009*. Paris; Karthala.

Ribot, J.C. and N.L. Peluso. 2003. A Theory of Access. *Rural Sociology*, 68(2): 153–181.

Rice, Xan. 'Ethiopia—country of the silver sickle—offers land dirt cheap to farming giants'. Guardian (Friday, 15 January 2010) Available at: www.guardian.co.uk/world/2010/jan/15/ethiopia-sells-land-farming-giants, Accessed 09/03/10.

Roymans, N., F. Gerritsen, C. Van der Heijden, K. Bosma, and J. Kolen. 2009. Landscape Biography as Research Strategy: The Case of the South Netherlands Project. *Landscape Research*, 34(3): 337–359.

Sarrasin, B. 2006. The mining industry and the regulatory framework in Madagascar: some developmental and environmental issues. *Journal of Cleaner Production*, 14: 388–96.

Scott, J. 1998. *Seeing Like a State: How Certain Schemes to Improve the Human Condition Have Failed*. New Haven and London: Yale University Press.

Seagle, C. 2012. Inverting the impacts: mining, conservation and sustainability claims near the Rio Tinto/QMM ilmenite mine in Fort Dauphin, Southeast Madagascar. *Journal of Peasant Studies* 39(2), 447–77.

Sikor, T. 2012. Tree plantations, politics of possession and the absence of land grabs in Vietnam. *Journal of Peasant Studies*, 39(3–4): 1077–1101.
Sikor, T. and C. Lund. 2009. Access and property: a question of power and authority. *Development and Change*, 40(1), 1–22.
Smaller, C., and H. Mann. 2009. 'A thirst for distant Lands: foreign investment in agricultural land and water.' International Institute for Sustainable Development (IISD) (May 2009).
Smillie, I., A. Brownell, and J. Létourneau. 2009. *Land Grabbing and Land Reform*. Partnership Africa Canada.
Snijders, D. 2012. Wild property and its boundaries—on wildlife policy and rural consequences in South Africa. *Journal of Peasant Studies* 39(2), 503–520.
Steinberg, S. 2008. 'Financial speculators reap profits from global hunger'. Global Research: Centre for Research on Globalization (24 April 2008). Available at: http://globalresearch.ca/index.php?context=va&aid=8794. Accessed 08.08.12.
Teyssier, A., L. Ramarojohn, and R. Andrianirina Ratsialonana. 2009/2010. Des terres pour l'agro-industrie internationale? Un dilemme pour la politique foncière malgache. *Echogéo*, 11.
Tsing, A. 2002. 'Land as law: negotiating the meaning of property in Indonesia', in F. Richards, *Land, Property and the Environment*. Institute for Contemporary Studies: 94–137.
Vidal, J. 2010. 'How food and water are driving a 21st Century Land Grab' Guardian Observer (7 March 2010). Available at: http://www.guardian.co.uk/environment/2010/mar/07/food-water-africa-land-grab, Accessed 06/08/10.
Vigh, H. 2009. Motion squared: a second look at the concept of social navigation. *Anthropological Theory*, 9(4): 419–438.
Von Braun, J. and R. Meinzen-Dick. 2009. 'Land grabbing' by foreign investors in developing countries: risks and opportunities. IFPRI Policy Brief 13, April 2009. Washington, DC: IFPRI.
Weis, T. 2007. *The Global Food Economy: The Battle for the Future of Farming*. London and New York: Zed Books.
White, B., Borras, S.M. Jr., Hall, R. Scoones, I. and Wolford, W. 2012. The new enclosures: critical perspectives on corporate land deals. *Journal of Peasant Studies* 39(3–4): 619–647.
Wolford, W., Borras, S.M. Jr., Hall, R. Scoones, I., and White, B. 2013. Governing global land deals: the role of the State in the rush for land. Development and Change 44(2).
World Bank. 2010. Rising global interest in farmland: can it yield sustainable and equitable benefits? Washington, DC: World Bank.
World Bank. 2003. Land policies for growth and poverty reduction. Washington, DC: The International Bank for Reconstruction and Development / The World Bank.
Zoomers, A. 2010. Globalisation and the foreignisation of space: seven processes driving the current global land grab. *Journal of Peasant Studies*, 37(2): 429–47.

SECTION 1

THE RECONFIGURATION OF RURAL LANDSCAPES AND LIVELIHOODS IN THE RECENT SCRAMBLE FOR AFRICAN LAND

CORPORATE LAND DEALS, DISPOSSESSION AND THE FUTURE OF FARMING

Ben White

INTRODUCTION[1]

Forty-five years ago the Polish economist Michal Kalecki, after visiting Egypt, Indonesia and some other postcolonial countries, noted the survival and apparent resilience of what he called the "intermediate classes" in agriculture and other sectors (by which he meant small- and medium-scale farms and other enterprises). He also raised the question whether, at some future moment, we would see their disappearance in final submission to the interests of big business (Kalecki 1967). Observing the current wave of large-scale, state-supported corporate acquisitions of contested lands and common lands today—in Africa, Asia, Latin America, and the former Soviet Union—one wonders whether Kalecki's moment has finally arrived.

In the last few years the useful fact-finding work and publicity on these land deals, both by mainstream international agencies and more critical NGOs has established beyond doubt that large-scale corporate land acquisitions and the accompanying dispossession of local people are occurring on an unprecedented scale (the studies and estimates are critically summarized by Cotula 2012). It sometimes appears that different agencies are competing to produce the highest estimates of the total area subjected to land 'grabs'—80 million hectares according the International Land Coalition (Anseeuw et al. 2012), 227 million hectares according to Oxfam (2011)—but as land deals are typically shrouded in secrecy, nobody really knows how much land is being acquired. All agree however that the greatest concentration of land deals—certainly more than 60 percent—is in sub-Saharan Africa (Cotula 2012: 650–656).

[1] This chapter is a revised version of the address "Who will own the countryside? Corporate land deals and the future of farming" presented at the NVAS International Conference Africa for sale: analysing and theorising foreign land claims and acquisitions, University of Groningen, 28–29 October 2010. Some parts are drawn from White 2011.

The academic world has been quick to respond to these developments. There is now quite an industry of academic, field research-based 'land-grab studies' underway, both by established scholars and also particularly by graduate students, and we will see an explosion of interesting dissertations, conferences, special issues of journals and so on in the coming years. When the Land Deals Politics Initiative called for papers for for the International Conference on Global Land Grabbing held in April 2011 at the Institute of Development Studies at the University of Sussex, and later for the 'International Land Grabbing II' conference at Cornell University in October 2012, in each case more than 400 abstracts were submitted, nearly all of them based on original field research.

As researchers we aim to go beyond fact-finding or general expressions of concern, and there are many kinds of questions to which the work of analysing and theorising foreign land claims and acquisitions might respond. First, why is it happening? And more specifically: why is it happening now? Second, how important is its transnational character? From whose point of view? Then, how does a corporate (transnational) land acquisition work? How is production organised in the newly enclosed lands? Who gains, who loses? What are the forms of local response (which may include both resisting and welcoming the presence of new investors) and how is resistance organised? What has been the international policy response? What is the role of states in welcoming or blocking foreign investment, and in shaping these processes more generally? And finally: if 'land grabbing' continues on a large scale, what are the implications for the future of global farming systems? The following sections touch briefly on each of these issues.

Why Do Land 'Grabs' Happen?

The current land rush, and the discourses of states, corporate investors and international agencies that come with it, is full of contradictions. On the one hand, most countries in the global south report declining farm sizes, land shortage and often food insecurity, while states and corporations justify the acquisition of large areas of land by claiming the availability of huge areas of "empty" or "unused" land in the same countries. These land deals are usually based on corporate promises to develop modern, industrial forms of agricultural production for food, feed, fuel, or fibre for export. Research has long ago shown, however, that such industrial (capital- and energy-intensive) forms of agriculture are unsustainable, and will accelerate global warming rather than slow it down (for example, many studies cited in IAASTD 2009). Meanwhile key international agencies, quite aware of this research and having themselves sponsored and published some of it, seem to have accepted that this form of agriculture is going to be the main motor of agricultural growth in the coming years.

The World Bank's policy report *Rising global interest in farmland—can it yield sustainable and equitable benefits?* (2010) embodies these contradictions. It includes several case studies commissioned by the Bank (including as African cases the Democratic Republic of Congo, Liberia, Mozambique, Tanzania, and Zambia). These studies document clearly that land investments are not fulfilling their promise of employment creation for local people, they are environmentally destructive, they disadvantage women, they ignore the proper legal procedures for acquiring land, and in many cases forcibly displace large numbers of people (Scoones 2010). But the same report proposes that any problems of governance, illegality and environmental destruction be prevented by the acceptance and implementation of a voluntary 'code of conduct' (further discussed below), after which corporate capital will behave more responsibly.

A number of authors have attempted to explain why the rapid increase in global land acquisitions is happening now. Annelies Zoomers (2010, see also this volume) has correctly argued that there are many different processes behind the current land rush, of which foreign investment in 'offshore farming'—which includes food, livestock feed and fuel feedstock development, makes up only one of several "drivers". Even within this one category of offshore farming, the reasons behind such foreign investments can differ widely. For example, East Asian or Gulf-state corporations, often set up by governments to make investments in food or fuel production in distant countries, may be driven by concerns to ensure food and fuel security at home in an era of recurrent shortages and rising commodity prices. Conversely, when a hedge fund (or my American pension fund) makes similar investments, investors are not at all worried about food scarcities or rising prices; on the contrary, they welcome global scarcity, they live by it and hope it will continue, as speculation over increasing land prices due to scarcity creates an opportunity for capital accumulation. Farm land has effectively become a relatively safe and attractive investment in today's turbulent global economy.

But besides asking why the corporate land rush is happening now, we could equally ask, why is it *only* happening now, or why did it not already happen long ago? Isn't this what we should expect in this (post-) neoliberal era of late capitalism? Is it not part of the free marketeers' dream that governments in the global south should follow the example of countries like the United States, the Netherlands or Australia (to name a few) where land markets have always been open to foreign buyers? The logic of the global market necessarily involves the free mobility of capital, such that markets in land (like markets in everything else) should be laid open to cross-border transactions and buyers. In a world in which every bit of the planet is potentially up for sale, or at least for long-term lease, to whoever wants to buy it, foreign land acquisitions are expected to even out spatial imbalances in the demand for and the supply of land and food. This vision of the benign influence and developmental potential of free markets in land ignores the fact that 'real' markets (whether at the village, regional, national or global level) are not sites where local land users, as willing sellers, meet willing buyers on an equal footing, to the benefit of each, but sites where unequal power is exercised, to the benefit of the more powerful. Indeed in many large land deals, those who cultivate the land are not the ones making the deals, and may not even be consulted about them, because of the state's claim to be the sovereign owner of public or common lands and lands held under customary tenure (Wily 2012; Cotula 2011).

Most regions of the global south have experienced a long history of large-scale land appropriations by both domestic and foreign actors; first by pre-colonial rulers during chronic internal wars and conflicts over territory, then by colonial governments and now, increasingly, by foreign or domestic corporations supported by government. In the early 19th century, outright sale by colonial powers of large tracts of land held in customary tenure was quite common, but this was often prohibited or limited by later colonial legislation such that longer term leases became the norm. In the post-colonial decades, both governments and civil society groups attempted to correct some of these historical distortions by implementing land reforms or other means so as to break up large private or corporate estates and re-distribute land to smallholders (see for example Warriner 1969, Sobhan 1993, Lipton 2010). This was often done with the support of international agencies, such as the World Bank, which was a major proponent of the dismantling of former colonial concessions in favour of small-holder based agricultural development strategies up to the 1980s. Paradoxically, these policies are now being reversed as governments support the acquisition of great expanses of land by large corporations, both foreign and domestic, usually in the form of long-term concessions or leases rather than outright purchase. Many of these deals, we now know, run on the margins of hundreds or thousands of hectares; and some of the contiguous areas of land designated by states for corporate land deals exceed millions of hectares. The (potentially) enormous scale and speed of expansion of these deals, which may be more rapid than previous agro-commodity booms in colonial or post-colonial history, may mean that they will have correspondingly greater impact.

We should remember that not all large-scale land deals actually result in anything, and in many cases it is too early to see what their impacts will be. A government-to-government land deal is often no more than a framework under which concrete deals between agribusiness corporations and local government for the leasing and enclosure of designated areas may or may not emerge. Potentially, however, these deals open the way to a truly wide-ranging global land reform; paradoxically though, in the case of the global land rush, it is an 'upside-down' land reform, where instead of equitable land redistribution to correct historical distortions, governments take land from the poor and give it (or lease it) back to the rich.

How Important Is the Transnational Character of the Global 'Land Grab'?

Views on the importance of transnationality in large land deals will probably differ widely, depending on the perspective and the level of analysis. We know that both domestic and foreign investors are currently driving the current land rush, often in collaboration with the state (see Adamczewski et al., this volume). In terms of international relations, it goes without saying that international land deals may have wide-ranging implications and may be the cause of significant international tensions between countries (Strauss, this volume). To some actors (including rural or urban-based political movements with strong nationalist sentiments) it may be particularly important to know whether the companies leasing out land for agro-industrial production of export crops are foreign or domestically operated—or (as is probably most common) a mixture of both. To local populations and farmers, however, the foreign or domestic origins of investment capital, ownership of the crops to be grown and destination of those crops—where they will eventually be sold as fuel, food, cosmetics, or other final uses—is often unknown and potentially irrelevant. Even if these facts are known by local people (which is often not the case), other issues appear to be of more interest, such as the forms in which the land they use is appropriated (or 'processes of dispossession', see Sapignoli and Hitchcock, this volume), and the ways in which they are excluded or incorporated, sometimes as producers, in global commodity chains (Hall 2011); if contracted by the company, many local people find themselves producing crops for export to faraway places on land which they believed to be theirs, and which used to be the source of their own subsistence and sense of identity (see chapters by Buchalik and Postel, this volume).

Certainly domestic corporations, with their links to people in high places, can be just as ruthless as foreign investors and probably less subject to critical scrutiny by international watchdog organisations. This raises the question of whether agrarian capitalism based on foreign land claims and acquisitions is in any way essentially different from other forms of capitalist agrarian monocrop production, and in turn whether the transitions involved (if any) require new tools of analysis (Adamczewski et al., this volume).

How Does a 21st-Century 'Land Grab' Actually Work?

While the media often focus on the role of foreign governments concerned with safeguarding supplies of agricultural products and raw materials, the actual "grabbing" of land—by which we mean the dispossession and exclusion of local people due to the enclosure of territory for sale or lease to a corporate investor—is commonly done by local governments, working together with investor corporations, and local elites.

In nearly all cases, the land appropriated in this way is the subject of contestation. In many countries, the planned expansion of corporate farming is based in the large areas of land which are not (yet) covered by the laws governing private property relations but have the status of "public" or "state" lands (Adamczewski et al., this volume). While these lands provide livelihoods to millions of cultivators and forest users under a wide variety of unofficial, semi-official or "customary", individual, or collective tenurial relationships, states claim sovereign ownership of the same land. The informal and insecure tenure under which many cultivators and forest users operate makes for vulnerability in contexts of globalisation and transnational or domestic corporate land deals (Wily 2012), which in turn has prompted calls for greater security of tenure, both by peasant activists and external organisations. At the same time, however, in many countries we have seen in the past few years active developments in national law-making and government regulations aimed at creating a legal framework that will facilitate the corporate acquisition of land held under customary title.

National and local governments and their foreign partners justify the enclosure and corporate appropriation of contested land with the use of an array of discursive tools which on the one hand portray the land as "marginal", "abandoned", "barren", "unused", "unproductive", "idle" or even "empty", and on the other promise a wide range of benefits to local people in the form of infrastructure development and particularly jobs (see the last section of this book, and particularly the chapter by Odoemene in the Nigerian state discourse of the "new Nigeria"). Those who oppose enclosure, using their own discursive tools (Tegomoh, this volume) which we should also analyse critically, can therefore be branded as being "anti-development".

One aspect of contemporary land deals is that they are typically shrouded in secrecy, and with some exceptions (Odoemene, this volume) the agreements or contracts themselves are rarely publicly available. As Lorenzo Cotula observed in a recent report: "Land deal negotiations are unfolding fast and behind closed doors. But secrecy and haste are no friends of good deals" (2011, 3). Cotula and his team analyzed the contents of contracts for twelve land deals in seven African countries (Cameroon, Ethiopia, Liberia, Madagascar, Mali, Senegal, and Sudan). These contracts are generally made between host governments and foreign investors, with local landholders or communities, or their representatives, having no formal role at all in the transaction.[2]

A short concrete illustration may help. Bakari Nyari of the Ghanaian NGO RAINS describes how a Norwegian agrofuel company, Agro Fuel Africa (a subsidiary of Bio Fuel Norway),[3] took advantage of Northern Ghana's traditional system of communal land ownership in an attempt to claim and deforest large tracts of land and create "the largest Jatropha plantation in the world". Nyari describes how strategies for acquiring land often take the following course:

The imaginations of a few influential leaders in the community are captured.

> They are told about prospects for the community due to the project and they were swayed with promises of positions in the company or with monetary inducements. The idea is that these people do the necessary "footwork" in the villages where they spread the word about job opportunities.

[2] The single exception was Madagascar, where one of the contracts analyzed involved representatives of 13 farmer associations.

[3] www.agrofuel.no

> A document is then prepared, essentially a contract, to lease the land to the company (Nyari 2008, 3)

The company co-opted local government officials, and together with them persuaded an illiterate local chief to sign away 38,000 ha of land, including several whole villages, with a single thumbprint. To obtain the temporary support of local communities, developers raised local hopes of jobs and income, which did not materialize. As forests were cleared, local people lost their income from forest products, and local leaders (chiefs) were made to appear 'anti-development' when they opposed the project. In this case, however, the opposition, led by RAINS, was able to use Ghana's Environmental Assessment Regulations to get the forest destruction stopped, but not before 2,300 ha of forests had already been stripped. Local women, being those with the most to lose, were the most vocal in opposition. One woman, in a meeting with the company, looked the Agrofuel Africa Chairman Mr. Finn Byberg in the face and asked him:

> Look at all the shea nut trees you have cut down already, and consider the fact that the nuts I collect in a year give me cloth for the year and also a little capital. I can invest my petty income in the form of a ram, and sometimes in a good year I can buy a cow. Now you have destroyed the trees and you are promising me something you do not want to commit yourself to. Where then do you want me to go? What do you want me to do? (Nyari 2008, 6)

In this case, Byberg expressed his regrets and a promise not to repeat the mistake. This outcome is indeed unusual, if we recall that many of the agro-industrial groups involved in these deals—both foreign and domestic, usually in some kind of joint-venture arrangement—are 'among the most ruthless in the world in terms of environmental destruction, labour conditions and human rights abuses'.[4]

How Will Production Be Organised? Who Gains, Who Loses?

Where will the land for these massive deals come from, how will production be organized, and for whose benefit? It is important for critical researchers, besides raising issues of land tenure, to ask further questions about the kinds of structures and labour régimes under which production is or will be organized in the new corporate farms. Under what conditions (whether smallholder contract farming or large plantations using

[4] As Almuth Ernsting reminds us for Asia (2007, 25).

wage labour) are the crops grown and processed? Who among the various actors involved benefits from the value added, generated in field production and the various stages of processing ? And what measures, if any, are in place to ensure that smallholder producers, or wage workers, benefit from their involvement?

This links to broader questions that have long been discussed in agrarian studies: why is it that large-scale plantations and areas where smallholder contract-farming is practiced are typically not zones of growing prosperity for ordinary people, but pockets of persistent poverty (Beckford 1972; Little and Watts eds. 1994)? This is not to argue that wage-work in large-scale agriculture, or contract farming for agribusiness, is always impoverishing—why should it be, if labour and farmers are well-organised and their rights, claims and contracts actively promoted and protected by government and the legal system? But under current conditions, there are grounds for serious concern about the quality of employment in corporate production, for both plantation wage-workers and contracted outgrowers.

These questions can be approached with the same tools of critical analysis that agrarian studies has applied to historical episodes of rapid expansion of large-scale, industrialized, capitalist, monocrop agriculture, in both its plantation and outgrower/contract-farming forms. Henry Bernstein neatly summarizes the research objectives of an agrarian political economy in terms of questions like: "who owns what? who does what? who gets what? what do they do with it?" (Bernstein 2010, 22–24). To these questions we should add: "what do they do to each other?" to capture the relational and political side of property and labour regimes, labour processes and structures of accumulation. A modern and flexible agrarian political economy also incorporates, in its exploration of these questions, dimensions that were relatively neglected in classical agrarian studies, such as the dynamics of gender, ethnicity, livelihood diversity, mobility, rural-urban links, and the environment (White and Dasgupta 2010, 599–600).

Responses and Resistance: Farmers, International Organizations and States

In many countries, national (state-sponsored) farmers' organisations have not been active in protecting small-farmer and farm-worker rights in the face of large-scale agro-industrial development (in the case of farmworkers' rights on private wildlife farms, see Andrew et al., this volume). Local agrarian movements are more often active, but are themselves weak and sometimes fragmented. In some cases, farmers' organisations and NGOs are themselves split into two camps, one opposing and the other supporting land deals. For those who support the deals, capitalist monocrop farming may not be their chosen vision of the agricultural future, but after decades of state neglect and the failure to provide even the most minimal infrastructure and support to rural areas, it may seem to be the only way in which roads, electricity, schools, health care, and even perhaps some jobs, will come to the communities in question.

Faced with the realities of environmentally and socially irresponsible behaviour of corporate agribusiness, large-scale mining (de Koning, this volume), private wildlife tourism companies (Andrew et al., this volume) and the appropriation of land for conservation purposes ("green grabbing", see Fairhead, Leach and Scoones 2012), the policy response of international agencies has been to propose the adoption of non-binding rules or principles for responsible corporate behaviour. These include the five-point Code of Conduct proposed by IFPRI experts, The World Bank's 'Principles for Responsible Agro-investment', or the FAO's 'Voluntary Guidelines on Responsible Governance of Tenure of Land and Other Natural Resources' (Von Braun and Meinzen-Dick 2009; www.responsibleagroinvestment.org; CFS 2012). The World Bank Group's seven 'Principles for Responsible Agro-Investment', for example, include: respecting land and resource rights; ensuring food security; ensuring transparency, good governance, and a proper enabling environment; consultation and participation; responsible agro-enterprise investing; and social and environmental sustainability.

Two questions should be raised here. First, why should we expect corporations to act on a basis of voluntary corporate 'social responsibility'? The experience of already-existing bodies such as the Round Table on Sustainable Palm Oil and similar set-ups for soya and mining gives no grounds for optimism on the capacity of voluntary guidelines and "codes of conduct" to protect the interests of local cultivators, gender rights, labour and the environment. Years after the establishment of the Round Table, only a tiny fraction of global palm oil production is certified and there is hardly any market for certified palm oil. Capitalist firms are not Boy Scouts, and they are unlikely to place moral codes above the interests and demands of their owners or shareholders (Borras and Franco 2010).

Second, the 'voluntary guidelines' discourse builds on earlier agendas to improve legal and bureaucratic mechanisms for land governance in 'weak' states (World Bank 2010). As I and my LDPI co-authors have argued elsewhere, such portrayals of states as fragile, weak or corrupt and of 'good governance' as a solution to the excesses of expropriation are too facile. They need to be replaced with more nuanced analyses of the ways in which power flows through the various disaggregated levels and functions of the state. States are themselves often active, calculating partners in land deals. While the formal institutions of state and governance are important, they are only one aspect of the multi-faceted relationships which make up states; we need to understand how land deals are shaped by, and shape, the institutions, practices and discourses of territory, sovereignty, authority and subjects (Wolford et al. 2013).

Third, as Olivier De Schutter, the UN Special Rapporteur on the Right to Food, has rightly argued, seeing the solution in terms of such guidelines—designed to mitigate the harm caused to local populations by the expansion of large-scale, capital-intensive farming—is to narrow the terms of the debate, accepting that future agricultural development will be based on large-scale, capital and energy-intensive, agro-industrial monocrop ventures and closing the door to other alternatives, in which small-scale, labour-intensive, environmentally friendly modes of cultivation remain the core units of feeding the planet and keeping it cool.[5] Professor De Schutter has become the single most important voice within the UN family arguing for a broader vision that 'goes beyond disciplining land deals and providing policymakers with a checklist of how to destroy the global peasantry responsibly' (De Schutter 2011, 275), promoting investment that reduces hunger and malnutrition, rather than aggravating them. In his official reports to the UN General Assembly and Human Rights Council (UN General Assembly 2010a, 2010b), but also in academic publications and numerous keynote addresses, media articles or interviews and press releases, he has taken a firm stance against the current narrow framing of the debate on 'land grabbing'. He has argued consistently that 'the most pressing issue regarding investment in agriculture is not how much, but how: what we need is not to regulate land grabbing as if this were inevitable, but to put forward an alternative programme for agricultural investment' (2011: 250). In a series of authoritative reports he has argued that alternative approaches must be based not on speculative large-scale acquisitions of farmland, nor on the creation of a market for land rights based on individual titling, but on security of tenure, agrarian reform where land concentration has become excessive, and reorientation of agricultural systems towards agro-ecological modes of production that are

[5] On this point, see also Borras & Franco (2010).

both productive, sustainable and contribute to the progressive realization of the human right to adequate food. De Schutter therefore arrives at a quite different set of 'principles', in which:

> Land investments implying an important shift in land rights should represent *the last and least desirable option*, acceptable only if no other investment model can achieve a similar contribution to local development and improve the livelihoods within the local communities concerned (UN General Assembly 2010a, 20, emphasis added).

Land Deals and Agricultural Futures

What about the alternatives? The Via Campesina, one of the most successful global networks of small-farmer organisations, campaigns against land grabbing with slogans like:

> "Land-grabbing causes hunger! Let small-scale farmers feed the world!"
> and—
> "Small scale sustainable farmers are cooling down the earth"

and therefore demands:

> 1/ The complete dismantling of agribusiness companies: they are stealing the land of small producers, producing junk food and creating environmental disasters.
> 2/ The replacement of industrialized agriculture and animal production by small-scale sustainable agriculture supported by genuine agrarian reform programmes.[6]

Is this romantic nonsense? These claims also need to be critically interrogated. In fact, quite authoritative support on the technical side comes from an important but almost unnoticed international study, the International Assessment of Agricultural Science and Technology for Development (IAASTD 2009). This report was commissioned by a number of UN agencies, including the World Bank and FAO, and drew on the expertise of about 400 specialists from all over the world. It argues that agriculture can and must be reinvented if it is going to feed the world's expanding population sustainably. It concludes that the dominant practice of industrial, large-scale agriculture is unsustainable, mainly because of the dependence of such farming on cheap energy, its negative effects on ecosystems, and growing water scarcity. Instead, industrial monocultures

[6] See various La Via Campesina position papers on http://viacampesina.org.

must be reconsidered in favour of agro-ecosystems that combine mixed crop production with conserving water supplies, preserving biodiversity, and improving the livelihoods of the poor in small-scale, mixed farming. Although the World Bank was one of the sponsors of this report, the findings are not mentioned in the Bank's (2010) seminal "land grab" report.

There are plenty of opportunities for states, international agencies and even corporate capital to invest in support of this new direction. These do not require the financing of corporate acquisition of land but rather investment in public goods, in rural infrastructure and various forms of support to small-scale agriculture. Farmers themselves still provide the vast bulk of investment in agriculture, dwarfing the expenditures of private foreign investors, governments and international donors. In recent decades, though, governments in the south and the north have placed their focus elsewhere. For the last decade or so, developing country states and the international community have been withdrawing more and more from their role of supporting small farmers and rural development more generally (FAO 2012).

One way to reflect on agricultural futures is to consider what kind of rural future lies ahead for the next generation of rural people.[7] While some local elders and elites may become rich by facilitating land dispossession and exclusion, and some cultivators may be seduced by, or feel no other option than to accept, immediate cash payments for relinquishing their land, we also need to consider what kind of future these land deals imply for the next generation in rural areas, those who will inherit this future.

Ethnographic studies of "traditional" rural African ways of growing up provide examples in which children and young people who want to farm were allocated a plot of land to farm themselves by parents or other adult relatives or village elders. In Zimbabwe, Elisabeth Colson observed in the 1950s that many Tonga children had their own fields. Unmarried boys or girls might be given a portion of a field belonging to either father or mother before obtaining their own fallowed land, and after harvest might have their own bins in which to store grain from these plots (1960, 79–89). A generation later, in the same region, Pamela Reynolds described how young boys often worked on, and were sometimes allowed to make, their own farms on the land of a parent or other relative, and thus 'actively direct their labour contributions in accord with various strategies that

[7] The ideas in the final part of this chapter on implications for the next generation are discussed in greater detail in White (2012).

maximize their chances of meeting current needs, and establishing links among kin and neighbours that will enhance future security' (1991, xxvii). But in how many countries and regions is it still possible for young people to slip themselves into independent agricultural production and earning in the way that these examples have shown? One reason why young people express a reluctance to farm may reflect not an aversion to farming as such, but to the long period of waiting that they would have to face before they have a chance to engage in independent farming.

Recent generations of young men and women are often confronted by the narrowing and sometimes complete closure of opportunities to gain access to a plot of land. Buchalik (this volume) describes how the generational transfer of farm land among the Voltaic peoples in Burkina Faso has undergone organic transformation in the face of construction of a national road network. This blocking or postponement of generational transfers may happen under all kinds of land tenure systems, whether land is held in private title, under customary tenure (in which use rights to farm plots are allocated by family or clan elders or chiefs) or as 'state lands'. Meanwhile the expansion of formal education and particularly secondary education contributes to a process of de-skilling of rural youth in which farming skills are neglected and farming is downgraded as an occupation, as Katz (2004, 143–151) has noted in Sudan. Young people are already moving to the cities in large numbers, and it is now widely assumed that young rural people are uninterested in agricultural futures,

Arguments for smallholder-based alternatives and against large-scale, capital- and energy-intensive corporate farming lose some of their cogency if the next generation of young men and women are genuinely not interested in farming. But this should not be taken for granted. Julian Quan summarising studies from various African countries observes

> ... limitations in young people's access to land, land concentration, and land sales and allocations outside the kin group by older generations can become highly problematic where alternative livelihoods are not available, and can trigger wide social conflicts (Quan 2007, 57)

Georges Kouamé (2010) describes such conflicts from Côte d'Ivoire, where Abure youth, angered at the way the old men preferred to rent the land out to Burkinabe migrants for pineapple cultivation rather than letting their own young people work it, destroyed the pineapple crops in the field.

Among the few scholars who have been arguing consistently for the need to find ways to make farming a better and more available option for young people are Paul Richards and his former student, Krijn Peters. Peters describes in detail the mismanagement and stagnation of the agricultural sector in conflict-torn regions of Sierra Leone, the false hope that education gave young people of recognition and success, and the vulnerability of young people to local seniors which was evident in the elders' control over customary courts, land, agricultural labour, and the allocation of marriage partners.

> The point is that the African rural setting is not only inhabited by landowning peasants, but increasingly by numbers of young people who lack the basic modalities even to be peasants [...] They cannot even mobilize their own labour to work the allegedly abundant land, since this would be vulnerable to extraction from them by marriage payments and court fines for infringements of a traditional code of behaviour regulated by elders. (2011, 224f.)

Peters argues that 'the dislike of rural youth [for agriculture] is not focused on agriculture as such, but on their vulnerability, in village conditions, to exploitation by local elites and gerontocrats' (2011, 203). Reviewing recent proposals for (bio)technical solutions to African agrarian poverty, Richards concludes '.....perhaps an even bigger focus for reform [than biotechnology] is the need to open up land to more intensive use by making it more readily accessible to young people, free from control by a local gerontocratic order' (2010, 560).

The issue of intergenerational transfer of land rights—or, when that does not happen, intergenerational dispossession when one generation's land is sold off which ought to have been passed on to the next—deserves our attention. If we are interested in small-farm based alternatives to industrial capitalist agriculture, there needs to be a generation of rural men and women interested to take up the challenge.

As I have tried to indicate, and as further chapters in this volume demonstrate, the current debate about "land grabbing" is in fact a debate about the future shape of farming and the fate of rural populations. There are real and important choices to be made, with important consequences for the coming generations. We might express them in this way: will young men and women still have the option, and the necessary support, to engage in environmentally sound, small scale, commercial mixed farming, providing food and other needs for their own society and others? Or will they only face the choice to become poorly-paid wage workers or impoverished contract farmers, in an endless landscape of monocrop food or fuel feedstock plantations, on land which used to belong to their parents, or to move to an uncertain existence in the informal sector of already crowded cities?

Bibliography

Anseeuw, Ward, Liz Alden Wily, Lorenzo Cotula, and Michael Taylor. *Land Rights and the Rush for Land: Findings of the Global Commercial Pressures on Land Research Project.* Rome: International Land Coalition, 2012.

Beckford, George. *Persistent Poverty: Underdevelopment in the Plantation Economies of the Third World.* New York: Oxford University Press, 1972.

Bernstein, Henry. *Class Analysis of Agrarian Change.* Halifax and Sterling: Fernwood Publishing and Kumarian Press, 2010.

Borras, Saturnino Jr. & Jennifer Franco. "From Threat to Opportunity? Problems with the Idea of a 'Code of Conduct' for Land-Grabbing". *Yale Human Rights & Development Law Journal* 13 (2010): 507–523.

Von Braun, Joachim and Ruth Meinzen-Dick. " 'Land grabbing' by foreign investors in developing countries—risks and opportunities". Policy Brief No. 13. Washington: IFPRI, 2009.

CFS. Voluntary Guidelines on the Responsible Governance of Tenure of Land, Fisheries and Forests in the Context of National Food Security. Final version, March 2012. Rome: FAO Committee on World Food Security. http://www.csm4cfs.org/files/2/vg_en_final_march_2012.pdf, accessed 12 July 2012.

Colson, Elizabeth. *Social Organization of the Gwemba Tonga*, Manchester: Manchester University Press, 1960.

Cotula, Lorenzo. *Land Deals in Africa: What is in the Contracts?* London: International Institute of Environment and Development, 2011.

——. "The international political economy of the global land rush: a critical appraisal of trends, scale, geography and drivers", *The Journal of Peasant Studies* 39 (3–4), pp. 649–680, 2012.

De Schutter, Olivier. "How not to think of land-grabbing: three critiques of large-scale investments in farmland", *The Journal of Peasant Studies* 38, 2 (2011), pp. 249–79.

Ernsting, Almuth. "Agrofuels in Asia: fuelling poverty, conflict, deforestation and climate change". *Seedling* (July): 25–33, 2007.

Fairhead, James, Melissa Leach and Ian Scoones. "Green grabbing: a new appropriation of nature?" *The Journal of Peasant Studies* 39 (2), pp. 237–261, 2012.

FAO. *The State of Food and Agriculture 2012: Investing in Agriculture for a Better Future.* Rome: Food and Agriculture Organization of the United Nations, 2012.

Hall, Ruth. "Land Grabbing in Southern Africa: The Many Faces of the Investor Rush". *Review of African Political Economy* 128, 193–214, 2011.

IAASTD. *Synthesis Report: Agriculture at a Crossroads: International Assessment of Agricultural Science and Technology for Development.* Washington: Island Press, 2009.

Kalecki, Michal. "Social and economic aspects of 'intermediate regimes'" in M. Kalecki, *Selected Essays on the Economic Growth of the Socialist and the Mixed Economy.* Cambridge: University Press, 162–169, 1972 (orig. 1967).

Katz, Cindi. *Growing up Global: Economic Restructuring and Children's Everyday Lives.* Minneapolis: University of Minnesota Press, 2004.

Kouamé, Georges "Intra-family and socio-political dimensions of land markets and land conflicts: the case of the Abure, Côte d'Ivoire", *Africa: The Journal of the International African Institute*, 80, 1 (2010): 126–146.

Lipton, Michael. *Land Reform in Developing Countries: Property Rights and Property Wrongs.* London and New York: Routledge, 2010.

Little, Peter and Michael Watts eds. *Living Under Contract: Contract Farming and Agrarian Transformation in Sub-Saharan Africa.* Madison: University of Wisconsin Press, 1994.

Nyari, Bakari "Biofuel land grabbing in Northern Ghana", 2008 http://www.biofuelwatch.org.uk/files/biofuels_ghana.pdf.

Oxfam. *Land and Power: The Growing Scandal Surrounding the New Wave of Investments in Land.* Oxfam Briefing Paper 151. Oxford: Oxfam GB for Oxfam International, 2011.

Quan, Julian. "Changes in intra-family relations" in L. Cotula ed., *Changes in "Customary" Land Tenure Systems in Africa*, 51–63. London: IIED/FAO, 2007.

Peters, Krijn. *War and the Crisis of Youth in Sierra Leone.* Cambridge: University Press, 2011.

Reynolds, Pamela. *Dance Civet Cat: Child Labour in the Zambezi Valley.* London: Zed Books, 1991.

Richards, Paul. "Do peasants need GM crops?" *Journal of Peasant Studies* 37, 3 (2010): 559–574.

Scoones, Ian. Investing in land: a commentary on the World Bank report. News item, www.future-agricultures.org, 16 September 2010.

Sobhan, Rehman. *Agrarian Reform and Social Transformation.* London: Zed Books, 1993.

UN General Assembly. *Report of the Special Rapporteur on the Right to Food.* New York: UN General Assembly, 65th session, August (2010a).

——. *Report submitted by the Special Rapporteur on the Right to Food.* New York: UN General Assembly, Human Rights Council, 16th session, December (2010b).

Warriner, Doreen. *Land Reform in Principle and Practice.* Oxford: Clarendon Press, 1969.

White, Ben. "Who will own the countryside? Dispossession, rural youth and the future of farming". Valedictory Address delivered on the 59th Dies Natalis of the International Institute of Social Studies. The Hague: International Institute of Social Studies, 13 October 2011.

——. "Agriculture and the generation problem: rural youth, employment and the future of farming", *IDS Bulletin* 43 (6), pp. 9–19, 2012.

White, Ben and Anirban Dasgupta. "Agrofuels capitalism: a view from political economy" *the Journal of Peasant Studies* 37, 4, pp. 593–607, 2010.

Wily, Liz Alden "Looking back to see forward: the legal niceties of land theft in land rushes", *The Journal of Peasant Studies* 39 (3–4), pp. 751–775, 2012.

Wolford, Wendy, Saturnino M. Borras Jr., Ruth Hall, Ian Scoones and Ben White. "Governing global land deals: the role of the state in the rush for land", *Development and Change* 44 (2), (in press, March 2013).

World Bank. *Rising Global Interest in Farmland: Can it Yield Equitable and Sustainable Benefits?* Washington DC: The World Bank, 2010.

Zoomers, Annelies. "Globalisation and the foreignisation of space: seven processes driving the current global land grab" *Journal of Peasant Studies* 37, 2 (2010): 429–447.

A CRITICAL REVIEW OF THE POLICY DEBATE ON LARGE SCALE LAND ACQUISITIONS: FIGHTING THE SYMPTOMS OR KILLING THE HEART?

Annelies Zoomers

This article provides an overview of the debate on foreign large-scale land acquisitions (FLA) and shows that there are urgent reasons to deepen and broaden the policy discussion. Whereas in the media and policy circles much attention is given mainly to improving land governance, with an emphasis on *protecting local rights* and *stimulating responsible investments*, I'll show that this will not be sufficient for turning the tide: current policies fight the symptoms while leaving the underlying causes unchanged; lessons from history are neglected; the speed and scale of the global land rush is highly underestimated; and sets of development-related policies are not consistent. While searching for ways for how to control large-scale land acquisitions, policies in the field of food security and climate change are generating claims for land, putting the land markets under pressure. In order to achieve equitable and sustainable development, policies need to be aligned.

Introduction

It is recently, since 2008/2009, that media reports were published on a rapidly appearing new phenomenon that developed in response to the food and climate/energy crisis: Capital rich countries with arable land scarcity such as Qatar, and other Gulf States, Saudi-Arabia, South Korea, Japan and China, searched for large areas of fertile land in Africa for the cultivation of *food* and/or *biofuels*. Following the food crisis in 2007 and 2008, and stimulated by the growing demand for bio-energy, these countries, but also investors from the EU and the US (as well as from South Africa, India and Brazil etc.), started to buy or lease millions of hectares of fertile land, in Madagascar, Ethiopia, Mozambique; but also Senegal, Tanzania, Zambia, Ghana; and a number of post-conflict countries such as Liberia, Sudan, DRC etc. Whereas most attention was given to Africa, land investments were also made in large parts of Asia and Latin America.

Based on this 'global land *grab*' (also called 'the global *scramble* for farm land; or more neutrally 'the global land *rush*' or 'large-scale land *deals*'), a discussion started about whether or not these (new) investments in land could become a positive force of development, and two opposite positions appeared (Cotula et al. 2009; Zoomers 2010; Borras and Franco 2010). On the one hand, the World Bank and other actors stressed the positive aspects, acknowledging that it was good that there was finally attention for the agricultural sector (also illustrated by the publication in 2008 of the World Development Report 'Agriculture for development') which had been neglected for almost two decades. Land was assumed to be unproductive and not used anyway (Cotula and Vermeulen 2009). Large-scale investments (and the use of 'empty' land) were expected to stimulate agricultural development—help improving food security and solving the climate crisis (through the establishment of climate sound agriculture); contribute to employment generation, bring in new *technology*, while offering new sources of *tax income* (Deininger and Dyerlee 2011).

On the other hand, also in response to the negative outcomes, organizations such as Via Campesina, but also the United Nations Special Rapporteur on the right to food (Olivier de Schutter), stressed the negative side (mostly from the human rights perspective), indicating that these investments were threatening local groups, who often did not have secure land titles and could hardly defend themselves. Processes of 'land grabbing' would almost inevitably lead to exclusion, fragmentation, displacement and enclosure (De Schutter 2009; also FIAN 2010). According reports published by the Oakland Institute (2011) 'these largely unregulated land purchases are resulting in virtually none of the promised benefits for native populations, but instead are forcing millions of small farmers off ancestral lands and small, local food farms in order to make room for export commodities, including biofuels and cut flowers' (http://www.oaklandinstitute.org). They—and others—also warn Africa of "new colonialism" from foreign investors (including hedge funds) and governments interested only in extracting the continent's natural resources to enrich themselves and not the African people. According to Cotula et al. (2009: 68) 'Land issues are emotive: large-scale transfers to foreign interests raise the spectre of the "bad old days" of colonialism and exploitative plantations' (....). International land deals may be perceived as bringing back the "bad old days" of colonialism, particularly in Africa. This is particularly so when rental fees are zero or close to zero (Cotula et al. 2009: 104).

Since the start of this debate, much discussion has taken place about the consequences. Organizations such as GRAIN (http://www.grain.org) and the International Land Coalition (http://www.landcoalition.org) are making attempts to collect information about what is happening on the ground (e.g. the construction of an online public data base on large-scale land acquisitions (and http://landportal.info/landmatrix); academics and journalists are currently actively involved reporting about the current situation and/or doing research (e.g. Cotula et al. 2009; Kugelman et al. 2009; Matondi et al. 2011; Deininger and Byerlee 2011; Harcourt 2011); there has been a boom in PhD projects[1] and many publications are currently under review.[2] Finally, policy makers and practitioners are looking for new policies (guidelines, codes of conduct etc.) to deal with this new phenomenon (see also http://www.IIED.org; htpp://www.landgovernance.org; and http://www.fao.org).

This chapter, based on several research projects in Africa,[3] as well as ongoing research in Indonesia (Susanti and Burgers 2011), Costa Rica (van Noorloos 2011), Vietnam (Pham Huu 2011), Argentina, Bolivia and Paraguay (Goldfarb 2011), aims to give a critical overview of the policy debate, providing an update of what we know today, but also showing that there are many reasons for concern. In order to stop land 'grabbing' (while also taking care of food security, energy needs and poverty alleviation), the current debate needs to be deepened and broadened. In policy debates much attention is currently given to improving land governance, protecting local people's rights, while stimulating responsible investment. However, are such policies enough to turn the tide and guaranteeing inclusive and sustainable development?

After a description of the state of the art, attention will be given to current policy initiatives, followed by a critical analysis of gaps an shortcomings, showing that current policy solutions are too limited. This is followed by a conclusion.

State of the Art: What Do We Know?

After the first media boom, a rapid start was made with many new research projects, and based on reports published by the World Bank, FAO, GRAIN, ILC, but also IIED, LANDac etc. (Deininger and Byerlee 2011; Cotula et al.

[1] In the Netherlands, various new research programmes on large-scale land acquisitions have been initiated at various universities in Amsterdam, Leiden, Utrecht and Wageningen.

[2] See for example special issues of the Journal of Peasant Studies, Feminist Economics, Development and Change and Geopolitics.

[3] Part of these projects are financed though LANDac (a partnership between of several academic institutions, private sectors and NGOs (see www.landgovernance.org).

2009 etc.), all kind of information was published about (a) the scale and area (b) the type of actors, and (c) and the implications on the ground.

a. *About the Scale and Type of Land*

Reviewing what kind of information we have about the extension of 'land grabbing', the World Bank (2010) counted in 2009 389 deals concerning 47 million hectares. At the same time, other sources mention larger amounts. The Global Land Project (Friis and Reenberg 2010) cites a minimum of around 10 million hectares in each of Mozambique, *DR Congo* and *Congo*, and in 27 African countries screened, it noted 177 deals covering between 51 and 63 million hectares. In recent research OXFAM/Novib estimates the total number of land deals on almost 1500 (80 million hectares), mostly used for the production of food (37%) or biofuels (35%).

But due to the lack of reliable statistics and the fact that land transfers are often invisible the truth is that no one knows how much land is involved or how many people are being affected. Reasons for why it is difficult to make reliable estimations include the lack of clarity about how to define land *grab* (what kind of land deals should be included) and the invisibility of land transfers.

> Land markets are not easy to elucidate. Land markets—or more specifically land transfers—are often not visible. Markets in *land* are in reality markets in land *rights*. In many cases, however, there may not be a transfer of documents because people do not have titles, or there is no land registration. Moreover, there may be no direct link between the official title and the real situation. Land ownership relations are often a layered reality in which earlier rights are still operative and the use rights of land do not always coincide with the use rights of water, trees and other resources (Zoomers 2003: 250).

Transferring land rights will thus often not have visible impacts and there is often a large time lapse between land acquisition and visible results. Planned investments are often slow and large areas of newly acquired land are used for speculation by, for example, international hedge funds. In other cases, investments are postponed, and thus there is no direct land use change.

At the same time, however, it is clear that the area involved is huge—and not restricted only to Africa. Large-scale land acquisition is taking place also in large areas of Asia and Latin America (Zoomers 2010). At least millions of hectares are covered by biofuels, sugar or Soya in Brazil, Argentina, Paraguay, Bolivia (Goldfarb 2011); oil palm in Indonesia

(Susanti and Burgers 2011) and the area involved is rapidly expanding.[4] Even though it is difficult to have detailed information about the number of hectares involved, it is clear that it is contributing to land use change: large-scale land acquisition has gone hand in hand with the rapid expansion of large-scale monocropping, often on the better agricultural land; it generally concerns the more fertile soils in areas with sufficient rainfall or good irrigation potential, and with better access to markets (Cotula and Vermeulen 2009). Loosing this land for local food production has obviously disproportionate impacts on food security and livelihoods. It is increasingly recognized that very little land is vacant or unused. Many of the areas involved are not empty, but occupied or used by various groups (see Alden Wily's 'Whose land are you giving away, Mr. President?') who utilize the land for various purposes, such as grazing animals and gathering fuel wood and contributes to local livelihood and food security of the poor.

In addition, large-scale land acquisition is also going at the cost of forest areas and is increasingly affecting ecologically fragile land; in Indonesia, for example, oil palm first went hand in hand with deforestation, but is nowadays going at the cost of peat lands, which is on the one hand less productive, and ecologically more vulnerability, on the other (Susanti and Burgers 2011).

According to the World Bank (2010) investors are deliberately targeting areas where government is weak. Much of the land involved is therefore located in post-conflict areas where parts of the populations are displaced and where ownership and/or governance relations are often not so clear (Mabikke 2011).

Making an effort to estimate area involved, it is important to acknowledge that the effects will not be restricted to the area of land leased and/or purchased: it will also have effects for other areas; rapid expansion of investments in oil palm in Indonesia, for example, were followed by fast immigration (opportunity seekers, interested in occupying the land and/or searching for new employment opportunities). Pressure on the local land markets are therefore often stronger that the pressure by the investments alone. This will in itself push other groups away who will

[4] We also know that land acquisition is not always about 'land'; land acquisition is also driven by the search for water and/or mineral resources (or land grabbing is driven by speculation). It is basically a process of 'resource' grabbing, so the area involved is probably larger than the 'land' grab alone.

search for new lands in (often more marginal) areas, generating a whole chains of displacement effects as if it were a water bed (Zoomers and van Westen 2011).

b. *About the Actors*

After the start of the land grab debate around 2009, positions have changed and the initial picture of 'Gulf states grabbing land in Africa' has become more nuanced and more diverse. In-depth research about what is happening on the ground shows that the range of actors tends to be very diverse: in addition to governments of countries such as South Korea or Qatar (who were amongst the first who were blamed for grabbing land in Madagascar and Kenya, respectively), there is a wide variety of other countries and investors (www.grain.org; www.landcoalition.org). Many firms, also from the US and the EU, are currently looking for land, not only in Africa, but also in the rest of the world. In addition to investments from the Gulf, China, EU and/or US, it is interesting to see that also Argentina and Brazil,[5] South Africa, India (but also Mauritius etc.) are actively involved in this search for arable land for food and/or biofuel/energy production.

In addition to the fact that the group of countries and/or businesses involved is more diverse than initially suggested, field research makes very clear that it is *not only foreign, but also domestic investors* who play an important role (see Sapignoli and Hitchcock, this volume). In addition to foreign and corporate capital, acquisition of land is also done by local domestic elites (see for West Africa Hilhorst et al. 2008). Land acquisitions are thus not necessarily about enormous tracts of land, or mega projects, but can also emerge from a conglomerate of smaller acquisitions. In practice, land acquisitions are often done by joint ventures, making the distinction between foreign and domestic capital rather artificial—investments are often a mix.

Research shows that in many countries (in Africa, but also Asia and Latin America) it is not right to speak about land *grabbing*, due to the fact that much of what happens today is *not illegal* at all. Host governments often support or enable these deals (i.e., land often being state owned). National governments regard these investments as a panacea (FIAN 2010);

[5] Brazil has recently signed agreement with for example Mozambique (and other 'Latin' African countries, often though or in collaboration with South Africa etc.) after having expanded in the direction of countries such as Bolivia, Paraguay (already during decades). See also Goldfarb (2011) for investments from Argentina.

in other words, a sound way to obtain foreign exchange, and with potential positive effects on infrastructure, rural job generation, technology transfer, growing of export crops, and improved food security (International land coalition 2010; FOE 2010). Governments such as in Ethiopia have high expectations about how foreign investors could help to initiate 'modernization' processes, and play central roles in setting up attractive regulating frameworks, negotiating the conditions and signing bilateral agreements etc. It is thus often part of official state policies to attract (foreign) investors who are offered state lands under favorable conditions with low cost leasing contracts between 50–99 years. The prices that investors pay for the land is often extremely low (between 1–5 dollars per hectare), and the 'modernization' effects (agricultural development, technology, employment etc.) are usually considered the main benefit (i.e., and not so much the direct land income).

In Africa (but also in Asia, and Latin America), the capacity of local governments to control grabbing is often rather limited—and local groups are often left out of negotiations; local groups often have high expectations about the benefits that will come and hope to profit from the employment that will be generated. These are reasons why the process is rapid and difficult to stop.

c. *About the Impact*

Since the start of the debate, much has been written about the impact of land grabbing, and today, three years after the start of the debate, it is increasingly clear that many of the expected benefits (employment etc.) have not (yet) crystallized; local people are often not informed—and have generally not (yet) been able to benefit. The 2010 World Bank report acknowledges that many of these so-called investment projects did no generate benefits, but in fact 'contributed to asset loss and left people worse off than they would have been without the investment' (World Bank 2010: 71). Land acquisitions until now did not inject much needed investment into agriculture and rural areas, but contributed in many places to the deterioration of the local situation (also environmentally). Local people lost control over their land[6] (von Braun and Meinzen-Dick 2009).

[6] In Africa, 90% of land remains outside the formal systems (FAO 2010) and many countries do not have legal or procedural mechanisms to protect local rights and take account of local interests, livelihoods and welfare (Cotula et al. 2009).

Practice shows the number of jobs generated by land investment usually is very small. Labor requirements for crops such as Soya is extremely limited. Chinese investors are often blamed for even bringing their own Chinese laborers (cf. http://www.grain.org). To the extent that large-scale land investment is based on outgrower schemes, payment and/or labor conditions are not necessary favorable (Cotula et al. 2009). Those places where investment is generating economic growth—for example, in Indonesia, as a result of investments in palm oil—will often attract large numbers of immigrants from surrounding areas with better education and more capital etc., who push local people aside (Susanti and Burgers 2011).

It is thus increasingly acknowledged that much goes wrong, with all kinds of unintended problems. Problems are in the first place caused by the 'myth of empty areas': lands presented as 'empty areas' are in practice often inhabited by local groups who are forced to move or are excluded from collective land or open 'commons' (pasture land, used by nomads etc.). It is now commonly acknowledged, also by the World Bank, that local populations are not part of the negotiation process. Local groups are *not informed* and do *not participate* in decision making; to the extent that agreements are made between governments and investors, arrangements are mostly confidential, and nobody is in a position to control (also not the Parliament). In addition, local groups do often not receive *compensation.* And if they do, the amount of money is not enough to buy new land, due to the increasing pressure on the land. *Rapid price increases* might be beneficial for people who are selling their lands, but it is pushing away people in the direction of more marginal low-cost areas (making them more vulnerable to climate risks of flooding, drought etc.). Another problem of rising land prices is that governments (willing to invest in social land reforms, social housing and/or nature conservation) are no longer able to do so. An example is Costa Rica where the government can no longer afford to buy land for nature conservation (van Noorloos 2011), even though private investors might at the same time acquire land to create their own 'paradise'.

Large scale land acquisitions are going hand in hand with growing tensions. As a response, some African countries, such as Mozambique, has decided to take a 'time out', imposing a moratorium on the purchase of land to non-citizens land with immediate effect, as an interim measure until appropriate legislation has been promulgated.

New Policy Initiatives by Donors

In general terms, to the extent that governments, NGOs and multilateral donor organizations are currently involved in policy formulation, much emphasis is given to improving land governance systems (in the context of 'good' governance), focusing on issues of *how to protect the rights of local people* (including the provision of compensation arrangements etc.); and *how to control the behavior of investors* through the development of 'codes of conduct'.

1. *Inclusive Land Policies and Protecting the Rights of Local People*

The Special Rapporteur on the right to food, Olivier de Schutter, has played an important role in bringing forward initiatives to improve the performance and limit the negative implications of large scale land acquisitions, pushing people's rights. In his report on the right to food (UN 2009), de Schutter proposes a set of core principles and measures for host states and investors to ensure informed participation of local communities, adequate benefit sharing and modes of agriculture that respect the environment. In addition, FAO has been working on the 'Voluntary Guidelines on the Responsible Governance of Tenure of Land, Fisheries and Forests in the Context of National Food, which was endorsed in 2012.

In the context of donor policies related to 'protecting local people's rights', much attention is given also to the need for land titling[7] and the creation of modern—low cost-land administration systems. Even though for a long time much attention was given to the need for individual and private titling (Deininger 2003; de Soto 2000 etc.), it has been accepted (also by the World Bank) that recognizing customary and/or collective titles are in many situations a more effective way of providing people with secure access. In practice, however, the contribution of land administration and land titling to land security tends to be limited: In many countries (even in countries like Mozambique with positive legal frameworks) due to capacity problems policy implementation is limited; local authorities who can control—but also civil society—are often too weak, opening

[7] In Africa, but also in Asia and parts of Latin America, to the extent that people have access to the land, this is often on the basis of informal and customary rights, but many lack formal titles. Tenure security is assumed to depend on having formal titles and transparent land administration systems.

Box 1: The voluntary guidelines

On 11 May 2012 the Committee on World Food Security (CFS) officially endorsed the Voluntary Guidelines on the Responsible Governance of Tenure of Land, Fisheries and Forests in the Context of National Food Security (http://www.fao.org).[8]

These Voluntary Guidelines (based on consultations in various countries and different stakeholders searching for 'national' consensus)[9] is intended to provide a framework for responsible tenure governance that supports food security, poverty alleviation, sustainable resource use and environmental protection. It sets out principles and internationally accepted practices that may guide the preparation and implementation of policies and laws related to tenure governance and much emphasis is on 'protect tenure rights to land, fisheries and forestry and to resolve conflicts; legal recognition of indigenous and other customary tenure rights, as well as informal rights (not only for land, but also other natural resources, including gathering rights. '(...) *States should protect tenure right holders against the arbitrary loss of their tenure rights, including forced evictions that are inconsistent with their existing obligations under national and international law; Promote and facilitate the enjoyment of legitimate tenure rights and provide access to justice to deal with infringements of legitimate tenure rights. They should provide effective and accessible means'* (pp. 3–4). The voluntary guidelines seek to improve governance of tenure of land, fisheries and forestries for the benefit of all, with an emphasis on vulnerable and marginalized people, with the goal of food security, poverty alleviation, sustainable livelihoods, social stability, housing security, rural development, environmental protection and economic growth' (p. 5). Guiding principles for responsible investment as formulated in the document are *Respect* (to recognize and respect tenure right holders and their right whether formally recorded or not); *Protect* (to safeguard tenure rights against threats; human rights are thus taken as a starting point, with much attention for consultation and participation); *Transparency* (i.e., providing information about rules and current situation) and *Accountability* (holding people and public agencies responsible for their actions and decisions).

[8] This initiative aims at supporting the progressive realization of the right to adequate food in the context of national food security, which were adopted by the FAO council at its hundred and twenty seventh session in November 2004, and the 2006 international conference on agrarian reform and rural development (ICARRD).

[9] During 2009–10, global and regional concerns regarding tenure governance were identified through an inclusive process of consultations. Regional consultations were held in Brazil, Burkina Faso, Ethiopia, Jordan, Namibia, Panama, Romania, the Russian federation, Samoa and Vietnam. These regional consultations brought together almost 700 people, from 133 countries, representing the public and private sector, civil society and academia. These consultations showed a strong consensus for an international instrument that deals with the governance of land, fisheries and forests (also in line with the MDGs).

the door for corruption and non-authorized transfers, in spite of attempts to improve the land policies.

In addition, land titling programs might generate some security (to those who get a title to their land), but will not translate into enhanced production capacity (due to the lack of credit facilities, lack of technical assistance and/or lack of fertile land). Even in the more positive circumstances, land titles might help the 'head of household' (male and/or female heads of households) to improve, but this is not a solution for the landless; or the youth who still rely on inheriting land; until inheritance they do not have other options than to work family-plots.

In the case of large-scale land acquisitions, providing local people with land titles might mean that they can stay on their lands, but this does not mean that they will benefit: immigrant groups of newcomers are often more successful in benefiting from the newly generated employment because they are better qualified. The local population (who could stay if their rights were acknowledged) is in many cases bypassed by newcomers—immigrants with higher levels of education, opportunity seekers who bring more capital and have better opportunities to benefit. In Riau (Indonesia), for example, investments in oil palm are mainly done by smallholder (Susanti and Burgers 2011); it is mainly the immigrants from Java and from the outside who are the 'winners' of development. After some time, it is will be increasingly difficult to define who the 'local' population is and who the external people or 'strangers' (van Noorloos 2011).

2. *Stimulating Responsible Investments and Codes of Conducts*

In addition to protecting local groups through the provision of land rights, others are focusing on *control the behavior of investors by applying notions of social corporate responsibility*. The World Bank has been working on a 'code of conduct' (or 'Principles') together with appropriate land policies (World Bank 2010). In addition, there are initiatives to create more responsible conduct of large investors such as the roundtable for sustainable oil palm or the round table for soy production. In these discussions until now, much emphasis tends to be given to the need for more consultation and mechanisms for benefit sharing, including compensation (Deininger and Byerlee 2011).

Developing 'codes of conduct' are of course positive in preventing exploitative relationships, but there are many limitations (Meinzen-Dick and Markelova 2009). First, codes of conduct might work (i.e., individual enterprises being forced to keep rules), but the outcomes (and the developmental impact) will very much depend on the negotiating power of the various stakeholders, and the capacity to control. Conditionality will be highly variable in space, creating a very heterogeneous situation and nobody is in a good position to control. Codes of conduct might help to stimulate development on a 'case-to-case' basis, generating development on a basis of negotiation, but there is a risk that this will lead to an extremely heterogeneous, fragmented and not transparent situation. Agreements are often made in the confidential sphere, and tools for exercising land rights are often very limited (also due to lack of democratic bodies).

Along with the codes of conduct and/or the promotion of 'responsible investments', there is a chance that new investments will be made in the social sphere (schools, medical services, housing etc.) which are very similar to the 'old fashioned' (and isolated) development projects. Whereas development organizations decided to turn away from the project approach (in favor of the Sector Wide Approach), there is now a risk that old-fashioned development projects return—leading to patchwork of islands of wealth, which are not sustainable in the long run. At the same time, codes of conducts might help to control the negative effects of large-scale land acquisition, but the impact will be limited to 'enlightened' investors who are willing to following these principles. It is clear, however, that not all the investors will be equally interested in or capable of following such principles (especially not at times of crisis). Even if investors adhere to principles—or accept new rules—they cannot be imposed on the whole sector and free-riding cannot be prevented.

Some Critical Reflections: Need to Deepen and Broaden the Debate

It is striking that in the current debate—and donor policies to deal with large-scale land acquisition- there is so much attention given to the need to improve the institutions: To the extent that large-scale land acquisitions are producing counterproductive results, this is explained by many as a consequence of weak governance and 'lack of rules'. According to the FAO, many tenure problems arise because of weak governance, and attempts to address tenure problems are affected by the quality of governance. 'Weak governance adversely affects social stability, sustainable use of the environment, investment and economic growth. People can be condemned to a life of hunger and poverty if they lose their farms, their homes and their livelihoods because corrupt tenure practices or implementing agencies fail to protect their tenure rights. People may even lose their lives when weak tenure governance leads to violent conflict' (http//www.fao.org). To the extent that active attempts are currently made to improve the situation (see above) all proposed solutions are related to institutional change, varying from voluntary guidelines, land titling, principles, codes of conduct etc etc.

There are several reasons, however, why 'blaming weak governance' and focusing on strengthening institutions as a tool for 'protecting local populations' (titling, land administration) and/or 'controlling investors/making investments more responsible' (codes of conduct etc.) will not be strong enough to turn the tide: current policies fight the symptoms while leaving the underlying causes unchanged; lessons from history are neglected, which will be discussed below; the speed and scale of the global land rush is highly underestimated; and sets of development-related policies are not consistent. While searching for ways for how to control large-scale land acquisitions, policies in the field of food security and climate change are generating claims for land, putting the land markets under pressure. In order to achieve equitable and sustainable development, policies need to become more coherent.

1. *Land Grabbing as a Logical Consequence of Earlier Policies: Fighting the Symptoms, Neglecting the Origins?*

It is striking that current land 'grab' is presented as *sudden* and *unexpected* issues (consequence of the food and energy crisis), without seeing it as a logical outcome of earlier policies. It should be acknowledged that current developments are the direct consequence of previous strategies (which were actively supported by donors).

In the early 1980s (when the state still played a central role in development *planning*), donor organizations played some role in land related matters by providing technical assistance; supporting 'integrated rural development projects' and other 'neutral' programs without having direct involvement in land reform and/or land-related policies (which were considered politically oversensitive by donors—better not to get involved). With the start of the neoliberal policies, along with the withdrawal of the state, agriculture and rural development slowly disappeared from the policy agenda leaving the development of these sectors increasingly to free market forces (even though NGOs played an increasingly important role in poverty alleviation).

It is interesting that in the context of neoliberal policies (especially in the early 1990s), donors started to play a direct role in land-related issues, something that had long been taboo. Along with the writing of de Soto (2000), donors started to invest increasing amounts of money in measures aimed at the liberalization of land markets, titling programs, and the creation of cadastres. Well-defined, secure land rights were considered crucial to creating incentives for investment and sustainable resource management, to facilitate low-cost transfers of land and credit access as the rural non-farm economy develops, and to allow the provision of public services at minimum costs (Deininger 2003; Zoomers and van der Haar 2000).

Later, when the agendas shifted from pure market liberalization toward good governance, donors and NGOs put effort into stimulating decentralization (strengthening local governments and stimulating participatory planning), while also pressing governments to create an enabling and stimulating business environment, as attracting foreign investment was seen as a necessary condition for pro-poor growth. In sum, in the last decade, donors played direct roles in stimulating governments to liberalize land markets (and in commoditizing land), attract foreign investment, and decentralize (while strengthening the capacity of local governments). It is not the food crisis or the demand for biofuels, but the whole set of earlier policies that is responsible for the current trends. Buying land became much easier, and increasing the level of foreign investment was presented as an indicator of success. However, local governments were often not strong enough to deal with these new outsiders.

What is interesting, but also confusing in the current debate, is that the type of solutions that are proposed today (land titling, codes of conduct) are basically a continuation of earlier policies, without any fundamental assessment of the underlying (neoliberal) ideas. Also striking is that in the current debate there is no discussion on the unexpected return of the state; it is now acknowledged that national governments have an important role to play, and hardly any reference is made to why decentralization failed. In fact, there is no discussion on a number of issues that really matter: Whether we should continue along this road of land commoditization (and stimulating free land markets); whether the emphasis should be on growth and attracting foreign capital (and how to incorporate private capital in development strategies); and whether we should reassess the role of the state and/or the importance of decentralization.

2. *Neglecting Lessons from the Past*

A second issue that I would like to raise is that in the current debate so little attention is given to the historical context, and that no attempt are made to learn from history. Even though that some refer to today's land rush in terms of new colonialism, it is a fact that no systematic analysis is made about questions such as 'what is old' and 'what is new'.

Focusing on the liberal period in the late 1800s, there were many examples of large-scale land acquisitions. A well-known example of such a large-scale land owner is the Argentinean Carlos Casado, who in 1886 secured ownership of almost 6 million hectares in the Paraguayan Chaco, an area larger than Switzerland (Kleinpenning 2009). Another interesting case involved land grabbing in early colonial Rhodesia, when the British government granted a royal charter to the millionaire Cecil Rhodes that 'gave him carte blanche for 35 years to exploit large territories we now know as Zimbabwe and Zambia' (Palmer 2010: 1). In the colonial and post-colonial time, many countries had extremely unequal patterns of land ownership, which were characterized by a high degree of concentration in the hands of a small minority. Also elsewhere, e.g., in the case of the Chagos islands, whole island groups were leased and people evicted in order to establish a new military basis (Evers and Kooy 2011).

Focusing on large-scale land acquisition today, it is relevant to acknowledge that in some countries current trends are opposite to earlier redistributive *land reforms* when governments made attempts to redistribute large land holdings in favor of small holders; but is sometimes also a repetition (or even a continuation) of earlier policies, e.g., the *green revolution* (introduction of new crop varieties, monocropping, mechanization etc.) and *agricultural colonization* (countries with considerable areas of 'empty' land trying to expand their cultivated area by settlement schemes). Many lessons can be learned: the Green Revolution (1950s) was evident of the strength of capital-intensive technological (new varieties, irrigation, rapid agricultural growth), but also the dangers and risks (salination of irrigated areas, growing inequality); land reforms (mainly in the 1960–70s) illustrate how difficult it is to change property relations—how politically sensitive the land issue is—and how creative (large) land holders can be to undermine or 'play with' rules (e.g., transferring land to their children for preventing expropriation etc.). Finally, agricultural colonization (1970s–1980s) demonstrated the myth of 'empty lands', but also the devastating environmental impact of horizontal strategies, leading to deforestation and environmental degradation (such as in the Amazon, but also in

Indonesia). It also showed how difficult it is to control the spontaneous mass-migration (large-scale land investment being followed by rapid processes of spontaneous colonization by people looking for land, leading to rapid deforestation etc.) (Kay 1998 and Dorner 1992 in Zoomers and van der Haar 2000, 19).

In assessing the land deals that are currently taking place in various countries, it is important to take into account the historical situation. In some countries (like Paraguay) current land grabbing is a 'continuation of history'; this is very different from the situation in countries such as Tanzania with a history of social land reforms (*Ujamaa*), and where current land deals are opposite to earlier trends (reversal of history). How current development relate to previous pathways of development is relevant (is it more of the same, or is it opposite to earlier developments).

3. *The Underestimation of the Scale of the Global Land Rush*

Another limitation is that in the current land debate there is a one-sided focus on agricultural lands (food and fuel). However, there are simultaneous forces that are also pushing people from their land, and pressures on (local) land markets are much larger than now suggested. Large-scale land acquisitions are also taking place for other purposes such as mining (often going hand in hand with pollution and/or destruction of the landscapes) (see de Koning, this volume), especially when concentration of minerals is low. In addition, large-scale land acquisitions take place also for nature conservation and REDD (Fairhead, Leach and Scoones 2012). Private investors, such as the Benetton family and other millionaires have bought millions of land in Patagonia which is now almost completely in private hands. In the Paraguayan Chaco, the 'Moonies' have become the owners of a huge tract of land providing them with the desired 'privacy' and entitling them to keep others out (Zoomers 2010).

There is a number of land claims that are usually not mentioned in the current debates, but which together consume large areas of land: acquisition of land for tourism (hotels searching for the best locations, often also influenced by UNESCO's world heritage sites)[10] and wildlife tourism (see Andrew et al., this volume). A space-intensive type of tourism is residential tourism: the baby boomers from US and EU buying apartments in 'gated' communities in countries such as Mexico, Panama and Costa Rica

[10] UNESCO world heritage sites are increasingly expropriated and managed by non-locals.

(van Noorloos 2011), but also in North Africa and Asia, where they hope for a long and 'sunny' life after retirement (Zoomers 2010).

In addition, along with globalization, *international labor migration* has also increased, with increasing numbers of people from the south migrating to far-away destinations in the north (or neighboring countries); migrants in diaspora are increasingly interested to use their remittances for buying new land/housing in their areas of origin, creating a real estate boom and putting local land markets under pressure. These diasporas (and presence of groups of migrants worldwide) play an important role also in facilitating investors (from US, EU etc.) to find their way in the direction of their areas of origin (e.g. the Chinese diaspora helping investors to open the doors in Africa and Latin America).

Finally, another important driver that is insufficiently taken into account in the current debate is urban expansion, and the fact that worldwide—especially in the surroundings of mega cities—agricultural lands are pushed away (also city centers are rapidly expanding due to foreign investments). Thousands of hectares of formerly agricultural land now lay idle, also due to speculation (hedge funds etc.). Given the speed of urbanization worldwide, this is one of the issues that need to be put central on the land governance agenda.[11] In Asia, in particular, pressures in the peri-urban sphere are rapidly increasing, due to large-scale land acquisition by the state who give priority to the establishment of *special economic zones* and/or the construction of airports and/or other infrastructural works (hydroelectric dams etc.) that are all related to the rapid economic growth.

The above-mentioned processes are producing both the obvious direct effects and the less visible indirect effects: The people who are displaced, whether voluntarily or forcibly, whether compensated or uncompensated, need to be re-established—and this is why the scale of land acquisition should not be underestimated. The earlier mentioned estimate of 47 to 80 million ha is only the tip of the iceberg, as local land markets are increasingly under pressure, especially in peri-urban areas. Codes of conduct or voluntary guidelines will not be enough to make a difference and/or guarantee responsible investment and/or inclusive development.

---

[11] In addition, it is time to bridge the gap between urban and rural debates. The 'right to the city debate' is taking place separately from debates about how to protect the rights of local people in the rural sphere, but it is basically about similar issues.

4. *The Mismatch between Parallel Debates: Policies are not Compatible*

Finally, another reason for concern is the inconsistency between simultaneous policy debates, all related to 'development'. Whereas donors were for a long time driven by goals such as development—sustainable development and/or poverty alleviation in the south, current concerns are much more fragmented and dispersed. There are many separate debates, each of them going in different directions. Policymakers and practitioners involved in pro-poor growth and poverty alleviation are, for example, concerned with questions such as how to achieve the MDGs (which in practice often translates in improvements in social infrastructure and services). Those involved in the food-security debate are much more involved in 'how to feed a world population of 9 billion in 2050'; in the debate about climate change all the attention is focused on mitigation and/or adaptation strategies etc. In each these debates, sub-groups of policy makers come up with their own set of recommendations (which are insufficiently compatible).

When looking at these debates from the perspective of land grabbing, it is striking (and problematic) that each ends up in 'competing claims' on land, stimulating the global land rush. Whereas policy makers in the land grab debate focus on how to prevent (further) land grabbing, protect local groups and/or control for the behavior of investors etc., colleagues in the food-security debate stress the need to expand frontiers of food production; some are in favor of the installation of new 'agro-hubs', the creation of large-scale agro-industrial complexes, including outgrowers schemes, while others plea for optimizing the link between small-holders and global commodity chains.

At the same time, policy makers working on climate change often give priority to investing in climate sound agriculture (which could of course be in favor of improving food security), but also stress the need for expanding the production of biofuels and/or investing in hydro-electric dams (green economy). The EU-targets for biofuel, the call for renewable energy (and the opportunities for countries to benefit from 'clean development mechanism') are responsible for the rapid expansion worldwide of oil palm, Soya, sugar etc. (often going at the detriment of food production); and large scale investments (by national governments) in hydroelectric power and dams, often going hand in hand with the displacement of populations (e.g. in Vietnam, Pham Huu 2011). In addition, large-scale land claims are currently made for reforestation projects as a direct consequence of donor interventions (NGO's stimulating REDD, REDD+, also as a consequence of the environmental lobby for biodiversity protection etc.).

There is an urgent need to bring these different policy discussions together. Policies aimed at food security, biodiversity conservation, sustainability, etc. are one of the drivers behind the global land rush, putting local land markets increasingly under pressure. At the same time, more attention should be paid to a number of problems that are currently not at the center of the debate, such as how to deal with increasing numbers of people living in dangerous locations (millions of people live in areas that are vulnerable to floods, drought, etc.). The current trend of the "foreignization" of land—namely its control by external actors—should be assessed, not only in relation to current and future demands for food and fuel, but also in relation to people's future maneuvering space, that is, space that will allow them to respond to the adverse effects of climate change; suitable resettlement locations should be identified in case they are ever required. Whereas poverty alleviation strategies are focused on achieving the MDGs (and persuading people to remain in their current locations by investing in local infrastructure and services), land grabbing and other factors are driving people away. In addition, it is dangerous that in donor debates, land is increasingly presented as a global public good, as this view is not shared by local groups who depend on their land as a source of identity and daily livelihood.

Final Reflections: Land Governance as a 'Balancing Act'

This chapter aimed to provide an update of the land grab debate (2009–now) and shows that there are urgent reasons to deepen and broaden the debate about land grabbing.

Land is a fundamental asset for various goals at distinct levels—having *secure* access to land is a necessary condition for achieving economic development; sustainable resource use (including the use of water); social justice and dignity (FAO Voluntary Guidelines: 3). Tenure systems define how to gain secure access to land and national resources and under what conditions; land tenure systems are defined and regulated by societies—formal policies, laws, but also customs and practices. Weak land governance can be one of the causes of economic stagnation, ecosystem degradation, poverty and inequality and exclusion. Land governance is highly relevant in current debates about how to achieve inclusive and sustainable development.

In this chapter, I argued that it is an oversimplification to suggest that the global land rush can be controlled by strengthening and/or improving institutions, as is often suggested in the land grab debate. Large-scale land acquisition is wrongly depicted as the consequence of a 'sudden' food and climate/energy crisis—it is the logical follow up of globalization, but also a direct outcome of earlier policies.

Reviewing current debates on large scale land acquisitions, discussions are rather shallow. In the media and policy circles all the attention is given to 'how to improve land governance', 'how to protect local rights' and/or 'how to control investments'. Much attention is given to the 'role of the state' and the quality of policy, legal and organizational frameworks (see Guidelines etc.): 'States should provide systems to record tenure rights (including registration, cadastre and licensing systems to improve tenure security and the functioning of markets (p. 22)). Implementing agencies should adopt simplified procedures and locally suitable technology to reduce the costs and time required for delivering services (p. 23); states should eliminate opportunities for corruption, particularly through publicizing requirements, fees, times for responses and through removing conflicts of interests and wide discretionary powers. Others stress the importance of restitution and compensation rules, 'codes of conduct' (FAO 2011).

The great challenge for land governance today is to deal with multiple pressures on land and competing claims, including powerful entrepreneurs and/or environmental actors clashing with local groups. Land governance needs to strike a balance between protecting rights and promoting the most productive use of the land; between economic progress, sustainable land use and social justice. Guidelines, principles, codes of conduct etc. might help, but land governance will always remain a 'balancing act'.

Given the scale and the speed of the process, it is not enough to improve land governance. In order to achieve inclusive and/or sustainable development, it is necessary to have more fundamental discussions about earlier policies (should we continue or stop the further commoditization of natural resources; do we want to proceed with 'horizontal' strategies etc.) but also looking forward: How to make parallel policies (climate change, food security, poverty alleviation etc.) more compatible; how to deal with increasing pressures on land as a consequence of globalization (tourism, migration) and/or autonomous processes of urbanization; and how to make sure that people who nowadays live in dangerous and vulnerable locations will have sufficient maneuvering space to adapt to climate change.

Whereas poverty alleviation was for a long time mainly the domain of NGOs and local actors (with increasing attention for local participation etc.), much of what happens today locally is determined from 'above' and from the 'outside'. Voluntary guidelines and codes of conduct might help to prevent excessive processes of land alienation, but will not help to stop 'commoditization of land' or reverse processes of globalization.

Bibliography

Alan, J.A. 1993. Fortunately, there are substitutes for water otherwise our hydro-political futures would be impossible. In *Priorities for Water Resources Allocation and Management* pp. 13–26. London, UK: Overseas. Available from: http://www.greenstone.org/greenstone3/nzdl?a=d&c=hdl&d=HASH18430b64ccdf12afd60ed4.np&sib=1&p.s=ClassifierBrowse&p.sa=&p.a=b, Accessed 18 January 2013.

Alden Wily, L. 2010. Whose land are you giving away, Mr. President? Washington, DC. Paper presented at the Annual Bank Conference on Land Policy and Administration, 26–27 April, 2010.

Borras, S.M. and J.C. Franco. 2010. From threat to opportunity? Problems with the idea of a "code of conduct" for land-grabbing. *Yale Human Rights and Development Law Journal*, 13, 507–523.

Cotula, L., S. Vermeulen, R. Leonard and J. Keeley. 2009. *Land grab or development opportunity?* London: IIED, FAO and IFAD.

De Schutter, O. 2009. Large-scale land acquisitions and leases: a set of core principles and measures to address the human rights challenge. Briefing note (Geneva: U.N. Office of the High Commissioner for Human Rights, 11 June 2009).

De Soto, H. 2000. *The Mystery of Capital: Why Capitalism Triumphs in the West and Fails Everywhere Else.* New York: Basic Books.

Deininger K. 2003. *Land policies for growth and poverty reduction. A World Bank Policy Report.* Oxford: Oxford University Press.

Deininger, K. and D. Byerlee. 2011. *Rising global interest in farmland: can it yield sustainable and equitable benefits?* Washington, DC.: The World Bank.

Dorner, P. 1992. *Latin American land reforms in theory and practice: a retrospective analysis*, Madison, Wisconsin: The University of Wisconsin Press.

Evers, S.J.T.M. and M. Kooy (eds.). 2011. *Eviction from the Chagos Islands: displacement and struggle for identity against two world powers.* Leiden: Brill Academic Publishers.

Fairhead, J., M. Leach and I. Scoones. 2012. Green Grabbing: a new appropriation of nature? *Journal of Peasant Studies*, 39(2), 237–261.

FAO. 2011. Voluntary Guidelines on the Responsible Governance of tenure of land, fisheries and forests. Zero draft. Rome, Italy. Available at: http://www.fao.org/docrep/016/i2801e/i2801e.pdf, Accessed 18 January 2012.

FAO (n.d.) Land tenure issues and requirements for implementing climate change mitigation policies in the forestry and agricultural sectors. 15–17 November, FAO head-quarters Rome, Italy. UN-REDD program. Summary of discussions. See also: http://www.fao.org/climatechange/65623.

Firmin-Sellers and P. Sellers. 1999. Expected failures and unexpected successes of land titling in Africa. *World Development*, 17, 1115–1128.

FIAN. 2010. *Land grabbing in Kenya and Mozambique: a report on two research missions—and a human rights analysis of land grabbing.* Heidelberg: FIAN International Secretariat.

Friis, Cecilie and Reenberg, Anette. 2010. Land grab in Africa: emerging land system drivers in a teleconnected world. GLP Report No. 1. Copenhagen: GLP-IPO.

Goldfarb L. 2011. The expansion of the Soya frontier in Argentina and beyond. PhD proposal, LANDac. International Development Studies, Utrecht University.

Harcourt, W. (ed.). 2011. Special issue 'global land grabs': challenges to sustainability. *Development* 54(1 and 2), 1–134.
Hilhorst T., J. Nelen and N. Traoré. 2011. Agrarian change below the radar screen: rising farmland acquisitions by domestic investors in West Africa: Results from a survey in Benin, Burkina Faso and Niger. Paper presented at the International Conference on Global Land Grabbing, 6–8 April 2011, Brighton, UK.
Kay, C. 1998. Latin Americas agrarian reform: lights and shadows, *Land Reform—Reforme Agraire—Reforma Agraria*, 2, 9–31.
Kleinpenning, J.M.G. 2009. *Rural Paraguay 1870–1963: a geography of progress, plunder and poverty* (Voume 1). Berlin and Madrid, Iberoamericana—Vervuert, pp. 703–712.
Kugelman M. and Levenstein, S.L. 2009. *Land Grab? The race for the world's farm land.* Washington: Woodrow Wilson International Center for Scholars.
Liverage, H. 2010. Responding to 'land grabbing' and promoting responsible investment in agriculture. IFAD Occasional paper. Available from: http://www.ifad.org/pub/op/2_e.pdf, Accessed 18 January 2013.
Mabikke, S. 2011. Escalating land grabbing in post-conflict regions of Northern Uganda: a need for strengthening good land governance in Acholi Region. Paper presented at the International Conference on Global Land Grabbing, 6–8 April 2011, Brighton, UK.
Matondi, P.B., K. Havnevik and A. Beyene (eds.). 2011. *Biofuels, land grabbing and food security in Africa.* London, New York: Zed Books.
McMichael, P. and I. Scoones. 2010. Special issue on biofuels, land and agrarian change. *The Journal of Peasant Studies* 37(4).
Meinzen-Dick, R. and H. Markelova. 2009. Necessary nuance: towards a code of conduct in foreign land deals. In: Kugelman and Levenstein (eds.) *Land Grab? The race for the World's farm land.* Washington, DC: Woodrow Wilson International Center for Scholars, pp. 69–81.
Oakland Institute. 2011. *Understanding Land Investment Deals in Africa.* Available from: http://media.oaklandinstitute.org/understanding-land-investment-deals-africa-ethiopia, Last accessed 18 January 2013.
Palmer, R. 2010. Would Cecil Rhodes have signed a code of conduct? Reflections on Global land Grabbing and Land Rights in Africa, Past and Present. Unpublished paper for the Biennial Conference, Oxford, 16–19 September 2010, African Studies Association of the UK.
Pham Huu, T. 2011. Dam construction and displacement in Vietnam. PhD proposal, LANDac, International Development Studies, Utrecht University.
Schoneveld G.C., L.A. German and E. Nutakor. 2010. Towards sustainable biofuel development: assessing the local impacts of large scale foreign land acquisitions in Ghana. Paper prepared at the World Bank Annual Conference on Land Policy and Administration, Washington, DC, 26–27 April.
Susanti, A. and P. Burgers. 2011. Oil palm expansion: competing claim of lands for food, biofuels and conservation. Unpublished paper for the ICCAFFE Conference 19–21 May 2011 in Morocco.
Van Noorloos, F. 2011. Residential tourism causing land privatization and alienation: new pressures on Costa Rica's coasts. *Development* 54(1), 85–90.
Von Braun, J. and R. Meinzen-Dick. 2009. Land Grabbing by Foreign Investors in Developing Countries: Risks and Opportunities. IFPRI Policy Brief, 13 April. Available from: http://www.landcoalition.org/pdf/ifpri_land_grabbing_apr_09.pdf, Accessed October 2008.
Von Witzke H. and S. Noleppa. 2011. EU agricultural production and trade: Can more efficiency prevent increasing land grabbing outside of Europe? Von Humboldt University and OPERA, Agripol, network of policy advisors.
World Bank. 2008. World Development Report 'Agriculture for development'. Available from: http://siteresources.worldbank.org/INTWDR2008/Resources/WDR_00_book.pdf, Accessed 18 January 2013.
World Bank. 2010. *Rising global interest in farmland: can it yield sustainable and equitable benefits?* Washington, DC: World Bank.

Zoomers, A. 2003. Land liberalisation and sustainable development in Latin America: Unravelling the land sales market of Santa Cruz, Bolivia. In: *International Development Planning Review* (IDPR) Vol. 25, no. 3, August 2003, pp. 245–263.
——. 2010. Globalization and the foreignization of space: the seven processes driving the current global land grab. *Journal of Peasant Studies* 37(2), 429–447.
Zoomers, A. and van der Haar (eds.). 2000. *Current Land Policy in Latin America. Regulating Land Tenure under Neoliberalism*, Amsterdam, KIT Press in collaboration with Iberoamericana/Vervuert.
Zoomers, A. and G. van Westen. 2011. Special Issue: translocal development, development corridors and development chains. *International Development Planning Review* 33(4), 377–509.

CHALLENGES AND RISKS FOR BILATERAL RELATIONS FROM FOREIGN LARGE-SCALE LAND TRANSACTIONS

Michael J. Strauss

Many states are currently allocating large parts of their sovereign territory to other states, alleviating the unequal distribution of land that has always been a factor in food shortages. This process is occurring amicably and unofficially, with no military conflicts, territorial cessions, or boundary changes. It is being done through business transactions involving vast areas of agricultural land that states are putting aside for the exclusive use of other states in exchange for financial or other compensation. These deals may be made directly between the states, or between a state and a private-sector actor in either the beneficiary state or the host state, or simply between two private-sector entities. The transactions may also involve partnerships or consortia, as well as actors that are not based in either the beneficiary or the host state but that act on their behalf (Strauss 2011, 198).

The practice appears to involve land in African states more than anywhere else, although it is also occurring in Asia and to a lesser extent elsewhere (GRAIN 2008). Africa is therefore likely to have the greatest consequences from the trend—positive and negative, expected and unexpected—and these will be important for the economic, social, and political situations in the countries involved. Consequences have already appeared in some African nations, most notably Madagascar. Meanwhile, the practice must be examined more broadly than in Africa alone because circumstances that arise from land transactions elsewhere in the world may provide lessons that are applicable to the African cases.

These so-called "land grabs" have emerged so recently and spread so rapidly that they are only now being studied as a major phenomenon. Much of the research focuses on their social, economic, political, and agricultural impact. This chapter assesses how the trend can affect international relations, and particularly the bilateral relations of the states that are concluding these deals with each other. While it focuses on land transactions made for food security, the observations it presents are equally valid for those concluded for other purposes such as mineral extraction, conservation, and agriculture for biofuels.

Many of the transactions comprising the trend remain obscure because they are not conducted publicly (Cotula et al. 2009, 68–69). Those involving private-sector actors often have confidentiality clauses to prevent competitors from obtaining information about them (Andrianirina-Ratsialonana et al. 2011, 6). The details that are known suggest that states are making these deals to address immediate food security concerns without giving much consideration to other domestic or international issues that can arise from them. The attitude seems to be "act now, worry about the consequences later" (Strauss 2010–1, 159).

In fact, the consequences can be great when geopolitical factors and the passage of time are taken into account. Bilateral relations between any two states may not be stable over lengthy periods like the ones that are often set for these agreements, such as 50 or 99 years (Cotula et al. 2009, 75–77). When one state uses part of another state's land for what it considers an essential need for its own viability as a state, and a deterioration then occurs in their bilateral relations (something that may be caused by the impact of the agricultural arrangement itself), questions can arise about both states' subsequent relationships with the territory involved.

This may eventually result in a state with farming rights on a large expanse of land in another state having an undesired presence there. Such situations do occur sometimes with more traditional territorial leases and servitudes that states conclude with each other for economic, military, or other purposes. These leasing arrangements have many parallels with the current agricultural land transactions, and states' historical experience with them can be instructive. Among the lessons is that when a bilateral deal involving territory turns sour, it can raise questions about territorial occupation, effective control, and even sovereignty. This problem arose with Cyprus, leased by the United Kingdom from the Ottoman Empire in 1878 and annexed by the British when the two states were on opposite sides of World War I, and with Guantanamo Bay, leased by the United States from Cuba since 1903.

The Challenge of Food Security

Food security is a challenge that every state must address on a continual basis. Many states are not able to produce enough grain or other agricultural crops necessary to feed their populations, and the few that have the potential to be self-sufficient in food may not be able to achieve this status consistently. Indeed, no state has ever been able to sustain its maximum crop output for more than brief periods. Weather conditions, social unrest, fuel price shocks, and government policies can disrupt agricultural production and cause large fluctuations in the size and quality of crops, and shortages sometimes occur.

The vital importance of food security to the viability of states once made it a source of warfare—it was among the factors that motivated states to desire more territory. For a time during the early twentieth century, some international relations scholars gave this an intellectual justification with the Lebensraum or "espace vital" theory, which equated a state's territory with the geographic space necessary for the preservation and development of its population (Rousseau 1956, 31–34).

Although the theory fell out of favour after it was implicated in Germany's behaviour during World War II (Smith 1980, 68), other developments were making it obsolete with respect to food security. The explosive growth of the global commodity trade during the post-war years made it possible for food crops to be transported around the world on a large scale, diminishing the role of food security in causing conflict. Many states became involved in trading agricultural commodities through government agencies that did business with each other and with private-sector commodity trading firms. What had once been accomplished by war was now being accomplished by business.

This system flourished for decades, reinforced by the increasing technological sophistication of commodity markets and by the spreading attitude that free trade was a favourable, if not always achievable, economic objective.

In 2007 and 2008, the system suffered a shock when international grain prices rose sharply due to a convergence of factors. World stockpiles of grain were not high, and several countries that frequently exported large amounts of grain had poor crops at the same time because of unfavourable weather conditions. Oil prices surged to record highs, raising the cost of producing and shipping crops and making some grain more attractive to sell as sources of energy instead of as food. Low levels of investments in agriculture during the preceding years limited the potential for some states to raise their crop output quickly, and the emerging international financial crisis was making it harder for farmers in parts of the world to obtain necessary credits (Austrevicius 2009).

The grain price surge threatened to create shortages not only in states that routinely imported grain, but also in some states that normally had enough to export. Many states that had become frequent suppliers of grain to the world acted to limit price increases in their domestic markets by restricting exports. According to the UN Food and Agriculture Organization, at least 25 nations imposed such export restrictions in 2008—an unprecedented development for the global market. Among them were major grain producers such as Argentina, Cambodia, China, Egypt, India, Kazakhstan, Pakistan, Russia, Ukraine and Vietnam (Demeke et al. 2009, 10). This intensified the rise in global food prices and exacerbated the problem for many states that had to import food crops.

A New Food Security Strategy

The situation prompted governments to reassess their policies on food security and diversify their efforts to achieve it. Many decided to reduce their dependence on the global commodity markets by making bilateral agreements that would ensure long-term food supplies from other states (Demeke et al. 2009, 25). Those states that routinely imported food crops by making purchases on the international market started buying or leasing large quantities of land in other states for the purpose of growing crops that could be exported back to themselves. African states were widely targeted for this amid perceptions that they had considerable amounts of land where agricultural activity could be further developed.

As the conceptual level, these land arrangements were nothing new for public authorities. As far back as 2,600 BC, the Babylonian city-state of Umma leased agricultural land from a neighbouring city-state, Lagash, and provided part of its crop to Lagash as payment of rent (the arrangement was not voluntary; it was imposed by a Babylonian king to settle a dispute over the land) (Saggs 2000, 61–62). During the middle ages, autonomous mountain valleys in the Pyrenees were leasing territory from each other for livestock grazing (Cavailles 1986); some of these leases stayed intact for hundreds of years, and one still exists, having been incorporated into an 1856 treaty that established the current boundary between France and Spain. In the last several centuries, modern states concluded a number of treaties that created land arrangements of this type.

What is new today is the way the concept is being implemented. Rather than state-to-state land purchases involving the acquisition of territorial title, or transfers of certain sovereign-like rights through the creation of leases and servitudes that are instruments of public international law, today's transactions frequently take the form of private purchases or leases of land and are subject to the domestic property laws and other regulations of the states where the land is located.

They are often done at the instigation of wealthier states, which emphasize the financial benefit for poorer states that have the land—the host states. These transactions are often treated as foreign investments, for which there may be financial incentives and other inducements for private sector entities to undertake; such incentives are offered not only by the state where the investment originates, but sometimes the host states seeking inward investment offer tax breaks and exemptions from customs duties to the investors (Cotula et al. 2009, 55, 80). Occasionally, the transactions involve additional commitments by the wealthier states, such as transfers of technology or the development of infrastructure in a host state (Cotula et al. 2009, 15, 100).

Indeed, many African host states recognized the trend as a tremendous opportunity to attract the kinds of large-scale investments that could yield long-term economic benefits—those "seen as capable of bringing new technologies, developing productive potential, facilitating infrastructure development, and creating employment and supply of food to local markets" (Cotula et al. 2009, 58–59). Consequently, some countries "are making strenuous efforts to attract and facilitate foreign direct investments into their agricultural sector" (Ogalo 2011, 10).

Moreover, the government of a potential host nation would certainly realise that shunning such investments while other countries sought them could enhance the relative strength of its economic or geopolitical rivals. Thus, even states that are wary of the trend's internal impact may have felt pressure to make land available to foreign interests. Having rights on African farmland has become so attractive that some host-state governments are offering land as a "sweetener" to attract foreign investments in unrelated sectors (Makoloo 2011, 5).

The Proliferation of Bilateral Transactions

These arrangements are seen mainly as agricultural and financial transactions—they are meant to improve food security for one nation and provide economic benefits to the other. But they are also political transactions, and it is the political aspect that may have the greatest impact over time.

As the scope of the trend was becoming evident, concerns arose among international diplomats and nongovernmental organizations. The United Nations special rapporteur on food, Olivier de Schutter, estimated in 2009 that 30 million hectares of land in developing countries had already been subjected to transactions of this type. "It's accelerating very rapidly, because all countries seem to be suddenly realizing that international markets will be less and less reliable and stable in the future, so they seek to insure themselves by either buying land abroad or encouraging their investors to invest in land abroad," he said (Rice-Oxley 2009). Researchers at the World Bank later estimated that transactions reported between October 2008 and August 2009 involved nearly 57 million hectares (Deininger et al. 2011, 51). Others have since given totals of more than 200 million hectares for international deals that have mostly involved agricultural land since 2007 (Anseeuw et al. 2012, 19; Zagema 2011, 5).

The degree to which these arrangements can impact domestic politics can be seen from two attempted transactions that were abandoned because of local opposition in the states where the land was located. One was in Asia, involving an agreement in 2007 that would have given China the right to grow rice for itself on 2.5 million acres in the Philippines, or about 10 percent of that country's arable land. The agreement was not publicly announced, but Philippine farmers learned of it as domestic rice supplies were tightening, and their outcry prompted the Philippine government to call off the deal (Brown 2009).

The other case, with much more dramatic consequences, involved a preliminary agreement in 2008 under which Madagascar would allow the South Korean company Daewoo Logistics Corp. to lease 1.3 million hectares of agricultural land for 99 years; the amount of land in question totalled more than half of Madagascar's farmland (World Bank et al. 2009, 48). The agreement called for Daewoo to invest $6 billion over 20–25 years to build infrastructure projects in the country, but resentment over the deal fuelled a military-backed coup in 2009 that ousted President Marc Ravalomanana and prompted his successor, Andry Rajoelina, to immediately declare the transaction void. "In the constitution, it is stipulated that Madagascar's land is neither for sale nor for rent, so the agreement with Daewoo is cancelled," he said (Lough 2009).

In fact, Madagascar's legal system did allow foreigners to have land usage rights—on the condition that they be obtained through long-term leases—and domestic farmers were exploiting only a small portion of the country's potential agricultural land; an estimated 90% had never been developed. (Randrianja 2012, 15). The government's agreement with Daewoo was not the only one of its type, but it was certainly the largest, and publicity about its existence gave it considerable symbolic importance (Rakotomalala 2012, 224).

The initial agreement, a contract that authorized Daewoo Logistics to identify appropriate land, was being implemented by the company through groups of topographers it had hired (Andrianirina-Ratsialonana et al. 2011, 6), but it never proceeded to a final accord. Daewoo later said it stood to lose millions of dollars from the investments it had made in connection with the project (Yonhap 2009), and cited the deal's collapse as a factor when it filed for bankruptcy later in 2009 (Kary 2009).

As part of its food security policy, "South Korea wants to grow a quarter of its food on foreign soil owned or leased by Korean companies" by 2030, according to Fred Pearce (2012, 244). The government has pledged to lend money and provide technology to companies that develop farming projects abroad to support this effort, and has mulled its own involvement: in 2009, agriculture minister Chang Tae Pyong said the country itself may try to obtain 50-year leases on agricultural land in eastern Russia (Oryza Rice News 2009).

Indeed, South Korea has been pursuing this policy aggressively and reportedly has agreed to farm 690,000 hectares in Sudan, which was eager to open up its territory to such deals, including some that involve other African states as counterparties. Egypt has an agreement to farm a large amount of Sudanese land for its own behalf, according to the Economist, which added that "an official in Sudan says his country will set aside for Arab governments roughly a fifth of (its) cultivated land" (Economist 2009), although it was uncertain whether that intent remained in place after the southern part of Sudan became an independent state in 2011.

Saudi Arabia is another state that is actively encouraging investors to engage in such transactions in Africa on its behalf. A group of Saudi investors reportedly spent $100 million to grow grain on land in Ethiopia that the government of that country has leased to them (Economist 2009), while Saudi interests have also agreed to farm 1.2 million acres in Tanzania (Food and Water Watch 2009).

It is important to note that African states can be on either side of these land transactions, given the continent's varied climates, topography, and agricultural potential. Among arrangements that have been reported is one in which Ukraine has agreed to permit Libya to grow wheat on 100,000 hectares, or about 1.4 percent of Ukraine's wheat growing area, for export back to Libya (Reuters 2009).

Benefits and Drawbacks

When states conclude transactions involving such large amounts of each other's territory, their bilateral relations are inevitably affected from the start. Among other things, the arrangements tie their economies together more closely by ensuring the development of large new trade flows. Their domestic social, political, and economic effects can be great enough to transform the interests of the states involved in ways that affect their relations both bilaterally and more widely.

Yet these agreements can cause one state's food security to be improved at the expense of the other state's food security, as large amounts of land can no longer be used to grow crops for the local market. Ethiopia is a case in point: it is among the world's largest recipients of food aid, but it has offered millions of hectares of land to foreign investors for their use—land with soil quality so good that a project manager said no fertilizer or herbicides are needed and that "there is absolutely nothing that will not grow on it" (Vidal 2011). The nongovernmental organization Food and Water Watch reports there are many other proposed or completed foreign land transactions in African countries where local food security situations are tenuous, including Kenya, Sudan, and Uganda, as well as in non-African states such as Myanmar (Food and Water Watch 2009).

The speed at which wealthier states have been acting to conclude these agreements is also causing misgivings among states where the land is located, as further "capacity building" may be needed for negotiations to occur on a more equal footing. According to the African Union, the pace of the transactions involving territory for farming has been so fast that some African states have entered into them without being prepared to bargain effectively and were essentially taken advantage of. It adds that other problems, notably riots and political instability, could develop if some of the arrangements displace local farmers (Malone 2009).

The NATO Parliamentary Assembly also warns of the threat of social problems in states where territory is put aside for farming by other states. "Although leased land can be formally owned by the state, it is often the case that local farmers have farmed land for generations and risk being kicked off it to make room for the investors. Cash starved states are sometimes willing to make land available to foreign renters even when it is already being farmed by local farmers. The practice naturally can spark social and economic tensions. Zambia and Madagascar have already undergone turmoil linked to these types of land deals," it said (Austrevicius 2009).

According to the World Bank, these bilateral farming arrangements are often described as a "win-win" strategy, with the wealthier investor acquiring land, access to the food produced on it, and financial returns on its investment, while the host state "receives an infusion of capital into its agricultural sector, leading to economic development." But it, too, warns that this can only be mutually beneficial if economic and social protections exist and if food security is maintained for both states (World Bank et al. 2009, 48).

The Impact on International Relations

These early observations make it clear that such transactions involve potential dangers that can affect the bilateral relations of the states that make them. Among the many scenarios that one can envisage:

- The foreign state's crop may be damaged or destroyed by social unrest, pollution, or other factors that emanate from the host state.
- Exports of the crop to the foreign state may be blocked by disruptions at ports or other facilities in the host state.
- The foreign state's crop may compete with host-state crops for resources that become limited, such as water during a drought.
- Food safety concerns can lead to restrictions on exports of crops from the entire host state, including the areas where the foreign state grows crops.
- A crop disease originating in the foreign state's crop may spread to harm the host state's crops, and vice-versa.
- In a season with unusually large crops, a foreign state that does not need all of the crop it grows in the host state may sell it on the world market in competition with the host state's crop, to the detriment of the host state.
- A foreign state that obtains the use of territory in the host state for growing crops may begin to use it for other purposes that are not covered in the agreement. The host state may not necessarily be aware of these activities if they are done covertly, as with the gathering of intelligence (Strauss 2010–1, 164).

It is also possible to envision geopolitical effects that go beyond the bilateral level. Ukraine's 2009 agreement to set aside a large amount of wheat-growing land for Libya was made in the context of several factors that changed dramatically within only two years: Ukraine's pro-western government was ousted by voters in 2010 and replaced by a pro-Russian government; and a severe Russian drought in the same year meant that Ukraine's routinely modest grain exports to Russia were poised to become very substantial

(Budrys 2010). The altered context also included Ukraine's own desire to limit grain exports due to the same drought (Tsukanova 2010), and a resurgence of Russian political influence in Ukraine (evidenced by the rapid renewal in 2010 of Russia's lease of a naval port in Sevastopol; Ukraine's previous government had refused to prolong the arrangement).

Whether these changes created pressures that affected the land deal with Libya is uncertain, as its details are not known, but it does show how the bedrock of such a transaction can be shaken by geopolitical events that involve states that are not party to the deal. By late 2010 the deal was still not implemented, and although Libyan authorities said it would proceed (Shuaib and Sarrar 2010), the situation changed further in 2011, when Libya's long-standing government was overthrown in a military conflict. The new government's position with respect to the Ukraine land transaction was not immediately clear.

Third-party states can affect foreign large-scale land transactions in other ways as well. Most ominously, a host state faces potential security risks if the state that uses its land becomes involved in a war at any point during the duration of the arrangement. This risk has long been recognized in a parallel context—foreign land transactions for military bases. When a nation uses another state's land for a military facility, the host state accepts the risk that part of its sovereign territory becomes vulnerable to attack in wartime (United States Naval War College 1912, 97). As food security can be as essential as military security for the survival of a state, the same risk can exist for agricultural land transactions.

"A land-use arrangement of this type erodes a traditional function of national boundaries: it permits the user state to reinforce its sovereign situation on its own territory through activities it performs outside of that territory. The experience of states with leased territories shows that the land itself may be perceived as a *de facto* territorial extension of the nation that relies on it, rather than as part of the nation where it is physically located" (Strauss 2011, 191). A typical case was the Canal Zone, leased by the United States from Panama between 1903 and 2000; it "was popularly perceived as 'American' territory" (Smith 2005, 142).

Land involved in foreign large-scale transactions can thus assume a supporting role in a conflict that involves the beneficiary state by contributing to its strength. This can compromise the host state's neutrality vis-à-vis the dispute, and draw it into an armed conflict in which it had no previous involvement or interest (Strauss 2011, 190).

Among other potential problems at the bilateral level, circumstances that arise from the land agreements but are not anticipated by their negotiators can have financial consequences or create issues in which liability may have to be determined. Cases in which land is used for purposes other than those specified by the agreement have actually occurred with territories that were leased under formal treaties (this was the case, for example, with the U.S. lease of Guantanamo Bay from Cuba; the range of U.S. activities there exceeded those authorized by the lease). All of these can become problems in relations between the states involved.

Indeed, it appears that the agreements establishing these land transactions often fail to take into account the range of contingencies that might arise. The World Bank notes, for example, that "capital locked up in land purchases and long-term leases cannot easily be freed up to buy food from other suppliers when there is bad weather or political disruptions in the host country" (World Bank et al. 2009, 49). Meanwhile, De Schutter, the UN rapporteur, calls the arrangements "extremely worrying" because the few transactions that the UN was able to examine were brief and did not address matters such as infrastructure investments or commitments to sustainable farming practices (Rice-Oxley 2009).

As noted earlier, these land transactions can generate issues that are similar to those that have already arisen with territorial leases and servitudes. The common aspects of these types of arrangements—the rights transferred between the states, the compensation paid to the host state, and the duration of the arrangement—can generate both problems and solutions (Strauss 2010–2, 97–108).

On the positive side, leases and servitudes often succeed in satisfying the desire of more than one state to have at least some rights on the same territory, and can strengthen bilateral ties by creating a jointly administered project. The current land transactions can do likewise, and in some cases they might prevent tensions over the land from developing.

But the transfer of rights can cause the sovereign host state to have little knowledge of, or control over, what actually happens on the territory, creating conditions for its misuse. Many foreign entities involved in large international land transactions use private security forces to protect their investments, and oversight of their actions can vary widely. The UN Department of Economic and Social Affairs recognizes the lack of oversight in a broader sense as a danger for the new land transactions: "To date, no investment contracts appear to have been made available to the public, and only a very few have been made available to intergovernmental and non-governmental organizations seeking to better understand and appraise these issues. The lack of transparency undermines government accountability, and increases the opportunity for corruption and other inappropriate acts," it warns (United Nations Department of Economic and Social Affairs 2010, 5).

Another lesson that can be drawn from leases is that the arrangement can, over time, change the character of the territory involved in ways that make subsequent reintegration with the rest of the host state problematic. An example of this occurred when the British lease of Hong Kong ended in 1997 and the territory reverted to China; changes that occurred during the U.K.'s stewardship were largely retained. The compensation aspect of leases has also created problems in some cases when the treaties fixed the payment amounts without taking into account possible changes that could occur over time in the value of the land involved or in the values of the currencies of the two states.

Some of the current land deals may encounter similar problems, and states can look to the experiences with leases for solutions to at least some of them.

Such problems can arise regardless of whether the foreign entity that obtains rights on the land is a state or a private-sector investor. However, in the case of a state, the magnitude of the impact can be much greater. A disagreement between governments that arises from a land arrangement may spill over into other areas of their bilateral relations, and tensions could mount to dangerous levels.

This was seen, for example, in a bilateral dispute over the use of a small zone in India called Tin Bigha, which lay between Bangladesh and a populated Bangladeshi enclave surrounded by Indian territory. The conflict became violent at times and "epitomised the way in which two antagonistic governments . . . could magnify a localised issue into one of considerable tension and emotive influence" (Jacques 2000, 45). Ironically, it was ultimately resolved by a bilateral lease—illustrating that this type of accord between states is not inherently "good" or "bad." What is more important is how the specific terms of the arrangement—something that is typically obscure in foreign land transactions—can affect the territory involved. "Due to its importance, problems related to territory have often caused serious disputes among States" (Menon 1994, 2).

A New Test of Sovereign Authority

At another level of international relations, states seeking territory in Africa or elsewhere for their food security may find they are competing with each other for the same land. This can generate tensions among states that are far from the land itself, as well as pressures to conclude deals quickly. And as some states rush to make these international farming arrangements, other states may feel forced to enter the fray.

In this respect, the process is similar to the rush by the world's former colonial powers to secure as much of the earth's territory as possible for their own economic benefit and development into more powerful states. Indeed, some critics are already referring to the new trend as neo-colonialism (Economist 2009).

Regardless of how close this parallel is in reality, a state that obtains the right to use a substantial piece of another state's land for an extended period of time will be able to influence events in the other state—and its influence may extend to matters that are not related to the issue of food security that led to the arrangement in the first place.

On the surface, these transactions reinforce the principle of territorial integrity because they allow states to address their agricultural and financial needs without altering any boundaries. But although the land covered by these arrangements stays under the sovereignty of the states where it is located, the process may eventually prove to be a test of their sovereign authority. It may even provide new challenges to existing notions of sovereignty itself.

Bibliography

Andrianirina-Ratsialonana, Rivo, Landry Ramarojohn, Perrine Burnod, and André Teyssier. 2011. *After Daewoo? Current status and perspectives of large-scale land acquisition in Madagascar*. Rome: International Land Coalition.

Anseeuw, Ward, Liz Alden Wily, Lorenzo Cotula, and Michael Taylor. 2012. *Land Rights and the Rush for Land: Findings of the Global Commercial Pressures on Land Research Project*. Rome: International Land Coalition.

Austrevicius, Petras, rapporteur. 2009. "Food Price Shocks and their Implications for Food Security." NATO Parliamentary Assembly. Last accessed 16 January 2012. http://www.nato-pa.int/default.asp?SHORTCUT=1779

Brown, Lester. 2009. "The Geopolitics of Food Scarcity." *Spiegel*, 11 March. Last accessed 16 January 2012. http://www.spiegel.de/international/world/0,1518,606937,00.html

Budrys, Aleksandras. 2010. "Russia grain imports to soar in 2010/11—analyst." *Reuters*, 19 August.

Cavailles, Henri. 1986. *Lies et passeries dans les Pyrénées*. Tarbes, France: Société d'Etudes des Sept Vallées.

Cotula, Lorenzo, Sonja Vermeulen, Rebeca Leonard, and James Keeley. 2009. *Land Grab or Development Opportunity? Agricultural Investment and International Land Deals in Africa*. London/Rome: International Institute for Environment and Development/United Nations Food and Agriculture Organization/International Fund for Agricultural Development.

Deininger, Klaus, Derek Byerlee, Jonathan Lindsay, Andrew Norton, Harris Selod, and Mercedes Stickler. 2011. *Rising Global Interest in Farmland: Can It Yield Sustainable and Equitable Benefits?* Washington: World Bank.

Demeke, Mulat, Guendalina Pangrazio, and Materne Maetz. 2009. *Country responses to the food security crisis: Nature and preliminary implications of the policies pursued.* Rome: U.N. Food and Agriculture Organization.

Economist. 2009. "The scramble for land in Africa and Asia." *Economist*, 21 May.

Food and Water Watch. 2009. "Global Land Grab Undermines Food Security in the Developing World." Last accessed 16 January 2012. http://documents.foodandwaterwatch.org/GlobalLandGrab.pdf

GRAIN. 2008. "Seized! The 2008 Land Grab for Food and Financial Security." *GRAIN Briefing* (Annex), October: 1–11.

Jacques, Katheryn. 2000. *Bangladesh, India and Pakistan.* Basingstoke, U.K.: Palgrave.

Kary, Tiffany. 2009. "Daewoo Logistics Wins U.S. Bankruptcy Protection (Update 1)." *Bloomberg*, 21 October.

Lough, Richard. 2009. "Madagascar's new leaders says Daewoo land deal off." *Reuters*, 18 March.

Makoloo, Maurice Odhiambo. 2011. "Foreign Direct Investment in Agriculture and Land Lease Contracting: A Critical Evaluation of Lease Contracts in Eastern Africa." Nairobi: Friedrich Ebert Stiftung. Last accessed 3 December 2012. http://www.fes-kenya.org/media/publications/FDI/FOREIGN%20DIRECT%20INVESTMENT%20IN%20AGRICULTURE%20AND%20LAND%20LEASE%20CONTRACTING%20A%20CRITICAL%20EVALUATION%20OF%20LEASE%20CONTRACTS%20IN%20EASTERN%20AFRICA.pdf

Malone, Barry. 2009. "Interview-AU: Africa not benefiting from foreign land deals," *Reuters*, 28 April.

Menon, P.K. 1994. "Title to Territory: Traditional Modes of Acquisition by States." *Revue de Droit International* 72:1–54.

Ogalo, Victor. 2011. "Foreign Investment in Agriculture in Eastern Africa: A General Overview of Trends and Issues." Nairobi: Friedrich Ebert Stiftung-Kenya. Last accessed 3 December 2012. http://www.fes-kenya.org/media/publications/FDI/overview-%20FDI%20in%20Agriculture%20in%20Eastern%20Africa_FES_VOO.pdf

Oryza Rice News. 2009. "South Korea To Encourage Farming Abroad," *Oryza Rice News*, 8 April.

Pearce, Fred. 2012. *The Landgrabbers: The New Fight over Who Owns the Earth.* London: Transworld.

Rakotomalala, Patrick. 2012. "Implicites de la crise 2009 et diplomatie française." In *Madagascar, le coup d'Etat de mars 2009*, edited by Solofo Randrianja, 211–238. Paris: Karthala.

Randrianja, Solofo. 2012. "Le coup d'Etat de mars 2009, chronologie et causes." In *Madagascar, le coup d'Etat de mars 2009*, edited by Solofo Randrianja, 13–41. Paris: Karthala.

Reuters. 2009. "Libya agrees deal to grow wheat in Ukraine." *Reuters*, 27 May.

Rice-Oxley, Mark. 2009. "G8: Does world need new rules on food security?" *Christian Science Monitor*, 8 July. Last accessed 16 January 2012. http://www.csmonitor.com/World/2009/0708/p06s17–wogn.html

Rousseau, Charles. 1956. *Cours de droit international public.* Paris: Les Cours de Droit.

Saggs, H.W.F. 2000. *Babylonians.* Berkeley: University of California Press.

Shuaib, Ali and Salah Sarrar. 2010. "Libya says Ukraine farm lease deal to go ahead," *Reuters*, 24 November.

Smith, Joseph. 2005. *The United States and Latin America: A history of American diplomacy, 1776–2000.* Abingdon: Routledge.

Smith, Woodruff D. 1980. "Friedrich Ratzel and the Origins of Lebensraum." *German Studies Review* 3:51–68.

Strauss, Michael J. 2009–1. "And When the Lease on Sevastopol Expires?" *International Herald Tribune*, 9 January.

——. 2009–2. *The Leasing of Guantanamo Bay.* Westport, Conn.: Praeger.

——. 2010–1. "Redistribuer le territoire des Etats pour éviter les pénuries alimentaires." In *Enjeux diplomatiques et stratégiques 2010*, edited by Pascal Chaigneau, 159–166. Paris: Economica.

——. 2010–2. *The Viability of Territorial Leases in Resolving International Sovereignty Disputes*. Paris: L'Harmattan.

——. 2011. "Land Leasing in Africa: The Geopolitical Risks." *African Geopolitics* 40:189–200.

Tsukanova, Anya. 2010. "Ukraine to limit grain exports due to drought: official." *Agence France-Presse*, 17 August.

United Nations Department of Economic and Social Affairs. 2010. "Foreign land purchases for agriculture: what impact for sustainable development?" *Sustainable Development Innovation Briefs* 8.

United States Naval War College. 1912. *International Law Situations with Solutions and Notes—1912*. Washington: Government Printing Office.

Vidal, John. 2011. "Ethiopia at centre of global farmland rush." *Guardian*, 21 March.

World Bank, United Nations Food and Agriculture Organization, and International Fund for Agricultural Development. 2009. *Improving Food Security in Arab Countries*. Washington: World Bank.

Yonhap. 2009. "Daewoo Logistics to lose millions after Madagascar coup." *Yonhap*, 19 March.

SECTION 2

THE CREATION OF FERTILE GROUND FOR THE STRUCTURING OF FOREIGN LARGE-SCALE LAND ACQUISITIONS: LAND REFORMS, PRIVATIZATION AND COMPETING JURISDICTIONS

LAND CONSOLIDATION AND THE EXPANSION OF GAME FARMING IN SOUTH AFRICA: IMPACTS ON FARM DWELLERS' LIVELIHOODS AND RIGHTS TO LAND IN THE EASTERN CAPE

Nancy Andrew, Femke Brandt, Marja Spierenburg, Dhoya Snijders and Nomalanga Mkhize

Introduction

The beautiful and hilly central regions of the Eastern Cape and the drier Karoo are now heavily populated with wild animals on game farms stretching from Grahamstown to Port Elizabeth and from there to Graaff-Reinet. Hundreds of kilometres of often electrified fences have been erected to enclose the wildlife, both far into the interior of the province and along the strip near the Indian Ocean. Sheep, goats and cattle still dot the landscape alongside chicory, pineapple, citrus, and dairy farms, but these farming areas are increasingly encroached upon by immense private game reserves. The establishment of game farms usually involves the merging of several properties; one of the largest hunting operations in the Karoo includes 13 former sheep farms and the largest private reserves for luxury tourism in the province occupy between 15 000 and 70 000 hectares. Game farms are also expanding through the large number of livestock and crop farmers in the region, who have diversified their activities by adding wildlife production and/or hunting as well as various types of tourist accommodations.

The acquisition of significant territory for game farming has meant considerable land consolidation, restructuring not only the physical landscape, but also the spatial and social relationships on the land. This has in turn raised important issues of and contestations over land use, particularly with regard to the impact of farm conversions on families living and working on those farms, whose labour is less in demand and whose livelihoods and connection to the land are either jeopardised or severed. These trends in the wildlife industry leading to private land enclosures represent one important form of land acquisition in South Africa within a continuing and more general tendency towards land consolidation into fewer large units since apartheid.

Unlike in many African countries, most agricultural land in South Africa has long been privately owned as a result of settler colonialism and the apartheid regime which engineered and enforced a rigid division between private land held by whites and 'communal' reserves or bantustans for black residents. White land owners controlled most of the agricultural land, and of the best quality, a pattern that is still prevalent today. The state plays a less important role in large-scale land deals in South Africa than in most of the cases presented in this volume, as most transactions in South Africa take place among private landowners and corporate actors. However, national legal and political structures, heavily influenced by the apartheid past and anchored in today's neoliberal environment[1] guiding the state's macroeconomic policies overall, continue to protect private property and to facilitate the concentration of land and production as well as land acquisitions themselves. This has created numerous political quandaries, including the central problem of landlessness and poverty within the black rural population, which post-1994 state policies have only slightly improved.

While land acquisitions primarily occur within South Africa's domestic private sector, the increased role of foreign investments in land and residential property transactions—as well as in the expansion of partially foreign-owned private game farms and tourism ventures—has received growing attention. Foreign land deals have fuelled longstanding and heated political debates over whether and how to change a land ownership system that has perpetuated such immense racial, social and economic inequalities and political discontent. The African National Congress-led state has been somewhat divided over how to handle foreign ownership and has introduced some restrictive conditions on foreign acquisitions of land and its use. The state straddles a dilemma: on the one hand it supports the drive for outside investments seen as a way to enhance the competitiveness of commercial agriculture within the global market and to facilitate the expansion of South African-based agribusiness and investment funds to other countries. On the other, state politicians make repeated promises to address the issue of a racially skewed distribution of land, and expand small-scale food production by and for black farmers and poor rural communities, which some within government argue is made even more difficult by the creeping number of partnerships with foreign investors.

[1] South Africa's neoliberal policies include fuller reliance on and integration into the world market economy, increased liberalization and privatization, fewer centralised state bodies than under apartheid, where the white minority regime played a determinant role in all sectors and the linkages among them. See Hart 2002, Shivji 2005, Terreblanche 2002 and Andrew 2009.

Tourism—alongside biofuel production, anticipated food needs in countries without sufficient land, the many forms of continued mineral and natural resources extraction (see de Koning, this volume), nature conservation and REDD,[2] and financial speculation—is one of many drivers of the international 'land grab' phenomenon in Africa.[3] The rapid spread of conversions to game farming in South Africa involves nearly one-quarter of all commercial farm operations. It cuts across various activities ranging from wild animal breeding and trading, the production of venison and other game products, to (trophy) hunting, other types of tourism such as game viewing and related hospitality and recreation, and personal leisure farms. Based on research conducted in the commercial farming areas of the Eastern Cape between 2008 and 2011, this chapter examines the ways in which two forms of wildlife-based tourism in South Africa—hunting farms and private luxury game reserves—have accelerated land consolidation and shifting land use and access patterns. It explores the effects of conversions to game farms on the large numbers of black families, referred to as *farm dwellers*, whose homes and ancestral graves are located on the commercial farms.[4]

After a brief historical overview describing the emergence of farm dwellers and their position in the agrarian economy, the chapter considers the changes in the property system and agriculture since apartheid that underpin the ongoing trend towards concentration of commercial farmland. Land reform is briefly addressed, followed by a summary of farmers' reasons for converting to wildlife production and the land acquisitions that accompany it in the Eastern Cape. An analysis of research findings then shows how game farming has affected farm dwellers' livelihoods and relationships to the land, drawing upon data collected primarily on

[2] Reducing emissions from deforestation and forest degradation.

[3] There is a growing body of literature on land grabs. See for example, Zoomers et al. (this volume), Fairhead et al. 2012, Cotula 2011, Benjaminsen et al. 2011, Borras & Franco 2012.

[4] The research project is entitled 'Farm dwellers the forgotten People? Consequences of conversions to private wildlife production in KZN and Eastern Cape provinces'. It is funded by the Dutch national research foundation NWO-WOTRO and involves six PhD students based at the University of the Free State, the University of Cape Town and the Vrije Universiteit in Amsterdam and a post-doctoral researcher. Subject areas include the effects on farm dwellers' livelihoods, labour and social relationships on hunting farms and within 'eco-tourism', sense of place and histories, interactions between private wildlife production and land reform, the quality of partnerships with local communities, the commodification of nature and of wildlife, the policy and institutional arena, as well as impacts on the local agrarian economy.

trophy hunting farms in the central Karoo district of the Eastern Cape and so-called private 'eco-tourism'[5] reserves in the Makana Municipality in the central-southern part of the province. A discussion of the role of the South African state and of foreign investors driving land consolidation and this change in land use provides further context for the social consequences for farm dwellers.

Farm Dwellers and the Legacy of Settler Colonialism

In order to understand the emergence of farm dwellers as a social category within the South Africa's rural population and related processes of marginalisation, it is important to consider the legacies of *settler* colonialism and ways in which African groups[6] were dispossessed of their land and subject to harsh labour conditions and repression. This began during the mid-17th century, when the first Europeans arrived with the Dutch East India Company (VOC) at the Cape of Good Hope. From then on, various forms of unfree labour, including slavery, were deployed by Europeans to explore and farm the Cape Colony. An extremely violent and patriarchal form of social relations between white 'masters', slaves and 'serfs' developed on the farmlands as a result of colonial conflicts over land and labour (Crais, 1992). The European *trekboers* moving into the interior regions of the Cape (now the Eastern Cape Province) were frequently attacked by the indigenous Khoi and San herders who fiercely resisted being expelled from their grazing and hunting grounds (a contestation which continues today, including in Botswana—see Sapignoli and Hitchcock in this volume). In the late 1700s the conflict over land and labour intensified as the expanding European colonialists encountered Xhosa people at the eastern border of the Cape Colony, leading to a series of frontier wars over the next hundred years.

The British occupied the Cape Colony at the turn of the 19th Century and soon implemented the English legal property system, awarding settler farmers freehold title that made them individual, private owners of land.

[5] Called 'eco-tourism' because it does not involve killing wild animals, although what constitutes 'ecological' in this context of huge tracts of rural land for private tourist businesses is certainly one of the debates.

[6] We refer to Africans as descendants of indigenous people living in those territories before settler colonization; following the racial classification under apartheid and the political movement against white minority rule, African has commonly come to mean all those who consider themselves black and in this chapter is used interchangeably with black in the contemporary period.

They also began to restrict the mobility and access to land of Africans, who were labelled as 'squatters' and 'vagrants' by colonial officials and landowners in need of labour. British settlers introduced Merino sheep for wool production, which built up commerce considerably and became one of the colony's dominant exports, attracting European capital investment in wool farms (Ross, 1986). With the expansion of early commercial farming in the region, European settlers were not only concerned about labour shortages; they also felt threatened by a successfully competing African peasantry tapping into opportunities created by the colonial economy.[7] Black peasant farmers in the eastern part of the Cape Colony were, however, increasingly constrained to produce on white farms in various forms of 'quasi-feudal' social relations. Through sharecropping, rent and labour tenancy arrangements, Africans were able to produce for themselves and the market. They also found ways to exert some degree of independence from and to resist colonial control.

The Cape colonial authorities and subsequently the South African state made great efforts to limit accumulation by African peasants in order to harness their labour for the white settler farms and early industry, especially diamond and gold mining. After the Union of South Africa was declared in 1910, the newly-forged national (Anglo-Boer) state introduced the notorious 1913 Natives Land Act, which prohibited Africans from buying or owning land outside of designated 'native reserves', or bantustans, on only 7% of the land surface (extended to 13% in 1936). The majority of Africans were drawn into a tightly controlled system of labour migration between the Transkei and Ciskei bantustans and enterprises requiring their labour. A growing number of black families also continued to live as tenants on the commercialising farms, pursuing peasant-like livelihoods within the constraints of their relations with European settlers. The apartheid state's legacy of 'legalising' and enforcing these rigid racial boundaries socially and spatially has left a major imprint upon the restructured post-apartheid state apparatus that the latter has not been able to efface.

Despite changes in agriculture over the past century and, more recently, in South Africa's political rule, together with reform policies, farm dwellers

[7] See also Postel's chapter in this volume. The independence and successes of the African peasantry in the 19th century are documented in Bundy's seminal work on the South African peasantry (1988); his analysis of the impact of the colonial economy upon African societies showed, among other things, that at the end of the 19th century Africans produced more wool in certain districts than European farmers. The resilience of the African peasantry and the advent of capitalist agriculture remain important subjects of debate among agrarian historians.

remain an important social group within the rural black population. The term 'farm dweller' is intentionally broader than 'farm worker', which alludes to a narrow legal status that dismisses people's historical associations with, and dispossession of, land (AFRA 2003). In this chapter, the term farm dweller refers to people living on farms, including workers, tenants and other rural dwellers who regard commercial farmlands as their home.

The particular shift to game farming is occurring in the context of the still very dominant racial and spatial organization of land and people inherited from the past—together with the distorted and uneven capitalist development in agriculture that accompanied it—as well as post-apartheid agricultural and land policies. Neoliberal, market-based land reform since 1995 has only barely chipped away at the edges of the foundation of this deeply entrenched land ownership system. Yet, in many ways, land reform has contributed to the overall process of consolidating landholdings among established white farmers and corporations rather than opening land back up to black small farmers. The post-1994 legal framework has also tended towards very minimal land rights for, and ineffective protection of, farm dwellers on the commercial farms who find themselves in an increasingly vulnerable position; in some ways this strengthens existing property owners' ability to evict, displace, retrench, or fire farm dwellers at will.

South Africa's Land Structure and Changes since Apartheid

The effects of the system of separate development, and the racial division of territory and land ownership that accompanied it underpinning colonialism and especially apartheid, continue to deeply affect the black rural population today. This land division has not changed significantly since 1994. The artificially-created, ethnically-based bantustans no longer exist officially and were integrated into the country's nine provinces in 1994; they remain a stark concentration and reminder of what apartheid society created and left behind, despite significant social differentiation in these parts of the countryside. A 20% growth in the population over the past decade and a half[8] has intensified land pressures, and the national government's neglect of former bantustan areas prompted the African

[8] StatsSA 2010. Black people make up 79.4% of the 49.9 million population, white people 9.2%, people of mixed race 8.8% and those of Indian origin, 2.6%.

National Congress (ANC) to renew a commitment to rural development at the time of Jacob Zuma's election in 2009 (ANC 2009).

Nearly two decades since the downfall of apartheid, 80% of commercial farmland continues to be owned by individuals—mainly white—with a range of corporations and agribusiness holding the rest (StatsSA 2005). Post-1994 land reform programmes have transferred only about 7% of white-owned land to black farmers (DRDLR 2010). Approximately one-third of the black rural population works as farm workers and labour tenants on commercial farms and represents the poorest section of the country's workforce. Social inequalities are visibly extreme in these farming areas, characterised not only by enormous differences in incomes and living standards, but also by the continuation of oppressive social practices and relationships on the farms stemming from the past.

From the mid-1980s, the state and leading players in commercial agriculture had already begun to shift towards economies of scale that depend on the concentration of landholdings in order to streamline the increasingly debt-ridden sector. This meant merging farms into larger units and eliminating less successful producers as well as beginning to cut back the substantial apartheid-era state subsidies and other advantages to white farmers that had kept many in business.[9] In addition, more finance capital was invested in an already highly centralised and overcapitalised sector[10] and development banks were privatised.

In the context of pivotal political decisions to follow a neoliberal macroeconomic strategy during the transition to a national unity government in 1994, the African National Congress deregulated further, closing marketing boards and doing away with export monopolies. Although the ANC's many political promises to the black population emphasised social redress and redistributing resources, including land, a key outcome of deregulation was the strengthening of the most powerful interests in agribusiness.[11] Fully in line with national plans for greater liberalisation, ending subsidies and boosting export production rather than domestic food crops, such policy shifts in agriculture—that fuelled land consolidation—tended to

---

[9] Some of these white farmers lost their land while others sold it or became managers on other farms.

[10] In 1992 the apartheid government under the National Party offered debt and drought relief pay-outs amounting to 3.4 billion rand, in order to help established grain and livestock farmers recapitalise (van Zyl & Kirsten 1996, 231).

[11] As described by Williams et al. (1998), greater market liberalisation allowed "producers, manufacturers and traders . . . to defend or even enhance the dominant positions which the whole range of statutory privileges had enabled them to establish".

reinforce the position of corporations[12] and farmers in the richer, export-oriented sectors closely connected to the world market. Price controls on agro-foods were removed despite the anticipated, harmful effect on food security for poor rural and urban households.[13]

Heightened pressures on commercial farmers to compete in a more liberalised environment, exacerbated by global crisis and its related dynamics, have taken their toll: since 1993 the number of commercial farming units has decreased by at least one third. In other words, the white landowning monopoly has shrunk in size—down to 40,000 in 2010 (SA Parliament 2010)—but it does not own *less* land, or only marginally less, which the failure of land reform underscores. In the 2009 Development Bank report, analysts Vink & van Rooyen write:

> Commercial farmers have adopted a wide variety of risk management strategies... that have been focused on income diversification (such as more part-time farming and investment in on-farm agro-tourism facilities) and on asset diversification... The result is a simultaneous consolidation of large commercial (industrial) farms with an increase in the number of smaller commercial farms, and an overall increase in the average farm size (DBSA 2009, 4).

Another form of 'diversification' in South African agribusiness is its expansion outside national borders to other African countries while still retaining home-based operations. For example, a deal was struck in 2009 between the commercial farmers union, AgriSA and the Democratic Republic of Congo government for 200,000 hectares of fertile land in that country, expandable to 10 million ha in the future. This arrangement is tax-free for five years with no export restrictions, including profits, although the ostensible goal is promoting food production for the Congo; negotiated privately, the state is secondarily involved through an inter-government agreement that protects the 1700 farmers involved from future expropriation (Sharife 2010).[14]

---

[12] While its corporate names have changed, a small, powerful group of central cooperatives previously controlling apartheid-era marketing boards and "organising" the monopoly interests of white agriculture remains closely tied to the functioning of other economic sectors, including services, processing and marketing of products, as well as insurance (StatsSA 2005).

[13] For discussion of changes in agricultural policy, see van Zyl et al. 1996, Greenberg 2003, Viljoen 2005.

[14] Other examples include the rapid expansion of South African sugar conglomerates Illovo (Mozambique, Zambia, Swaziland and Kenya) and Tongaat-Hulett (Mozambique and Zimbabwe); see company websites.

Liberalisation also had major consequences for the workforce, both in agriculture and other sectors of the formal economy, which experienced a large net loss of jobs commonly attributed to the implementation of the macro-economic policy called GEAR (Growth, Employment and Redistribution).[15] The consolidation of agricultural production and land contributed to a decline in the number of jobs on the commercial farms between 1985 to 1995, followed by a slight increase up until 2002, before declining again (Vink & Kirsten 2003). New minimum wage laws were introduced in the sector in 2001, and many farmers who were used to paying very minimal labour costs either tried to reduce the number of tenants and/or farm workers on their farms or find ways to stall complying with the new laws.[16] In addition, there has been a significant tendency to downgrade employment to casual labour,[17] and in some agricultural sectors farmers are using lower-paid, women's labour or hiring women as casual workers. This trend towards precarious contract labour arrangements is felt strongly within the context of recent shifts to game farming as well, as will be discussed below in the research findings.

These national priorities set the terms for the debate over land reform in the early 1990s and, most importantly, would shape to a large extent the outcome of the land reform programme itself.

Investment management funds are also very active. The Pretoria-based joint venture Emvest, manages the African AgriLand Fund, which uses private equity to invest in "undervalued" land in Africa for industrial agricultural projects. The Fund has holdings producing mainly for export in Zimbabwe and owns the 5th largest private farming company in Swaziland, El Ranch, producing baby vegetables for European markets. Emvest leases land in the E. Cape to grow tomatoes, soya and wheat and in Mozambique it is involved in jatropha for biofuel production, tilapia for export as well as plantation agriculture near the Limpopo River and in Zambia, benefitting there from a 99–year lease. See www.emvest.com, www.oaklandinstitute.org/land-deal-brief-deciphering-emergent%E2%80%99s-investments-africa and www.emergentasset.com/?func=PageAfricanLandFund.

Agribusiness investment fund AgriVie (headquartered in Cape Town with offices in Mauritius and Kenya, composed of SP-aktif and Sanlam Private Equity), together with the Development Bank of Southern Africa, the Industrial Development Corporation and the Kellogg Foundation, invests in multi-country agricultural projects in Botswana, Tanzania, Uganda and Kenya. This consortium provides a glimpse of the concentration of agricultural production and processing, processing, as AgriVie is involved in dairy, vegetables, food & beverages, forestry products as well as seeds and fertilisers (www.AgriVie.com).

[15] The effects of GEAR and successive macroeconomic frameworks have been widely debated: see Makgetla 2006, Viljoen 2005, Mather 1997. Government's 'New Growth Path' and 'National Development Plan 2030' under discussion continue to try to attenuate this problem.

[16] Field interviews in 2005 and with Department of Labour 2011.

[17] The number of non-permanent jobs rose from about one-third in 1991 to almost half in 2002. See Aliber et al. 2007 for more on casualisation trends in agricultural employment.

The volatile issue of land reform in South Africa constituted an important symbolic expectation of the political transition in 1994. It continues to be at the heart of discussions over the agrarian economy and the goals of rural development as well as what further social transformation is needed. Although constrained by the priorities to maintain the structure of the commercial farming sector overall, the political discourse of land reform was originally aimed at the poorer, landless groups within the rural black population, including women, farm workers and labour tenants with a high interest in land. It fostered hopes that widespread colonial and apartheid dispossession would be partially compensated through the land restitution programme, through tenure reform in communal areas and rights to land for farm workers and labour tenants, as well as through redistribution of large tracts of commercial, white-owned farmland to new or existing black farmers.

In reality, land reform's role in pushing forward the promised transformations of the rural economy and land system inherited from apartheid has proven to be extremely modest, both quantitatively and qualitatively. Only a small percentage of white-owned land has been transferred back to black farmers.[18] A major focus of critique[19] has been the fact that all aspects of reform are closely tied to the land market itself, which is not a neutral regulator and has fuelled speculation and price rises while channelling state money towards purchase rather than for development and support of new farmers. In addition, existing private property is protected by the Constitution, which together with limited political will cast a deep shadow on meaningful new land rights for black South Africans.

The very premise of the redistribution programme, organised on a willing buyer/willing seller basis, has been a continued target of criticism because it requires black farmers—with government assistance—to buy land back from the white landowners who they often perceive as having stolen it from them in the first place or acquired it under white minority rule. Critics argue that simply removing racial prohibitions to the land

[18] Redistribution beneficiaries had to be able to match government grants, tending to favour better-off black farmers, although subprogrammes have accommodated poorer applicants, including a relatively small number of women. Restitution cases (rights-based) straddled a range of communities and socio-economic strata; very few farm workers and labour tenants have received land through reform.

[19] There is a large body of literature on the problems and achievements of South African land reform. See for example South African Parliament 2009, Andrew 2009, Lahiff 2008, Ntsebeza 2007, National Land Summit 2005, Borras 2003, DoA 2001, DLA 1999.

market—overwhelmingly the domain of the more prosperous, white landowning minority—does little to redistribute land. An important but hardly surprising result is that it has essentially excluded the poor, farm labour among them. Increasingly, redistribution has become geared towards a small, somewhat wealthier section of black farmers considered to have the potential to contribute to commercial agriculture; this has sometimes been referred to as the 'deracialisation' of the sector. At the same time, new land reform projects have often been too large and lacked sufficient training and support to carry them through. Land subdivision has been avoided as an alternative, and state efforts have been at best erratic in developing and supporting small-scale initiatives more oriented towards real opportunities for the poor to improve their livelihoods and meet food security needs. These trends have occurred elsewhere in Africa, such as Mali—where the smallholder agricultural sector faces mounting pressure from large-scale, domestic and foreign investments in land (see Adamczewski et al., this volume).

The commodification of land, already longstanding in South Africa, accelerated through the process of state-led reform relying on the land market. A predictable outcome of this, as with other similar land reforms in the global South where resale had not been prohibited, is the reconcentration of *redistributed* land. Even if low-income farmers are relatively marginal to its core functioning, the market economy also intensifies pressures on those farmers to sell land they cannot afford to develop themselves, or who are choked by debt. In South Africa, such land frequently returns to better capitalised (mainly white) farmers eager to buy it. A reported *one-third* of redistributed land nationally has 'leaked back to white owners', Rural Development and Land Reform (RDLR) Minister Nkwinti revealed, reducing the total amount of white commercial land and state land transferred (from 7%) to only 4.5% (Boyle 2010).

As regards land reform aimed at farm workers and labour tenants, legislation was passed in 1996 (Labour Tenants Act) and in 1997 (Extension of Security of Tenure) to protect farm dwellers from arbitrary evictions and ostensibly to establish their rights to lodge claims on portions of land they have lived and worked on. However, according to a 2005 study, waves of evictions occurred between 1996 and 2001 and less than *one percent* of evictions were legally handled, showing the continued weight of unequal power relations in the countryside and the bias of legal structures (Wegerif et al., 2005). Very few substantive rights for farm dwellers have been realised in the preceding decade and a half, and as the case of private game reserves and farms illustrates, after farm dwellers are evicted or displaced, the burden rests entirely on their shoulders to fight for reinstatement on the farms and for potential land rights.

Game Farming and Land Consolidation in the Eastern Cape

Land consolidation for various forms of wildlife production is occurring in the context of these broader land concentration dynamics and large-scale production. Nationally, wildlife is produced on nearly 10 000 commercial farms, half of which continue their previous crop and/or livestock activities as well (NAMC 2006). In the Eastern Cape, more than 90% of mainly white commercial farmers and private landowners have diversified; game ranching has been added to ongoing—though sometimes scaled-down—conventional agriculture. About 7% of the commercial farms in the province have converted entirely to wildlife production.[20] Due to the fact that land ownership and forms of land use are not always registered with the government, or only with certain departments, the exact land surface involved in private wildlife production and tourism is not clear,[21] although estimates vary from 13 to 16.8% of South Africa's total land surface (NAMC 2006).

A high proportion of game farm revenues stem from hunting, especially trophy hunting, which caters to a wealthy, mainly international clientele. Hunting revenues have been estimated to account for 60% to 80% of total income to the wildlife industry (Du Toit 2007; AFRA 2003), with between 600 million and nearly one billion rands[22] flowing into state coffers (Carroll 2010). Other landowners are developing private so-called eco-tourism ventures, offering game viewing drives and occasionally demonstrations of 'traditional' culture in a range of packages ranging from family recreation to a high-end market targeting a very specific section of affluent leisure consumers. Mass marketing includes both claims of offering an experience of 'unspoiled wilderness' in private reserves, highly contentious conservation messages[23] and openly ideological appeals to a 'lifestyle' reminiscent

[20] P. van Niekerk, Nelson Mandela Metropolitan University (South Africa).

[21] In terms of statistics, game farms tend to fly below official radar. They are not categorised or counted separately by government departments, which makes it impossible to precisely say how many there are, how much land they occupy or how many jobs they provide. As a result, most figures are produced by industry-sponsored research.

[22] The South African Rand fluctuates around 10 ZAR to 1 Euro or 8,5 ZAR to the US dollar.

[23] For discussion of conservation and commoditised landscapes, see Brooks et al. 2011, Wolmer 2007 and Neumann 1998.

of a grand colonial era. One specialised hunting outfitter in Cradock, for example, advertises:

> Sundowners are enjoyed in the quaint colonial underground pub or around a campfire under the star filled African Sky. Candlelit hunting cuisine, with fine South African wines, is served in old colonial comfort, with classic China, antique silverware and crystal.[24]

Interviews with local game farmers and the wildlife industry representatives provide testimony of multiple motivations centred on a common thread of the desire to 'hold onto' the land. This may be in order to use land as an asset to sell, to invest in, or as a way of legitimizing their 'place' in society. A common view is that land value increases when it is used for wildlife production. Many explained that stock farming is no longer profitable and that game farming requires fewer permanent workers (and thus resident black farm dweller families). They consider this an attractive option, particularly in light of higher labour costs since new labour laws were adopted in recent years, and state attempts to protect land rights of farm dwellers—even though in practice these attempts have been seriously flawed. Others, however, argue that game farming creates employment opportunities and hope that this, in combination with conservation practices, will enhance the reputation of game farms and protect farm owners from land reform. The wildlife industry has financed influential studies which fuel assertions that game ranching will ultimately provide a substantial boost to the national economy as well as stimulate growth, job creation and corporate concerns for social upliftment of disadvantaged (black) rural residents (Langholz & Kerley 2006, J. DuToit 2007). Still others have heavily invested in the logic of nature conservation, and argue that game farms are contributing to the return to 'natural wilderness' and maintain that this is how most of the province should be—conveniently ignoring the history of pre-colonial livestock husbandry and other forms of land use. A related but distinct idea was expressed that only commercially-managed, private wildlife reserves are viable forms of nature conservation, and that what they consider to be poorly-run, public game parks (especially provincial ones) are really only adequate for the local population's use and enjoyment.

Whether commercial farmers decide to change entirely or merely add wildlife production to their ongoing agricultural activities may well

---

24 Http://www.southern-cross-safaris.co.za/manor.html. Accessed in 2011.

depend on the ways in which landowners have chosen to amalgamate or reorganise properties. Many game farmers have been buying up adjoining farms—on average six to seven,[25] but some purchase even more properties—or are forming partnerships or conservancies with neighbouring farms and removing the internal fencing to create larger wildlife habitats. Some have been expanding family-run businesses this way, while other game farms have become part of larger corporations.

Alongside primarily domestic investments, an area that has received less attention in studies on large-scale land acquisitions, foreign capital also appears to be increasingly mobilised by commercial farmers and landowners.[26] Some farmers are seeking capital injections to launch or move their operations into wildlife production, not only for land purchase but also for the costs of stocking and/or raising 'wild' animals, building fencing, adhering to regulatory policies, and marketing their business. In addition, as in the case of many of the large, private 'eco-tourism' reserves catering to top international services and accommodations standards, massive capital investment is required and a number of the prominent reserves have joined large international corporate groups. One of the most famous private wildlife reserves, Shamwari, is part of the Mantis group which owns eco-lodges and luxury hotels in Africa but also in Europe. Kwandwe, another large—22,000 hectare—private reserve, belongs to '& Beyond', a corporation that operates 35 safari lodges throughout Africa and has recently branched out to India.[27]

Advertisements for upscale reserves seeking supplemental international capital flows urge potential individual investors to 'Own your own slice of game reserve paradise' with exquisite photos of 'Big 5' animals,[28] beautiful landscapes and ultra-plush lodging.[29] Precise data on levels of

---

25 See also Langholz & Kerley 2006.

26 South African estate agent websites directly target foreigners, promoting investment returns from 50 up to 500% on game farms. They argue that land is still relatively cheap there and the growth of wildlife tourism will increase its value. Yet one game farmer interviewed in the Makana area (March 2011) felt with the recession 'eco-tourism' had peaked and plummeted; his neighbours were getting low prices on land they resold.

27 See www.andbeyond.com. In 2008 Dubai World Africa became a major shareholder in the Mantis Group; the latter has since sold its shares. (cf: Hotel Newswire: http://hotel-executive.com/newswire/12759/dubai-world-africa-buys-into-mantis-collection). *The Herald Online*, 4 January 2012.

28 The 'big five' include elephant, lion, buffalo, rhino and leopard.

29 For example, www.rizeestates.co.za/etengolodge.html. A range of shareholding possibilities are on offer at many of South Africa's private game reserves, including plots of land and residence packages accruing rental percentages.

domestic and foreign investments in game farms or private reserves, however, are difficult to obtain, given the above-mentioned problems with land ownership and registration. Most private game farms involved in one or another form of tourism manage bookings through their websites, but these seldom provide ownership details. In fact, on these websites and during interviews, many game farmers present themselves as owners; while they may have owned the core property on which the game farming venture started in the past, we later discovered that some were actually managing the game farm on behalf of investors.

At the same time, similar to global trends, financial investment and speculation in land in South Africa are not necessarily tied to a particular form of land use. Although the state is not playing the role of broker, foreign investors have faced few restrictions up until now. Some government officials accuse foreign investors of not just taking over land, but of provoking higher land prices, making it unaffordable for others—even for the government to purchase for land reform.

Growing concern about foreign ownership has led the government to include clauses which ostensibly limit land sales to foreigners on the basis of long leasehold instead of freehold in new national land reform draft papers released in late 2011. Proposed conditions include partnership with South Africans, restrictions on quantity and absentee landlordism, as well as excluding 'sensitive and national security land such as communal, coastal, heritage, rural, agricultural, environmentally-sensitive, security-sensitive, and borderlands'.[30] Game farms are not specifically mentioned, despite previous government documents suggesting they would be included in restrictions on leisure activity areas, golf estates, etc.

Conversions to Game Farming in the Eastern Cape: Consequences for Farm Dwellers

Our research findings confirm the important point made in this volume's introduction that landscapes are actively being produced and that they are contested. While hunting and eco-tourism enterprises have different labour requirements, overall, farm conversions to wildlife production reduce employment possibilities, and invariably affect labour relations

[30] See the DRDLR's *Draft Green Paper on land reform*, released on 25 August 2011, p. 16. These conditions are not spelled out in the final *Green paper*, released a few days later, but are still apparently being discussed.

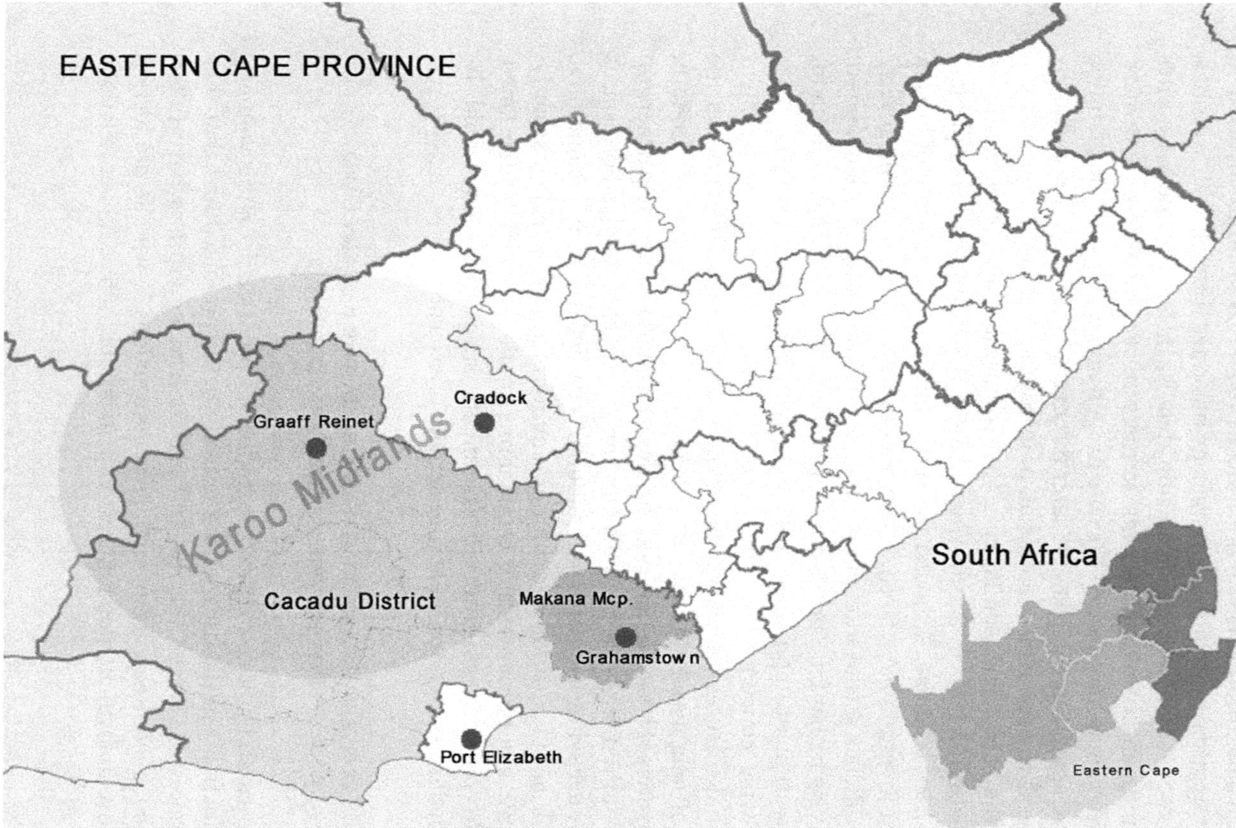

Source: Adapted from www.demarcation.org.za

Map 1. Karoo region and Makana Municipality (fieldwork areas) Eastern Cape Province.

and settlement patterns on the farms. The consolidation of land associated with the establishment of game farms results in increased displacement of farm dwellers to nearby rural and urban townships, changed livelihoods and in many instances, loss of access to any agricultural land. The histories and relations on the farms are not identical in all localities; they reveal how colonial and apartheid legacies shape the ways in which South Africans situate themselves and others in post-apartheid rural landscapes. Our two case studies also analyse the contradictory and inconsistent role of the state in relation to the expansion of game farming, land consolidation and what this means for farm dwellers.

Research was conducted between 2008 and 2011, in two different geographical areas of the Eastern Cape Province (see map 1), namely the Karoo Midlands and the area including Makana Municipality and the coastal strip up to Port Elizabeth. A concentration of trophy-hunting farms is found in the Karoo, whereas in the Makana area private game reserves (PGRs) specialising in safari- or eco-tourism activities are dominant. Many of the latter target the upper end of the tourism market and offer animal viewing and luxury accommodation. These businesses rely heavily on tourist facilities like airports and road networks that tend to become scarcer inland, where the enormous Karoo hunting properties are often accessible only by unobtrusive gravel roads. Contrary to eco-tourism places, hunting places are not promoted on billboards along the national roads. Yet, the trained eye recognizes the high fences and the wandering game species in the *veld* indicating wildlife production farms.

Numerous interviews were conducted with game farm owners and managers, farm workers and dwellers, government officials, NGO staff, and other relevant parties. It is worth noting that we often had difficulties speaking with farm workers and/or dwellers *on* game farms or large private game reserves since access depended on the owner's or manager's permission. They were sometimes apprehensive due to the political sensitivity of topics dealing with labour relations, land reform, and nature conservation, along with existing tensions between farmers and workers, as well as among workers themselves. In the Karoo, researchers carried out ethnographic study after considerable efforts to establish relations with landowners and negotiate access to a number of game farms in order to explore the meanings various stakeholders attributed to farm conversions to game farming in the region.

1. *Disruptions of Livelihoods for Farm Dwellers in Changed Hunting and 'Eco-tourism' Landscapes*

The notion of creating wilderness based on the idea of 'pristine nature' is an important feature of both hunting and 'eco-tourism' landscapes. Landowners assume that tourists prefer to see as little human interference in the landscape as possible.[31] This particular landscape imagery has consequences for the space and place of farm dwellers living on these farms. In most cases the creation of both types of wildlife-based businesses meant moving farm dwellers off the farms that had been sold or merged with neighbouring properties. The impacts of these displacements on farm dwellers' specific relations to the land, to landowners and to the farms vary, depending on somewhat different regional historical processes of dispossession and labour arrangements.

In the Karoo, agriculture has been a crucial sector for employment since the establishment of white-owned commercial farms during the 19th century. Formal jobs have stagnated since 1995 (Inxuba YeThemba 2008). The region is popularly known for its Merino wool and Angora mohair production on the vast livestock farms that cover hundreds or even thousands of hectares. The more intensive crop and mixed farms that cover less surface area are situated along the Fish River. Heightened competition and droughts stimulated some sheep farmers to shift to game farming already in the 1970s and with the increased deregulation of the agricultural sector starting in the late 1980s, many livestock farmers followed their example.

With the amalgamation of farms into single properties for game production—a process which is also occurring in commercial livestock and crop farming—employment opportunities in the area have been decreasing since 1995 (Inxuba YeThemba 2008). This has led to a migration pattern that continues today, in which a steady influx of farm dwellers move into the townships[32] of rural towns. While many game farm owners and managers claim they have employed more workers since their shift to

[31] Concepts of 'pristine nature' devoid of human presence can be traced back to post-Enlightenment ideas and romanticism, which assume a strong nature/culture divide. These ideas have continued to influence nature conservation practices, and have justified many evictions from state-run conservation areas (see Brockington & Igoe 2006). Lately, 'pristine nature' has been redefined as a scarce resource that can—and should be—commodified (Castree 2008a; 2008b). For a more detailed discussion of the role that ideas about 'pristineness' play in private wildlife production, see Brooks et al. (2011).

[32] The townships are equally a legacy of the colonial and apartheid eras. Especially during apartheid, the influx of black residents to towns and cities was tightly restricted and controlled through pass-laws. Separate areas were designated for black residents,

wildlife production, they often compare the number of jobs on the game farm as a whole to that on the smaller property they owned before the conversion, ignoring the livelihoods lost on the additional properties they acquired. Those farm workers who manage to stay on the game farm are frequently performing work quite similar to that on the sheep and goat farms, such as managing grazing and maintaining water points and fences; fencing, however, is increasingly contracted out to teams of local casual labourers. Some are trained to track wildlife and prepare trophies but this is often learned on the job and it only rarely leads to a significantly higher wage.

Nevertheless some male permanent workers on hunting farms receive wages above minimum wage level. At the time of fieldwork in 2009, full-time permanent farm workers on trophy-hunting farms reported incomes ranging from a minimum wage of 1238 ZAR per month up to 1800 ZAR (or an average of about 175$ at 2012 rates). They were paid the same as workers on other types of commercial farms and did not benefit from higher hospitality sector wages, even though trophy hunting farms involve hospitality work. Farmers typically subtracted the legally allowed 10% deductions for provision of electricity, housing, and game meat from the wages of farm workers living on the farm. In some cases farmers deducted money from workers' wages without providing the facilities or products they were charging for.

Overseas clients often leave generous tips to supplement the incomes of hunting farm staff, but in practice some farm owners 'save' these tips and pay them out to workers as an 'extra bonus' in December. The farmer decides who deserves how much tip money according to traditional farm institutions based on the ideology of paternalistic authority. The informal bonus system does increase workers' incomes, but the arbitrary method of distribution causes distrust between farmer and workers because there is no transparency about the total income that the farmer has pocketed from tips. As a result, working and living on a trophy-hunting farm perpetuates workers' dependence on the farmer's way of managing and controlling farm labour. The division of labour between men and women on hunting farms is similar to the local livestock farms. Men work outside in the field as trackers, skinners and general farm workers and women are employed (often part-time) as domestic workers in the farm houses and/

'locations' or townships, often far away from town centres and residential areas reserved for white residents. This spatial lay-out still persists today.

or lodges for visitors. Children of farm workers residing on the hunting farms are typically sent to live with relatives in town by the time they start attending school.

Contrary to the hunting farms, the large-scale private eco-tourism game reserves generate more employment than the cattle, goat and sheep farms they replace. How stable those jobs are and how many farm workers have been hired in this relatively new workforce is not clear. It would be useful to compare large PGRs more closely with the more intensively cultivated crop farms in the area. Some of the PGRs make a point of employing mainly local residents—usually restricted to the lower echelons of the workforce—whereas others deliberately recruit from outside the region. One of the largest reserves in the area, which resulted from the merging of 11 livestock farms, claims to employ about 300 people compared to the roughly estimated 70 to 80 workers who previously were in service on the farms, but some employees and other PGR owners disputed this figure. About 60% are women, most working as chamber maids, cleaners or in the kitchen, and the majority are between 20 and 40 years of age. While job opportunities for women have increased, those for men were quite limited and tended to be on a casual, seasonal or precarious basis—both on farms and game farms. A few former farm workers obtained part-time work repairing fences or carrying out other maintenance, and some are employed as security guards on the game reserves. Due to the recession, occupancy rates at some of the luxury lodges have declined, resulting in retrenchments. Overall unemployment in the informal rural settlements and townships remains very high.

In terms of adherence to labour legislation—a continual and widespread problem on the white-owned commercial farms, including on hunting farms—these large properties running high-end tourist operations appear in the main to be paying the minimum wage. Hospitality workers on game farms receive higher wages than those paid for general farm work and are provided with some kind of pay slip (very often *not* the norm on commercial farms). The way game farm managers treat overtime and tips is a continually sore subject, since for many they are key in rounding out a meager month and many respondents feel these extras are neither fairly nor transparently handled.

Unionisation is very low. None of the farm workers on the hunting farms studied belonged to a union, nor did they know where to go with their complaints or to seek relevant information about labour laws, land rights and other issues. In the Makana Municipality we were told about a union at only one out of seven large PGRs—an independent one, not affiliated with the ANC or its trade union federation, COSATU (Confederation of South African Trade Unions)—although discussions were underway at a second private reserve. Farm worker union organisers and some employees reported that workers caught promoting a union were harassed; they described being searched for stolen goods as they left work or intimidated with threats of withdrawing transport or the extra water provided to poorly serviced rural settlements, or being replaced with one of the thousands waiting for their job. Union staff had the legal right to access game reserves and farms to speak to hospitality and general workers, but were often turned away by security or the gates were locked, thus limiting contact with employees to their periodic visits to town.

In addition to 'gendered' shifts in employment, the composition of staff in both types of wildlife-based operations was changing at the time of research, intensifying the divisions and tensions. Regular incidences of violence revealed symptoms of extremely unequal power relations on farms. On trophy-hunting farms in the Karoo, several game farmers had employed Zimbabwean men as chefs to cook for hunting clients, while some of the eco-tourism PGRs also preferred to employ non-South African employees. Zimbabwean workers are stereotypically described by game farmers as 'educated, hard working and well-behaved' people compared to South-African workers. The preferential treatments of Zimbabwean workers in the eyes of South African workers, and language barriers between them, create tensions. Some game farmers use these tensions by claiming, as one respondent did, that "South African staff do not like the Zimbabweans because they won't back them up when they are stealing, lying and cheating" (Interviews, March 2009). These kinds of statements suggest that farm dweller communities on hunting farms were intentionally disrupted to prevent any form of solidarity or trust among workers there.

Stark contrasts mark the PGR eco-tourism sector. Smiling, cocktails in hand, one young woman at an opulent 5-star lodge greeted and served arriving international guests who pay from $600 to $2500 per night during high season. At the end of her shift she would be transported by a local mini-van business back to her shack settlement that has neither electricity nor running water. It was unclear if managers for these luxury PGRs had ever visited the poor rural settlements where their 'general' and hospitality staff are residing. While PGR owners present their operations as modern, they rely on many of the institutionalised structural inequalities and social practices stemming from the colonial and apartheid eras.

The managers and public relations staff stress the capacity-building and community development that PGRs can provide. Training programmes are offered to 'skill up' what they considered to be uneducated farm labour, yet interviews with members of all of the parties involved in this relationship suggested that these initiatives ended up in promotions for only a very small minority of black staff who rarely become rangers or join management at some level. A notable exception was one family-run game reserve, which forms a part of a much larger conservancy offering 3- and 4-star accommodation. The owners had made a concerted effort to integrate their dozen or so farm dweller families into the hospitality and safari end of the tourism operations, including positions such as chef and lodge manager. An important aspect of the arrangement is allowing staff to continue to live across the road on the owners' livestock farm, where the workers have access to land for gardens and for grazing cattle and small animals.

The presence of farm dwellers in hunting and eco-tourism landscapes, as well as their vulnerable position in the agrarian economy in which these landscapes are rooted, are both increasingly temporal and contested.

2. *Farm Dwellers' Sense of Belonging on Game Farms, Attachment and Rights to Land*

In the introduction to this volume, Evers, Seagle and Krijtenburg discuss the relationship between changing landscapes, or certain features of landscapes, and changing social meanings imbued to them. In the Eastern Cape today local patterns of dispossession, labour recruitment and land tenure all influence the way in which attachment to land and to rural spaces are understood and contested.

In the Karoo African labourers have worked and lived on white-owned commercial farms for generations, often moving from one farm to the other in search of (slightly) better living conditions. Farm workers' lives depended on farm owners' choices; if a farmer went bankrupt—which occurred regularly in this arid region—or re-established his farm elsewhere, or when one of his children moved to another farm, part of the workforce was expected to relocate as well. As a result, farm workers and farmers in this part of the province have been highly mobile throughout history. Workers have resisted dependency on agricultural work by leaving farms to seek other livelihood options in town; yet since there were very few ways to make a living there, they often had to return to the farm. Although farm dwellers in the Karoo did not seem to have strong attachments to particular farms, many respondents felt that they belonged to the area and considered it 'home'. Despite government promises to improve tenure security for farm dwellers, they also felt that their place on the farms was becoming more insecure; as 'belonging' on these farms becomes more difficult, they anticipate their perceived inevitable departure from the farms by building or investing in housing in a nearby rural township:

> We have to get a house in [town], [so that] when we leave Sir then we know we have a place to go to. Because if you don't have a place to go to, you should not build a shack. You have to have your own home, and you shouldn't stay with your mother, you need you own house.....Look at [other female farm dweller]; if she gets her pension from Sir, she needs to go to her own house, that's how we do it. (Farm dweller in Karoo region, August 2009)

Populations in these townships are growing, resulting in severe problems of access to services, businesses, healthcare facilities, roads, transport, and space. Without alternative job possibilities, capital or other assets to start up an enterprise in town, the livelihood choices for people coming from the farms are very limited.

A similar pattern of movement was found in the Makana Municipality and coastal area. Especially during the earlier wave of conversions to private wildlife production farm dwellers experienced outright evictions and retrenchments (ECARP/SCLC 2006). More recently, displacement has often taken the form of pressuring families to leave 'voluntarily' through various means. These included terminating farm dwellers' jobs along with any services such as transport, closing off access to the farms with new fencing and (digital) locks, demolishing farm dwellers' housing on the farms, waiting until their lack of income and their fear of wild animals drove them to leave, or offering them small sums of money to leave. Many farm dwellers interviewed during research in 2011 had relocated to nearby townships (Paterson, Alicedale, Port Elizabeth, Grahamstown) within a radius of 70 kilometres of the farms on which they had grown up or worked. There they hoped to find a job or share a house with relatives. Numerous other families had moved to un-serviced or poorly serviced informal rural settlements. They had built shacks for their extended family and often were surviving on only one part-time wage and a pension with support from family and social networks. Farm dwellers' histories in the Makana Municipality differ to some extent from those in the Karoo; many families have lived and worked on the same farm for generations and often consider that particular farm their 'home'. Ancestral graves and ritual places strengthen these ties to the land and the farms (see also Postel in this volume).

Both early historical dispossession in the province and the prevalence of extensive livestock raising (along with major, intensive horticulture centres) have meant that the process of reducing labour and displacing farm workers and tenants has been a gradual, ongoing one. While waged farm work is more common today than labour tenancy arrangements, many farm dwellers interviewed in Makana Municipality and the coastal area described having previously had access to patches of land for gardens and grazing on the farms where they had lived, as labour tenants often did. The allocation of huge stretches of land converted to wildlife tourism elicited quite some resentment among those interviewed. Asked if he thought that game farms and tourism would help develop the area, one respondent stated:

> Personally, I'm not for it. It's against our dignity to use all this land for animals. These animals live in such nice conditions and have so much space but with us, a single candle can burn down all our houses and we lose everything... (March 2011)

Only a few respondents were willing to discuss land rights for farm dwellers openly. For large private game reserve owners land rights for former farm workers in the area were not a real issue and they considered 'irreversible' property mergers to have sealed their fate. In fact, the displacement or removal process *had* already severely jeopardized farm workers' rights to portions of commercial farms they had previously lived on and cultivated for years. However, the 2011 Land Tenure Security Bill still under discussion in South Africa—which aims to provide more substantial protection of and rights to farm workers and tenants than previous legislation—is stirring up some contention; as one landowner who had diversified into game production and hunting stated unambiguously and ominously (despite his need for the farm dweller families working on his farm): "We will get them off our land altogether, if that thing is passed, you can count on it!" (Game farm owner, March 2011).

In the Karoo we observed that farmers provided their own solution to control the presence of farm dwellers on their farms and to secure their own terms of belonging within the post-apartheid regulatory framework. Several trophy-hunting farmers use a private labour consultant to manage labour contracts, disputes and evictions within the boundaries of the law, thereby assuring that they operate legally and, in doing so, help to 'formalise' the relations between farmers and workers. It is a profitable type of consultancy, tapping into needs of commercial farmers who generally perceive state regulations as hostile and struggle to reconcile the implementation of new workers' rights with old social habits centred around 'farmers' laws'. Indeed, farm workers' lives still very much depend on the farmers' will. The farmers' practice of relying on a private consultant to mediate between them and their workers is deeply resented by the workers, who feel their side of the story is not taken into account during dispute resolution, only strengthening the farmer's power over their lives.

A story that seems consistently neglected in the main discourses on wildlife farming is farm workers' concerns about their physical security on the game farm, especially those inhabited by dangerous game like buffalo or rhino. Because they walk in the field without rifles and often do not live in enclosed areas like the farm owners and the farm guests, they see the potential encounters with wildlife as a serious risk to their personal safety. They feel they have nothing to protect themselves with—no guns for self-defence in the wildlife habitat, no insurance arrangements to support the family and very little means to challenge this situation. Within the boundaries of the game farm, fencing and the absence of fencing also indicates who belongs in certain spaces, and who does not. As landowners gradually convert these landscapes into private "wildernesses", the place of animals is central, such that they 'belong' there, whereas for farm dwellers the right and possibility to belong in the same spaces appear to be fading or disappearing, with little recourse to state mechanisms for protection and for enhanced social and property rights.

3. *The Contradictory Role of the South African State*

State actors and legislation have played an ambivalent role in the spread of farm conversions to game farms. Policies aimed at assisting farm dwellers' to obtain land rights and labour regulations on farms have been very poorly implemented or enforced, and sometimes cause unintended consequences. The introduction of minimum wages and labour rights for example, facilitated casualization/externalization processes and the formalization of labour arrangements on farms. Combined with the persistence of arbitrary rule by farmers, the post-apartheid legal framework in some ways places farm labourers in a more vulnerable position and demonstrates the ineffectiveness of labour laws in addressing unequal power relations on farms.

The failure of the state to empower or improve farm dwellers' situations is evidenced in the ways they perceived local government institutions such as the Department of Labour to be corrupt and staffed with bureaucrats acting on behalf of farmers' interests. It must be noted, however, that the local branches of the Department of Labour are seriously understaffed, and that inspectors experience severe problems in accessing farms, since owners resent the interference of government in their farm organisation. At the same time, labour inspectors told us that most commercial farmers have learned how to 'pass' the very perfunctory inspections and then the state no longer bothers them, whether or not changes beyond the payment of a minimum wage have been made on their farms.

As regards access to land rights, the state has invested some effort into disseminating information but this has been quite uneven. In the Karoo Midlands farm dwellers were not aware of possibilities to claim land through the Extension of Security of Tenure Act and none of the game farms was under claim for restitution or targeted for redistribution. The few local NGOs in the Karoo Midlands devoted to supporting farm dwellers were understaffed and underfunded. Among farm dwellers interviewed in the Makana Municipality—who were frequently unhappy with the way in which rural spaces where they lived and worked are shrinking before their eyes and are now home to wild animals—there was also very little awareness of land reform and farm tenant rights even many years after they were introduced. Few people knew about how tenure security reform under discussion might apply to them and who to approach, and furthermore, most had not been involved in organised attempts to resist efforts to move them off the farms. A few restitution cases, challenging rights to land on the basis of apartheid-era dispossession or forced removal, were underway in the central-southern part of the province—although the Rural Development and Land Reform department was reluctant to discuss these cases—and only a small number of rural claims had been settled at the time of fieldwork in 2011. One respondent recounted how the creation of a large PGR and subsequent eviction of families from the area had fractured the farm dweller community. In that case, most people had ended up accepting a small pay-out offered by the new landowner, but his father, who refused the money, resisted and was finally settled in a house on a small farm. He then died very shortly afterwards. The son's family began a chicken project with others from the removed farm dweller community, but this was some distance away from the area they had lived in and are seeking to be restored to them.

From their 'relocated' position in one of the Grahamstown townships, several families are continuing their legal and political struggle to return to a piece of the land they consider home, which happened to be a highly-prized, fertile strip near the Fish River; respondents contended that a local game farm owner illegally 'incorporated' the land into his purchase of several farms near there. Significantly, all land rights cases encountered during research had been assisted, in one way or another, by non-governmental legal centres or land sector organisations.

With regard to the redistribution component of the South African land reform programme, an official from the provincial Rural Development and Land Reform department stated that she knew of 'no redistribution cases on private game farms' within our study areas, inadvertently indicating that buying any private game farms in the area for the purpose of reaching the government's target of redistributing 30% of land to new black farmers in each province was not currently in the cards. Increasing prices for game farm land may add to the government's land reform dilemma.[33]

A variety of government and civil society respondents, including farm dwellers themselves, expressed considerable concern over the extent of land consolidation in the province due to the expansion of game reserves and were in general highly sceptical of the benefits of tourism for the rural black population. PGR owners and managers, together with a small but vocal minority of supporters within academia and some long-time Department of Agriculture members who served under the apartheid regime, generally blamed farm dwellers and their lack of non-farm skills for their situation, while somewhat disingenuously criticising the current ANC government for 'incompetency' and the poor results of promised rural development.

Municipal officials all reported that the influx of evicted or displaced farm workers was putting enormous pressures on local township resources, services and land. In the Makana Municipality, hugely expensive (and insufficient) water tanks were being delivered to some farms and rural black settlements that needed clean water, yet the building of basic infrastructure seemed to encounter numerous bureaucratic and financial problems. PGR owners said they had few water-related difficulties in an otherwise water scarce area, often erecting dams to supply water for game, which at least one municipal employee reported to be causing shortages on the other side of the highway. Various well-intentioned but frustrated provincial government officials felt that old power structures were too entrenched and the obstacles too great to improve farm

[33] An official from the Eastern Cape Provincial Department of Economic Development and Environmental Affairs informed us that the price per hectare in some of the most coveted areas for game farming had risen to 20,000 ZAR, while agricultural land can be bought for 8,000 ZAR per hectare.

dwellers' lives in significant ways. Among those we spoke to, it was primarily the community-based organisations and rural development organisations that were closely familiar with the deteriorating quality of life and livelihood prospects of workers and dwellers moved off of the farms and thus able to see more clearly the political and social consequences of farm conversions.

In addition, a number of respondents raised concerns about the shift in land use to non-food producing activities on vast stretches of farmland; they considered this to be contributing to higher food prices which are increasingly centrally controlled by large supermarket chains that negatively impact local small farmers' food production,[34] a trend occurring in many African countries (see Evers et al.). The wildlife industry argues it is providing dried and fresh game meat on the market (Dry 2011), but farm dwellers told us they could not afford to buy it.

Government departments, on a national as well as provincial level, have also displayed ambivalent attitudes towards game farming and the resulting land concentration and changes in land use. Some officials purport that wildlife tourism on private land is a motor for local economic development and that game farming benefits conservation programs. Others criticise game farming for either wasting productive land or for creating playgrounds for the rich. A former minister of Agriculture and Land Affairs questioned the production value of game farms and suggested a moratorium on them at the 2005 National Land Summit. Rural Development and Land Reform Minister Nkwinti described game farms as 'elitist' and said they amounted to a 're-colonisation of the countryside' (Haywood 2007: 195). The Department of Agriculture (DoA), which manages commercial farming, holds a more ambiguous position as it appears to be endorsing the wildlife industry as a profitable form of land use, while some DoA officials consider it to be negatively affecting national food production and have accused the industry of spreading diseases (Govender 2005).

Nonetheless, no policy has curbed game farming as of yet. On the contrary, the state has benefitted from rising revenue streams and the Department of Environmental Affairs (DEA) has tended to facilitate the growth of the wildlife industry. An increasing number of animals can be hunted in South Africa, with the Eastern Cape topping the list at 56 huntable species. The Eastern Cape Province's permit fees alone amounted to 66.83 million rand in 2009 (Caroll 2010), a figure which does not include other

34 See Baipethi and Jacobs 2009.

environmental policy revenue such as transportation permits, daily fees, taxidermy exportation fees or fees for keeping wildlife on private land. Environmental policy has been contested by landowners and the DEA has criticised game farmers for harmful conservation practices. Yet it is DEA policy which prescribes the high game fences that have led to disputed borders and in effect reinforce farm owners' claims to land and wildlife. Politically and legally, the policy placed wildlife species into new [private] property regimes that facilitate the privatisation and commodification of game, thereby contributing to expansion of game farms (Snijders 2012).

The quality of life and livelihoods of farm dwellers and workers rarely figure in the policy debates, in industry studies or among the reasons farmers give for shifting to wildlife production. Farm dwellers' family graves are often on the land occupied by game ranches, and farm dwellers' social networks are connected to the towns around the farms; however, their personal ties to the land and the nature of their social networks reflect varying regional and historical developments. All of this underscores the importance of analysing the neglected social impacts of land consolidation and land use changes on farm dwellers.[35]

Conclusion and Discussion

This chapter has shown that the spread of game farming and wildlife-based tourism is actively producing new landscapes with important cultural, social and economic consequences for farm dwellers. We have highlighted how these changes are embedded in broader structural dynamics at work in South Africa; while not a linear process, land consolidation—in the context of an already highly centralised commercial agricultural sector—has followed a definite pattern in the wake of strategic macroeconomic decisions negotiated during the period leading up to and during the political transition in 1994. Both increased liberalisation and agrarian reforms—prescribed within a neoliberal course of development and its reflection in policy—have had the effect of bolstering large-scale

[35] For more on evictions and abusive farm conditions for dwellers, see the 2005 study by Wegerif et al, the S. African Human Rights Commission's *Inquiry into human rights violations in farming communities* (2003) http://us-cdn.creamermedia.co.za/assets/articles/attachments/00738_farming.pdf and the update in 2008 www.sahrc.org.za/home/index.php?ipkContentID=15, as well as the 2011 Human Rights Watch report *Ripe with Abuse. Human Rights Conditions in South Africa's Fruit and Wine Industries.* www.hrw.org/sites/default/files/reports/safarm0811webwcover.pdf.

agriculture and thus the concentration of both land and production. In a sector seeking to develop high value exports within a highly competitive global market, the largely unsuccessful market-based land reform programme has not significantly countered this tendency.

The African National Congress-led state has sought to expand the number of black farmers gaining access to land, but has aimed to do so on the basis of preserving the commercial farming sector more or less as it was structured. Organised white landowners have strongly opposed reforms and particularly the subdivision of private land. Rather than the state actively breaking up large units from the outset in order to facilitate changing the racial imbalance of ownership as part of transforming the countryside in general, primarily land concentration has resulted in the form of fewer but larger commercial farms.

Due to the extensive privatisation and monopolisation of land by white settlers historically, land acquisitions and current trends in land consolidation in South Africa take place mostly within the domain of the private land market rather than through the state as broker. At the same time the state, together with its protection of private land constitutionally and practically, provides an enabling political and legal environment, sometimes at variance with its own development policies. Land deals, in our view, are but one aspect of the vertiginous and mostly negative effects of globalisation on small farmers. Real estate websites give the impression that South Africa too is 'for sale', with marketing pitched seductively to foreign investors—both individual and corporate.

Private game farming provides a graphic example of this process of land consolidation, land use changes and restructuring the rural social landscape, all of which operate against expanding small scale agriculture and non-commercial food production acutely needed in the poor areas of the countryside, where many cannot afford prices set by large retail food suppliers.

The majority of the game farms visited for this study, both in hunting and 'eco-tourism', emerged through the amalgamation of several farms in order to establish large enough habitats for wild animals and to create a sense of ultimate wilderness for tourists. Gaining greater control over land and private ownership of wildlife through the further commodification of land and nature is all quite legal, with very little direct interference from the state, and is increasingly supported by foreign investors interested in developing hunting and tourism initiatives aimed primarily at a wealthy international clientele. The proportion of domestic to foreign investment is difficult to ascertain, but it is clear that most of the largest hunting farms and 'eco-tourism' reserves in the province are turning to multiple investment sources, including a substantial number from abroad. In light of recent land acquisition trends worldwide, this land consolidation process—related to the expansion of game farming and foreign land ownership debates in South Africa—is arousing further qualms regarding its social costs. Government departments' reactions to game farming and land consolidation are ambivalent, with some stressing potential profitability and trickle-down effects, while others express concerns about small-scale food production and available land for reform.

The social impacts of conversions to wildlife production on farm dwellers vary somewhat by region and by mode of wildlife utilisation. In the arid Karoo, where mobility from farm to farm has been greater, the shift to game faming feeds into an ongoing process of farm workers seeking to establish homes in rural townships, thus increasing pressures on the already meagre service delivery in these areas. Hunting farms dominate in the Karoo, involving less labour and accelerating evictions and displacement. In the area between Port Elizabeth and Grahamstown, however, the largest properties are private 'eco-tourism' game reserves requiring more labour than livestock ranches and hunting operations and generally paying higher wages for the hospitality work for which more women than men are hired. Some tourism operations do employ local residents and occasionally farm workers who lived on the farms before conversion, while others deliberately recruit from outside the region.

In terms of livelihood options, jobs are not the only issue. Farm dwellers have strong connections to the farming areas. Moreover, their removal from the properties means they lose access to land for grazing and cultivation. The degree to which farm dwellers engage in stockholding and crop production, aside from working for white commercial farmers, differs by region, and to some extent by farm. In the Karoo this dependence and foothold on the land appeared to be less common than further south in the Makana area. In both areas farm dweller removals sometimes lead to conflict over land while sometimes they are largely invisible. Power relations on white-owned farms remain extremely unequal. Once farm dwellers are gone it becomes even more difficult for them to establish potential rights to that land. Numerous farm dwellers have been evicted but often their displacement is more gradual, induced by withholding certain basic services, refusal to employ them, destroying their dwellings and introducing dangerous game without any protection for them. Those who resist are channelled through the appropriate government department, where their cases often reach an impasse.

This significant change in land use and ways that land is acquired and consolidated to create private hunting farms and safari or 'eco-tourism' reserves pose an important central question as to whether or not these activities really represent much development potential for black families who have been the backbone of labour for the white commercial farm sector and whose lives are rooted in the land. This is particularly questionable for those who have been displaced, whose livelihoods have been disrupted or abruptly ended, and whose rights to land remain tentative to virtually non-realisable in the current framework. And for those farm dwellers still living and working on commercial farms, including game farms, this will also continue to be a highly contested landscape.

Bibliography

African National Congress (ANC). 2009. *Election Manifesto: Working together we can do more*. Johannesburg: ANC.

Aliber, M., M. Baipethi, P. Jacobs. 2009. "Agricultural employment scenarios." In *Another Countryside? Policy options for land and agrarian reform in South Africa*, edited by R. Hall, Cape Town: PLAAS.

Andrew, N. 2009. "Reforming South Africa's land system: the conflict that won't go away." Institut Français des Relations Internationales (IFRI), *Notes de L'IFRI*, Paris, December.

Association for Rural Advancement (AFRA). 2003. Investigation of the effects of conservation and tourism on land tenure and ownership patterns in KwaZulu-Natal. Phase 1 Report, 15 September. Pietermaritzburg: Mclntosh Xaba & Associates.

Baipethi, M., P. Jacobs. 2009. "The contribution of subsistence farming to food security in South Africa", *Agrekon*. 48 (4): 459–482.

Benjaminsen, T.A., I. Bryceson, F. Maganga, & T. Refseth, 2011. Conservation and land grabbing in Tanzania. Paper presented at the Global Land Grabbing Conference, IDS Sussex, 6–9 April.

Borras, S. 2003. "Questioning Market-Led Agrarian Reform", *Journal of Agrarian Change* 3(3): 367–394.

Borras, S. & J. Franco. 2012. Global land grabbing and trajectories of agrarian change: a preliminary analysis. *Journal of Agrarian Change*, 12(1): 34–59.

Boyle, B. 2010. "New land laws aim to speed up redistribution", *Sunday Times*, 13 September.

Brandt, F. 2011. "Contemporary struggles over land, power and labour in the context of private trophy-hunting farms in the Eastern Cape, South Africa". Paper presented at ECAS4 Uppsala, 15–18 June.

Brockington, D. and J. Igoe. 2006. "Eviction for conservation: A global overview". Conservation and Society 4 (3): 424–470.

Brooks, S., M. Spierenburg, L. van Brakel, A. Kolk, K.B. LuKhozi. 2011 "Creating a commodified wilderness: Tourism, private game farming, and 'third nature' landscapes in KwaZulu-Natal". *Tijdschrift voor Sociale en Economische Geografie*. 102(3): 260–274.

Bundy, C. 1988. *The Rise & Fall of the South African Peasantry*. London: James Curry.

Carroll, T. 2010. "The Department of Environmental Affairs 2009 Hunting statistics". Presented at the 2010 Annual General Meeting of the Professional Hunting Association South Africa at Zulu Nyala Country Manor Fourways, 16 November.

Castree, N. 2008a. "Neoliberalizing nature: The logics of deregulation and reregulation". *Environment and Planning A* 40 (1): 131–152.

——. 2008b. "Neoliberalizing nature: Processes, effects, and evaluations". *Environment and Planning A* 40 (1): 153–173.

Cotula, L., 2011. The outlook on farmland acquisitions. Policy Brief, published by the International Institute for Environment and Development (IIED), Edinburgh.

Crais, C. 1992. *White Supremacy and Black Resistance in Pre-Industrial South Africa: The Making of the Colonial Order in the Eastern Cape, 1770–1865*. Cambridge: Cambridge University Press.

Department of Agriculture (DoA). 2001. Strategic Plan for South African Agriculture. From website: http://pretoria.nda.agric.za/docs/sectorplan/sectorplanE.htm.

Department of Land Affairs (DLA). 1999. *Annual Report*. Pretoria: DLA.

Department of Rural Development and Land Reform (DRDLR). 2011, *Green Paper on Land Reform 2011*. 31 August.

——. 2011 *Draft Green Paper on Land Reform*. 25 August.

——. 2010. Strategic Plan 2010–2013. Pretoria: DRDLR.

Development Bank of South Africa (DBSA). 2009. "The economic performance of agriculture in South Africa since 1994: Implications for food security". Paper #17.

Dry, G., 2011. Commercial wildlife ranching's contribution to a resource efficient, low carbon pro-employment green economy, 7th International Wildlife Ranching Symposium, Kimberly, October.

Du Toit, A. 2004. 'Social exclusion' discourse and chronic poverty, a South African case study, *Journal of Peasant Studies*, 35(5): 987–1010.

Du Toit, J.G. 2007. Role of the Private Sector in the Wildlife Industry. Pretoria: *Wildlife Ranching South Africa*, 30 August.

Eastern Cape Agricultural Research Project/ Southern Cape Land Committee. 2006. "Advancing positive land rights and sustainable livelihoods for rural communities". Unpublished Report, Grahamstown.

Ewert, J., J. Hamman. 1999. "Why Paternalism Survives: Globalization, Democratization, and Labour on South African Wine Farms". *Sociologia Ruralis* 39(2): 202–221.

Fairhead, J., M. Leach and I. Scoones. 2012. Green Grabbing: a new appropriation of nature? *Journal of Peasant Studies*, 39(2): 237–261.

Greenberg, S. 2003. "Land reform and transition in South Africa". *Transformation: Critical Perspectives on Southern Africa* 52(1): 42–67.

Govender, P. 2005. "Minister considers stopping all new golf estates and game farms." *Sunday Times*. http://allafrica.com/stories/200508070155.html (Accessed 28 May, 2011).

Hart, G., 2002. *Disabling globalization. Places of power in post-apartheid South Africa*, Berkeley, Los Angeles: University of California Press.

Haywood, M. 2007. "Re-wilding or hyperwilderness-plus ca change?", *South African Journal of Art History*, 22(1): 195–203.

Inxuba YeThemba Municipality. 2008. Local Economic Development Strategy, 12 December.

Langholz, J., G. Kerley. 2006. "Combining conservation and development on private lands: an assessment of eco-tourism-based private game reserves in the Eastern Cape." Centre for African Conservation Ecology Report no.56. Port Elizabeth: Nelson Mandela Metropolitan University.

Lahiff, E. 2008. "Land Reform in South Africa: a Status Report." PLAAS Report 38.

Luck, K. 2005. "Farm workers and land tenure reform: The case of game farming in Hope Fountain in the Eastern Cape". *Social Dynamics* 31(1): 84–103.

Makgetla, N. 2006. "Is growth plan the main dish or just a starter?" *Business Day*, 10 February.

Mather, C. 1997. "Agriculture slips out of Gear", *Mail & Guardian*, 9 May.

Mkhize, N. 2010. "Private game farms and the tenure security of farm workers and dwellers: Lessons from Cradock, Eastern Cape". Paper presented at conference: Overcoming structural poverty and inequality in South Africa: Towards inclusive growth and development. 20–22 September.

National Land Summit. 2005. "Draft recommendation on the principles of 'willing buyer willing seller' and government's approach to land reform". July.

Neumann, R. 1998. *Imposing wilderness: struggles over livelihood and nature preservation in Africa.* London, Los Angeles: University of California Press.

Ntsebeza, L. 2007. "Land redistribution in South Africa: the property clause revisited". In *The land question in South Africa: The challenge of transformation and redistribution,* edited by L. Ntsebeza and R. Hall, 107–132. Cape Town: HSRC Press.

Ross, R. 1986. "The origins of capitalist agriculture in the Cape Colony" in *Putting a plough to the ground: Accumulation and dispossession in rural South Africa, 1850–1930,* edited by W. Beinart, P. Delius & S. Trapido. Johannesburg: Ravan Press.

Sharife, K., 2010. "SA-Congo 'land grab': Exploitation or salvation?", *Mail & Guardian,* 12 March.

Shivji, I. 2005. "The Changing Development Discourse in Africa", *Pambazuka News,* 224.

Snijders, D. 2012. "Wild Property and its boundaries—on wildlife policy and rural consequence in South Africa", *Journal of Peasant Studies,* 39(2): 503–520.

South African Parliament. 2009. "Willing buyer, willing seller model doesn't work—Land affairs minister Gugile Nkwinti", 20 June.

——. 2010. "39,982 commercial farmers in SA—Minister", 30 August 2010 National Assembly—written reply to question 2019, 6 August, 2010.

Statistics South Africa. 2005. Census of Commercial Agriculture 2002 Financial and Production Statistics. Pretoria: StatsSA.

——. 2010. Mid-year Population estimates. Accessed online at www.statssa.gov.za, P0302 online.

——. 2011. General Household Survey 2010. www.statssa.gov.za/publications/P0318/P0318June2010.pdf

Terreblanche, S. 2002. *A History of Inequality in South Africa,* 1652–2002. Pietermaritzburg: University of Natal Press, 2002.

The National Agricultural Marketing Council. 2006. Report on the investigation to identify problems for sustainable growth and development in South African wildlife ranching. Pretoria: NAMC.

Van Zyl, J., J. Kirsten, H.P. Binswanger. 1996. *Agricultural land reform in South Africa: policies, markets and mechanisms.* Oxford University Press Southern Africa.

Viljoen, M.F. 2005. "South African agricultural policy 1994 to 2004: some reflections". *Agrekon* 44(1):1–16.

Vink, N., J. Kirsten. 2003. "Agriculture in the national economy" in *The Challenge of Change—Agriculture, Land and the South African Economy,* edited by L. Nieuwoudt and J. Groenewald, Pietermaritzburg: University of Natal Press.

Vink, N., J. van Rooyen, 2009, The economic performance of agriculture in South Africa since 1994: Implications for food security. Development Bank of South Africa.

Wegerif, M., B. Russell, I. Grundling. 2005. *Still searching for security: The reality of farm dweller evictions in South Africa.* Nkuzi Development Association.

Williams, G., J. Ewert, J. Hamann, N. Vink. 1998. "Liberalizing markets and reforming land in South Africa". *Journal of Contemporary African Studies.* 16(1).

Wolmer, W. 2007. *From wilderness vision to farm invasions: conservation and development in Zimbabwe's south-east Lowveld.* London: James Currey.

Interviews conducted between 2008 and 2011.

DEVELOPMENT AND DISPOSSESSION: IMPACTS OF LAND REFORM IN BOTSWANA

Maria Sapignoli and Robert K. Hitchcock

Introduction

The shift from communal to individualized systems of land tenure is a process that has occurred throughout Africa. During the 20th and early 21st centuries there were at least 40 major attempts to reform the basis of land tenure in various African countries (Sanford 1983; Hunter 2004; Anseeuw and Alden 2010). Relatively few of these efforts could be described as successful; many of them exacerbated social inequities, increased poverty and resulted in environmental degradation (Sanford 1981; Peters 1994; Rohde et al. 2006; De Sagte 2011).

A useful example of the costs and benefits of African land tenure reform is that of the Republic of Botswana in southern Africa.[1] Botswana is an interesting case for a number of reasons. First, it differs from its neighbors in southern Africa because it was not a settler state in the classic sense of the term. As a protectorate, the process of colonization of Botswana was somewhat different from its neighbors (Picard 1985). Relatively small areas of land were allocated to European settlers as commercial farms, totaling approximately 5 per cent of the country, as opposed to 43 per cent of the land of Namibia, 40 per cent of Zimbabwe, and 87 per cent of South Africa. Second, in the 1970s, 1980s, and 1990s, when Botswana had become relatively well-off economically as compared to other African countries, the government sought and received substantial foreign direct investment (FDI) in the form of loans from the World Bank and other international donors for large-scale land reform and livestock development projects (Leith 2005). Third, the government of Botswana does not have a general policy of encouraging foreign land acquisition (FLA); foreigners do, however, get access to land through behind-the-scenes arrangements with

[1] For discussions of the importance of Botswana as an example of grazing land reform, see Hitchcock (1980); Picard (1981); Lawry (1983), Sanford (1983), Merafe (1988), Dickson (1990); Tsimako (1991); Peters (1994).

Batswana who have obtained land through purchase (in the case of freehold land) or allocation through land boards (in the case of tribal land).

This chapter considers changes in land tenure over time in Botswana, looking first at the processes of change in land distribution and land tenure reform that occurred in the colonial (1885–1966) and post-colonial periods (1966–present). As we will show, some of the land in Botswana was converted into cattle ranches as part of large-scale livestock development programs, while other land became wildlife reserves, national parks, and towns (see also Andrew et al., this volume).

Two general processes of change in land tenure are considered: (1) the establishment of freehold areas under the colonial government, and (2) the post-colonial reform of land tenure in the tribal lands, which saw leasehold ranches established on what had been communal land. We begin with a discussion of the colonial transformations in land tenure, then address the post-independence land reforms. In the process, we consider the various factors that led to dispossession of sizable numbers of poor people in Botswana, with many of the benefits of these programs going to better-off members of the society and to foreigners. Particular emphasis is placed on the processes of dispossession of some of the poorest people in Botswana, the San, or, as they are known in Botswana, the Basarwa.

In an effort to assist the people in rural communities, the Botswana government initiated several programs: the Remote Area Development Program and Social and Community Development (S and CD), which provided food and other support. Credit schemes were available through the Financial Assistance Policy (FAP) and the Arable Lands Development Program (ALDEP). The initiation of a Community-Based Natural Resource Management program encouraged communities to embark on CBNRM activities, which in some areas included the integration of crops, livestock, and wildlife (for a critical discussion of CBNRM, see Dressler et al. 2010). In this chapter, we examine the ways in which these programs have worked (and not worked), drawing on examples from Ghanzi, the Western Central District, and southern and western Ngamiland, places San are in the majority.

Land Reform and Livestock Development

The background of Botswana land reform has roots in its colonial and post-colonial past. In the late 19th and early 20th centuries, some of the land in the country was allocated by colonial authorities to European individuals and companies on a freehold basis, notably the Ghanzi Farms in western Botswana, the Tati Concession in northeastern Botswana, and the Tuli Block along the Limpopo River in eastern Botswana (Schapera 1943: 7–15, 1971; Parsons 1973; Mazonde 1991; Tlou and Campbell 1997; Manatsha and Maharajan 2010). Local impacts of these decisions included the dispossession of sizable numbers of people who had resided on that land for generations but whose services were not needed by the farmers or companies who got title over the land. The reduction in access to land meant that in some cases, the livelihoods of people, especially the poor, were reduced.

With the establishment of the British Protectorate over Bechuanaland, portions of the country were set aside as Crown Lands, notably the Western Crown Lands, comprising what are now the Ghanzi and Kgalagadi Districts (approximately 30 per cent of the country), and the Northern Crown Lands, covering the northern portion of what was the Ngwato Tribal Territory and Chobe (see Figure 1).

In western Botswana, partly in response to a request of Cecil John Rhodes and the British South Africa Company, land was set aside for farms, partially as a buffer between German South West Africa and the Bechuanaland Protectorate. In 1895, a Lt. Fuller and a contingent of Bechuanaland Protectorate Police along with 25 Afrikaner families trekked across the southern Kalahari and arrived in Ghanzi on 24 April. They hoped to move on to settle in Ngamiland but were rebuffed by the Tawana chief, Sekgoma Letsholathebe. In 1896 Lt. Fuller submitted a request to the Bechuanaland Protectorate Administration that Ghanzi become a farming area for European settlement (Botswana National Archives [BNA] file C.O. 417/141). The Bechuanaland Protectorate Administration agreed in 1897 to set up a farming block of land that would be allocated to individuals. Eventually 41 farms of approximately 5,000 morgen (4.284 sq km) were allocated to Afrikaner and English farmers who trekked out of South Africa to Ghanzi in 1898–1899 (Russell and Russell 1979: 12–15; Guenther 1986). The Ghanzi Farms were expanded in the 1950s and 1960s, when additional farms were surveyed and allocated. Today, there is a total of 172 Ghanzi freehold farms, the vast majority of which are owned by Batswana, some of them of English and Afrikaner heritage.

Over time, a substantial portion of the Ghanzi San population, which numbered at one time in the thousands, became what in effect were landless laborers on land that was granted to other people. Pressures were exerted on San who were not working on the farms to leave. Many of them did so, in some cases moving to the main administrative center of the region, the town of Ghanzi. In the 1960s, San and other groups who

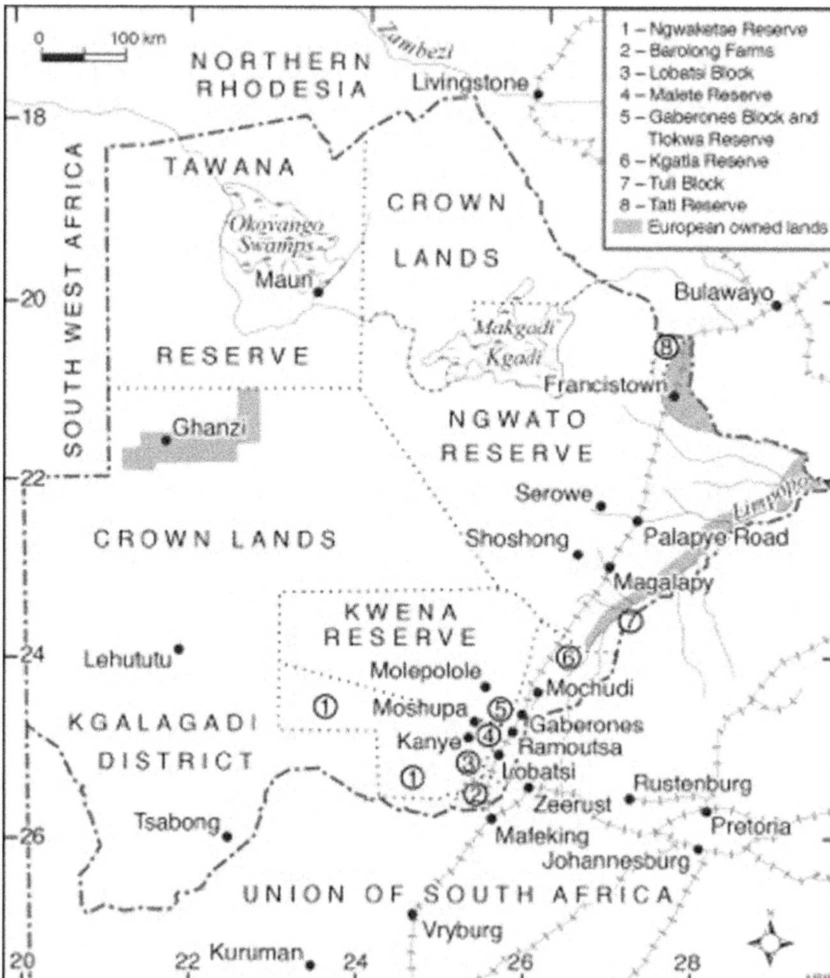

Figure 1. Map of the Bechuanaland Protectorate

were defined as squatters were removed from Ghanzi, their homes being burned by district administration officials. Similar removals from squatter camps took place in Francistown at the behest of the Tati Company and the British Protectorate Administration. San in the Northern Crown Lands were removed from the areas that they occupied by the Protectorate Administration and the Ngwato tribe in the mid- to late 1940s after incidents of alleged lawlessness occurred (Hitchcock 1991; BNA file S.198/2). Not long after the removals, the Bechuanaland Protectorate Administration granted the Commonwealth Development Corporation (CDC) the rights to a set of commercial cattle ranches in the Northern Crown Lands in the same area from which the San had been removed and relocated to the areas to the east and south of the Nata River. The establishment of settlement schemes for San was a feature of both colonial and post-colonial state policy in Botswana.

Another aspect of state policy in Botswana was the creation of protected areas, including national parks, game reserves, and monuments. These areas were set aside to protect the natural and cultural heritage of Botswana (Campbell 1973). One of these areas, established in 1961, was the Central Kalahari Game Reserve, established in part to protect wildlife and habitats but also to allow the residents of the reserve to continue their hunting and gathering activities (Silberbauer 1981; Hitchcock 2001, 2002; Sapignoli 2012). By the time of independence in September, 1966, Botswana had set aside some 17 per cent of its land as national parks, game reserves, and other kinds of protected areas.

Post-Independence Land Reforms

In July 1975, Sir Seretse Khama, the first President of Botswana, announced a long-term program of land reform and livestock development for the country, the Tribal Grazing Land Policy (TGLP) (Khama 1975; Republic of Botswana 1975). This program, which was supported by the World Bank and the European Development Fund as well as by the government of Botswana, had three main aims:

(1) to stop overgrazing and degradation of the range;
(2) to promote greater equality of incomes in rural areas;
(3) to allow growth and commercialization of the livestock industry on a sustained basis.

Table 1. Land zoning categories in Botswana

Type of land	Land zoning category	Amount of land (sq km)	Percentage of country
Freehold land	Freehold farms	32,970	5.7
State land	Parks and reserves	101,535	17.4
	Other	32,455	5.6
Tribal land	Communal	173,432	29.8
	Commercial	51,094	8.8
	Wildlife Management areas	129,450	22.2
	Leasehold ranches	3,351	0.6
	Remote area Dweller settlements	3,523	0.6
	Other	53,945	9.3
Total		581,720	100.0

Note: Data obtained from the Ministry of Local Government and the Ministry of Lands and Housing, Government of Botswana. The category "other" includes land in towns and land set aside for government purposes (e.g. trek routes, quarantine camps for livestock).

The best way to achieve these aims, it was argued in a government white paper (Republic of Botswana 1975), was through the granting of exclusive rights to individuals and groups who would then have an incentive to manage their grazing in appropriate ways.

The customary forms of land ownership that remained under the Tribal Land Act of 1968 and the TGLP white paper stipulated that (1) individuals had the right to land for residential, business, grazing, and agricultural purposes; (2) individuals could not own land (i.e. have *de jure* tenure rights) in communal areas, (3) traditional authorities (chiefs and headmen) no longer had the right to allocate land; instead this right was ceded to district land boards; (4) individuals seeking land or water rights from Land boards had to apply for it, and (5) there were no individual entitlements in communal land, only in freehold and what was defined as commercial (leasehold) land.

Under customary law in Botswana, open surface water (e.g. rivers, springs, pans with water in them) was free to be used by anyone who wished to use it (Schapera 1943: 243–244). This was also true for dams that were constructed through collective labor. In the past, people were supposed to seek permission from the chief (*kgosi*) or grazing area headman (*modisa*) for the right to develop a water point (Schapera 1943: 244). Where water was obtained through the expenditure of private labor or the use of capital, as in the case of well-digging or borehole sinking, people were able to keep the water for personal use. In the 20th century and especially during the new millennium, there were cases in which individuals transferred the rights over water points to other individuals, some of them foreigners, in exchange for some kind of cash or in kind payment.

Since the passage of the *Tribal Land Act* individuals had to seek permission for a water right from the district land board. If an individual bought a private freehold farm such as one in Ghanzi or in the Tuli Block in eastern Botswana, he or she had rights of ownership of the water points on that farm. Once an individual got a water right, either through getting permission to establish a water point from the land board, or through purchasing a private farm, he or she also had access to the grazing land surrounding the water point. If people wished to appeal decisions of the Land board about a water point, they had to lodge such an appeal with the Minister of Lands and Housing (in the past, the Minister of Local Government and Lands). Conflicts over water rights are not uncommon in the communal areas of Botswana, and they were a source of friction between groups and individuals in the past as well (see also Adamczewski et al., this volume).

One of the major issues that arose during the course of TGLP implementation revolved around the numbers of non-water right holders and non-livestock owners residing in the areas that were designated as commercial leasehold ranches. While attention was paid in the White Paper to protecting "the interests of those who own only a few cattle or none at all" (Republic of Botswana 1975: 6) and it held that "planning will aim to ensure that land development helps the poor and does not make them worse off" (Republic of Botswana 1975: 2), things did not work out that way. When it was found that many of the sandveld areas had existing water points and people in them, planners responded by zoning the land either commercial or communal. The criteria used were (1) the numbers of water points and cattle posts that existed in them, and (2) the presence or absence of villages and towns. No land was zoned as reserved because it was felt that there was sufficient land for communal use already.

Thus, in spite of the fact that the 'reserved areas' were the only 'safeguards for the poorer members of the population' (Republic of Botswana 1975: 7), it was decided to forgo zoning land in this way. Instead, some of the land was left un-zoned pending further investigation. As the zoning process evolved, it was noted that some of the land had substantial numbers of wildlife. Since only a portion of those areas where wildlife was found was protected in the form of national parks and game reserves, it was recommended that a new land zoning category be created: Wildlife Management Areas (WMAs).

By the early 1980s, the zoning and land use planning process had resulted in the country being divided into a number of different categories including (a) commercial land, (b) communal land, (c) reserved land, (d) Wildlife Management Areas, (e) specialized leasehold farms, (f) national parks and game reserves, and (g) land left either un-zoned or categorized as 'investigation areas' (Wily 1981). The latter were areas where insufficient information was known to make a land zoning designation. It is important to note that virtually no land whatsoever was set aside as reserved; thus, the 'safeguards for the poor' were dispensed with completely. Essentially, the 'reserved' areas would have provided land for people who did not have cattle or practice agriculture to continue to maintain their customary activities, which included foraging, and would have prevented these areas from being turned into commercial cattle ranches or designated as communal areas.

At the time the Tribal Grazing Land Policy was declared (1975), it was felt that the granting of exclusive rights would lead to greater efforts at conservation. What has happened, in a number of cases, however, is that ranches were stocked heavily, and the grazing was reduced significantly. Individuals who had leasehold rights maintained their rights to grazing in the communal areas; as a result, when their ranches were overgrazed, they simply moved their livestock back to the communal grazing areas, thus exacerbating the grazing problems in these areas. This system of dual grazing rights posed serious problems for environmental quality in both the commercial and communal areas (White 1993; de Sagte 2011).

The situations on commercial ranches were complex. People living there were generally not allowed to graze their own animals on the ranch, unless specific provision was made for that by the ranch lessee. Fences constructed on the peripheries of the ranch (border fences) restricted the movement of livestock out of the ranch area. If the grazing was overexploited, or if a fire burned off much of the grazing or a drought hit and grazing resources were reduced, cattle owners were faced with a dilemma: because of the existence of private or leasehold ranches nearby, they could not simply move their cattle to an adjacent area. They had to move them back to the communal areas, which meant that their animals were competing with other people's livestock for grazing and water. It also meant that they had little control over the breeding activities of their animals.

Based on fieldwork in TGLP ranch areas in the 1970s–1990s (see Hitchcock 1978; Campbell, Main and Hitchcock 2006; Perkins 1991), people residing on the ranches generally wished to plant some vegetables and food crops (e.g. sorghum, maize, water melons). With the ranch lessee's permission, they would prepare small gardens for vegetables or plough larger fields, often using the cattle or donkeys belonging to the ranch lessee. They then had to protect their gardens and fields from marauding goats, donkeys, cattle, and wildlife using brush fences. In many cases, however, people who had TGLP ranches would not allow their employees or their families to plant crops on their ranches because they assumed it would mean that their workers were pursuing their own interests and not taking good care of the livestock on the ranch.

The costs of fencing, borehole drilling and equipment have increased greatly over time, thus making the question of the economics of ranching a major issue. Data on livestock production (measured in terms of weight gain and numbers of calves born) suggest that communal area cattle posts in a number of cases had higher productivity levels than did the leasehold ranches, according to the Animal Production Research Unit of the Ministry of Agriculture (Ministry of Agriculture 1983; see also Behnke, Scoones, and Kerven 1993; White 1993 for discussions of this point). The costs of setting up and running a ranch in the remote areas of Botswana are quite high, and as a result many cattle owners decided not to fence. Some water source owners also refused to sign leases over the land surrounding their boreholes since they did not feel that it was in their best interests. They felt this way because they saw no reason to pay even a minimal amount of money for land which they essentially had exclusive rights over anyway, in line with government land legislation passed in 1991 (the National Policy on Agricultural Development, Republic of Botswana 1991). It should be noted that much of the funding for the commercialization of the livestock industry in Botswana in the 1970s and 1980s was provided by the World Bank (see Table 2). Additional funders included the European Development Fund, the U.S. Agency for International Development, and the African Development Bank. It is also interesting to note that many of the loans made to individuals who obtained leasehold ranches were written off by the NDB, thus allowing cattle owners, some of them well-to-do, to essentially be subsidized by international and national funding agencies, something that was not the case for the poor who were removed from ranches. It is important to note that of all minority groups in Botswana, numbering approximately 37–40, the San have the lowest percentage of

Table 2. World Bank funded livestock development projects in Botswana

Project	Title	Dates	Finance
LDP 1	Livestock development project 1	1972–76	US$5,400,000
LDP 2	Second livestock development project	1977–1982	US$13,400,000
LDP 3	National land management and livestock development project	1985–1988	US$17,800,000
TOTAL	3 projects		US$36,600,000

land board certificates, which means that they have the highest potential of being dispossessed. Very few, if any, San have been allocated grazing or water rights by land boards.

Social Equity and Land Development in Botswana

The question of social equity is still a contentious issue in Botswana. Over 40,000 people resided in the tribal areas that were zoned as commercial. Some of these people were required to leave the ranches; compensation, if it was given at all, was in the form of cash and was relatively minimal. The argument that compensation should be provided in the form of land was accepted only to a limited degree by the land boards. When there were conflicting rights over commercial ranches, the land boards opted for de-zoning (declaring the area communal). In an effort to offset problems of dispossession,the alternative strategy was to set aside blocks of land either within or adjacent to commercial ranching areas where people who are required to leave leased land could gain access to social services and some land for production purposes. In practice, the area that was declared Communal Service Centers (CSCs) constituted a small amount of land (1,058 square kilometers) (see Section 20 in the revised edition of the *Tribal Grazing Land Policy Guidelines*, Ministry of Local Government and Lands 1984). Communal service centers were found in western Central District (Mmaletswai), the Hainaveld region of Northwest District (Ngamiland), northeastern and western Kweneng District, Southern District (Tankana), Kgalagadi District, and Ghanzi District (see Figure 2).

However, most people who were evicted from the ranches opted not to go to the communal service centers, in part because they saw them as too small in area, too crowded, and unlikely to provide opportunities for subsistence and income generation. Instead, they decided to move to other communal areas where there was more space, Their decision to relocate

Figure 2. Map of Botswana showing districts, major towns, protected areas, and remote area settlements

to other communal areas may also have been an expression of discontent over the government's policy to move them out of the ranches. In fact, this is what actually happened in the context of the Central Kalahari Game Reserve in the 1990s and the early part of the new millennium. People removed from the CKGR did not all go to the resettlement sites, but chose to go to other communal areas near the Central Kalahari; others went to towns or to freehold farms where they had relatives or friends.[2]

In total, some 4,000 people occupied these communal service centers, and their numbers increased as ranches failed and were abandoned, and ranch-owners reduced the numbers of residents on their ranches. One of the problems was that neither the communal service centers nor the remote area settlements were officially gazetted under Botswana government legislation. Consequently, cattle owners and other people could freely move into them with their animals. The result of this situation were increased conflicts and a decline in livelihoods and well-being of many of the residents of the settlements and communal service centers (Malopi and Batisini 2008; Good 2009; Hitchcock, Sapignoli, and Babchuk 2011).

Until today, pastoralists (e.g. Tswana, Herero, Bakgalagadi) move into the Remote Area Dweller settlements and communal service centers, so as to take advantage of grazing grounds and government-subsidized water. It is anticipated that this trend will increase with climate change and environmental degradation.

Land and Labor in Ghanzi District

Much of the district's land is freehold land, commercial livestock ranches or Wildlife Management Areas (in the case of the latter, the area totals 26,342 sq km (2,624,200 hectares), or 22.34% of the district's land). Including the Central Kalahari Game Reserve, the largest protected area in Botswana, (52,313 sq km, 5,231,300 hectares), the land devoted to wildlife-related purposes in Ghanzi District totals almost two thirds of the entire

[2] For discussions of the resettlement sites created as a result of the Botswana government's decisions to move people out of the Central Kalahari Game Reserve in 1997 and 2002, see Kiema (2010); Hitchcock, Sapignoli, and Babchuk (2011); Sapignoli (2012). The CKGR and areas to the east, including the Western Sandveld region of Central District, have substantial symbolic significance for the people who call it their home. This symbolic significance is seen in the ways that they describe it: "This is my land," "This is my *g!u*" (G//ana for territory), "This is the land of my ancestors and the place where they are buried," "It is the place where I was born" (Kiema 2010: 23; see also Silberbauer 1981: 95–9, 141–142). The name for the Central Kalahari Game Reserve is Tc'amnqoe (Kiema 2010: 11).

district (see Figure 3). In these areas, the primary utilization of the land is for wildlife-related enterprises, such as tourism and game ranching (see also Andrew et al., this volume) At the same time, small communities of people carry out a variety of livelihood activities in these wildlife areas.

One of the ways in which the Ghanzi District Council and the government of Botswana dealt with the issue of the large numbers of poor people on freehold farms in Ghanzi District, as well as those who were squatters in the Ghanzi Township and those who were told to leave leasehold ranches (i.e. at Makunda and in the south eastern Ghanzi District) was that they resettled these groups in what came to be called Remote Area Dweller settlements. Theoretically open to anyone in the country who wishes to settle there, these settlements are characteristically in communal areas or in Wildlife Management Areas. Most of the settlements are 20 by 20 km (40,000 hectares), which is smaller than the area generally needed to support full-time foraging as a lifestyle (Hitchcock 1978; Wily 1979, 1981, 1982). All of them have been provided with social and physical infrastructures by the Ghanzi District Council or central government (e.g. water points, schools, teachers' quarters, health posts, *dikgotla* [i.e. meeting places for community members and officials, among others], and areas of land for residences and, in some cases, gardens, fields, and kraals) and places for keeping livestock.

Even if today, sizable numbers of San (as well as members of some other groups such as Bakgalagadi, Tswana, and Herero) can be seen to work on Ghanzi freehold farms and on TGLP ranches and cattle posts, security of tenure has deteriorated for them. The main reason is that the number of people who are allowed to remain on farms has been reduced, in part because of labor costs and because some Ghanzi and leasehold area farmers have added fences -which reduces the need for herders (*badisa*)—and have established boundaries around farms, so as to exclude farm workers from them.

In fieldwork carried out by both authors in the Ghanzi Farms in 2011 and 2012, it was found that many of the people on the farms were concerned about the future, saying, for example, "We have no security here. The farm owners can remove us at any time."[3] There was evidence to support these

[3] Fieldwork on issues involving land in Botswana was carried out over a period from 1975 to 2012. Maria Sapignoli conducted field work in Ghanzi, Gaborone, and Lobatse in July–September, 2006, with follow-up work in Ghanzi in 2010–2011 and 2012. In July–August, 2011 Sapignoli and Hitchcock conducted field work in northern Ghanzi District on Ghanzi farms and some of the settlements (Kuke, Roobrak, New Xade) as part of an assessment of

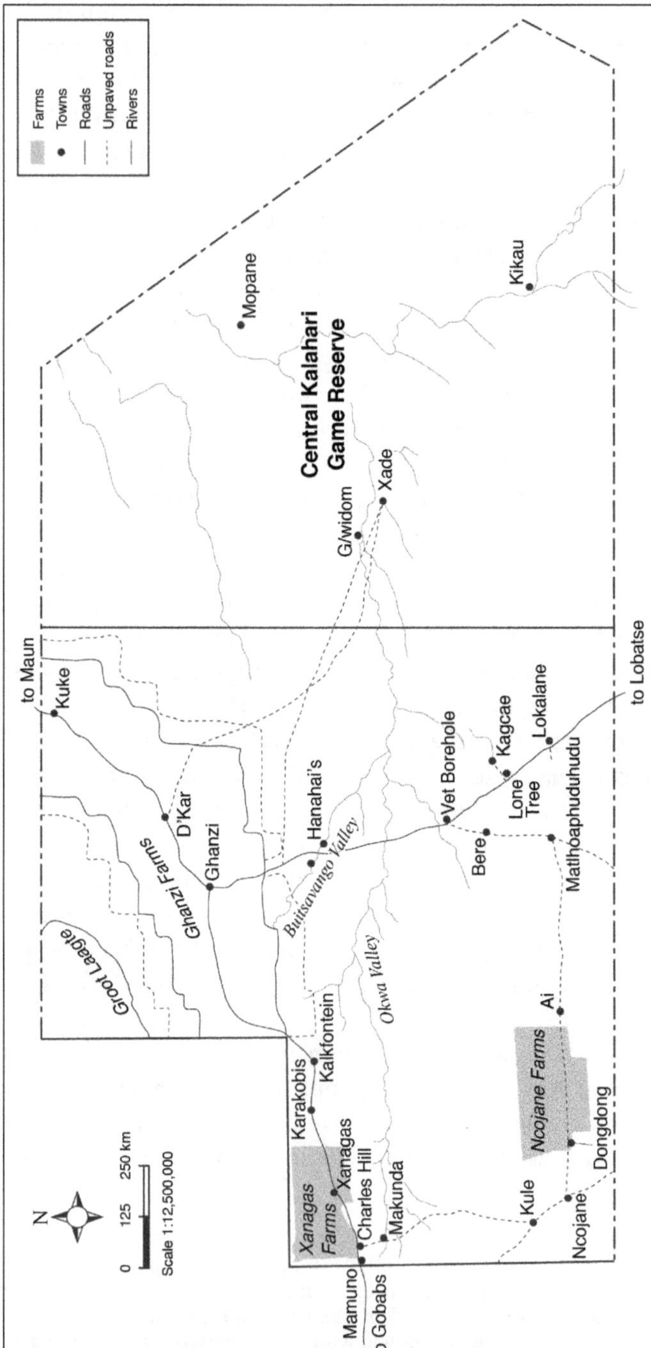

Figure 3. Map of Ghanzi District and the Central Kalahari Game Reserve

concerns. An assessment of a sample of Ghanzi farms revealed that the numbers of San farm workers had been reduced from 10–12 per farm in the 1970s and 1980s, to 5–6 per farm in 2011. Fewer of the farm laborers, who in the past could be termed generational farm workers—i.e. people who lived their entire lives on the farms and were totally dependent on the farm owners for support—were San. Exacerbating the position of San workers is the fact that a significant portion of the farm worker population on some Ghanzi Farms is made up of Bakgalagadi, Herero, Tswana, or Zimbabweans (Sapignoli and Hitchcock 2011). Farm owners say that while they may appreciate the long-standing connections they and their families have had with San, 'new workers' are "more efficient and cost less".

The Western Sandveld Region of Central District, North West District and Land, Livestock, and Wildlife Development

In the 1970s, with the introduction of the Tribal Grazing Land Policy, the government of Botswana and the Central District Council designated what became known as the Western Sandveld region as a commercial first development area (see Figure 4). Originally, there were plans for 300–400 leasehold ranches, but after lengthy surveys and investigations and evidence showing that people had customary rights to land in much of the area, it was decided to set aside only 18 commercial ranches, arrayed along a veterinary cordon fence, notably the Makoba Fence. In the early 1990s, the government decided to allow individuals who had water rights (i.e. the possession of boreholes) to get leasehold rights over the areas surrounding their boreholes, averaging 8 km by 8 km in size (64 sq km or 6,400 hectares). Some of the water right holders opted to fence the areas around their boreholes, with funding from the National Development Bank. Under TGLP, 342 commercial ranches were demarcated and allocated to individuals and groups (Republic of Botswana 1989; Mathuba 2003). By the late 1980s, approximately 4% of Botswana's land area was devoted to TGLP ranches. The TGLP approach was expanded and reinforced by the 1991 National Agricultural Development Policy (Republic of Botswana 1991). By 2006, an additional 602 leasehold ranches were demarcated. This meant that approximately 8% of the country's land

---

potential copper mining impacts (see Sapignoli and Hitchcock 2011). Hitchcock's work on the western Central District was carried out between 1975 and 2012 (see Hitchcock 1978, 1980; Campbell, Main, and Hitchcock 2006).

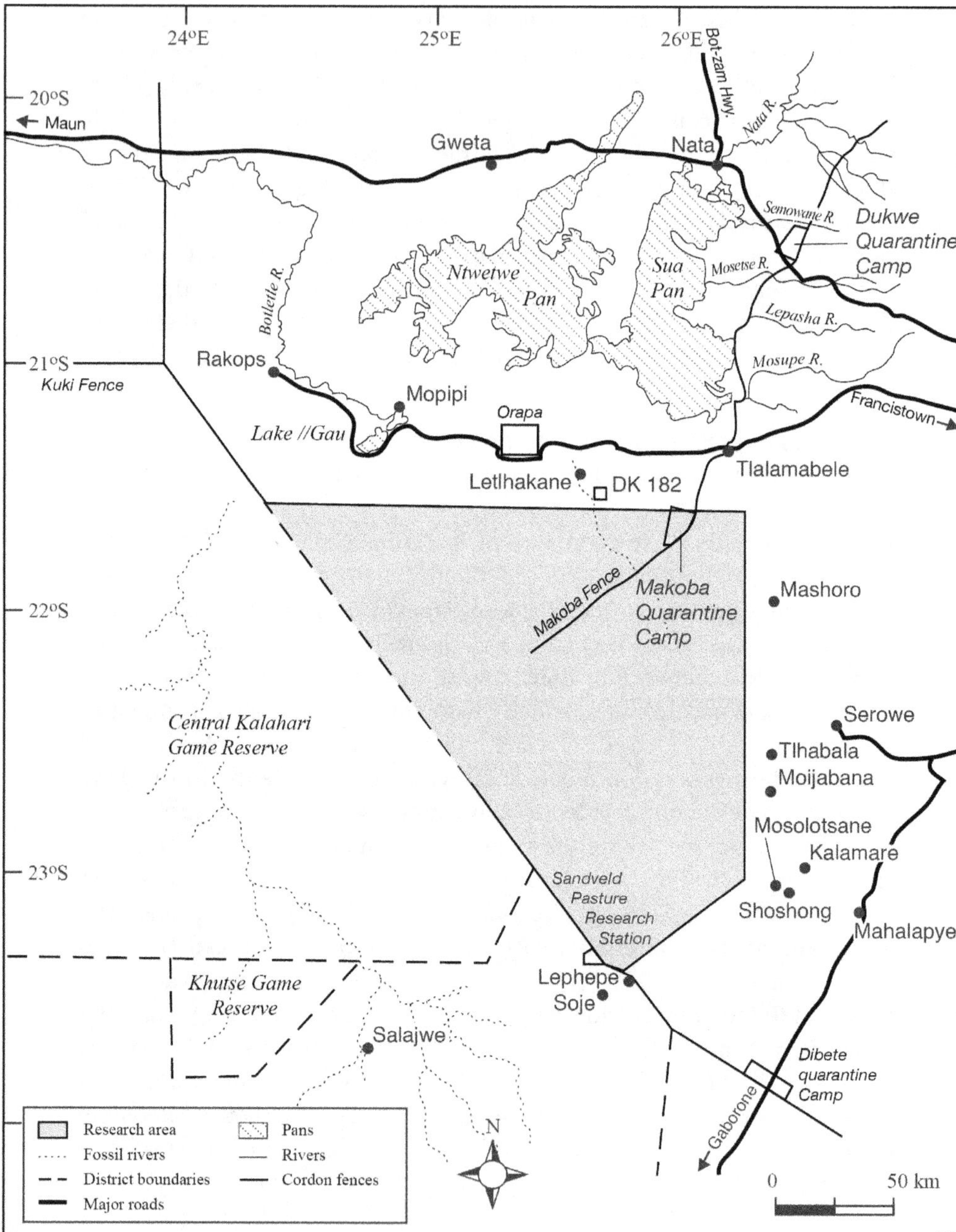

Figure 4. Map of the Western Sandveld Region of Central District, Botswana showing the research area

had been converted from communal (common property) to private leasehold land.

In fact, by the early 21st century nearly all of the approx. 300 commercial leasehold ranches in the Western Sandveld region of Central District were owned by individuals who lived outside of the region. Research by a team from the University of Sussex (Sporton and Thomas 2002), revealed a trend toward expansion of commercial cattle ranches along with a wide range of social, economic, and environmental impacts, the causes and consequences of which were contested. At the same time, questions were raised about the long-term impacts of livestock on the range, the degree to which cattle grazing contributed to local environmental change and the socioeconomic impacts of ranching programs on common property resource management systems (Perkins 1991; Dougill 2002; Campbell, Main, and Hitchcock 2006; Cullis and Watson 2009). A detailed study of the Makoba Ranching block and assessments of ranch communities (see Figure 5) revealed that some of the individuals who got leases for their land, opted to tell the residents of the ranches, including ranch workers and their families as well as non-workers, that they had to leave the ranches. Many of these residents were San. When livestock had been removed from the ranches, former employees moved to areas on the periphery of the ranches. There they attempted to earn a living through a mixture of foraging, working for other people, doing piecework (e.g. building fences, clearing roads), and engaging in formal sector employment (e.g. working at the diamond mines of Orapa or Letlhakane). Some received rations from the government as part of Botswana's drought relief, Remote Area Dweller, and destitute support programs.[4] Other ex-ranch residents moved to towns to the east, or went to live in the Central Kalahari Game Reserve. Moving into the Game Reserve was a risky strategy since the government had already told the people living in the reserve that they would no longer be allowed to live there nor use the wildlife and other natural resources in the reserve (Hitchcock 2002; Sapignoli 2012).[5] Still others opted to leave the region altogether. In the wake of this migration families could be seen to split up; men went to work in towns or in

[4] So-called destitutes are individuals who lack the means of supporting themselves.

[5] Information obtained from people in the eastern part of the Central Kalahari Game Reserve who had moved back into the reserve from the Central District after the 2006 CKGR court case indicated that some of the CKGR residents had come from the Botletle River region and from the settlements around Kedia, south of Lake //Gau (Xau), which had been established for remote area dwellers in the 1970s, and Xeri, one of the CKGR resettlement locations established in the early part of the new millennium.

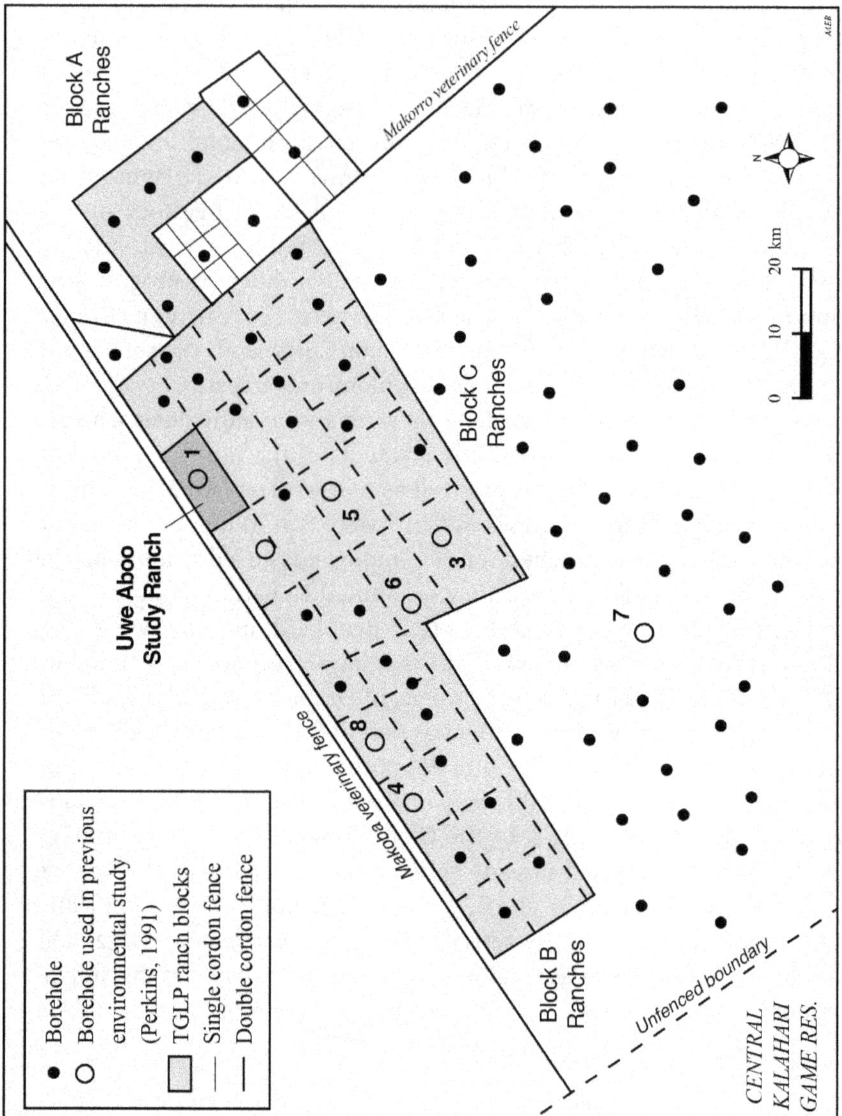

Figure 5. Map of Tribal Grazing Land Policy Ranches in the Western Sandveld Region of Central District

the mines, leaving behind their wives and children. Many of these female-headed households were without land, livestock or other resources.

In the early 21st century, new commercial ranches were established in the area both northwest and southwest of the Makoba Veterinary Cordon fence, where the original block of 18 TGLP ranches had been demarcated in the 1970s. The new ranches attracted local people as well as foreigners, in search for jobs as herders and pumpers. In some cases their families came with them. One of the trends in the early 21st century, however, was that many of the jobs were taken up by individuals who did not have families on site, but who instead sent money to them at their homes in Botswana and Zimbabwe.

From Ranch to Game Reserve

In order to qualify for one of these ranches with the sub-district land board, individual applicants had to have a management plan. Many of these plans, as it turned out, were done by professional consultants, and the ranch applicants themselves were frequently unaware of the provisions of the plans (Motlopi 2006: 25). In the bidding process, citizens and citizen-owned companies were given preference over non-citizens in the land board criteria. This, however, did not prevent non-citizens from purchasing ranches from others who had been allocated them.

In the case of the 72 TGLP ranches in the Hainaveld region in North West District (Ngamiland), just to the north of the Central Kalahari Game Reserve, some of the ranch lessees formed a conservancy (a block of ranches which had a common management plan aimed at conservation, game ranching, and commercial wildlife management) and advertised on the web for willing buyers; the price for the conservancy in 2011 was over US$3,951,150 for a conservancy area some 26,341 hectares in size (www.bestrealestate.com/go/en, accessed on May 28, 2011). Several foreign companies sent representatives to Botswana to assess the potential of the conservancy in 2010–2011, a number of them from China. Such efforts were being encouraged by the government of Botswana through its land policies and its policy on game ranching (Republic of Botswana 2002). In several areas, ranchers sold off their livestock and replaced the domestic animals with wild animals, of which a number were bought at auctions. Some of the ranches established hunting operations and made arrangements for foreign hunters to come to their ranches to hunt, usually for substantial payments of foreign exchange. Thus, both in freehold farm areas (e.g. the

Ghanzi Farms) and in commercial ranching areas such as those in Central and North West Districts, there was a transformation in land use and management and a shift in control, with relatively wealthy land owners, ranch lessees, and companies consolidating their hold on land, while poor occupants of those lands were largely excluded. A number of the hunting operations are carried out by San who have been engaged as hunting guides for generations in Botswana. By and large, however, few San have management positions in safari companies, and no San own safari hunting or tourism companies in Botswana.

In Ngamiland some communities were given wildlife rights, under Botswana's Community-Based Natural Resource Management Policy (Republic of Botswana 2007). In order to get these rights from the Department of Wildlife and National Parks, the communities had to come up with a land use and management plan, a constitution, and a community trust board. CBNRM was considered by some in the country a "foreign grown" concept and one that was expatriate driven (Rihoy and Maguranyanga 2010: 58). Part of the early work on CBNRM was funded by the U.S. Agency for International Development (USAID) and implemented by a private company working in conjunction with the Department of Wildlife and National Parks. Later on, the World Conservation Union and SNV, the Netherlands Development Organization, got involved in CBNRM in Botswana (Rozemeijer 2001; Arntzen et al. 2003). By 2012, there were some 160 community trusts in Botswana, many of which were engaged in various kinds of natural resource-related activities, some of which generated substantial revenues.

In North West District, there are nearly a dozen community-based organizations, most of which were working with private joint venture partners. A list some of these CBOs and their activities is presented in Table 3. There were a number of challenges that these community trusts faced, including (1) getting a joint venture partner through a fair and transparent bidding process which was willing to work cooperatively with the community, (2) ensuring that the joint venture partners, some of which were foreign-owned, did not take advantage of the local community by honoring their agreements (e.g. providing the community trust with agreed-upon royalties, not overshooting their licenses), and (3) ensuring full community participation. Some safari companies promised communities that they would hire specific numbers of local people and that they would provide training, something that they did not always do. There have also been cases where safari companies bribed community trust members in an effort to get the lease.

Table 3. Community trusts in Botswana's North West District involved in ecotourism and integrated conservation and development activities

Name of trust and founding date	Controlled hunting area, Size in km²	Composition of population, population size	Project activities
Jakotsha Community Trust, 1999	NG 24, 530 km²	Mbukushu, Herero and G//anikwe San, 10,000 people, multiple villages	Community tourism, *makoro* (canoe) poling, basketry and other craft sales
Khwai Development Trust, 2000	NG 18, 1,815 km² and NG 19, 180 km²	Bugakwe San, Tawana, and Subiya, 360 people, 1 village	Ecotourism, craft sales, work at private safari lodges, auctioning off hunting quota portion, setting up a of a community-owned tourist lodge
Mababe Zokotsama Community Development Trust, 1998	NG 41, 2,181 km²	Ts'exa San, 200 people, 1 village	Ecotourism, craft sales, and safari tourism
Okavango Community Trust, 1999	NG 22, 580, km², NG 23, 540 km²	Bugakwe, Wayeyi, Mbukushu, G//anikwe, Dxeriku, BaTawana, 2,200 people, 5 villages	Safari hunting and photo-based tourism
Sankuyo Tshwaragano Management Trust (STMT), 1995	NG 34, 870 km²	Wayeyi and Subiya, 345 people, 1 village	Ecotourism, safari hunting concession, craft sales, campsite
Teemashane Community Trust, 1999	NG 10 and NG 11, ca. 800 km²	Mbukushu, Wayeyi, Bugakwe San, G// anikwe San, 5,000 people,	Community tourism, campsite, cultural trail, craft sales
/Xai/Xai (Cgae Cgae) Tlhabololo Trust, 1997	NG 4, 9,293 km² NG 5, 7,623 km² (16,966 km² total)	Ju/'hoansi San, Mbanderu, 450 people, 1 village	Leasing out of portion of wildlife quota, crafts, safari hunting and tourism

Note: Data obtained from the North West District Council, the North West District Land Use Planning Unit, and the Kuru Family of Organizations. NG stands for Ngamiland.

For their part, the community trusts have had their own challenges, such as handling funds in a transparent and accountable manner, providing broad community benefits, listening to community members' opinions, and responding to community requests for assistance (Rihoy and Magurananga 2010). Also, from the government side they have been challenged.

During late 2011 and the first half of 2012 some San community trusts were barred from operating by the government as a result of alleged mismanagement. Moreover, government officials have said that the Botswana government is considering shutting down commercial safari hunting in the country altogether (Gaotlhobogwe 2011b, data from Ministry of Environment, Wildlife, and Tourism, 2012).

Conclusions

It is clear from this assessment of land reform in Botswana that local people, notably the San, have been affected in a variety of ways by State-led changes in land policy since the colonial era. The land reforms included setting aside areas for private use by individuals, so-called freehold areas, which were established under the Bechuanaland Protectorate. In cases where lands were set aside for freehold purposes, sizable numbers of local people, many of them members of minority groups, were dispossessed, while other people, many of them non-local or foreign, were able to benefit from the land (e.g. through raising of livestock, engaging in commercial agriculture, or participating in safari hunting with private clients, many of them from abroad). Similar kinds of situations occurred in the case of the land reform efforts made under the Tribal TGLP and the National Agricultural Development Policy of the post-colonial Botswana government, which saw a substantial portion of the country set aside as commercial cattle ranches, resulting in the dispossession of tens of thousands of people, a sizable proportion of them San, many of whom moved into the already over-crowded communal areas.

The third kind of land reform was the division by the Botswana government of the Wildlife Management Areas into areas for commercial use, that is, for private safari companies, and those for community use. In North West District, for example, three quarters of the so-called Controlled Hunting Areas (CHAs) ended up in the hands of private companies, while only a quarter of the CHAs became Community-Controlled Hunting Areas (CCHAs) (data from North West District Land Use Planning Unit and the North West District Council, 2011).

As for future developments, the people of Cgae Cgae (/Xai/Xai) and Dobe in the community-controlled hunting areas NG 3 expressed significant concern to planners and biologists working with them in 2012 about the selling of leases for 8 km by 8 km (64 sq km, 6,400 hectares) farms in the NG 3 area. Boga Thura Manatsha, a Motswana researcher, told reporter

Ephraim Keoreng of the Botswana newspaper *Mmegi Wa Dikgang* in June, 2012, when asked about what Botswana was facing in the future: "The main challenge is that the government seems to turn a blind eye on the now disturbing buying and selling of land by foreigners." Professor Manatsha went on to say the following:

> The other difference between Botswana and other countries is that here, cattle barons, bureaucrats and politicians, and (now) property developers are working in collusion. Therefore, it becomes difficult for the poor to articulate their land rights. Botswana has become a country where wealth is made through acquiring land cheaply from the poor and weak (Keoreng, 2012: 1).

Like many in Botswana, Manatsha is concerned that land in the country will soon be auctioned for commercial, industrial, civic, and community use, putting an end to land applications. The provisions for this new approach are contained in the new draft Botswana Land Policy which was tabled in the Botswana Parliament session that ended in 2012 (Gaotlhobogwe 2012a).

The issue that remains to be solved is what rights local people will have to ensure that they benefit from the presence of commercial cattle ranches, private hunting concessions or mining operations on the lands which they have fought so hard to retain. As an informant put it in an interview in Ghanzi in August, 2011, "We have had enough of the government giving away our land and resources to wealthy individuals and foreign companies. It is time that we got our own rights to the land, legal rights which cannot be sacrificed in the name of 'development' by the state or by big companies." While the companies that have prospecting licenses, leases and title deeds in the Kalahari maintain that they have progressive policies in place to safeguard the rights of the local communities, as well as the environmentally and socially sustainable exploitation of natural and human resources, local people continue to worry, given the long, complex, and difficult history of land reform and sub-surface resource extraction and development in Botswana.

Acknowledgments

We wish to thank the government of Botswana for permission to conduct the research discussed here. Some of the financial support for the research by Maria Sapignoli for this paper came from the Sociology Department of Essex University in the United Kingdom. Financial support to Robert

Hitchcock was provided by the U.S. National Science Foundation (grants SOC75-02253 and BNS76-20373), the Danish Ministry of Foreign Affairs, the Norwegian Ministry of Development Co-operation, the U.S. Agency for International Development, and Hivos (The Netherlands). We want to express our appreciation to the San and other advocacy and development organizations in Botswana, including First People of the Kalahari, the Kuru Family of Organizations, the Working Group of Indigenous Minorities in Southern Africa, the Botswana Khwedom Council, and Ditshwanelo, the Botswana Center for Human Rights. We also wish to thank the people of Botswana and the various companies, organizations, communities, and individuals who provided us with information and shared their insights on land, resource, and development issues. Useful suggestions were made for improving this article by the editors and several external reviewers, to whom we are very grateful.

Bibliography

Anseeuw, W. and C. Alden, eds. 2010. *The Struggle for Land in Africa: Culture, Politics, and Change*. Cape Town: Human Sciences Research Council Press.

Arntzen, J.W., D.L. Molokomme, E.M. Terry, N. Moleele, T. Tshosa, and D. Mazambani. 2003. *Main Findings of the Review of CBNRM in Botswana*. CBNRM Support Program, Occasional Paper No. 14. Gaborone, Botswana: IUCN Botswana and CBNRM Support Program (IUCN/SNV CBNRM Support Program).

Behnke, R., I. Scoones, and C. Kerven, eds. 1993. *Range Ecology at Disequilibrium: New Models of Natural Variability and Pastoral Adaptation in African Savannas*. London: Overseas Development Institute.

Bolaane, M. 2004. "The Impact of Game Reserve Policy on the River BaSarwa/Bushmen of Botswana." *Social Policy and Administration* 38(4): 399–417.

Campbell, A. C. 1973. The National Park and Reserve System in Botswana. *Biological Conservation* 5(1): 7–14.

Campbell, A., M. Main, and R.K. Hitchcock. 2006. "Land, Livestock, and Labor in Rural Botswana: The Western Sandveld Region of Central District as a Case Study." In *Updating the San: Image and Reality of an African People in the 21st Century*, R.K. Hitchcock, K. Ikeya, M. Biesele, and R.B. Lee, eds. Osaka, Japan: National Museum of Ethnology, 183–228.

Childers, G.W. 1976. *Report on the Survey/Investigation of the Ghanzi Farm Basarwa Situation*. Gaborone, Botswana: Government Printer.

Cullis, A. and C. Watson. 2009. *Winners and Losers: Privatizing the Commons in Botswana*. London: International Institute of Environment and Development.

de Satge, R. 2011. "Botswana," in *Decentralized Land Governance: Case Studies and Local Voices from Botswana, Madagascar, and Mozambique*, K. Kleinbooi and R. de Satge, eds., with C. Tanner. Cape Town: Institute for Poverty, Land, and Agrarian Studies, University of the Western Cape. 14–47.

Devitt, P. and R.K. Hitchcock. 2010. "Who Drives Resettlement? The Case of Lesotho's Mohale Dam," *African Study Monographs*, 31(2):57–106.

Dougill, A. 2002. "Ecological Change in Kalahari Rangelands: Permanent or Reversible? In *Sustainable Livelihoods in Kalahari Environments: A Contribution to Global Debates*, D. Sporton and D.S.G.H. Thomas, eds. Oxford: Oxford University Press. 91–110.

Dickson, W.L. 1990. *Land Tenure and Management in a Developing Country: The Case of Botswana 1966-1975*. Gaborone, Botswana: National Institute of Research (NIR).
Dressler, W., B. Buscher, M. Schoon, D. Brockington, T. Hayes, C. Kuill, J. McCarthy, and K. Stresnay. 2010. "From Hope to Crisis and Back Again? A Critical History of the Global CBNRM Narrative." *Environmental Conservation* 37(1):5–15.
Gaotlhobogwe, M. 2012a. "Botswana Land Up for Auction." *Mmegi wa Dikang*, Vol. 13, no. 32, 27 August 2012.
——. 2012b. "Basarwa, Bakgalagadi in another Forced Relocation." *Mmegi wa Dikang*, Vol. 29, no. 40, 15 March 2012.
——. 2011a. "Trophy Hunters' Paradise." *Mmegi Wa Dikgang*, Vol . 13, no. 24, 25 June, 2012.
——. 2011b. "Wildlife Hunting to Cease in Botswana." *Mmegi wa Dikang*, Vol. 28, no. 4, 15 July 2011.
Good, K. 2009. *Diamonds, Dispossession and Democracy in Botswana*. Johannesburg: James Currey and Jacana Media.
Guenther, M.G. 1986, *The Nharo Bushmen of Botswana: Tradition and Change*. Hamburg, Germany: Helmut Buske Verlag.
Gulbrandsen, O. 2012. *The State and the Social: State Formation in Botswana and Its Precolonial and Colonial Genealogies*. New York and Oxford: Berghahn Books.
——. 1987. *Privilege and Responsibility: On Transformations of Hierarchical Relations in a Tswana Society*. Bergen, Norway: Department of Anthropology, University of Bergen.
Hitchcock, R.K. 2006. " 'We Are the Owners of the Land': The Struggle of the San for the Kalahari and Its Resources." In *Updating the San: Image and Reality of an African People in the 21st Century*, R.K. Hitchcock, K. Ikeya. M. Biesele, and R.B. Lee, eds. Osaka, Japan: National Museum of Ethnology. 229–256.
——. 2002. " 'We Are the First People': Land, Natural Resources, and Identity in the Central Kalahari, Botswana." *Journal of Southern African Studies* 28(4):797–824.
——. 2001. " 'Hunting is Our Heritage': The Struggle for Hunting and Gathering Rights among the San of Southern Africa." In *Parks, Property, and Power*, D.G. Anderson and K. Ikeya, eds. Osaka, Japan: National Museum of Ethnology. 139–156.
——. 1991. "Kuakaka: An Early Case of Ethnoarchaeology in the Northern Kalahari." *Botswana Notes and Records* 23:223–233.
——. 1980. "Tradition, Social Justice, and Land Reform in Central Botswana. *Journal of African Law*, 24(1):1–34.
——. 1978. *Kalahari Cattle Posts*. Gaborone, Botswana: Ministry of Local Government and Lands.
Hitchcock, R.K. and T. Nkwe. 1982. "Social and Environmental Impacts of Agrarian Reform in Rural Botswana," in *Land Policy and Agriculture in Eastern and Southern Africa*, J.W. Arntzen, L.D. Ngcongco and S.D. Turner, eds. Tokyo: United National University Press. 93–99.
Hitchcock, R.K., M. Sapignoli, and W.A. Babchuk. 2011. " 'What about Our Rights'? Settlements, Subsistence, and Livelihood Security among Central Kalahari San and Bakgalagadi." *The International Journal of Human Rights* 15(1): 62–88.
Hunter, J. ed. 2004. *Who Should Own the Land? Analyses and Views on Land Reform and the Land Question in Namibia and Southern Africa*. Windhoek: Konrad Adenauer Stiftung and Namibia Institute for Democracy.
Keoreng, E. 2012. "How Foreigners are Buying Land like Magwinya." *Mmegi Wa Dikgang*, Vol. 13, no. 46, 1 June 2012.
Khama, Sir S. 1975. *Launching the Tribal Grazing Land Policy*. Gaborone, Botswana: Government Printer.
Kiema, K. 2010. *Tears for My Land: A Social History of the Kua of the Central Kalahari Game Reserve, Tc'amnqo*. Gaborone: Mmegi Publishing House.
Lawry, S.W. 1983. *Land Tenure, Land Policy, and Smallholder Livestock Development in Botswana*. LTC Research Paper No. 78. Madison, Wisconsin: Land Tenure Center.
Leith, J.C. 2005. *Why Botswana Prospered*. Montreal: McGill-Queens University Press.

Lindsey, P.A., P.A. Roulet, and S.S. Romanach. 2007. Economic and Conservation Significance of the Trophy Hunting Industry in Sub-Saharan Africa." *Biological Conservation* 134:455–469.

Malope, P. and N. Batisini. 2008. "Land Reforms that Exclude the Poor: The Case of Botswana," *Development Southern Africa* 25(4): 383–397.

Mathuba, B.M. 2003. Botswana Land Policy. Paper presented at the International Workshop on Land Policies in Southern Africa, Berlin, Germany.

Manatsha, B.T. and K.L. Maharajan. 2010. "The Politics of Land Question in North Eastern Botswana in the Context of Southern Africa." *The Social Sciences* 5(2): 128–138.

Mazonde, I. 1991. *The Enterprise of Ranching in the Tuli Block: A Study of Cultural Adjustment and Social Change in Botswana.* Gaborone, Botswana: National Institute of Research.

Merafe, Y. 1988. "Social and Economic Effects of the Tribal Grazing Land Policy in Botswana with Particular Reference to Livestock Production," in *Botswana: Education, Culture, and Politics*, Alan Barnard, ed. Edinburgh: Center of African Studies, University of Edinburgh. 55–63.

Ministry of Agriculture. 1983. *Agriculture for Botswana.* London: Macmillan Education.

Ministry of Local Government and Lands. 1984. *Tribal Grazing Land Policy Guidelines.* Gaborone, Botswana: Ministry of Local Government and Lands.

Mogalakwe, M. 1986. *Inside Ghanzi Freehold Farms: A Look at the Conditions of Basarwa Farm Workers.* Gaborone, Botswana: Applied Research Unit, Ministry of Local Government and Lands, 1986.

Motlopi, K. 2006. Privatization of Rangelands, Ranch Development, Management, and Equity: The Case of Area 4B, Botswana. MA Thesis, Norwegian University of Life Sciences Department of International Environmental and Development Studies.

Perkins, J. 1991. The Impact of Borehole Dependent Cattle Grazing on the Environment and Society of the Eastern Kalahari Sandveld, Central District, Botswana. Ph.D. Dissertation, University of Sheffield.

Peters, P. 1994. *Dividing the Commons: Politics, Policy, and Culture in Botswana.* Charlottesville, Virginia: University Press of Virginia.

Picard, L.A. 1980. "Bureaucrats, Cattle, and Public Policy: Land Tenure Changes in Botswana." *Comparative Political Studies* 13(3):313–356.

——, ed. 1985. *The Evolution of Modern Botswana: Politics and Development in Southern Africa.* Lincoln: University of Nebraska Press and London: Rex Collings.

Republic of Botswana. 2007. *Community-Based Natural Resources Management Policy.* Gaborone, Botswana: Government of Botswana.

——. 2002. *Botswana Game Ranching Policy.* Government Paper No. 5 of 2002. Gaborone, Botswana: Government Printer.

——. 1991. *National Policy on Agricultural Development.* Government Paper No. 1 of 1991. Gaborone, Botswana: Government Printer.

——. 1989. *Report on the Review of the Tribal Land, Land Policies, and Related Issu*es. Gaborone, Botswana: Government Printer.

——. 1986. *Wildlife Conservation Policy.* Government Paper No. 1 of 1986. Gaborone, Botswana: Government Printer.

——. 1975. *National Policy on Tribal Grazing Land.* Government Paper No. 2 of 1975. Gaborone, Botswana: Government Printer.

——. 1968. *The Tribal Land Act.* Gaborone, Botswana: Government Printer.

Rihoy, L. and B. Maguranyanga, 2010. "The Politics of Community-Based Resource Management in Botswana." In *Community Rights, Conservation, and Contested Lands: The Politics of Natural Resource Governance in Africa*, Fred Nelson, ed. London and Washington D.C.: Earthscan. 55–78.

Rohde, R.F., N.M. Moleele, M. Mphale, N. Allsopp, R. Chanda, M.T. Hoffman, L. Magole, and E. Young. 2006. "Dynamics of Grazing Policy and Practice: Environmental and Social Impacts in Three Communal Areas of Southern Africa." *Environmental Science and Policy* 9(3):302–316.

Rozemeijer, N. ed. 2001. *Community-Based Tourism in Botswana: The SNV Experience in Three Community Tourism Projects*. Gaborone, Botswana: SNV (Netherlands Development Organization).

Russell, M. 1976. "Slaves or Workers? Relations between Bushmen, Tswana and Boers in the Kalahari," *Journal of Southern African Studies* 2(2):178–197.

Russell, M. and M. Russell. 1979. *Afrikaaners of the Kalahari: White Minority in a Black State*. Cambridge: Cambridge University Press.

Sanford, S. 1983. *Management of Pastoral Development in the Third World*. New York: John Wiley and Sons and Overseas Development Institute.

——. 1981. *Review of World Bank Livestock Activities in Dry Tropical Africa*. Washington, D.C.: World Bank.

Sapignoli, M. 2012. *Local Power through Globalised Indigenous Identities: The San, the State, and the International Community*. Ph.D. Dissertation, University of Essex, Colchester, United Kingdom.

——. 2009. "Indigeneity as Expert Witness: Negotiating Identity in the Case of the Central Kalahari Game Reserve", In *Law and Anthropology*, Michael Freeman and David Napier, eds, Oxford and New York: Oxford University Press. 247–268.

Sapignoli, M. and R.K. Hitchcock. 2011. *Social Impact Assessment Anthropological Analysis of the Ghanzi Copper Project Area, Western Botswana*. Gaborone: SIAPAC and Loci Environmental.

Schapera, I. 1971. "The Native Land Problem in the Tati District." *Botswana Notes and Records* 3:219–268.

——. 1943. *Native Land Tenure in the Bechuanaland Protectorate*. Alice, South Africa: Lovedale Press.

Scudder, T. 2005. *The Future of Large Dams: Dealing with Social, Environmental, Institutional, and Political Costs*. London: James and James Science Publishers.

Silberbauer, G.B. 1981. *Hunter and Habitat in the Central Kalahari Desert*. Cambridge: Cambridge University Press.

Sporton, D. and D.S.G.H. Thomas, eds. 2002. *Sustainable Livelihoods in Kalahari Environments: A Contribution to Global Debates*. Oxford: Oxford University Press.

Tlou, T. and A. Campbell. 1997. *History of Botswana*. Third Edition. Gaborone: Macmillan Botswana Publishing.

Tsimako, B. 1991. *The Tribal Grazing Land Policy Ranches: Performance to Date*. Gaborone, Botswana: Socio-economic Monitoring and Evaluation Unit, Ministry of Agriculture.

White, R. 1993. *Livestock Development and Pastoral Production on Communal Rangeland in Botswana*. Gaborone, Botswana: The Botswana Society.

Wily, E.A. 1982. "A Strategy of Self-Determination for the Kalahari San (The Botswana Government's Programme of Action in the Ghanzi Farms)." *Development and Change* 13(2):291–308.

——. 1981. *The TGLP and Hunter-Gatherers: A Case Study in Land Politics*. Gaborone, Botswana: National Institute of Development and Cultural Research.

——. 1979. *Official Policy Towards San (Bushmen) Hunter-Gatherers in Modern Botswana: 1966–1978*. Gaborone, Botswana: National Institute of Development and Cultural Research.

DOMESTIC AND FOREIGN INVESTMENTS IN IRRIGABLE LAND IN MALI: TENSIONS BETWEEN THE DREAM OF LARGE-SCALE FARMING AND THE REALITY OF FAMILY FARMING

Amandine Adamczewski, Perrine Burnod, Hermine Papazian, Yacouba Coulibaly, Jean-Philippe Tonneau and Jean-Yves Jamin

Introduction

Plans for large-scale land acquisitions by private investors have drastically increased, especially in Africa, which appears to be the new, privileged destination of land-grabbing (Cotula et al., 2009; Von Braun & Meinzen-Dick, 2009; World Bank, 2010). Targeting mostly developing countries that are not self-sufficient in their food production, these investments put at the forefront issues of food and land security. More broadly, they renew the debate on what kinds of agriculture, for which farmers and with which business models, could favor economic and social development.

In Mali, the *Office du Niger* (ON) area is presented as rich in land and water resources. Foreign states as well as foreign and local private companies target land in this zone (Cotula et al., 2009; Diallo et al., 2010; Brondeau, 2011). Irrigation schemes currently cover approximately 100 000 hectares (ha), and could potentially cover up to one or even two million ha. This area has thus always been at the heart of Malian agricultural development policies. During the past 20 years, it benefited from substantial economic growth; family farmers—mostly smallholders—were, and still are, the main actors of this economic success. Rice being the main urban staple food in Mali, they manage to massively produce rice (Bonneval et al., 2002), supplying half of the national market (Bélières, 2011).

Despite this success, since the 1960s, Malian decision makers have continued to promote large-scale farming, though without real results. Since 2000, the situation has changed. Numerous investors regularly approach the government in the hope of implementing large, land-based investments in the ON area. Those requests (from Libya, China, South Africa, Canada, Malaysia, USA, etc.) represent therefore a great opportunity for the Malian government, not only to develop large-scale farming but also to finance the extension of the irrigated area, a state dream since the 1930s. However, the benefits from those investments prove to be less obvious for smallholders themselves. The development of large-scale farming might encroach on smallholders' land, as their land rights are not secured, neither (i) in the irrigated zone, where the available area per family (in average 3 ha per household of 13 members) is decreasing, due to population growth, nor (ii) in the neighboring dry lands where they cultivate rain-fed cereals and have cattle pastures. Large-scale farming might also jeopardize smallholder access to other main resources like water and fuel wood. Competition over natural resources, especially land, is currently the main issue. Moving beyond the debates that often oppose large-scale agriculture against smallholders farming, this chapter analyzes policies and regulations that may impact on investment and land issues in the ON area. It questions to what extent family farming and large-scale farming can coexist in this context. The first section presents the status of land investment projects in the ON area. A second section analyzes the role of the government in promoting and regulating foreign and domestic investments. The following section then focuses on the social opposition to these large-scale investments. Finally, the last section discusses the impact of large-scale agribusiness on family farming and the unequal competition between smallholders and large companies. The conclusion highlights the existing, sharp contrast between the current poor results of large-scale farming and the effectiveness of small-scale, family farming.

Scarce information is available on large-scale agribusiness projects. Access to information is limited for Malian citizens and decision makers, as well as for international organizations. This is due to investor discretion regarding their plans, but also sometimes because of very vague business transactions. Diffusion of information is hindered by the sensitive nature of land issues in political debates. This chapter uses the results of previous studies (Burnod et al., 2010; Cotula et al., 2009; Diallo et al., 2010; Adamczewski et al., 2011) and field data collected from 200 interviews held in 2010 with agents from public institutions, regional or local governments, private developers, NGOs, farmers associations, trade unions, local populations, and other key informants. The interviews were conducted in the capital city, Bamako, and in the ON area. In addition, data was gathered from juridical laws, political orientations, and project documents.

What Kinds of Investments Are Implemented or Planned in the ON Area?

The whole ON area is state-owned, and land is officially titled in the name of the State. The *Office du Niger*, a public institution created in 1932 and reorganized by the Ordinance 96–188/P of 11 July 11 1996, manages and controls water and land access for all users, from small family farmers to big investors, notably through land leases or land permits. Hence, in the irrigated area, tightly managed by the State through the *Office du Niger* institution, farmers only have formal use rights, providing that they were awarded a land lease or a land permit. In rain-fed areas, smallholder land rights, based on local rules and custom, are not legally recognized. These areas, loosely controlled by the Office du Niger, are managed by village authorities and the commune. According to the official estimations, two and a half million hectares could be irrigated in the area (map 1). But until now, only 5% are effectively developed under irrigation schemes. These 98 000 ha are mostly cultivated by family farmers. Since 2004, in order to develop the costly irrigation infrastructures required to encourage large-scale, "modern" farms, the government has been implementing incentive policies. Consequently, and notably since 2007, the number of private agricultural investment projects drastically increased, with 10 in 2002, and more than 200 in 2009. During the 2004–2009 period, various entities—from Malian family farmers or entrepreneurs to big private national and foreign companies—have applied for land leases on more than 870 000 ha, almost 10 times the currently developed surface (Map 1). All of them have not yet obtained the land; according to projects, land allocation is at different stages.

The Targeted Land Area Totals 870 000 ha: 45% by National Investors, 55% by Foreign Investors

In the ON area, domestic entrepreneurs, which have not been taken into account in previous studies on land-grabbing in Mali, target about 400 000 ha altogether. The vast majority of them (80%) seek to gain access to a land area ranging from 1 to 50 ha, with one-third looking for less than 5 ha. This group includes mainly family farmers, sometimes organized in association. They often intend to extend their existing irrigated farm or to settle on a new farm to grow rice and market gardening products. Schematically, land is mostly acquired on a 5 ha basis for an individual farmer and on a 50 ha basis for an association. While these land holders are labeled as *investors* by the *Office du Niger*, as investment is needed to develop land for irrigation, they own little capital. There are also small entrepreneurs applying to get a land lease (from 10 to 20 ha). They are mainly officers in Bamako or Ségou, or Malians who used to live abroad and plan to invest in agriculture and to delegate the management to a third part.

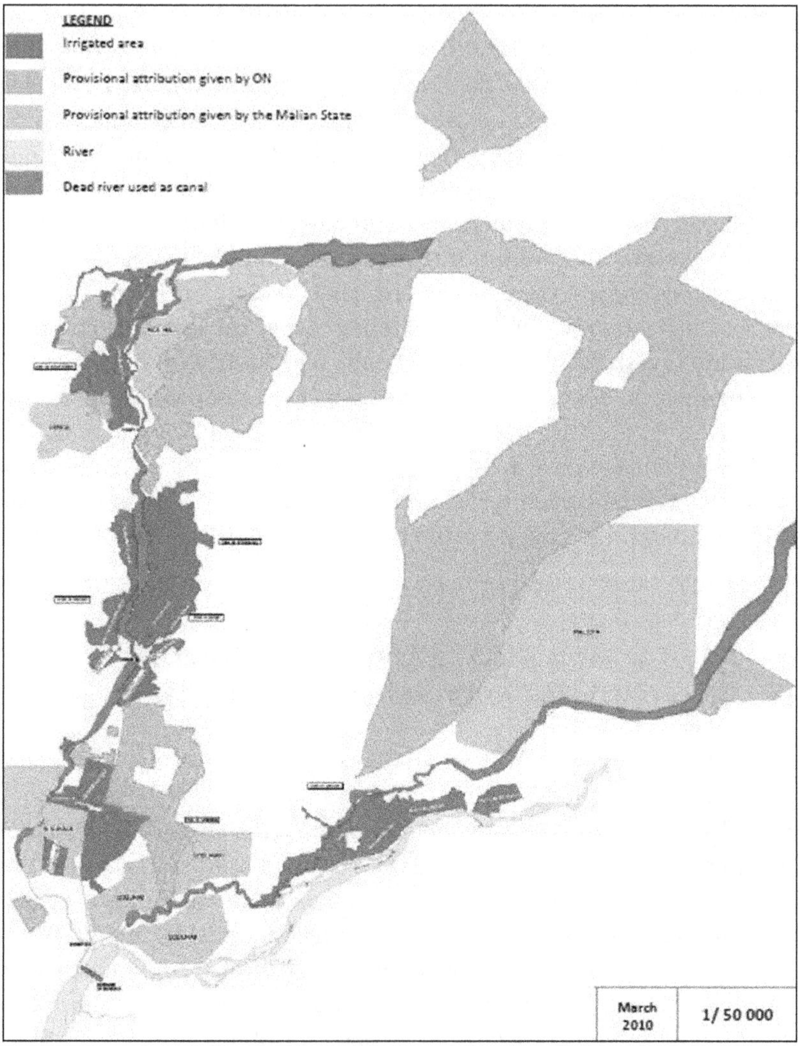

Map 1. Irrigated zones and future projects in the ON area

Table 1. Main Malian investors (hidden name due to confidentiality issues)

Investor	Requested surface	Planned activity	Progress
A.O.	10 000 ha	Oil crops	unknown
B.M.	10 000 ha	Jatropha	Liable to cancellation
S.	10 000 ha	Jatropha	Signed Lease Study in progress
B.	10 000 ha	Oil crops	Liable to cancellation
G.M.	10 000 ha	Jatropha	Liable to cancellation
S.N.	15 000 ha	Oil crops	Finalized study No crops installed
C.	20 000 ha	Rice	Liable to cancellation
A.S.	20 000 ha	Oil crops	Liable to cancellation
S.O.	20 000 ha	Oil crops	Liable to cancellation
A.E.	40 000 ha	Oil crops	Unknown
Tomota	100 000 ha	Oil crops	Study in progress (850 ha cultivated with rainfed crops)
TOTAL	255 000 ha		(Total for all national investors, 400 000 ha)

In contrast with those small farmers or entrepreneurs, about twenty domestic investors want to lease large plots, from 500 to 100 000 ha (see Table 1). Those domestic investors generally claim to hold the capital needed to develop the land; only a minority of them is trying to get funding from outside. For this group, the targeted land area totals about 300 000 ha (80% of the area targeted by Malian nationals). These private Malian investors, already acting in agriculture (GM, Tomota) or newly arrived in this sector, plan to develop oil crops for food or agrofuel markets (e.g., *Jatropha curcas*). They want to implement a large-scale farming model based on mechanization and wage system, a model far removed from that utilized by small-scale Malian investors, which are anchored in family farming practices.

As widely discussed in the media, big foreign investors are also well represented in the Malian land rush. They are eighteen in total, all coming from diverse origins and having different status in Mali. Each foreign investor applies for a lease ranging from 2 500 to 100 000 ha; in total, foreign investors have appealed for nearly 440 000 ha altogether (Details and nationalities in Table 2). The majority plans to develop large-scale plantations; nine foreign private companies aim to produce oil crops, and four foreign States (Libya, Saudi Arabia, China and Burkina Faso) intend to

Table 2. Main foreign projects

Project name	Investor	Requested surface	Planned Acitvity	Progress
Projects carried out by foreign states (total = 127 500 ha)				
Malibya	Libya	100 000 ha	Rice, vegetables, cattle	Finalized study (but not matching legal rules) Main irrigation canal constructed
Foras	Saudi Arabia	5 000 ha (maybe 100 000 ha)	Rice	Study in progress Factory under construction
N'SUKALA II	China	20 000 ha	Sugar can	Study in progress
?	Burkina-Faso	2 500 ha	rice	Unknown
Projects carried out by private investors—total = 245 000 ha				
PSM	South Africa (and Malian government)	40 000 ha	Sugar can	Finalized study 140 ha irrigation test
SEEDROCK	Canada	40 000 ha	Oil crops	Study in progress
LOHNRO	Panafrican Conglomerate	20 000 ha	Rice	Study in progress
BALY SBB BIO	Burkina Faso	10 000 ha	Rice	Unknown
PETROTECH	USA	10 000 ha	Jatropha	Leased signed
SOUTHERN GLOBAL	USA	10 000 ha	Oil crops	Study in progress
FAYEZ	Sudan	5 000 ha	Oil crops	Liable to cancellation
Gonzales	Spain	5 000 ha	Oil crops	Liable to cancellation
A.A.M.	Lebanon	5 000 ha	Jatropha	Unknown
Agro ED	France		Oil crops	Cancelled
Roxwell Invt. Group (OYT)	Malaysia	100 000 ha	?	Liable to cancellation
Projects carried out by inter-states organization—total = 51 000 ha				
CEN-SAD		40 000 ha	Food crops	Unknown
UEMOA		11 000 ha	Rice	Study in progress
Projects carried out by foreign aid agencies—total = 16 000 ha				
MCA-Mali	MCC – USA	16 000 ha	Rice	Land title—1 000 ha cultivated 5 200 ha developed
TOTAL = 440 000 ha (Total for all foreign investors, 470 000 ha)				

grow cereals or sugar cane. Three other investment projects are public in nature: two are led by African inter-state organizations (Cen-Sad and UEMOA) and one is run by a foreign aid agency (MCC—based in the United States).[1] These three latter intergovernmental or development projects are designed to redistribute the developed land back to small investors or family farmers, in response to the government bid for projects aimed at producing rice for national and sub-regional markets. Once again, the envisioned models of agricultural development advocated by the state stand in stark contrast to both those promoting family farming and private investments geared towards intensive and large-scale farming.

Out of the 870 000 ha targeted altogether (including Malian and foreign investments), 50% are planned for rice production (415 000 ha), 38% for oil crops (sunflower, soybean, and peanut: 290 000 ha; Jatropha: 35 000 ha), 6% for sugar cane, and 1% for wheat (Figure 1). The *Office du Niger* selected specific areas for the different investors. Spatial distribution of the diverse projects depends on the type of crop; investments related to oil crops are mainly located in areas that are not yet developed, with no existing irrigated schemes or roads, such as Kareri, Kokeri and East Kouroumari (see map 1). Rice projects, both small and large, are located next

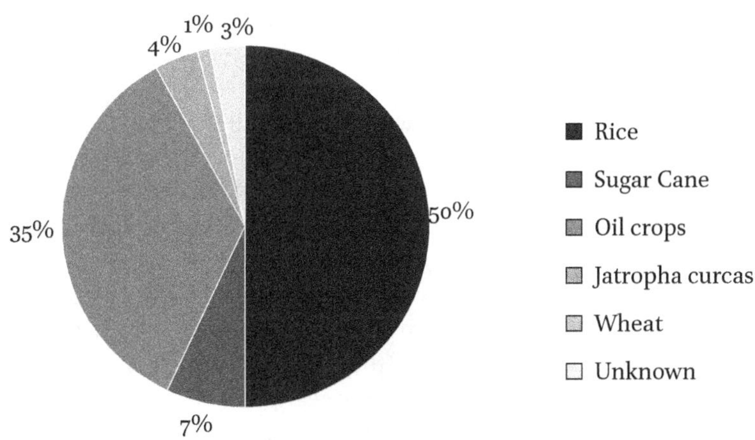

(Source: project documents and surveys, 2010)

Figure 1. Crops planned by domestic and foreign investors (surface) %

[1] The aim of the MCC project is to distribute 5 to 50 ha developed land plots to existing and new farmers, in order to run intensive rice production. MCC project obtained 16 000 ha of potentially irrigable land from the Malian government.

to existing irrigated areas and thus close to water and road infrastructures (for example, near the M'Bewani, Macina and Kouroumari areas). Sugar cane projects (60 000 ha) are concentrated next to existing sugar cane plantations in the M'Bewani area, where sugar cane has been cropped since 1960. Most large-scale land projects are located in areas far removed from existing infrastructures. Due to the added expense of roads and canals, the investment cost is very high: from 5000 to 7000 Euros per ha. These huge amounts, often underestimated by investors, probably explain the slow progress of the projects.

From Announcements to Effective Implementation

The vast majority of the operators have not yet begun project implementation on the terrain. Most operators have not yet signed the final land lease; only 108 land leases have been signed (covering 50 0000 ha in total). It was found that just three land leases were signed by foreign investors (for only 55 ha). The first was signed by a French investor to develop Jatropha, the second by a Chinese investor for rice crops (but the investor has recruit family farmers to cultivate the land), and the third by a German investor (already owner of a hotel in Mali), for tree plantations. The other projects developed by foreign investors are in the process of being finalized by a convention (for example, the Malibya Project, Sosumar and Sukala), or by a land title (as in the case of the MCA project).

Hence, about 820 000 ha (94% of the requested area) will be allocated on the basis of temporary agreements. If the project submitted is validated, investors receive a lease agreement which becomes effective if, within a period of one year, they conduct additional studies (such as an Environmental and Social Impact Assessment (ESIA) and other technical and economic feasibility studies) (see Figure 2).

However, taken with the above legislation, by the end of 2009, 90% of these provisory engagements may have never been enforced (for a land area of about 450 000 ha), as the developers neither provided the compulsory technical and socio-economical studies to the government (mentioned above) which are requested within the first year following the initial approval, nor built the irrigation infrastructures demanded in the three first years. This could be notably the case for half of the biggest investors (7 domestic ones out of 11 and 6 foreign ones out of 18). There is thus a great deal of flexibility observed in the enforcement of the procedures. Some agreements signed five years ago remain valid even though none of the mandatory social and technical studies have been carried out.

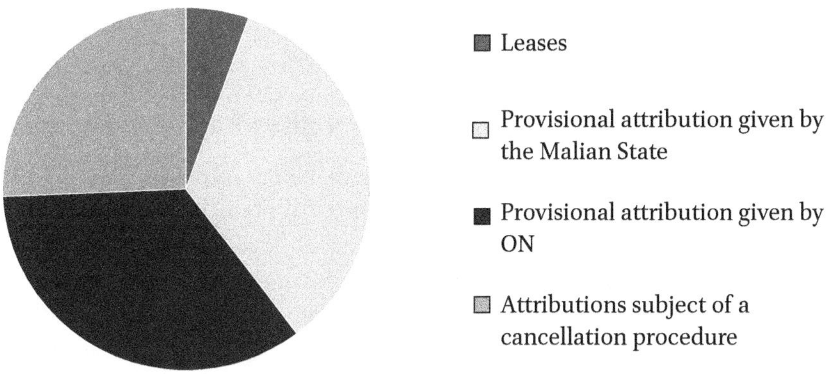

(Source: ON data, May 2010)

Figure 2. Status of different land attributions in the ON area.

In fact, this absence of land access formalization does not seem to really hinder the developers. Some foreign operators, without any finalized land lease contract, have already implemented irrigation infrastructure construction and agricultural works. Nevertheless, in 2010 and in 2011, several provisory engagements were cancelled for projects respectively covering 224 000 ha and 57 000 ha.

On the other hand, very few operators have built significant infrastructure or valorized the land. As of 2010, only 2% of the 870 000 ha sought had been exploited. Out of the 50 000 ha assigned through leases (the first lease being delivered in 1998), only 11 000 ha are now cropped: two thirds by a longstanding sugar company, and one third facilitated through informal and illegal sublease contracts with small farmers. Indeed, the Chinese investor who has obtain a lease to cropping rice, rent his land to small farmers to take some profit on. Subleasing is officially forbidden, but implicitly tolerated by the *Office du Niger* institution. Frequently, when a scheme is developed, investors or farmers who are not able to crop their land let or sub-let it. Thanks to these arrangements, they hope to get a minimum return on their investment or at least enough capital to cover the water fees paid to the *Office du Niger*. Out of the 820 000 ha provisionally allotted to large-scale investors, only two promoters (MCA-Mali and PSM) have really begun cultivating irrigated crops on roughly 2 000 ha (less than 3% of the total attributed area). The sole major work, completed in the recent years, is the construction of a new canal intended to irrigate 100 000 ha for the Malibya Project. However, this very large canal (the fourth largest canal of this type built since the creation of the ON) is not currently used because no irrigation system was developed downstream.

The Role of the Government: Strong Promotion of Investment but Weak Regulation

1. *The Malian State Promotes Large Investment*

In newspapers (The Guardian 8/06/2011; Irish Times 22/06/2011, New York Times 21/09/2011, Le Monde 18/10/2011), southern countries are often presented as victims of the new foreign investment flows. But in many cases, governments really promote foreign direct investment (Cotula et al., 2009). In Mali, during the last 10 years, the government has been implementing an active incentive policy to promote domestic and foreign investments. Malian State and international donor investments are indeed no longer sufficient to develop the irrigation sector—as costs were estimated at about 366 million Euros for developing an additional 50 000 ha (Hydropacte, 2010). The government aims not only at attracting investors to finance irrigation infrastructures, but also entrepreneurs to manage large-scale and intensive farms. Following this new policy, attracting private and foreign investors became a priority. Conversely, this reveals a loss of confidence and lack of interest in family agriculture on the part of the state.

The government implemented this policy through the creation of a one-stop office for investors (*Agence Pour l'Investissement*, API) in 2005, the adoption of the Economic and Social Development Project (PDES) in 2007 (urging the government to "identify, promote and support private projects able to create new production units") and various appeals to private and public investors in 2008. Its objective is currently to develop 120 000 ha by 2020 (www.office-du-niger.org.ml). Given that only 100 000 ha were developed during the past 80 years, the government needs substantial investment to accomplish this goal and hopes for rapid developments.

2. *Office du Niger, the Official Land Manager*

The *Office du Niger* is the institution in charge of managing land and water access. It has the role of centralizing all requests for land access. This institution holds the power to allot plots located in irrigated areas and to stop the land lease contract if the tenants do not pay the water fees. As all irrigated land is already occupied, new land allocations are now severely limited. Tenants are family farmers and the average cropped area is, as mentioned earlier, roughly 3 ha per family, each family consisting on average of 13 persons (Coulibaly et al., 2006). Almost all family farmers are small holders: two thirds, if not completely landless, hold an area inferior to 2,5 ha; the biggest smallholders, considered as "rich" by the others, hold 5 to 15 ha, and represent only 10% of all farmers (Bélières, 2011). The decrease by two-thirds of the average area per family during the 10 last years (Bélières et al., 2003) and the dynamism of the informal land market (Coulibaly et al., 2006) prove that land pressure is very strong. Foreign and local investors do not compete directly with small holders for existing irrigated plots. The competition is more on lands that could be developed for irrigation.

The *Office du Niger* also holds the power to allot plots outside of existing irrigation schemes as well, in areas with high irrigation potential. In accordance with legal rules, all investors must present themselves at the *Office du Niger* in order to obtain a 'letter of agreement'. This letter is supposed to be delivered only after a preliminary field investigation to identify existing resources and their uses, and to avoid encroachment upon already allotted plots. After the realization and validation of technical and environmental impact assessments required by the government, and after fulfillment of various other requirements, such as infrastructure development, investors can sign a 30-year lease (known as an ordinary lease or *bail ordinaire*—BO) or a 50-year lease (emphyteutic lease or *bail emphytéotique*—BE). In line with the legislation, even if it is far from being systematically enforced, the *Office du Niger* can cancel the contract if the operator does not develop at least 50% of the allotted surface within the first 3 years (renewable once) or does not respect the irrigation specifications.

Because the *Office du Niger* had full control over land, water and men in the area, it has been described for a long time as a state within the state (Jamin and Doucet, 1994). However, its power is now weakening. In these last years, the biggest investors have enjoyed privileged land access without first addressing the *Office du Niger*. Higher levels of state authority are indeed now involved in land management; the *Office du Niger* is then becoming a simple local state service, tightly supervised, and even sidestepped by central government.

3. *When the Central State Takes Its Power Back*

Legally, the *Office du Niger* is the sole decisional and operational public service in charge of water and land allocation to small and large investors. Despite this, the government directly allotted nearly 300 000 ha (30% of the total targeted area) to foreign investors through conventions and then by-passed the *Office du Niger*. The UEMOA and Malibya projects were approved via a signed agreement with the Ministry of Agriculture; PSM

(South Africa) worked with the Ministry of Industry and Trade; Sukala SA (China) dealt with the Ministry of Housing, Lands & Urbanism; and the MCA project (USA) directly signed an agreement with, and exceptionally received a land title document from, the President of the Republic. In April 2009, the government created a specific Secretariat of state to manage the integrated development of the ON area (MDDIZON), later, upgrading it to Ministry status. This new Ministry, directly reporting to the Prime Minister, now supervises the *Office du Niger* institution, thus replacing, for this function, the Ministry of Agriculture. From the government's point of view, this creation was necessary to increase the level of coordination between the different ministries in charge of, and involved in, different investments in the ON area. The MDDIZON conglomerate reflects the government's desire, through a one-stop service authority for large-scale land investment, to hijack decision-making power from previously de-centralized institutions. This re-centralization of power in Bamako, far from the field, partly explains the ineffectiveness of regulatory framework (cf. infra).

4. *State Institutional Competition and Ineffective Formal Regulation*

The State plays an important role in promoting investments, but its regulating role appears more limited. The procedure for accessing land in the ON area is based on three different legislative documents: the Land Tenure Code, the Investment Code and the Law on Pollution. Moreover, the presence of large investors has set the regulation system in motion, inducing the revision of the environmental decree, the setting up of an environmental and social impact assessment (ESIA)—compulsory to obtain the environmental license, the formalization of a formal compulsory management plan, and the internal reorganization of the *Office du Niger* services. But in the field, practices reveal that these regulation tools are not yet effective.

Firstly, procedures for and authority over land management are not well established. The government and the *Office du Niger* have allotted a total area of 820 000 ha to investors even though they plan to lease about 200 000 ha by 2020. In addition, various land areas have been assigned without reference to the 2004 irrigation development master plan (called SDDZON), in other words, without taking into account neither the water availability in the Niger River (very limited during the dry season, from February to June), nor the water transport capacity of the existing infrastructures.

The land allocation procedure was sometime implemented too hastily and without any rigorous follow-up, inducing in some cases instances of double allocation. In 2009, the World Bank launched a project to develop 2500 ha (PAPAM Project) to install small and medium investors in the M'Bewani area. In this region, some plots were allotted twice; the *Office du Niger* first allocated land to national citizens (Malian entrepreneurs, village communities and peasants) and later the state allocated the same area to the PAPAM (international) project. This resulted in the cancellation of prior allocations such that the World Bank funded PAPAM project could continue. The fact that different government representatives (e.g. the President of the Republic, Ministers of various departments, and the CEO of the *Office du Niger*) sign, or signed, conventions with investors, reveals the tensions between foreign operators and the *Office du Niger* services. These conventions parallel the letters of agreement normally delivered by the *Office du Niger*. Moreover, foreign investors frequently consider them as a land lease contract—even if it is not legally the case, and carry out field development without doing the prior studies legally required by *Office du Niger*.

In January 2010, the *Office du Niger* reorganized its services in order to better analyze the contents of investment projects. It created a new department, Land Management and Development, designed to re-concentrate the analysis of all land projects in the Niger Office. But, at the same time, the MDDIZON Department, also recently created, reduces the *Office du Niger* institution's power and interferes with its selection and supervision attempts. The result is a lack of serious project selection, giving the opportunity to promoters to access land, even without competencies in agriculture or irrigation, without knowledge of the local social and economic context, or without the financial capacity to complete the technical and social assessment (which costs about 1500€ per hectare). In 2007, a land lease commission was set up (made up of *Office du Niger* representatives) to determine whether or not the operators respect the land access procedure. However, until 2010, this commission was only able to process 5% of the requests and the commission's members have rarely carried out the field visits necessary to prevent local conflicts opposing operators and local farmers.

Secondly, the API agency, also designed to regulate the investments, struggles to guide investors. This investment 'one-stop' office was originally meant to simplify the administrative procedures to be followed for investment projects, but in fact created an additional administrative step for investors. Consequently, operators, notably foreigners, bypass it altogether. Moreover, they prefer negotiating land and water access directly with the Presidency or one of the ministries such that they can enjoy the following advantages: i) *convention* instead of *letter of agreement*; ii) significant decrease in hydraulic fees—justified by the fact that investors substitute the state for investing in infrastructure; iii) priority water access during the dry season, when the Niger River is at its lowest level (as is the case for the Malibya, PSM and Sukala projects).

Thirdly, since 2000, and according to a new environmental decree, all promoters must carry out an environmental and social impact assessment (EISA) for any project covering an area exceeding 10 ha. But the outcome of the ESIA, enforced since 2008, does not appear to impact upon actual project content. Public consultations usually entail a project summary presented by the promoter but do not create the conditions for real exchanges between the *Office du Niger* agents, local levels of government and populations living on the area requested by the project. Requirements are scarce and not enforced due to the absence of funds allocated to the Ministry of Environment, which is in charge of controlling them; as a result, some investors have already cleared forest, mined or carried out polluting activities without paying any fees. The government still has not decided on the level of tax intended to benefit the Ministry of Environment; however, one proposition is that fees could be equal to 1.5% of the sum invested by the operators.

As a result of these weak regulations, local land rights, based on local practices and customs, are generally not respected. Local land uses include rain-fed agriculture, extensive breeding and wood exploitation. Even when theses uses are recognized by the population and allowed by the *Office du Niger*, no national directive exists, detailing and guaranteeing compensation for the affected populations. The only reference is the World Bank operational policy on involuntary resettlement (OP 4.12),[2] but no company or project has actually fully implemented it, and many companies do not refer to it (e.g. Malibya and Tomota projects). The MCC project is the only one to comply with most of the OP 4.12 procedures.

Compensation for the populations affected by the project (*PAP*s in the World Bank vocabulary) is defined on a case-by-case basis. Some operators (MCA and Sukala II projects) finance or are expected to finance compensation for PAPs, whereas for other investors (Malibya and PSM), the government is in charge of covering costs for compensation. In the

---

2 http://siteresources.worldbank.org/INTFORESTS/Resources/OP412.pdf

latter case, costs fall to the State in exchange for investments made in infrastructure, such as factories, roads and canals. Some investors claim that differential treatment should not exist in order to try to avoid paying compensations, arguing that some other investors are not charged for this. Hence, the slow pace at which the political negotiations intended to define the entity who will have to provide such compensation (promoter or state), and the total amount of this compensation, as well as the State's difficulties in securing the necessary budget, are significant obstacles to the overall efficiency of the procedure.

While the government was quite effective in promoting investments in the area, and as a result many investors are now planning or already implementing projects, the state is unable to enforce existing laws and regulations to regulate investor activities, as coordinating or controlling institutions are still trying to find their place in this new and constantly shifting investment landscape.

Can Family Farmers' Pressure Help Regulation Emerge?

1. *Large Investors Favored at the Expense of Family Farms?*

The State wants to promote private large-scale and intensive agricultural farming, viewed as more efficient than family farming, to contribute to the country's food security. But the development of large-scale agribusiness, potentially complementary to family farming, is thus far been far from a driver for family farming. Instead of favoring family farming systems, which already face significant demographic, financial and land constraints, large-scale land deals reduce the land and financial resources that could have been allotted to small-holders. During the past 25 years, the average rice cropped area fell from 7–8 ha per family to 2–3 ha; even if poverty is less important in the ON area than in the other parts of the country, farmers express great concern about their future, particularly on land issues (Belieres et al., 2011). Indeed, the rules regarding access to land and water are very unequal; whereas investors obtain, in a few months time, provisional attributions on thousands of hectares and enjoy favored access to water, family farmers struggle to obtain a few hectares and are forced to pay water fees to keep their land lease contract valid. These inequalities are all the more strong, even in cases where large investors have not yet cropped land lots. When some hectares are effectively cropped, the work is partly done by family farmers or based on family farmers' practices. Despite this very unbalanced dynamic, the situation remains the same as it was 10 and 20 years ago: small-holders are producing rice (and vegetables) for home consumption and the domestic market, whereas the few active private companies are specializing in sugar production.

The intense competition for land marginalizes family farmers with low financial, social and political capital compared to national or foreign private operators. Nevertheless, small-holders are progressively becoming aware of the scope of the current land rush, even if access to information is another critical issue; there is very little information available to family farmers, and it is nearly impossible to know how many hectares are allocated to a particular project, where the project will take place and especially with what kinds of conditions (e.g. compensation, fees, water rights, etc.).

2. *But Family Farming Is Still Active*

Family farmers are not totally forgotten in the current rush for land. The State and some few international donors continue to give small-holders some access to newly established irrigation schemes—even if the amount of developed surfaces and the distribution patterns do not fit the needs and requests of the family farmers. For example, the Millennium Challenge Account (MCA) project seeks to combine family farming with the installation of small and medium-size farms; however, beneficiaries are selected on the basis of capital assets, thereby excluding a large portion of the candidate farmers who cannot claim for traditional land rights in the project area.

Family farmers are also proactive. They have developed several strategies to expand their irrigated lands, some developing "low cost" irrigation schemes. Modeled after the current irrigation scheme, farmers make pirate connections to divert water from existing irrigation or drainage systems to dry lands. These informal and low costs schemes have enabled many farmers to access irrigated land outside the regulations of the *Office du Niger*. Farmers try also to develop new strategies to protect their interests in this context mounting large-scale land acquisitions, and small-holders are actively organizing themselves to fight against land monopolization.

Local leaders are attempting to organize farmers in order to obtain additional land leases necessary to develop small irrigation schemes. These new local initiatives, mobilizing family groups, district or village organizations, reveal a real desire on the part of farmers to increase their productive capacity and keep control of their land, even if their level of land access is insecure compared to the guarantees given to the private sector. Lastly, these initiatives, which may be promising or remain isolated, show that family agriculture is far from being completely passive.

3. *First Social Claims, First Implementation of Formal Rules*

The dry lands where the government intends to develop irrigation schemes are State-owned lands managed by the *Office du Niger*. Legally considered as *'vacant and free of uses'*, in practice they are used for many activities: rain-fed cropping (e.g., millet, sorghum, and cowpea), cattle breeding (local and transhumant pasture use as well as tracks and watering points), fuel wood collecting, hamlets and villages settling. Investors located in the area are thus a source of potential and actual conflicts related to land and water resources.

In four cases, some local groups publicly expressed their strong opposition to land deals. In the first case, without having conducted any technical or environmental assessment, a Malian firm, Tomota, cleared 1400 ha of savannah. The company did not take into account traditional land rights, even though they were formalized in, and then partly secured by, an agro-pastoral plan jointly developed in 2006 by the local communities and the State. Local agro-pastoralists were forced to move their cattle to distant grazing areas: *"Around the village, there are trucks and sunflower fields, our animals are forced to leave or to remain in the boxes, but we have no means to give them fodder"* (an agro-Pastoralist in Monimpébougou, September 2010). Local claims, supported by traditional authorities and elected representatives, have been directly addressed to the government. Negotiations are still ongoing, though a compensation scheme is being discussed. A second case of opposition concerns the PSM project, initiated in 2002 by the Schaffer Global Group in collaboration with the Malian government, which will develop 20 000 hectares of sugar cane. In the concerned area, prior to the land acquisition, villagers were cropping rain-fed cereals. Some of them expressed their discontent and presented themselves to the village leaders and local representatives of government to defend their cause. They also requested the help of the *Office du Niger* representative, without any success, the latter having few details about the PSM project at all. In 2008, as municipal elections approached, opposition to the PSM became an argument used by the candidates. But, due to economic and political lobbies, the elected mayor was the one candidate in favor of the project.

In 2009, the Shaffer Group received funds from the African Development Bank (AfDB). But when AfDB was informed of local claims (relayed by the media), following its own procedures, it imposed a public consultation and compensation packages (for example, rice plot allocations). In this case, the intervention of a supra national authority was necessary to enforce the legislation and to take into account the farmers' voices, formerly hushed by political and economic interests. The defined compensation scheme is debatable, but it exists. While affected people will lose their land, they will be invited to sign an agreement with the company for cropping sugar cane on a small plot (in the irrigated zone), as compensation for their lost rain-fed plots. By now, the project has only developed 140 ha. Many uncertainties about the future of these farmers persist: the content of the farming contracts, absence of agricultural alternatives to rain-fed cereal crops, and uncertainty of employment opportunities in the sugar plantations. But the project is declared to be a government priority, thus making oppositions difficult to emerge.

A third case of opposition concerns a Malian entrepreneur. In 2010, a Malian investor, being one of the largest businessmen in Mali, obtained 7400 ha to grow wheat. He secured land access adjacent to the PSM sugar cane project. Work began without local people being informed. The farmers, already affected by the PSM, were strongly opposed to this new investment encroaching again upon their crop land and pastures. Demonstrations took place on site, which were relayed by the local press (Malijet, November 2010). The *Office du Niger* representatives tried, without any success, to negotiate with the claimers. The investor, thanks to his various political connections, used the police to remove people with the approval of state officials. The local press denounced the violence of the repression. Nevertheless, the Malian businessman, facing strong social pressure and being afraid of getting a bad reputation, gave 1000 hectares to the claimers. Part of the village is now employed by the investor, who has developed 500 ha and now cultivates 240 ha. The project is displayed by the *Office du Niger* as a best-selling agribusiness. In this case, once again, claims were successful thanks to the media.

In the last case, that of Malibya, a Libyan company installed infrastructure without considering the existing villages and drovers' paths (Brondeau, 2011). Thanks to engineering studies and interventions by the *Office du Niger*, the construction plans changed, such that a planned canal required the removal of only 4 villages instead of 16. However, dwellings and gardens near the canal were destroyed without any compensation. In Kolongo village, the new canal divides the village into two parts, and no bridge was constructed. As a result, the people living on the other bank must now walk four to six km to access to basic infrastructures (school, market, community hall, health centre). Local groups began to stand up for their rights, organized themselves at local level and got the support of local and regional government representatives. Eventually, their claim was taken in account, and an ESIA was carried out. After several months of negotiation, individuals were either compensated or resettled by the Government. There was no additional cost for the promoter of the project, as the convention between Mali and Libya (renegotiated when the problems began occurring with local farmers), states that this kind of issue is to be settled by the Malian partner, with Malibya arguing that it was already investing in public infrastructure for Mali and the state should handle compensation. Two years after the infrastructural work started, the government only paid 6% of the compensation schemes defined by the ESIA, and only for houses and gardens. Nothing has been done to compensate the loss of the farmers' fields and the cattle breeders' pastures.

Farmers' local and national trade unions and organizations are beginning to mobilize local, national and international opinions. Thanks to the local campaigns and demonstrations, slight but important changes appeared: the realization of ESIAs, negotiations of compensation schemes, and more equitable land distributions. But compensation schemes are still considered as insufficient by some farmers and union representatives and, as exemplified in the Malibya case, not really enforced. In addition, ESIAs and negotiations are still not implemented in a systematic way, and local land rights and interests are far from being taking in account and recognized. This low impact is mainly explained by political lobbies and also by the poor echo among media, the poor coordination between the various local claims, and the divergent points of view at local level. Some local groups and elected representatives indeed support large-scale land projects with the hope of getting jobs and financial resources at the commune level (for example, the Malibya project states that it will develop 10 000 jobs, and Sosumar 4 700 jobs).

Conclusion

The Malian State has played a key role in promoting domestic and foreign investment in the *Office du Niger* (ON) area. It sees private and foreign investors as the new solution to develop Malian agriculture and, as such, gives less support to family farming, even if smallholders have until now been the only producers of food crops.

Moreover, the State has not added an effective regulatory framework to its incentive investment policy. Formal regulations exist, but are not enforced or are severely constrained by political stakes and tensions among State services. As a result, no investment selection is carried out. Numerous investors have not yet gone further than an application to obtain a land lease and very few, even among the biggest operators, have already started cropping. The question of the capacity of these supposedly efficient entrepreneurs to improve local farming systems still remains. In the mean time, family farmers actively valorize the private investors' land though subleasing plots or innovating upon previous agricultural methods, such as for example developing "low cost" irrigation schemes. The absence of effective formal regulations induces the eviction of local people and risks to create numerous conflicts, of which four were outlined in this chapter.

The main pressure to make the regulations effective seems to come from the local communities themselves. As a result of their protests and claims, and with the support of unions and local representatives, they manage to make the central government act. Even if progress is still modest, in many cases this led to the realization of at least small compensation schemes offered to the affected local groups, and the enforcement of (theorically compulsory) environmental assessments. Much progress is yet to be made in order to really inform and involve local populations in the land management of the ON area. Real advancements and debates seem only possible if countervailing powers are organized. But building a strong lobby is difficult in an area where local interests are quite diverging among rain-fed farmers, irrigated farmers, herders, citizens, elected representatives, and local state authorities. Building a strong lobby is also difficult in a context where the representatives of state authority (central, regional and local government) supported domestic and foreign investments for diverse economic and political reasons, and have hijacked and re-centralized the management of the ON area.

Despite the success of family farming in implementing new techniques and crops and in supplying the domestic cereals markets, the Malian government focuses its development policy on large farms, hoping that they will quickly develop infrastructure and increase production. But, for the moment, few private companies are actually meeting these objectives. The few hectares allotted to big private companies and cultivated are already being cropped by family farmers. Family farmers sometimes operate as subcontractors (as in the Chinese project) or as future landowners (such as the MCA project, which seeks to develop family farming).

But only a few development projects funded by international donors promote family-based agriculture and offer them alternative to irrigable land access which displacement is involved.

Despite the win-win scenario promoted by the government, agricultural development policies do not ensure any complementarities between agribusinesses and family farmers. The Malian government has not enacted adequate laws to ensure real protection of the environment and populations at risk with agribusiness investments. Conflicts already occurred between investors and local inhabitants on several occasions. Their number will likely increase, with the construction of new irrigation systems and the unequal distribution of water, privileging investors, during the dry season. Moreover, in the short and medium term, conflicts related to water allocation might also appear. Even if violent strikes led to some financial compensation for confiscated land, local people are still not involved in the design and planning of irrigation schemes. Civil society remains poorly organized and represented in the debate on land management, partly because its different components do not share the same interests.

The stake is to undertake real negotiation about land and water issues (two aspects that are considered separately today) with all stakeholders involved: investors, donors, government officials, rainfed and irrigated local farmers, stock breeders, but also local people representatives, the rural communities: the latter are indeed in charge of land tenure everywhere in the country, except in the ON area.

Bibliography

Adamczewski, A., Jamin, J.Y., Tonneau, J.P. 2011. Investisseurs versus paysans locaux: vers quelle agriculture irriguée au Mali?: L'exemple du secteur sucrier. Transcontinentales (10–11) (article n°5): 10 p. [20111118]. http://transcontinentales.revues.org/1113

Bélières, J.F., Coulibaly, Y., Keita, A., Sanogo, M. Caractérisation des exploitations agricoles de la zone de l'Office du Niger en 2000. Ségou: URDOC/ON Nyeta Conseils, 2003.

Bélières, J.F., Hilhorst, T., Kébé, D., Keïta, M.S., Keïta, S., Sanogo, O. Irrigation et pauvreté: le cas de l'Office du Niger au Mali. Cah Agric 20: 144–9. doi: 10.1684/agr.2011.0473, 2011.

Bonneval, P., Kuper, P., Tonneau, J.P. *L'Office du Niger, grenier à riz du Mali: succès économique, transitions culturelles et politiques de développement,* Cirad/Karthala, Montpellier-Paris, 2002.

Brondeau, F. L'agrobusiness à l'assaut des terres irriguées de l'Office du Niger (Mali). Cah Agric 20: 136–43. doi: 10.1684/agr.2011.0472, 2011.

Burnod, P., Gautier, D., Gazull, L. Les agrocarburants au Mali: Nouveau Produit, vieilles recette ? Une analyse de l'émergence et des enjeux du système d'innovation « Agrocarburant ». Montpellier: ISDA, 2010. http://hal.archives-ouvertes.fr/hal-00533380/

Cotula, L., Vermeulen, S., Leonard, R., Keeley, J. Land grab or development opportunity? Agricultural investment and international land deals in Africa. London/Rome: IIED, FAO, IFAD, 2009.
Cotula, L. (ed). Land and water rights in the Sahel. Tenure challenges of improving access to water for agriculture. Issue Paper 139, IIED, 2006.
Coulibaly, Y.M., Bélières, J.F. et Koné, Y. Les exploitations agricoles familiales du périmètre irrigué de l'Office du Niger au Mali: évolutions et perspectives. Cah Agric 15(6): 562–9, 2006.
De Janvry, A., Gordillo, G., Platteau, J.P., Sadoulet, E. (eds). Access to Land, Rural Poverty and Public Actions. Oxford: Clarenton Press, 2001.
Diallo, A., Mushinzimana, G., Wehrmann, A., Üllenberg, A. Foreign Direct Land Investment in Mali, Work of Division 45—Agriculture, fisheries and food, Eschborn: GTZ, 2010.
HYDROPACTE, Etude de formulation des besoins de financement des actions du Schéma Directeur de Développement de la zone ON-SDDZON, 2010.
Jamin, J.Y., Doucet, M.J. La question foncière dans les périmètres irrigués de l'Office du Niger. Les cahiers de la recherche développement 38: 65–82, 1994.
Office du Niger. Schéma directeur de développement de la zone office du Niger, 2008.
Samaké, A., Bélières, J.F., Bosc, P.M. et Sanogo, O. Les implications structurelles de la libéralisation sur l'agriculture et le développement rural au Mali. Première phase du programme RuralStruc. Bamako: CEPIA / Banque Mondiale & Coopération française, 2007.
SEDIZON. Situation des attributions de terres en bail dans la zone Office du Niger, 2010.
Toulmin, C., Quan, J. (eds). Evolving Land Rights, Policy and Tenure in Africa. London: DFID/IIED/NRI, 2000.
Vermeulen, S., Cotula, L. Over the heads of local people: consultation, consent and recompense in large-scale land deals for biofuels projects in Africa. Journal of Peasant Studies, 37(3), 2010.
Von Braun, J., Meinzen-Dick, R. '"Land Grabbing" by Foreign Investors in Developing Countries: Risks and Opportunities'. IFPRI Policy Brief 13, April 2009. Washington, DC: IFPRI, 2009.
World Bank. Rising global interest in farmland: can it yield sustainable and equitable benefits? Washington, DC: World Bank., 2010.

CONFLICT BETWEEN INDUSTRIAL AND ARTISANAL MINING IN THE DEMOCRATIC REPUBLIC OF CONGO (DRC): CASE STUDIES FROM KATANGA, ITURI AND KIVU

Ruben de Koning

Introduction

The mining sector in the Democratic Republic of Congo (DRC) is widely regarded as the key engine for post-conflict reconstruction. To attract foreign investment, the government in 2002 enacted a new mining code that makes it easier for foreign companies to obtain industrial mining titles. Within a few years exploration concessions covered about a third of the country. Meanwhile, exploitation rights to the most important proven deposits were converted to new joint-ventures between foreign investors and Congolese state mining companies. The rapid attribution of mining titles has, however, not lead to a resumption of industrial mining on the scale the central government and its foreign donors had hoped for. Apart from a few copper and cobalt mines in the southern Katanga province, mineral production in the rest of the country, but also in Katanga, remains largely artisanal. Artisanal mining employs up to two million people across the country and largely takes place on concessions where industrial mining is supposed happen (Wold Bank 2009). In many of these artisanal mining areas and particularly in the eastern DRC state functions have almost completely eroded during two consecutive civil wars. Artisanal miners often work in dangerous conditions and are forced to pay numerous illegal taxes or to work for the military and rebel forces that control mines. At the same time, the local power complexes that emerged around artisanal mining operations have withheld large scale industrial investment, thereby preventing displacement of artisanal miners from concessions.

Despite the negative investment climate, some foreign mining companies try to start exploration and exploitation activities in their newly acquired concessions in the eastern part of the country. Potential profits evidently outweigh security and reputational risks. Some of these risks have reduced in recent years because of the gradual integration or defeat of rebel forces. But as companies move on the ground they are often confronted with protest and sabotage by local mining communities who fear resettlement.

This chapter seeks to provide better understanding of the different ways in which mining companies gain or attempt to gain access to their concessions in the eastern and southern parts of the DRC, with particular attention to how they deal with artisanal mining communities and the role that local governments can play in accommodating multiple interest. The chapter argues that the current regulatory framework in the DRC fails to provide guidance to solving problems arising from overlapping claims to mineral resources—this despite the mediation efforts of local governments and the increasing pressure on and occasional goodwill of companies to accommodate the interests of artisanal mining communities on their concessions. Case studies are based on analysis of government documents and news articles, as well as personal interviews conducted between January and March 2010 with stakeholders in government, industry and civil society.

The chapter is structured in three parts. The first part presents the new mining regime that the 2002 Mining Code introduced, e.g. its provisions, the level of implementation and the disparate effect on providing legal security to industrial and artisanal miners. The second part provides three case studies introducing three foreign companies operating in three different areas in the DRC: Group Forrest International (GFI) in the copper and cobalt sector of the southern Katanga province; AngloGold Ashanti's gold exploration activities in Ituri district in Orientale province; Kivu Resources in the North Kivu province. The third part of the paper clarifies the need for regulatory reform and identifies ways to better accommodate industrial and artisanal interests in order to reduce potential conflict.

A New Mining Regime in DRC

Home to significant share of the world's reserves of copper, cobalt, gold and a range of other precious metals, the Congolese mining sector has from colonial days onwards formed the backbone of the national economy. Since president Mobutu nationalised the economy in then Zaire, the Congolese mining sector has been run almost exclusively by state owned enterprises, also known as parastatals. Dropping commodity prices and mismanagement of these parastatals in the beginning of the 1980s set in motion a long period of economic decline and hardship for millions of people. In response, in 1982 the Mobutu government deregulated the mining sector, allowing minerals to be held transported and sold by private persons. This had generated a first wave of informal artisanal mining and mineral trading activity particularly in eastern and southern parts of the country (De Koning 2009, 2). During the 1980s, Mobutu's advice to the population to cope with economic difficulty was 'debrouillez vous' ('fend for yourself'), encouraging people to ignore the law in order to make ends meet (Bayart, Ellis and Hibou 1999). In the final years of Mobutu's rule in the mid 1990s, the regime further privatised the sector through allowing the first joint venture contracts to be signed between parastatals and foreign mining companies (NIZA/IPIS 2006, 31). After Mobutu was removed from power in 1997 privatisation took up speed in order to generate revenues for the new regime in power under president Kabila in the form of royalty payments.

On-going fighting in the eastern Kivu and Orientale provinces from 1997 onwards further entrenched artisanal mining in the local economy. As most rural infrastructure was destroyed, artisanal mining of gold, tin and tantalum ore in many places became the only viable livelihood option for unemployed youths, creating new multi-ethnic communities in often inhospitable and previously scarcely populated environments devoid of any decent roads, sanitation facilities and other basic services (De Koning 2010). In the southern Katanga and Kasai provinces where industrial production of respectively copper/cobalt and diamonds came to a standstill in 1997, miners laid off by parastatals now massively turned to artisanal mining in the concessions they had previously exploited on an industrial level (NIZA/IPIS 2006). The same happened in Ituri district in the north-east of the country, where industrial gold mining was concentrated.

While privatisation of the Congolese mining sector during the 1990s fits with a wave of similar efforts in Africa associated with World Bank-guided Structural Adjustment Programmes, its trajectory is unique. It came about rather independently from outside pressure and was greatly influenced by the 1997 regime change and ensuing civil war in the east. During this period, both the central government in Kinshasa and rebel governments in the east introduced new contractual agreements for industrial mining and modified or renegotiated existing ones, all this over the heads of an ever increasing number of artisanal diggers, transporters, traders, and their dependents.[1] It wasn't until 2001 that the World Bank stepped

[1] The World Bank estimated in May 2008 that about 90 per cent of the DRC's mineral resource production relies on the artisanal mining sector, which employs between

in to supervise the government's mining policy, leading to the enactment of a new mining law in 2002. The same year the parallel rebel government in the eastern DRC was formally dissolved as part of the global and inclusive peace agreement between the central government and Congolese rebel and militia groups in the east. The new law and its accompanying mining regulations of 2003 provide the legal framework for acquiring rights to explore, exploit, process, and trade minerals in the DRC. The law distinguishes between three categories of exploitation: industrial, semi-industrial or small-scale mining, and artisanal mining—each of which is subject to a different tax regime and permit system (DRC government 2002). Importantly, the law and regulations also regulate the transfer of existing mining rights to joint ventures between private companies and state mining companies. The principal intention of the law was to provide a clear legal framework that would, on the one hand, transform the role of the state from mine operator to regulator, and on the other, attract foreign investments needed to reinvigorate industrial mining.

As intended, private companies have progressively replaced the state's central role as a mine operator following the enactment of the new law. Although the largest share of 30 year valid but renewable exploitation permits—308 out of 471 as of May 2008—is still in the hands of state-owned companies, the 33 most feasible and lucrative titles are subject to a partnership agreement by which exploitation rights are leased by a private company or transferred to a new joint venture between a private company and a state-owned company (World Bank 2008, 41). The majority of the mining rights transferred to private–state joint ventures belonged to the state copper and cobalt producer, Gécamines. Gécamines usually has a 12.5–17.5 % share in joint venture companies that actually exploits the concession. In addition, nearly all exploration permits—4 246 out of 4 353 as of 2007—are in the hands of private enterprises that have no contractual agreement with any of the state-owned enterprises (Ibid., 17).

While a range of foreign companies have entered the Congolese mining sector, investment plans have generally lagged behind. As of March 2008, only 10 of all exploration permits allocated to 642 mining companies had been converted to exploitation permits (*Africa Mining Intelligence* 2008).

500 000 and 2 million people, depending on the season and demand. With each miner having on average four or five dependants, the livelihoods of 2.5–9 million persons, out of a total population of 66 million, depend on artisanal mining (World Bank 2008, 56).

According to a few commentators, some companies have no genuine investment plans but have rather used their mining rights to resell or raise their own share prices (Mazalto 2008). Meanwhile, many foreign mining companies that have entered joint venture operations with state mining companies and foreign investors (60 in total) are not delivering on their investment plans. Their contracts have taken several years to be reviewed and renegotiated, and only a handful has been confirmed to date. In addition to legal insecurity, worldwide economic downturn since late 2008 has slowed down investment. In December 2008 the IMF adjusted its projection of Foreign Direct Investment in the DRC for 2009 from $2.5 billion to $800 million (Miningmx 2008). These investments are concentrated in copper and cobalt mines in the south of Katanga Province.

Since 2002 the national ministry of mines and the central mines cadastre in Kinshasa have prioritised the attribution and transferral of industrial titles, thereby failing to widely implement the provision of artisanal mining in the new mining code. By March 2008, 43 Artisanal Mining Zones (AMZs) were delimitated countrywide, not nearly enough to accommodate a significant proportion of artisanal miners.[2] Few were created afterwards. Widespread delimitation of AMZs is much hampered by the fact that almost all mineral rich lands have been awarded to companies in the form of industrial exploration or exploration concessions, leaving very little space available. The government would simply have to wait until a first exploration period expires before it can reduce the size of the concession in order to open up space for artisanal mining. However, the government rather prolongs the duration of the first period of 4–5 years for exploration concessions. As a result, most artisanal mining still takes place in areas where it is illegal, either within existing concessions or outside concessions where there is no AMZ. Artisanal mining activities in exploration concessions are hardly ever contested by the titleholder or state authorities unless they interfere with drilling activities that usually take place in a restricted area within the concession. Government or private policing of active exploitation concessions is usually much stricter.

[2] In the 2002 Mining Code, artisanal Exploitation is defined as: "Any activity by means of which a person of Congolese nationality carries out extraction and concentration of mineral substances using artisanal tools, methods and processes, within an artisanal exploitation area limited in terms of surface area and depth up to a maximum of thirty meters."

The illegality of artisanal mining does not mean that it is unregulated. State mining services are usually present to register miners, record production and issue transport authorisations to licenced traders. In many sites customary chiefs attribute plots of land to miners that often have come from elsewhere and levy taxes on local production and trade taking place around the mines. Furthermore, artisanal mining is often authorised at sub-national level. Provincial mining authorities legally incorporate artisanal miners' cooperatives, and at times sanction agreements between parastatals and cooperatives that permit the latter's access on concessions, often in return for a share of the production (De Koning 2009, 6). Provincial and territorial authorities have also issued 'unofficial' mining titles that may overlap concessions falling under exploration permits issued by central mining authorities. The new mining law states that mining rights are exclusive, but does not specify any procedures or respective responsibilities of companies and state authorities to deal with title-less users of the land that the mining permit covers.

The inconsistency between central and provincial mining policies and practices could be considered as a factor inhibiting industrial revival of the sector. At the same time, the above mentioned sub-national agreements are an almost logical response to the overdue recovery of industrial mining in many exploitation concessions, especially given the fact that there is little activity in many exploration concessions and the delimitations of artisanal mining zones to accommodate masses of artisanal miners is limited.

Company Case Studies

The stage of mining development in DRC much depends on the past and present security situation. In southern Katanga, the civil war suspended industrial production between 1997 and 2002. Although infrastructure decayed, it was not fully destroyed and industrial copper and cobalt mining resumed in 2002. In the Ituri district (Orientale Province) war subsided in 2004 after French peacekeepers intervened under the flag of the European Union (EU). By the time of writing, no industrial production had taken place but foreign companies were starting to get mining infrastructure underway at designated locations where they had acquired exploitation rights. In the provinces of North Kivu and South Kivu, war has not come to a definite end despite several peace agreements. Most mining companies in the Kivus are yet to transfer their exploration titles into actual mining rights. This is much due to presence of armed groups at mine locations as a result of which companies have not been able to access the terrain to carry out exploration activities.

1. *Forrest in Katanga*

The oldest and largest foreign economic operator in Katanga is the Belgian group, George Forrest International (GFI). Its mother company, *Entreprise Generale Malta Forrest* (EGMF) has been active in the country since 1922. The group is probably the biggest private taxpayer in the country; in 2007, it paid almost $47 million, of which almost $19 million came from its mining operations. And with 15 000 people on the payroll, the company is also the largest private employer in the country (GFI 2008, 1).

Compared to international mining giants like Lundin, Anvil and First Quantum—that are also active in Katanga, GFI is probably the holder of the most important mining portfolio in DRC. During and right after the years of civil war, GFI radically expanded its mining possessions through a number of joint venture agreements with the state mining company, *Gécamines*. After having acquired some smaller mines—including that of Luiswishi—the company in 2004 obtained the rights to one of the most lucrative mining concessions in the country, that of Kamoto. After a merger acquisition with UK registered Nikanor in 2007, the company was estimated to hold 70% of the available copper reserves in Katanga.

The company's favourable position, however, received a blow in 2008 when it was put under pressure by the government to hand over two important concessions (not yet in production) near the Kamoto mine back to *Gécamines*, in order to bring them into a joint-venture with Chinese partners (Marysse and Geenen 2009).[3] The same year, GFI had to sell the larger share of its stake in the Kamoto project to the Swiss-based commodity trader, Glencore, in order to raise capital to continue operations in other active concessions.[4]

Conflict over Luiswishi

At the end of 2009, the company's activities in its concession in Luiswishi received criticism from local human rights organisations (ACIDH 2009, ASADHO 2009). This criticism focuses on alleged company complicity in

---

[3] In exchange the company will either receive 825 million USD compensation, or two new concessions by 2015 (Marysse and Geenen 2009, 393).

[4] But the project itself continues to be operated by GFI subsidiary Katanga Mining.

forceful evictions and demolition of property of 'illegal' artisanal miners on the concession, but also of local populations in the adjacent town of Kawama. To understand these confrontations, we must go back more than a decade.

In 1998 a joint project involving EGMF, *Gécamines* and the American OM Group started treating tailings from Luiswishi open-pit mine and resumed full industrial production in 2000. In 2003 the mine accounted for about half of the country's total cobalt and a quarter of copper production (Coakley 2004, 10.6–10.8). In 2004 a new joint venture was agreed between EGMF and *Gécamines*, thus creating the *Companie Miniere de Sud Katanga* (CMSK) that has exploited the Luiswishi mine to date. Production after 2004 remained stable at about 12 000 tonnes of copper and 4 500 tonnes of cobalt, representing about 10% of world consumption (Yager 2010, 11.8).

Beyond the mine itself, which covers five square kilometres, small numbers of artisanal miners have exploited the perimeters of the concession since 1997 (Kumbwimba 2009). In 2007, CMSK and provincial authorities discussed a strategy to secure the concession against artisanal miners, following concerns about radioactivity. No concrete steps were taken at the time (*Le Potentiel* 2007). The problem of artisanal miners on the concession became more pressing in the beginning of 2009, when about 1 000 miners were displaced from the nearby Ruashi concession, according to a company spokesperson. This happened at the same time that exploitation in Luiswishi was suspended due to fall out of world demand for copper following the economic crisis.

Gécamines' unarmed Industrial Guards, responsible for guarding the concession, did not have the manpower to secure the entire perimeter. Furthermore, the police stationed near the mine let artisanal miners pass after payment, according to an independent journalist in Lubumbashi. By mid-2009 there were about 3 000 artisanal miners working on the concession according to the government's Small-scale Mining Assistance and Training Service (SEASSCAM). The CMSK spokesperson holds that the intensified presence of artisanal miners generated several safety concerns, such those arising from landslides. But artisanal miners allegedly also attacked and wounded 30 CMSK employees. In November 2009 the company asked the provincial Ministry of Interior to find a solution for artisanal mining and protect its properties.

On 23 November the police searched houses in the village of Kawama for minerals. Some villagers objected and subsequently burned a truck, vandalised a bus belonging to CMSK, and barricaded the main road.

According to a local human rights organisation, the provincial Minister of Interior responded by deploying a range of public security forces, including the mining police—set up to intervene in mining related conflicts—but also riot police and some army element to quell the protest. The Minister allegedly also sent a special brigade to demolish the houses of illegal artisanal miners.

The readings of CMSK on one side and human rights advocates on the other, as they concern the details of the demolition operation, are different on two important points. First, according to CMSK there had been no involvement of CMSK personnel or equipment. Human rights advocates on the contrary claim that, in addition to public security forces, the operation involved the *Gécamines*' Industrial Guard, as well as four bulldozer operators of CMSK. Secondly, according to CMSK, only houses situated on the concession, and identified by the customary chief of Kawama, had been demolished. Meanwhile, human rights advocates claim that 221 houses in Kawama belonging to citizens not involved in mining had been demolished. The UN mission in the DRC (MONUC) also undertook investigations. According to a representative almost 600 houses had been demolished in and near Kawama village by the local police, but with the aid of equipment belonging to the CMSK mining company.

Partial Resolution of Conflict

Following artisanal miners' protests in Lubumbashi, the provincial Governor Moise Katumbi on 25 February 2010 promised that he would personally take care that delocalised miners would be compensated (*Katanga News* 2010). Indeed, SAESSCAM had thereafter received the financial means—possibly from CMSK according to a GFI spokesperson—to provide 300 dollars compensation for each dislocated miner. In addition, the governor initiated negotiations between miners and *Gecamines* to resettle dislocated miners in the inactive concession of Kasombo, according to A SAESSCAM representative in Lubumbashi. Whereas 1 600 illegal miners had been compensated by the end of February 2010, families whose houses had allegedly been demolished outside the concession had—by March 2010—not received any compensation, according to human rights activists.

Assessing Forrest's Response in Luiswishi

Intensified law enforcement in Luiswishi must be seen against the backdrop of CMSK's financial difficulties at the end of 2009. The company was also under pressure from the government to continue to make a profit from Luiswishi, as it is the one of the only partnerships that generates fresh cash to *Gécamines* (Lutundula Commission, 2006, 27). If industrial production would hamper, the government could be tempted to use its current contact review process to remove the concession from CMSK and give it out to new investors.

The sense of urgency to find a solution for artisanal miners prompted the company to put pressure on the government to take measures. With the law being unclear of how to deal with artisanal miners occupying a concession after the concession has been allocated, the government can take any course of action. In this case, it sent a range of security services—including those with no clear mandate—to intervene on mining concessions. Any excessive use of force is not the direct responsibility of the company, but the company could have insisted on minimal force deployment, and initiated resettlement negotiations prior to the demolition of property.

Going beyond the *ad-hoc* response in the Luiswishi case, neither CMSK nor GFI as a whole has any specific policy of resettlement or engagement with artisanal miners. The company does run an extensive community development programme—i.e. supporting the revival of agriculture region, providing electricity and drinking water in Kawama, and building educational and health facilities—but it is unclear if such support has targeted artisanal miners. In its summary of corporate responsibilities on the GFI website the company refers to Global Compact and the ILO conventions, particularly on the issues of corruption and child labour (GFI 2009). There is no reference to International Finance Corporation (IFC) performance standards that, amongst other things, deal with resettlement, or the Voluntary Principles on Security and Human Rights that concern interactions between extractive industries and public and private security forces.

2. *AngloGold Ashanti in Ituri District*

In the gold rich district of Ituri, AngloGold Ashanti Kilo (AGK) explores industrial gold production. AGK is a joint venture between the South African AngloGold Ashanti and the state mining company *Office national des mines d'or de Kilo-Moto* (OKIMO). AGK holds Ituri's key mining concession, which contains approximately 71 tonnes of gold worth $2.3 billion (AngloGold 2009, 7). The contract has since 2007 been under review and was only confirmed in March 2010. By April 2010 the company had not yet started mine construction.

AGK's history in Ituri has been tainted by allegations of supporting the *Front des Nationalistes Integrationnistes* (FNI) militia group. Between

2003–5 the FNI was the dominant force around the town of Mongbwalu where AGK is based. According to UN experts in 2005, company representatives admit to have provided housing to the then FNI leader, Floribert Njabu, treated some of its soldiers at the AGK clinic, and paid taxes and fees to the FNI at the airport (United Nations 2005, 33). A year later UN experts concluded that the violations were isolated cases and did not reflect the company's overall corporate strategy (United Nations 2006, 22). After the neutralisation of most militia in 2006, community development and artisanal mining are the main post-war 'soft security' challenges for AGK in Ituri.

AngloGold and Community Development

With regard to community development, the company encountered problems late 2005 when it tried establishing an elected stakeholder forum. This forum was not supposed to include (former) combatants and political activists. However, as a result of self-nomination of individuals involved in 'questionable activities' the mayor of Mongbwalu suspended the forum (Kapelus 2006).

The forum was reinstated in 2006 with the main task to identify community development projects, keep the community up to date with developments, and offer local people the opportunity to raise concerns. Local civil society groups have since questioned the independence of the forum from AGK. To address this concern additional information sharing meetings have been scheduled with wider civil society presence. Still it has been argued that local people are not fully informed about mine development and potential consequences of industrial mining for local livelihoods (Barnett 2010).

An AGK spokesperson maintains that as long as there was no approval of the final renegotiated contract with OKIMO, the company could not share any definite plans about exploration sites that are to be exploited and areas that are likely to be sealed off. The company also failed to share preliminary options for resettlement, as reflected in an external project review. The company states that it is committed to avoiding resettlement where possible and relocating people in accordance with IFC performance standards. The delays in communicating mine development plans, however, generates anxiety among the populations living near exploration sites, according to researchers that assessed the situation in Mongbwalu in May 2009.

To take away some of this anxiety, AGK has initiated several development projects. It built a school, improved the hospital, provided money for medicine, salaries for medical staff and teachers, and undertook extensive road development projects with MONUC. To further address demand for jobs, AGK also intended to undertake a $1 million project to treat and extract gold from tailings—the rejected material from previous mining and screening operations—that could employ 300 people. Unfortunately, this project has been cancelled because it was not economically viable. The cancellation of the tailings project is likely to disappoint miners who are eager to find formal employment with the company, and now have to await job creation at future industrial sites.

AngloGold and Resettlement of Artisanal Miners

Besides limited employment creation, the company's role in closing artisanal mining opportunities is a source of suspicion among Mongbwalu's estimated 25,000 miners.[5] About 2 000 miners lost their work when in December 2007 Congolese authorities ordered the closure of the Adidi mine, ostensibly for health and safety reasons.[6] Because AGK was likely to meet resistance if it would try to close the mine itself, the company had for several months lobbied the mayor and city government to close the mine. There appeared to be little political will due to commercial involvement of local politicians in artisanal mining activities. The Governor of Orientale province was called in to exercise the necessary authority to close the mine. Through radiobroadcasts, direct engagement with managers of artisanal production, and promises to artisanal miners to offer alternative employment opportunities, AGK dissuaded miners to resist the Governor's decision. After the closure, AGK paid the national police to guard the entrance of the mine until it was sealed. To this end a written protocol was agreed between AGK and the police, following the Voluntary Principles on Security and Human Rights to which the company signed up in 2007. Dislocated miners seem to have moved to other artisanal mines, including equally dangerous ones such as Makala and Senzere. There are no plans under way to close these mines as well.

The reason for AGK to lobby for the closure of the mine, that is for safety reasons, can be disputed. There is a good possibility that future mine development will take place in or in the vicinity of the old Adidi mine.

[5] There are about 50,000 and 60,000 artisanal miners in concession 40, with perhaps half of this number active around Mongbwalu (Fahey 2008, 361).

[6] The total number of people going out of work is disputed, ranging from 1,500 (Hayes and Ziulkowski 2009, 20) to 5,000, when including transporters, traders, and suppliers (Fahey 2008, 363).

According to the company itself most advanced drillings takes place at Mongbwalu and Adidi (AngloGold 2010). Furthermore, an independent researcher found that Adidi mine remained accessible to AGK workers for more than a month, contrasting AGK's claims that it sealed the mine four days after miners were shut out (Fahey 2008, 378). This could indicate the company is undertaking exploration activities in Adidi, which could be seen as the actual reason for calling upon authorities to shut down the mine.

Again, there is no procedure spelled out in the Congolese Mining Code of how to handle artisanal miners on concessions. In this case, resettlement plans were well communicated, did not involve the use of force and therefore did not lead to any mass protest, as some had expected it would.

Assessing AngloGold in Mongbwalu

With regard to community relations, living up to all expectations will be practically impossible for AngloGold in Ituri. Transparency is likely to be more important. For several years, local communities have been in a waiting position as a result of the pending contract with OKIMO. Despite the fact that the company has tried to built good relations, it did not share the most critical information about future mine development and consequences for resettlement. Now that its contract has been approved the company must quickly present and discuss its plans and overcome points of disagreement. It is recommended here that this takes place prior to carrying out its social and environmental impact assessment, which is a legal obligation before starting mine construction.

When it comes to resettlement and compensation, the case shows that the Adidi experience may not be the best example to follow. Although the closure had been non-violent, AGK could be accused of not living up to promises of creating employment, particularly now the tailings project is cancelled, and of hiding behind the government to reassert control over its concession. Resentment over these issues risks being expressed more vehemently in case of potential future closures of mines where displaced miners have resumed their activities.

3. *Kivu Resources in North Kivu*

The provinces of North and South Kivu hold important deposits of cassiterite (tin ore), coltan and wolfram, as well as gold. Industrial mining was never the dominant mode of production of these metals. The civil war halted all industrial activity due to inaccessibility, pillaging and withdrawal of foreign investment. This is the situation to date; some of the private companies that have secured exploration rights have plans to start (semi) industrial mining processes, pending a reliable source of electricity and improvement of the security situation (Garret 2008).

Kivu Resources is registered in Mauritius and owned largely by South-African and British shareholders. Its 100% subsidiary, Mining and Processing Congo (MPC) holds a licence to purchase minerals from artisanal miners, as well as exploration rights over the country's main cassiterite mine in Bisie, North Kivu. In the course of 2010, it shifted its strategy in Bisie from mineral trading towards mineral exploration.

Competition over Qwnership of the Bisie

MPC was awarded a research permit covering the Bisie mine in September 2006. In December of the same year the company entered into an informal agreement with traditional chiefs. The agreement committed the company to the provision of services (including housing, dispensaries, schools, and some student fees) to their local communities, as well as revenues to the local government per unit of purchased minerals (Tegera and Johnson 2007, 22). As such the agreement was meant to generate local goodwill necessary to access the cassiterite market.

The company's ability to buy from Bisie has been undermined from the beginning by a rival company, *Groupe Minier Bangandula* (GMB), which was established by Congolese businessmen, and 50% owned by Alexis Makabuza, a former member of parliament. In 2005 GMB entered into several lease agreements with SAKIMA, the state mining company. At the time GMB was under the impression that one of these included Bisie. Provincial administrators recognised the lease agreements. However, the agreements had bypassed the Ministry of Mines in Kinshasa. On top of this, SAKIMA's contracts were to be revoked as an outcome of the 2007 mining contract review (*Le Potentiel* 2009).

Although the central government formally recognised the legal title of MPC, GBM continued to act as dominant purchaser of minerals in the period 2005–2008. During this period, the GBM worked with a renegade army unit, the so-called 85th Brigade. Together they levied taxes on artisanal mining operations and trade from the mine (Garrett 2008, 6). Their collaboration had the support of the territorial administrator with whom GBM entered into a formal agreement in August 2006. According to this agreement GBM provided the administration with a guaranteed share of local production and associated revenues, in return for security provision, presumably by the 85th FARDC Brigade.

To strengthen its power base in the mine after MPC was granted formal exploration rights, GBM mobilised miners to form a cooperative, COMIMPA, through which to sell to GMB. This cooperative was installed in Bisie under the supervision of the territorial administrator. While largely representing GBM shareholders, the cooperative also drew support from miners that feared they would loose access to the mine once MPC would start industrial processes in the future. Although having been under physical attack by the 85th Brigade in October 2006, MPC stuck to its plan to build industrial mining units in the area. Meanwhile, MPC did agree to COMIMPA's installation at the mine, since the cooperative also agreed to sell part of its production to MPC (Ibid., 27).

In October 2008 MPC called *force majeur* on its exploration operations as a result of the deplorable local security situation, putting $28 million investments on hold (*Metal Bulletin* 2008). It also stopped mineral purchases from Bisie according to a company representative. At the time of writing this chapter, the company saw no opportunity to lift the *force majeur* status of the project because the security situation has remained largely the same despite the mine changing hands. According a senior manager of the company the regular army brigade which replaced the renegade 85th brigade is equally engaged in illegal taxation and mining activities.

Paving the Way for Industrial Development

Despite many difficulties the MPC has not abandoned the idea to develop the mine in the future. In order to reduce the risk of local resistance to future exploration activities, the company entered into discussions with cooperatives, traditional authorities, mining authorities, and other administrators to find a way to develop the mine in the future. In February 2010, MPC, three cooperatives and a body representing traditional authorities signed a protocol agreement in Goma, under the supervision of mining authorities.

The agreement, amongst other things, indicates that MPC does not interfere with artisanal mining as long as it does not hinder exploration activities, and that the company will assist in transferring miners to a legal Artisanal Mining Zone (No 5261), that was delimitated just south of Bisie. With regard to current trading activities the agreement indicates that cooperatives are charged with bringing minerals to trading points outside the concession and that traders are not authorised to carry out their activities at the mining site.

Whether the agreement will improve the security situation—allowing MPC to enter the terrain—is very uncertain. According to a representative of MPC, the Minister of Mines is committed to putting pressure on the Defence Minister to remove all military from the mine upon the signing of the agreement. How the agreement could provide an incentive to do so is however unclear.

Assessing Kivu Resources in Bisie

Kivu Resources has been confronted with persistent military infiltration in mining activities in areas under government control. The DRC government does not provide clear guidance on whether and how to operate in such areas. Meanwhile advocacy groups demand companies to ensure their activities do not contribute to the conflict in any possible way. The mine of Bisie takes centre stage in on-going discussions, because of its economic importance and the fact that it fuels conflict despite being under control of government forces.

The inability to guarantee the security of personnel motivated MPC to put investments on hold. Reputation damage may have played a role in the decision to stop mineral purchases from Bisie. The attack on company personnel was a demonstration of soldiers' commitment to protecting the interest of the rival company. But it may also have been an attempt to prevent any industrial processes, which go against the interests of artisanal miners. Under these circumstances it seems logical for the company to first take away the most immediate perceived threat of interfering in commercial activities, by stopping purchasing. The next step is to negotiate its entry for more long-term exploration and exploitation activities once the area is demilitarized.

Because the company has not entered into a marketing or protection agreement with the controlling military, UN experts have never typified MPC as one of the companies that have taken advantage of the militarization of the Bisie mine. Instead, the government, the UN and donors consider the company to be a credible partner in their efforts to regularise mineral production and trade in the area. Whether the company is able to live up to its promises made in the agreement with mining cooperatives will only become clear in the future, but the intention to accommodate multiple interests prior to actual engagement deserves recognition.

Conclusion

Mining companies that do business in the DRC are the first to realise that the formal rules and institutions that are supposed to govern their operations insufficiently guarantee actual access to properties. There is a clear dualism between central mining authorities that provide formal licences to industrial operators, and local state authorities that tend to defend vested interests (including its own) that are tied to artisanal mining operations. The risk of violence hides in the fact that security actors are mobilised or act independently in defence of one or the other claimant. In the North Kivu case, militia forces opposed the industrial investor. In Katanga, state security forces acted on its behalf.

Yet, case studies also show that conflicts between industrial and artisanal mining can be managed and resolved in a non-violent manner and with positive involvement of state authorities. Above case studies provided examples of how local (mining) authorities facilitate agreement between industrial investors and artisanal mining communities. In Katanga this took the form of unofficial allocation of inactive concessions mines by local government authorities. In Ituri the governor's intervention led to a more spontaneous relocation of artisanal miners. In North Kivu a more formalised resolution was attempted in the form of a protocol agreement involving resettlement in a designated artisanal mining zone.

Whether these solutions are sustainable for both companies and artisanal mining communities is yet another question. Often the problem is merely relocated to another area, which may come under industrial mine development in the near future. And in case legal space *is* provided, it remains to be seen whether artisanal miners accept to resettle, since AMZs are usually delimited in unexplored areas where it is uncertain whether alluvial deposit are sufficient. A further risk is that artisanal miners are used as free prospectors, and will be pushed out by the new legal titleholders once lucrative alluvial deposits are discovered. It should be noted that AMZs are established for one year only and that although licenses are renewable, zones can be closed the moment industrial mining is considered suitable. To date this has not yet happened. However, in Katanga province some private companies that previously traded minerals produced in illegal artisanal mining sites have obtained industrial exploitation concessions covering these sites.

The illegal nature of artisanal mining complicates constructive, peaceful engagement by the foreign mining companies that recently entered the DRC or resumed mining operations after the war. Most companies do not crack down on artisanal activities but tolerate them as long as they do not affect their operations. To defuse tension between artisanal and industrial mining possible companies can take the initiative to delimitate part of their concessions for artisanal mining during a certain period of time, improve artisanal production methods, and enter into a formalised supply agreement with artisanal miners. The Mining Code does not yet allow for such arrangements.

More structurally, AMZs need to be created in lucrative areas in order to offer compensation for potential displacement from industrial concession. The government could withdraw permits from companies that are not able or have no intention to execute their management plans submitted upon the attribution of their title. Alternatively the government may condition the transfer of an exploration right into an exploitation title upon the delimitation of a viable AZM within the concession area. Besides delimiting more AZMs, the durability of AMZ needs to be assured by law so to allow entrepreneurs to invest in artisanal production and potentially scale activities up to semi-industrial production and obtain a small-scale mining permit that is valid for five years and renewable once.

The options outlined above represent a more gradual and cooperative evolution from artisanal to industrial mining than the process envisioned by the government in 2002, which aimed at rapidly replacing one by the other. Officials of different agencies within the mining department are increasingly sensitive to the argument that the artisanal mining sector should be legalised and supported in order to help alleviate poverty and sustain economic growth. The economic crisis that hit at the end of 2009 demonstrated that artisanal mining may be more resilient to price shocks than the industrial sector. This would be the right moment to push for the necessary legal and policy reforms.

Bibliography

African Association for the Defense of Human Rights (ASADHO), "Violation de droit des populations environnant les sites minier" [Violation of populations' rights surrounding mining sites], press release N°006/2009, December 2009.

Action Against Impunity for Human Rights (ACIDH), "La malediction des richesses minieres frappe les habitants du village Kawama" [The curse of mineral richness hits the inhabitants of Kawama village], press release N°ACIDH/04/11/2009, 3 December 2009.

AngloGold Ashanti, "Anglogold Ashanti Limited announces the pricing of its equity offering and mandatory convertible bonds offering and cautionary announcement", September 15, 2010.

——, "DRC country Report 2008", September 30, 2009.

Sara Barnett, "Golden Opportunity or False Hope? AngloGold Ashanti's Proposed Gold Mine in the Democratic Republic of Congo", Catholic Overseas Development Agency, February 2010.

Jean-François Bayart, Stephen Ellis, Béatrice Hibou, "From Kleptocracy to the Felonious State?", in *The Criminalization of the State in Africa*, eds. Jean-François Bayart et al. (Oxford: James Currey, 1999), 1–31.

George J. Coakley, "The Mineral Industry of Congo (Kinshasa)", in *2003 Minerals Yearbook*, United States Geological Survey, 2004.

Dan Fahey, 'Le Fleuve d'Or: the Production and Trade of Gold from Mongbwalu, DRC', in *L'Afrique des Grands Lacs. Annuaire 2007–2008*, ed. Stefaan Marysse et al. (Paris: L'Harmattan, 2008), 357–384.

Democratic Republic of Congo, "Special National Assembly Commission Charged with the Examination of the Validity of Economic and Financial Conventions Concluded during the Wars of 1996–1997 and 1998: The Lutundula Commission Report", National Assembly of the Democratic Republic of Congo, February 26, 2006.

——, "Loi no. 007/2002 du 11 juillet 2002 portant Code minier" [Law no. 007/2002 of 11 July 2002 on the Mining Code], published in *Journal officiel de la Republic democratique du Congo*. Accessed July 15, 2002. http://www.glin.gov/view.action?glinID=151167.

Nicholas Garrett, "*Walikale: Artisanal Cassiterite* Mining and Trade in North Kivu", June 2008. Accessed January 12, 2009. http://www.artisanalmining.org/userfiles/.../CASM_WalikaleBooklet.pdf.

Groupe Forrest International, "Communiqué du Groupe Forrest: Fiscalité 2007 et ITIE" [Communication of Groupe Forrest: Fiscality 2007 and EITI], May 27, 2008.

——, "Corporate Responsibility". Accessed July 4 2009. http://www.forrestgroup.com/uk/chap04/index.html.

Karen Hayes and Aaron Ziulkowski, "Building Bridges not Walls: Promoting Human Rights through Community Based Security in the Democratic Republic of Congo", *Leading Perspectives*, Spring (2009): 19–21.

Paul Kapelus, "AngloGold Ashanti in the Democratic Republic of Congo: Management Challenges and Responses to Operating in a Weak Governance Area" (paper presented at the Fourth International Learning Forum Meeting of the UN Global Compact, Ghana November 22–24, 2006).

Ruben de Koning, *Artisanal mining and post-conflict reconstruction in the Democratic Republic of Congo* (Stockholm: Stockholm International Peace Research Institute, October 2009).

——, Demilitarizing mining areas in the Democratic Republic of the Congo: the case of Northern Katanga province, (Stockholm: Stockholm International Peace Research Institute, January 2010).

Musao J. Kumbwimba, "La Problématique de L'exploitation Minière Artisanale dans la Province du Katanga, Cas du District de Kolwezi" [The Problem of Artisanal Mining exploitation in the Province of Katanga, the Case of Kolwezi]. Accessed June 23, 2009. http://www.memoireonline.com/12/09/3006/m_La-problematique-de-lexploitation-miniere-artisanale-dans-la-province-du-Katanga--cas-du-distr13.html.

Stefaan Marysse and Sara Geenen, "Win-win or Unequal Exchange? The Case of the Sino-Congolese Cooperation Agreements", *The Journal of Modern African Studies* 47 (2009): 371–396.

Marie Mazalto, "La Réforme du Secteur Minier en République Démocratique du Congo: Enjeux de Gouvernance et Perspectives de Reconstruction" [Mining sector reform in the Democratic Republic of Congo: governance stakes and perspectives for reconstruction], *Afrique Contemporaine* 227 (2008): 53–80.

Netherlands Institute for Southern Africa (NIZA) and International Peace Information Service (IPIS), *The State vs. the People: Governance, Mining and the Transitional Regime in the Democratic Republic of Congo* (Amsterdam: NIZA and IPIS, 2006).

Aloys Tegera, and Dominic Johnson, *Rules for Sale: Formal and Informal Cross-border Trade in Eastern DRC* (Goma: Pole Institute, 2007).

United Nations, "Report of the Group of Experts on the Democratic Republic of Congo", S/2005/30, January 25, 2005.

——, "Report of the Group of Experts on the Democratic Republic of Congo", S/2006/53, January 27, 2006.

World Bank, *Democratic Republic of Congo, Growth with Governance in the Mining Sector* (Washington DC: World Bank, 2008).

——, "Democratic Republic of Congo: Country Brief." Accessed June 23, 2009, http://web.worldbank.org/wbsite/external/countries/africaext/congodemocraticextn/0,,menuPK:349476~pagePK:141132~piPK:141107~theSitePK:349466,00.html.

Thomas R. Yager, "The Mineral Industry of Congo (Kinshasa)," in *2008 Minerals Yearbook* (United States Geological Survey, 2010).

"Congo", *Miningmx*, December 18, 2008. Accessed June 24, 2009. http://www.miningmx.com/wts/914296.htm.

"Les Conclusions de la Revitisation des Contrats Miniers", *Le Potentiel*, November 17, 2009. Accessed December 12, 2009. http://fr.allafrica.com/stories/200911170394.html.

"Les Creuseurs de Kawama Dédommagés" [Diggers of Kawama Compensated], *Katanga News*, February 27, 2010. Accessed May 4. http://katanganews.cd/fr/index.php?option=com_content&task=view&id=103&Itemid=31.

"Lubumbashi : Examen de la Situation de Radioactivités du site Luiswishi" [Examination of Radioactivity of the site of Luiswishi], *Le Potentiel*, June 22, 2007.

"Kivu Resources declares force majeure on DRC tin project", *Metal Bulletin*, October 13, 2008. Accessed January 12, 2009. http://www.metalbulletin.com/Article/2028615/NonFerrous/Kivu-Resources-declares-force-majeure-on-DRC-tin-project-.html.

"Vers une Revision du Code Minier au Congo" [Towards a Revision of the Mining Code in Congo], *African Mining Intelligence*, March 26, 2008.

SECTION 3

STAKEHOLDER INTERACTIONS AND COMPETING VALUATIONS OF LAND

SHIFTING PATTERNS OF LAND USE AND OWNERSHIP IN BURKINA FASO WITH A CASE-STUDY OF TWO KURUMBA VILLAGES—BOURZANGA AND POBE-MENGAO

Lucjan Buchalik

Introduction

Burkina Faso is currently undergoing a dynamic and distinctive transformation within the framework of land possession and the attitude towards it. Essentially, these changes are observed in the provinces that have largely remained on the outskirts of modernisation. Traditionally, land in these provinces has a defined geographical and ontological status, independent of external influences. However, the decision of the central administration in the capital of Ouagadougou to construct a tarmac road in the area triggered an unprecedented dynamics of mediation of land perceptions between the State and the local Kurumba people.

The present discussion explores these dynamics in the local context of two villages in Kurumba land, Bourzanga and Pobe-Mengao, over a period between 1997 to 2009.[1] These two villages have been selected because their settlement lay-outs have been used as blueprints for (re-)planning other Kurumba villages. Describing the changes in the lay-outs of the two villages, the discussion particularly focuses on how local and outside developments have impacted on the physical and socio-cultural structure of the land. In this context, the physical manifestations of 'tradition' and the State, i.e. traditional buildings and graves versus the tarmac road, can shed some specific light on the local negotiation of 'foreign' perceptions of land that for centuries had been in the custody of traditional authorities. To be able to gain insight into the dimensions of the changes, the case-study is set within the wider socio-cultural and political context of the Voltaic peoples, among who the Kurumba are one.

[1] Kurumba land is a compact area in which the dominant ethnic group is the Kurumba. It covers the northern part of Burkina Faso, the provinces of Bam in the Central-Northern region, Soum in the Sahel region, Yatenga and Loroum in the Northern region.

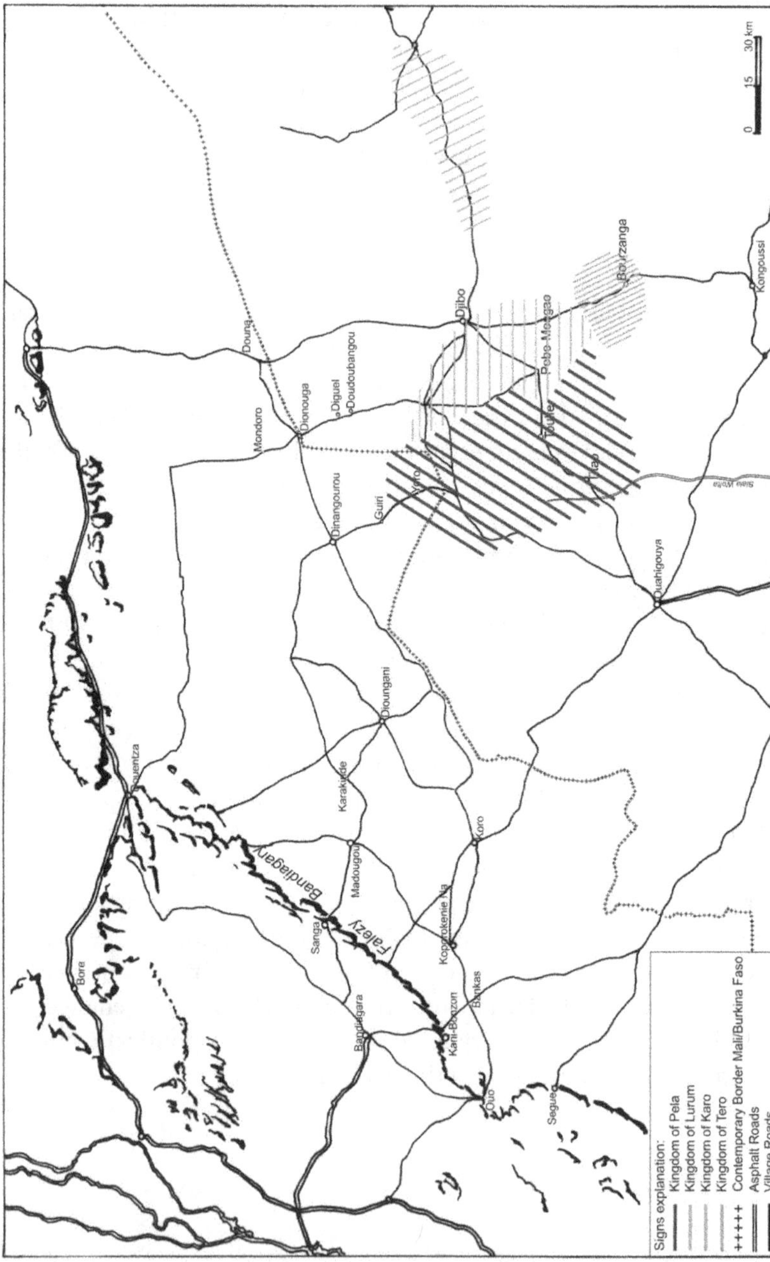

Map. 1 The area inhabited by the Kurumba

The Voltaic Peoples in Socio-Historical Context

The geographical area discussed in this chapter lies within the basin of the Volta River and the Niger, which meanders first to the north, towards the desert, and then sharply turns to the south (also referred to as the Niger Bend), to eventually drain into the Gulf of Guinea. The area is often hit by droughts, which is one of the reasons for its poor economic development. The northern part of the Niger Bend is mainly inhabited by herdsmen, and more towards the south by small farmers, classified as the Voltaic peoples, amongst whom the largest groups are the Mossi, Gurmantche, Bobo, Gurunsi, Dogon, Yarse, Marka and Kurumba. The lack of clear borders between areas inhabited by different peoples results in the occurrence of multi-ethnic villages.

By the end of the twentieth century, the Voltaic peoples numbered 12 million, constituting a majority of the population of Burkina Faso (Komorowski 1994, 67).[2] In the past, the Voltaic peoples formed many states, linked together by loose bonds of interdependence. These states were set up by chiefs, who were surrounded by an aura of divinity. Traces of this elevated status have survived until the beginning of the twenty-first century. Each local community had additionally a ritual headman called 'the master of the land', who was responsible for maintaining good relationships with the land, thus ensuring the prosperity of the people. The role of the master of the land, or the master of the water in the case of fishermen, was performed by the head of the lineage (usually the oldest man) that first occupied the land. Being the master of the land or water involved distributing the rights to the use of land or water (a river or a lake). In other words it was necessary to obtain permission from the appropriate master of the land (or water) to be able to fish in a particular water, cultivate land or build a house. These roles ought not to be perceived in terms of ownership (as owners of the land in the European sense), but in terms of guardianship—as guardians responsible for the land.[3]

According to G.P. Murdock (1959) the political organization of the Voltaic peoples derives from the religious idea of the deification of the earth. The chief is the head of the lineage that traditionally first occupied the

[2] The Voltaic peoples also live in Mali, Niger, Ghana, Togo, Benin and Ivory Coast.

[3] In central Chad, some Hadjarai people also recognize the role of the 'master of the mountains', performed by members of the lineage that first settled in a particular area. After they left the mountains and moved their dwellings to the valleys, this role started to disappear. At present, it is only remembered by the oldest members of the community.

land.[4] In the past, a chief used to maintain an elaborate court in his dwellings; currently, the term 'capital town' refers to the quarter occupied by the lineage of the chief. The religion of the Voltaic peoples has undergone considerable changes over the centuries; however, worship of the earth and ancestor veneration are still very strong today. The role of the master of the land is hereditary. His task is to carry out duties related to the ancestors and the earth. Another task is bringing rain, since fertility rites and beliefs that only a sacrifice made by the master can ensure prosperity and a good harvest are still very common. The master of the land is also responsible for burials of chiefs who carry out priestly duties and are honoured as gods.

Although land was used for collective usufruct, the rights to it were held by the descendants of the first occupants of the land. In fact, this is still the case in older villages, where the former masters of the land, descended from the people who originally occupied the land, are highly respected figures. Inhabitants of the villages set up nowadays, however, have a distinctly different attitude towards land ownership. What can be observed today is a sharp departure from tradition in community life (Murdock 1959, 77–87).

Traditionally, the Western idea of ownership of land is alien to the Voltaic peoples. Farmers are only using the land, whereas the original occupants are controlling it and are responsible for its fertility. Land belongs to the community, and, above all, the family. In order to understand this concept clearly, it is necessary to define the very term 'family'. People who are rightful members of a family are not only the kinsmen living today, but also the ancestors, who cultivated the land in the past and bestowed it upon the family, as well as the generations who will be cultivating the land in the future. Since the land belongs both to the departed and those who are not born yet, in reality it is not possible to contact the owners, hence—the land cannot be sold. However, changes in the economy have affected the attitude towards land ownership, as exemplified in the case-study below.

[4] Various sources also use the term 'king', and call the land he ruled 'a kingdom'. African pre-colonial states are often called kingdoms, despite the fact that the land is owned collectively by the community, that the ruler is not an exclusive owner of the land and he cannot grant the land to his vassals.

People of the Earth versus People of the Rule

The Kurumba live in northern Burkina Faso and the border areas of Mali. Its population was estimated at 196,100 people in 2001 (Lewis 2009). They probably came to the area in the thirteenth or fourteenth century. Since then they have established a number of chieftaincies, some of which still exist today.

If you had asked a Kurumba person in the 1950s, "Does land belong to anyone?", "Can it be divided?", he would have promptly answered that land had no owner, only that the Sawadogo lineage was guarding it. This is because the Sawadogo lineage was the first to settle on the land currently occupied by the Kurumba, according to the myth of origin of the Kurumba. There are many versions of this myth, but the most generally shared one says that the 'house of iron', in which the Kurumba descended from the sky, emerged in the forest, in a small grove of baobabs, not far from today's town of Oure Rimaibe. The area was already occupied by the Sawadogo, who found the house, and opened it with a double-bladed axe. The five people who came out of the 'house of iron' were the chief Sandigsa from the lineage of Konfe and his court. An argument broke out between the Konfe and the Sawadogo, and each side wanted to prove their superiority and dominate the other one. This led to a power struggle, which resulted in one member of the Konfe becoming the chief and referred to as *Ayo*, whilst the eldest of the Sawadogo became the master of the land—*Asendesa*. This division of power created a particular pattern of social organization and a certain form of diarchy. Until today, the Konfe have the role of rulers governing people, and each appointment of the new *Ayo* needs to be validated by the Sawadogo, masters of the land.

In short, *Asendesa* (always the eldest of the Sawadogo) controls the land, and *Ayo* (chosen from among the Konfe) is the chief holding political and religious functions vital to community life. As a result of this organisation, a certain opposition arose between 'the people of the earth' (the Sawadogo) and 'the people of the rule' (the Konfe). Neither side has absolute power, and in order for the Kurumba community to function properly, cooperation between the two lineages is essential. *Ayo*, being the chief, has his household in the centre of the village. This also visually emphasizes the social status of the head of the lineage. On the other hand, the household of *Asendesa*, which is connected with the earth, needs not be located in the centre of the village. In the kingdom of Lurum, it was not until the middle of the twentieth century that *Asendesa* moved to the capital of the kingdom; before that, he used to live in Gargaboulli, a village located over 10 km away. *Asendesa* holds power over the arable and settled land (villages), i.e. the whole territory. However, his power only relates to parcelling out of land and maintaining order. This ownership perception of land has remained the same over the ages.

In the mid-20th century, the earth was equated with a woman. Even today, some of the informants still say that 'earth is a woman', and a woman cannot be 'owned' or 'sold'. Hence, just like a woman can not have an owner, neither can land. The idea that earth is a woman and has a soul comes from a prayer, which *Asendesa* says whilst blessing the land: "the wife of the sky, the earth—take, eat, and give (land); go to your husband who is up above and share this sacrifice with him; they (the sky and the earth) enjoy health and corporal vitality".[5] In other words, the earth is thought to be the wife of the male sky. This union of male and female, the earth and the sky, is there to provide life-giving food. The cultivation of land not only has an economic aspect, but also, and perhaps above all, has a religious dimension. Earth is sacred, earth gives life, and so it needs to be respected. Defiling the earth is the greatest crime among the Kurumba.

Controlling and Serving the Land

Since arable land is the basis of a farmer's livelihood, the distribution of land is extremely important. Until the mid-20th century, *Asendesa* and some older members of the community would know the borders of the area belonging to each village. They passed this knowledge onto the chosen members of the next generation. As a result a select group that belonged to the inner circle of the Asendesa had access to this information.[6]

One of *Asendesa's* tasks is to protect the rights of individual farmers regarding the use of land. Whoever wants to claim a parcel of land which has been cleared from bush and wants to use it for agriculture, needs to ask *Asendesa* for permission. Only the bush which—as far as the oldest members of the community can recall—has never been cultivated before can be used for agriculture by this person. *Ayo* also holds the right to

[5] The full text of the prayer can be found in Schweeger-Hefel and Wilhelm Staude (1970, 309).

[6] At present, *Asendesa* has ceased to be the governing factor in the parcellation process of military grounds, despite taking part in it. His participation is nevertheless a gallant compliment from the government administration towards tradition.

parcel out land for agricultural use; however, he needs to discuss the issue with *Asendesa* beforehand, or at least inform him. This makes *Asendesa* a kind of 'living cadastre'. Therefore, newcomers who want to settle down in the village need to obtain permission from the two headmen—both *Ayo* and *Asendesa*. *Ayo* can dispossess a family of the land they are using, and give it to the newcomers, so that they can settle. *Asendesa* needs to then allocate the dispossessed family a different plot of land. If a plot is left untilled, and someone wants to start cultivating it again, they need to obtain official permission from *Asendesa* (Schweeger-Hefel and Staude 1970, 310).

The right to a plot of land is acquired through cultivation. Such a plot can be handed over for cultivation to one's successors. The same principle applies to land designated for dwellings. In the mid-20th century, a person who wanted to set up a new household had to ask *Ayo* for permission. *Ayo* could only grant a permission after having discussed it with *Asendesa* and after having obtained his consent. *Asendesa*'s authority concerning these permissions is underscored by a ritual act performed by the head of the family that wanted to set up a new household. The head had to perform a sacrifice to the earth, in the form of a hen or a sheep, before the building work began. After the building had been completed, the host would organise a special celebration to which he invited guests, including all the people who helped construct the buildings. The head of the family was only a representative of the rights for using the land held by the whole family, and was also the person who organized field work.

According to tradition, land could not be sold, but a family could lend someone the right to use their plots. Such an arrangement did not involve fees, lease payments or voluntary gifts. According to the Austrian ethnologists Annemarie Schweeger-Hefel and Wilhelm Staude (1970), this free lease of plots was a logical consequence of the idea that land will never be owned by the cultivator. In effect, the leasing of land became the first step in acquiring land. This evolution contributed to the development of the idea of an individual family, which sought independence from the extended family (which normally made all the decisions when it came to land cultivation). This meant that young married couples could gain independence from the extended family sooner than before. If a family was neglecting their plots, *Asendesa* could take the land from them, but could not allocate it to a different person—he could only hold it for his own use (Schweeger-Hefel and Staude 1970, 234–235, 310).

In sum, the land belonged to the community, but whatever required work in the field was owned by an individual—this applied especially to fruit trees, wells, man-made bodies of water and gardens. As a result, some wells and bodies of water were accessible for all the members of the community, and some were privately owned. Schweeger-Hefel and Staude (1970, 235) noted that in 1961 in Pobe-Mengao there were 25 private water intakes; by 1965 the number had grown to 35–40. This was the result of an increase in the number of privately owned gardens, in which the owners grew plants that required greater amounts of water. These days, since wells are drilled with money from foreign and domestic sponsors, they are widely accessible. In fact, nowadays, only wells that are situated within a private garden are owned by the gardener.

There were also exceptions from the traditional idea of the 'collective ownership' of land. Schweeger-Hefel and Wilhelm Staude (1970, 310–311) indicate that a man could acquire private ownership of land if—with *Asendesa's* consent—he cleared a hitherto uncultivated part of the bush. A father could give the private plot thus created to his sons. The harvest of the field, and also the money from selling it, were private property. These private plots could only be cultivated and looked after in addition to work in the family fields. Private plots did not fall under the decision-making power of *Asendesa*, and he could not dispossess a family of such fields, unlike the fields owned collectively, as described above. In fact, land that was not subject to dispossession must have been perceived as the property of the person who cultivated it. Fathers who wanted their young 10–12-year-old sons to understand the notions of responsibility and ownership would give them a small plot of land for cultivation.[7]

Being the descendent of the original occupants of the land and carrying out the responsibilities of *Asendesa* did not only involve decision-making in matters relating to land. Above all, *Asendesa's* responsibilities concerned the land, and thus inevitably concerned the people who inhabited and cultivated it. By making offerings to the earth, masters of the land ensured its fertility. They were also responsible for bringing rain, if no rain had fallen for a long time.

---

[7] These traditional views and principles are becoming blurred due to political relationships between Kurumba and Peul. The whole land around Pobe-Mengao was conquered by the Fulbe in the course of wars that were fought in the past. Until now, the Fulbe consider themselves to be the rightful owners of the land. The Kurumba people have to—at least formally—rent the land from them, although they do not make any lease payments or give presents. The Fulbe people can theoretically demand the land back, although they have never done that. They are rich and own a lot of land, so, if there is a need, they can start cultivating a plot of land that is currently untilled (Schweeger-Hefel and Staude 1970, 310–311).

Tradition at the Time of Great Changes

The mid-20th century brought significant changes in the community practices of land ownership. A farmer, previously considered to be the user of the land, now became its owner. The changes were accelerated by the introduction of the monetary economy, e.g. through taxation. Nevertheless, the new pattern of ownership was still giving priority to the inheritance of land within the family of the owner. A number of new, transitory forms of regulating ownership also emerged; for example, the original owner, wanting to keep his responsibility over the land, reserved a right to buy the land back. Also, a man who sold his plot enjoyed a life-long right to redeem the land, provided he returned the money he had received. This arrangement, however, was losing its significance as time went by. The heir of the seller enjoyed this right for a certain period of time, but if he did not exercise it, the transaction was considered completed. In case of the death of the owner, unless he left special instructions, his properties were passed down to his eldest son, whose responsibility it was to provide for his brothers or provide them with a fair share of the legacy. In case the heir was a child, the younger brother of the late father would act as a guardian.

One last characteristic of the Voltaic people's use of land is the phenomenon of wandering villages. Since time immemorial villages moved, but what was left behind was the remembrance of the original occupants—the autochthons. Most often, the only trace of a relocated village was a slight elevation of land in a characteristically different colour, where earth from the washed-away households tinted the surrounding ground. New residents remembered the old village and its people. In their view, the first inhabitants remained masters of the land (e.g. the Tellem for the Dogon people). In the past, the most common cause for the relocation of a village was the depletion of soil, which forced farmers to look for land further away from the village. When the distance became too big, new quarters were built, or the village was moved altogether. In this respect, a village did not have a permanent territory nor clear-cut borders—it was people that constituted the village, not buildings or the location.[8]

---

[8] The situation was slightly different in the Bandiagara Escarpment occupied by the Dogon. Until the mid-20th century, the area was very dangerous, with local wars and attacks being a common phenomenon. This explains why the Dogon people did not want to leave their fortified villages. It was not until the time of French colonial rule, when the land of the Dogon was pacified and that Dogon people started to cultivate land also in the plateau.

Nowadays, the traditional perception of land ownership creates certain problems in terms of rural development. Traditionally, dwellings formed compact hamlets. The roads that went through them were winding and narrow, which made it impossible for bigger motor vehicles to go through. For instance, in the mid-20th century, when motor vehicles were rare, a road ran through the centre of Toulfe (the capital of the kingdom of Pela), close to the market and the chief's dwellings. The road linked Ouahigouya and Titao with Djibo. Describing Toulfe after the road construction, Schweeger-Hefel and Staude (1970) characterised Toulfe as a vibrant village benefiting from trade and transit, while they wrote about Pobe-Mengao, one of the two villages in this case-study, that it was a small village, only significant for being the chief's residence.

In 1982 the government built a new road from Ouahigouya to Djibo. In order to preserve the old part of Toulfe, the road was laid out 500–600 metres away from the old part of the village, where the chief had his household. As a result, a new centre sprang up, which was separated from the old village by a body of water. The new centre included administration buildings, a school, a village dispensary and a mosque. There were not many residential buildings, and hardly any shops or commercial facilities; those remained in the old part of the village. Traffic was shifted away from the old centre, but the new centre did not provide any transit facilities. A different road layout was proposed in Pobe-Mengao. Here, the road ran 200 metres away from the chief's household and 200 metres away from the market. No new centre sprung up, but the village moved closer to the road, and the area along the road became a centre of trade and services. As a result of the different lay-out of the road, the situation of the present-day village is very different from the one described by the two ethnologists. In the 1990s, it was Pobe-Mengao that seemed to be a wealthy village (by Burkina Faso standards), and Toulfe was, and still is, small and poor.[9]

Benefits coming from building a road were also appreciated by the farmers of Bourzanga. Since 2007, as a consequence of the government's infrastructural development programme, the road running from Djibo through Kongoussi to Ouagadougou was upgraded and widened. Bourzanga became easily accessible for large delivery vehicles, and farmers, who have since been selling more of their agricultural produce. Meanwhile, the number

[9] Author's evaluation takes into consideration, among others, the presence of schools, dispensaries, accommodation facilities, restaurants, bars, telephone services, photovoltaic panels, access to mobile networks.

of lorries passing by (mainly on their way to the goldmine in Inata) has grown tremendously and with it the number of drivers stopping by. The increase in the number of travellers has encouraged the development of trade and services. This can be illustrated from the sudden increase of eating places. In the late 1990s, there was only one bar selling drinks in the village. It was very difficult to find a place where food was served. By the end of the first decade of the twenty-first century, when the road was there, this picture had changed dramatically. Now, there are several places where a traveller can eat and drink, and there is also a petrol station. Along the road, a number of small shops were built, mostly targeting travellers. The nearby market is open once every three days, and shops are open daily.

Changes of Perceptions on Land Partitioning in the 21st Century: Bourzanga and Pobe-Mengao

The two Kurumba villages are a vivid example of practical, technical and social solutions being applied in connection with the construction of the new tarmac road. Thus, an event that at first sight may seem to have only beneficial economic effects on the village, in reality causes a whole spectrum of socio-cultural impacts. More generally over the last 30 years, between 1980 and the first decade of the 21st century, striking changes in the way of handling the village space can be observed, each change impacting differently on existing local social structures. For instance, as was mentioned before, there is a notable difference between the settlement plan applied in Pobe-Mengao in the 1980s and the one implemented in Bourzanga in the years 2007–2009. This difference illustrates how much the approach to land ownership, the division of land, traditional and central authority and, most of all, the organization of local communities has changed.

The serious interference in the village lay-out in the form of the new road construction incited, in both cases, a process of social negotiation. In Pobe, road construction was restricted to the previous lay-out of the old gravel road. Its boundaries were respected for the well-being of the village inhabitants. In Bourzanga, 25 years later, the decision was made to exceed the road boundaries and accept the changes that would come as a result. This difference in tackling the lay-out of a major road signals already the profound change in the approach towards tradition and social organization over time; it also illustrates how the relations between the central authorities in Ouagadougou and the citizens-inhabitants of the villages have become closer.

Bourzanga, a village with a population of about 5,000 people situated on the route from Kongoussi to Djibo, offers a telling present-day example of the subtle mediation of government and local perceptions on land in the context of a road construction. The existing road had already been slightly widened. In the 1980s roads were planned to run through the village joining this road, purportedly making it much easier to travel around the village. In the process, some land had to be parcelled out and some buildings knocked down. First consultations with the residents of Bourzanga began before the road was upgraded in 2007. The building work was commissioned by the government administration and supervised by the local government administration; traditional authority representatives were consulted in the process and involved in the new land division, which was, beyond a doubt, only a form of respect from the government officials towards tradition.

While the first plan of the proposed parcellation was drawn up, the layout of the roads that were going to run through the village was established, and buildings were selected for destruction. Some other buildings were provisionally marked for demolition in case a need for further changes arose. Only the village's oldest quarter, where the chief's residence is—Tong'dene—was not parcelled out. The residents of Bourzanga saw this development as an opportunity to progress and to modernisation. When asked about whether parcellation should also encompass old quarters occupied by the chief and the master of the land, they answered firmly: "There are places where fetishes are; there are sacred places; they must not be touched; they must be left as they are." The traditional quarter occupied by the chief of Bourzanga was not touched, since it was perceived as sacred. The cemetery situated on a nearby hill was not touched either—the road was laid out at some distance from the cemetery.[10]

In the village of Pobe-Mengao, a slightly different problem arose. Next to one of the narrow paths in a quarter called Nenkate, there was a grave

[10] This respect for the old parts of the settlement with a sacred character is not uncommon in Voltaic peoples in general. In the land of the Dogon, similar respect is paid to the houses of the *Hogon* shrines, homes for the elderly *togu-na* and others. On the way from Bandiagara towards the escarpment, several kilometres away from the town, the road makes a sharp turn. A driver might think it pointless and absurd, because there are no major physical obstacles on the way. Yet, there is a cultural obstacle. If the road went straight ahead, it would damage the remains of an old *togu-na*, which the local community would definitely dislike.

of a male Sawadogo—the lineage of masters of the land. When people or donkeys walked along the narrow path, they did not damage the grave. However, when motor traffic came, the cars driving along the path were damaging the laterite blocks of the tomb. By way of protection the grave was surrounded by a wall which became a serious obstacle for cars passing the grave.

In this case the construction of a road did not become an impulse for far-reaching changes. The result of such a solution was a limited interference with the area, exemplified by the old road being covered with an asphalt layer. As a consequence the authority structure was preserved—in Pobe, *Asendesa* still plays a leading role as opposed to Bourzanga where his position has been weakened. Another visible illustration of a tradition-modernity negotiation is the village of Namsiguya. When the aforementioned road from Kongoussi to Djibo was being upgraded, an old cemetery was destroyed in Namsiguya. The only trace left of it—still visible today—is a large heap of pottery.[11] The question is: why was a sacred place not respected in this particular location? The answer seems fairly simple—the memory of the people buried here had faded; they disappeared from the consciousness of the people living today.

In Bourzanga, people whose dwellings will be knocked down are allocated new plots of land by the mayor. These residents now become the owners of plots that are situated on the outer edges of the village, thus contributing to the natural expansion of the village. This is a clear break with traditional village planning, which until 2009 was more compact and dense, the lay-out forming part of the village's defences. After parcellation, the village takes on a different character: it is more spacious, households are dispersed at some distance from one another, and the middle can be reached by a road several metres wide. This leads to a development of a new type of habitation and pattern of settlement—which can be seen in the villages that have already undergone parcellation. Looking at the contemporary development of Ouahigouya (the capital of the kingdom of Yatenga of the Mossi people), one can easily notice a special area occupied by the palaces of former rulers and the present ruler *Naaba* Kiiba, and in some distance, the new residential and commercial quarters. This pattern of settlement, i.e. leaving the old quarter to the ruler and building new residential quarters nearby is also pursued in Bourzanga.

---

[11] Corpses were buried in clay pots.

When asked, farmers from Bourzanga emphatically stated that parcellation was necessary, and that it was the first step to economic development and modernity. But they also pointed out a number of problems that the relocated residents will have to face. Not everyone believes that they will get a new plot of land entirely free of charge. Some people are expecting that 'extra' payments will have to be made to the mayor. Another complicating factor is that relocated families will not receive any financial compensation for building a new homestead, and what makes it worse contemporary buildings are much more expensive than traditional clay ones (in French called *banco*). The new homesteads are built using modern building materials, such as cement, reinforcement bars and corrugated sheets. Round huts made of hand shaped earth, with conical thatched roofs, are considered obsolete. Contemporary houses are rectangular and generally have two rooms. Each room has a window made of corrugated sheet. The house has a flat roof, and the door is locked with a padlock or an industrially manufactured lock. Each homestead is comprised of at least two such houses. This makes contemporary buildings—freed from the traditional compactness of villages—more spacious and comfortable, which is what inhabitants from Bourzanga often emphasize. Certainly, it is also one of the reasons why they give up their old homesteads so readily.

Another consequence of parcellation and the implementation of new building solutions is the division of families. A traditional household consisted of the parents and their sons with their own families. When a household could not house all of the newborn grandchildren, a decision was made that only the oldest son would remain with the parents. The other sons had to become independent, which happened relatively late. The new type of settlement meant that sons, who built their own homesteads and thus became independent fairly quickly, were starting up their own autonomous families.[12] Young residents of villages due to undergo parcellation stress the fact that they will be the ones to do the building work and decide on "how to set up my own homestead". Others (sometimes even the elderly) argue that old houses are not sustainable[13]

[12] As opposed to the traditional settlement which meant that sons lived together with their father in one homestead for a very long time, and therefore completely dependent on his will.

[13] Traditionally, buildings made of *banco* needed to be renovated and replastered every year. Modern buildings are plastered with cement, and so they are more sustainable.

or aesthetically pleasing. Therefore, they consider parcellation an opportunity for improvement.

At the time of the author's fieldwork, residents of Bourzanga hoped that as soon as the tarmac road would be ready (completed by the end of 2010), it would take much less time to reach Kongoussi and Ouagadougou. This means that more tradesmen will come to the village to buy agricultural products. The new road will also bring tourists, and, no doubt, in time a hotel will be built. In spite of a general acceptance of these changes among local communities, they perceive certain dangers as well. A rich farmer owning a modern farm can see more than merely the bright side of parcellation and broadly understood modernity. He argues that he can sense a certain danger to tradition. The *Imam* from Toulfe thinks that "modernity can be a threat". On the other hand, the parish priest from the parish in Djibo thinks that "building roads and the parcellation of land bring significant changes to our lives, but this is the way of progress. We are facing a difficult challenge. We must make up our minds as to which path we want to follow."

Conclusions

The parcellation of land and the construction of a new tarmac road are multi-faceted issues, of major socio-cultural impact at the local level. As has been demonstrated in the case of the villages of Bourzanga and Pobe-Mengao, they involve changes not only in the perception of land ownership, but in perceptions of social organisation more generally. Although changes of perceptions of land ownership started in the mid-20th century, shifting from land as common property to leased property, the most dramatic impact on local understandings of land ownership happened simultaneously with the construction of a major national road network in the late 20th and early 21st centuries. The construction of new roads started a parcellation process, which could be seen to include entire villages and the land around them.

The physical interference of the road with the village lay-out gave rise to the creation of new living areas outside the village. The reduction of the number of houses in the ancient village centres in favour of the outer edges of the villages was demonstrated to be a characteristic feature. In the process conceptual connections were made between State—i.e. government administrative—and local perceptions on land ownership. While before only the younger sons of a family were given land outside the village into ownership, the construction of the road through the village necessitated a more heterogeneous group of villagers to abandon the village and access this type of land. Thus, privately owned property was facilitated to a much larger group than before.

In the process of planning land parcellation and road construction, the State could be seen to leave the areas of some of the traditional power structures untouched. Although, from the formal point of view land is a state property, in practice the descendants of the first settlers remain involved in matters of land division and property rights, although it is undoubtedly more ceremonially than practically.

Characteristic for both villages—and this is a general phenomenon among villages that are affected by the construction of the national road network in the region—is that the area of the chief's residence has not been parcelled out, but has remained in the centre of the village as a symbol of traditional power. However, this does not automatically imply that the chief's residence is the current centre of power. In fact, the physical width of the tarmac road that runs through the two village centres has resulted in two different sets of social negotiations, in Bourzanga disturbing and possibly marginalising the chief's position in future.

While the new road in Pobe-Mengao has not impacted the village setup, being laid out within the boundaries of the old road, in Bourzanga the road has exceeded the width of the old one and has necessitated the destruction of houses. A new residential area was developed outside the village centre, with houses of a rectangular design. Due to their more spacious lay-out Bourzanga inhabitants can be seen to readily exchange their more traditional and cramped circular huts for the new houses outside the village. In the process potential new successors of power are removed from the centre of the village.

Despite all these implicit socio-cultural dilemmas, it seems that building roads and parcellation can go hand in hand with traditional perceptions on and relations to land, and that it is possible to work out a new model of cooperation between the traditional structures of power and the State, in which the State becomes the mediator in land trading and the initiator of deep changes in the organization of agricultural land investments. The construction of new tarmac roads imposing new land parcellation is a direct impulse. It induces changes not only within the structure of land ownership but above all within the regulation of individual ownership rights.The examples of both places—Pobe-Mengao and Bourzanga—in the context of state politics exemplify one way of solving the ownership rights problem. Finally and on a more general note, the case-study has hoped to demonstrate that an ethnography of land ownership rights can make a valuable contribution to forging legal regulations that recognize socio-cultural dimensions of land ownership rights (Delville 2010).

Bibliography

Delville, Phillippe L., "Registering and Administering Customary Land Rights: Can We Deal with Complexity?" In *Innovations in Land Rights Recognition, Administration, and Governance*, edited by Klaus Deininger, Clarissa Augustinus, Stig Enemark, and Paul Munro-Faure, 28–38. Washington: The International Bank for Reconstruction and Development / The World Bank, 2010. Paper presented at The Annual Conference on Land Policy and Administration, Washington, April, 2010. Accessed June 28, 2012. http://siteresources.worldbank.org/INTARD/825826-1111150255516/22560754/InnovLandRightsRecogFINALv3.pdf.

Komorowski, Zygmunt. *Kultury Czarnej Afryki*, Wrocław-Warszawa-Kraków: Zakład Narodowy im. Ossolińskich, 1994.

Lewis, M. Paul (ed.). *Ethnologue: Languages of the World*, Dallas: 2009. Accessed October 11, 2011. www.ethnologue.com/show_country.asp?nameBF.

Murdock, George Peter. *Africa. Its people and their culture history*, New York-Toronto-London: McGraw-Hill Book Company Inc., 1959.

Schweeger-Hefel, Annemarie, and Wilhelm Staude. *Die Kurumba von Lurum*, Wien: Verlag A. Schendl, 1970.

List of Informants

Naaba Baongo Badini Boureima, chief of Bourzanga
Koob Naaba Badini Elisé, garden manager in Bourzanga
Badini Jean-Paul, farmer from Bourzanga
el-hadj Ganame Alodi, *imam* from Toulfe
Ganame Mammoudou, teacher from Toulfe
Irge Alou, master of the land from Belehede
Konfe Amadi, farmer, member of the council in the village of Pobe-Mengao
Konfe Hamidou (Medo) *Lurumyo Sigiri*, chief of the kingdom of Lurum in Pobe-Mengao
Revd Ouedraogo Blaise, parish priest from Djibo
Asendesa Sawadogo Sino, master of the land from Pobe-Mengao
Sisse Amadou, farmer, head of the association *Kaptaluelo* (Fight against hunger) from Pobe-Mengao
Zoungrama Gabriel, farmer and tailor from Namsiguya
Zoungrama Jean-Baptiste, farmer, retired religion teacher from Namsiguya

BEING A FOREIGNER IN ONE'S COUNTRY: MOBILITY, LAND ACQUISITIONS AND INVESTMENTS IN CAMEROON

Evelyne N. Tegomoh

Introduction

Cameroon is a country where politics of belonging are quite crucial to making individual achievements meaningless if not appreciated and endorsed as collective success by the group, i.e. your home village or ethnic group (Nyamnjoh 2002: 115–116). In particular, representation, mobility, being in touch with 'global' streams of information as well as the use of newly acquired knowledge to boost local 'visibility' are driving forces for aspiring individuals. In the process of bringing something new into the villages, these individuals' identities are constantly being negotiated at the local, regional and state levels. In this chapter the focus will be on one particular manifestation of identity negotiation, which can be seen to occur in the context of large-scale landed investments in the Western highlands of the North West region of Cameroon. Historically, people of this area have been mobile and their agro-pastoral activities characterized by conflict, relative scarcity and infertility of land. This mobility is translated in specific cultural and social forms related to the exploitation of resources, for instance in tenure regimes, power relations and ideologies.

Apart from bringing along their networks, mobile individuals contribute to their communities in such a way that the links between the individual and his home are maintained or strengthened. From the perspective of the communities in the home area, those who move have to show their worth back home through their socio-economical and political investments. With the coming of a multi-party system, the concept of 'belonging' shifted. People regrouped themselves into ethnic associations, because it mattered who was voted in or out from the home region. In fact, the issue of belonging became crucial for those aspiring to become part of the political elite. (Geschiere and Gugler 1998; Monga 2000; Englund 2002; Nyamnjoh 2005; Geschiere and Jackson 2006; Hebinck and Lent (eds) 2007, Barten 2008 and Ndjio 2009). This has led to unusual situations, such as politicians-to-be coming back to what they call their 'home' for the first time since they were born and raised.

This chapter explores one particular type of mobility that can be observed among Cameroon's national politicians, which are large-scale land acquisitions outside their home areas. Since these lands are not within the 'home' boundaries, the generally observed politics of belonging no longer seem to apply and therefore 'belonging' no longer a distinctive aspect of the politician's identity. By tracing the land acquisition histories of three politicians from the Western highlands (the so-called grasslands) the discussion examines the impact this recent phenomenon has on socio-cultural perceptions of belonging, Honourable Yoyo, El Hadji Dan Pullo and Ni John Fru Ndi are all from the grassfields of the North West region. All three have humble beginnings; their lives started on farms/ranches with their families. They became successful basically because they travelled around the world and therefore acquired the asset of formal and informal new knowledge. However, each of them negotiated belonging in the context of large-scale landed investments outside their home area to different degrees and in different ways. This also explains why they are the subject of this chapter. The mix of similar geographical and socio-economic backgrounds, and different landed investment strategies, different relations to employees and the different opinions people have on the three politicians offer a perfect context for exploring and comparing how each of them mediates belonging.

Socio-Historical Context

1. *Politics of Belonging*

In Cameroon's history awareness of identity and belonging was very pronounced during the colonial regimes of the Germans, British and French, as peoples were divided without their historicity taken into account. With the birth of a major political party coming from the English speaking part of the country in 1990, new political reconfigurations had to be made and in the process identities and belonging were being redefined. This caused further divides with name calling as 'cam-no-go' as well as a proliferation of ethnic associations.[1] Membership of ethnic associations was on the basis of connections back in the home villages, resulting in some people

[1] 'Cam-no-go' or 'strangers' refers basically to those people from the Western grassfields who migrated to the coast as workers on the various plantations and ended up making landed and human investments, on farms. As a result of establishing their families in the coastal area it was difficult for them and their offspring to return to their villages. Originally

finding themselves to be outsiders. One could be included or thrown out depending on the circumstances under which identities were defined. Concerning a male adult, the society had some clear expectations; building a house, marrying and bringing forth children and keeping his social relations alive through active participation in the life of the community were among them. These are the standards by which a man was and still is to some extent considered successful and therefore to belong. (Geschiere and Gugler 1998; Monga 2000; Englund 2002; Gugler 2002; Nyamnjoh 2002 and 2005; Geschiere and Jackson 2006; and Ndjio 2009).

In view of the above, it may be argued that a politics of belonging is engrained in the everyday life interactions of the people in Cameroon. In combination with newly acquired knowledge from without, it has taken on unprecedented dimensions; political elites have been able to negotiate and amass vast terrains of agricultural land. Communal land has been affected, in particular, being sold to 'sons of the area' for agro-industry.

2. *Land Law Reforms*

The reunification of Cameroon in 1972 provided a platform for the harmonization of the reforms of the different land tenure systems since colonial times. Ordinance No. 74-1 and 74-2 of 6 July 1974 classified land as Private, owned by individuals and corporate entities, groups or the state. This type of land must be titled and registered. Also there is Public land—for instance, highways, parks, waterways—which is held for the common good by the state. Lastly, there is National land, which is generally unoccupied land, held by communities under customary law, informal settlements and grazing land. The state has the power to allocate use rights to individuals or groups, or convert such land into the state's private or public property.

From this division of land into three types of ownership, the following tenure types are recognized by formal law. One is ownership, where landowners have rights to exclusive possession and use of their land, the right to mortgage the land, and the right to transfer the land. Two, the state can grant usufruct rights to occupants of national land especially to unregistered community land. Lastly, leaseholds can be granted by private parties or the state, under terms agreed to by the parties. Leasing, rental arrangements and share-cropping are some common deals made on the

'cam no go' is a pidgin phrase used in reference to a particular species of skin rash which is very itchy and resistant to treatment.

ground; profit or licence includes the right of customary communities to benefit from products of unoccupied national land until assigned to a particular use by the state.

Most land in Cameroon has been obtained through purchase, leasing, borrowing, inheritance, or allocation by traditional leaders. Since the registration process is generally considered cumbersome, expensive and time-consuming, the vast majority of the population depends on customary law. Additional gaps in the land administration process and infrastructure have contributed to slowing down the transition from customary property rights to private ownership of property. Finally, reports of multiple sales of the same land, false land certificates, and inaccuracies in boundary definitions suggest growing land registration corruption, conflicts and disputes over land being frequent. Hence, it may not be surprising that banks, landholders or buyers do not rely on the official land registration system. Their practices are silently endorsed by the state, which in its efforts to modernize agriculture has made land available to politically and economically powerful individuals and entities (GOC Land Law 74-1 1974; Halle 2006; AfDB 2009; USAID 2011). It should be noted that the agricultural sector of Cameroon produces over 20% of GDP, and that the country has been a long time producer of cash crops such as coffee, cocoa, rubber, banana etc. Until the 90s the government invested consistently in agriculture through agro-pastoral shows, schools and research schemes, and institutions such as the Upper Nun Valley Development Authority, UNVDA Ndop, the Institute for Agricultural Research for Development, IRAD, and the Institute of Zoo-technical Research, IRZ, in Garoua, and Ngaoundere, Ekona Bambui. Additionally, there were two major agricultural funding schemes, the National Fund for Rural Development, FONADER and the North West Development Authority, MIDENO. These institutions produced significant results both at the local and national levels. When funding was gradually reduced/abandoned projects came to a halt, which, among others, led to migration to the urban centres (Fonjong, 2004). However, during the last decade the government has been revamping these institutions, re-instating the agro-pastoral show, which took place in 2011, and privatizing some agro-industries to, arguably, improve management. These developments have received mixed reactions from the local communities.

In the Western Highlands, the region under discussion here, land is still considered to be customarily held. Land belongs to the Fon (Divine King) who distributes it to his subjects and friends as need arises. Usually after identification of the location of the land requested, one goes to see the

Fon to present one's case.[2] Usually these vast terrains are fallow, or only bits of them used for cultivation. The amount of hectares one can acquire depends on the individual's negotiation skills, personal relations/connections and financial viability.

Three Land Acquisition Biographies

1. *Emmanuel Yoyo Mohmbanka*

Honourable Yoyo, as he is popularly called, is a retired police commissioner, a former parliamentarian and mayor of Ngoketunjia division, Ndop, where he is a resident. During his years of service with the government as a police officer, he travelled across the country a lot, holding different posts of responsibility in public and border security stations. In 1980, he constructed his first house in his home village of Baba 1 in the Ndop plain, as is expected from any son of the community. This house is on land that belongs to his father's lineage. He was given it by a paternal uncle, when he had indicated it was his place of preference among other propositions to build his house. It was only afterwards that he acquired other pieces of land in Bamenda, the provincial headquarters of the North West region. There he built houses for commercial purposes. In 1990, his current residential home was constructed in the divisional headquarters of Ngoketunjia, Ndop, which is about 20km from his home village, Baba 1. He retired in 1995 to stay closer to home, the ranches and farms he had acquired before. During this period, while he was out of government service, he joined the main opposition party, SDF. He then ran for the mayor's ticket of his division, Ngoketunjia. He won the parliamentary elections twice, thus having two terms in office as mayor, from 1997–2007.

Honourable Yoyo had started cattle rearing, which he considers a family trade, as far back as 1974. He started off by using the family and communal grazing fields before acquiring land (approx. 160 hectares) from other places to facilitate the process of transhumance in December. His ranch and farms are located in Bamessing, which he recently gave up to focus on that in Babungo, one of the neighbouring villages to Baba 1. The latter as

[2] In the case of Fon Voga Simon II of Big Babanki land allocation had disastrous consequences. He was dethroned and burnt to death by his people, partly because he had sold off some fertile land to Dan Pullo (see below) against their consent (Fai 2006; Halle 2006; Mbunwe 2006).

well as Baba 1 were acquired during the past 10 years. His farms, which are located within his ranch, were first mapped out for commercial purposes. He used to farm about 24 hectares of maize for sale, which was mainly bought by maize dealers from Bamenda. This farm is situated in the main farming land of Baba 1. Because of the availability of water sources, the area is nowadays mostly used by his cows during the dry season. He has given up this stretch of land to concentrate on the over two hectares of farm land close to his home in Ndop. Using the cow dung left behind by his herds of cattle (over 500) to enrich the land, he plants mostly maize and vegetables for home consumption. After the distribution of corn to family and friends, the surpluses are sold to maize dealers. With at least ten permanent salaried workers, his ranch and contracts for the construction and reconstruction of water catchments, schools, bridges and roads keep him quite busy and in touch with the government.

Before, during and after his tenure as a parliamentarian, he has been one of the biggest contributors, not only in cash, to the various developmental projects at home. Most recently, he has completed a road running from the market square up to the palace of Baba 1 towards the border with Oku sub-division. This has won him other bigger contracts in the division. His workers are more or less treated by him as family members, participating in a variety of occasions organised by their boss. They also profit from the produce of the farms, and herdsmen are in control of the milk production from the cattle.

2. *El Hadji Dan Pullo*

El Hadji Dan Pullo is a big business magnate without formal education. He owns and runs businesses at home and abroad (South Africa, Europe and America). He is of a mixed descent, Fulani and Kom. He considers himself a Fulani man of the grassfields, even though he is also considered Kom, because of his matrilineal descent. He uses his mixed parentage in a rather complex and intricate way, one of which is to mix in the higher circles of power in the government. He is thought of and seen as a personal friend of the president, Paul Biya. He is therefore a staunch supporter of the ruling political party, Cameroon's People Democratic Movement (CPDM) and a member of the central committee of the party. Over the years he has made huge financial contributions to the running of CPDM affairs. It is said that through his connection with the president he was able to buy the tea plantations of Djutitsa, Ndu and Tole, jointly referred to as the Cameroon Tea Estate (CTE), while disguising himself as the representative of a non-existent South African firm, Brobon Finex (Eko, 2003 and Konings, 2008). The tea estate, formerly managed by Cameroon Development Cooperation (CDC), cuts across vast locations in three geographical areas, North West, South West and West Regions covering over 60.000 hectares.

The Bakweri Land Claim Committee (BLCC) claimed that the estate, originally valued at 4.5 billion CFA, was sold at a give-away price of 1.5 billion CFA with the consent of the privatization committee. Additionally, it found that during the process of negotiation the sales of tea had been suspended, thus leaving the creditors of CDC unpaid. When the local population realised that El Hadji Dan Pullo was behind the take-over of the CDC tea plantations and there was no such company as Brobon Finex of South Africa, a public outcry against him was unavoidable. Public strikes with road blockages, deaths and court cases followed, as the public witnessed a massive transfer of public and private property into the hands of one individual, in the name of agricultural modernisation. Tensions were rife in the South West region, as much as in those parts of the West and North West regions that were affected by the deal (Eko 2003; Adams 2006; Nana and Mbom 2006 and Konings 2008: 56–57). The output from the tea estates has dropped considerably. Claiming unpaid dues and salaries, workers of the Tole tea estate could be seen to camp out at the regional delegation of Labour and Social Security in Buea. Meanwhile, Dan Pullo is involved in several court cases, which is usually a protracted process in the Cameroonian legal system.

Although Dan Pullo is the owner of many houses scattered over the country, his home is Ndawara Tea Estate in Belo, Boyo division of the North West Region. Within this over 2,500 hectares of land are his family's living quarters, a health unit, a school, a police post and a hotel/guesthouse for tourists. Spreading out over multiple hills and valleys, his ranch has become one of the tourist attractions of the area. As for the police post, its presence raises questions, because normally police posts are created at the divisional level. Connections at the top probably made it possible to have such a unit. With a private police force at his hands, Dan Pullo is able to ward off protest and violence at his estate by the people who have been dispossessed of their lands—communal and possibly privately owned land—and deprived of their livelihoods. These precautions seem to relate to earlier outbreaks of violence on his Santa tea nursery (North West region). The 2006 outbreaks were the result of failed negotiations on co-habitation between the local population of Santa Njong and the estate management.[3] In fact, after the CDC deal the general public had become more sceptical about Dan Pullo's land ownership ambitions. When he nonetheless managed to negotiate his way through the system and acquired a vast area of land in the Santa area, this caused a public outcry. People destroyed and blocked the entrance/exit of a traffic circulation in/and out of the region. Since Santa is a central hub in the regional infrastructure—located on the borders between the West and North West region and on the main high way connecting the area with the rest of the country—police action followed promptly. This police intervention led to arrests and even deaths. Later, law enforcement officers were dispatched to the scene to ensure calm, as part of the regional headquarters had been paralysed (Eko 2003; Adams 2006). It was a big news item in Cameroon, with all the top administrative officials and military officers coming out to plea for calm and normalcy.

In general, El Hadji Dan Pullo has been qualified by the news media as a land expansionist, dispossessing people of their land and livelihoods and leaving them with little or no option but to work for him under harsh conditions. However, as the biggest agrarian investor of the region, he has also been applauded for his efforts as a 'true son of the soil'. He has been acclaimed for fostering development, employing youths of the region, as well as providing social facilities like roads, schools, health units etc. During the Ramadan of 2006 he was given the highest mark of appreciation by almost 200 Fons and some political big wigs of the region that visited and blessed him on his Ndawara estate (Mbunwe 2006).

Being a Fulani, cattle rearing has always been an essential element of his life. Within his Ndawara estate, there is a big cattle ranch with a select breed of cows, mainly from Ngaoundere in the Adamawa region. There are also horses and ponies, some of which are used by tourists to go across the fields; there are sheep and a large poultry farm with, among others, ostriches. The mixed farming on his ranch and estates is done by some of his over one thousand permanent workers, for cash crops and for their own subsistence. Tea covers the bulk of this land, with specialists, plants and machineries brought in from India for production and quality control. Tea produced from these estates is distributed nationally and internationally.

[3] Wamey, P. 2005, on the Santa Njong's peoples' protest against the CTE extension plan and the negotiation process that preceded it.

Through his investments especially in Ndawara he has created roads to the farms, and thus can easily distribute farm products on the local and national markets. Danpullo is considered one of the biggest private employers of the region. However, the pay package of his workers is considered below standard; some even describe working on his estate as slave labour. His investment strategy clearly demonstrates 'mobility', in the sense that knowledge, services, goods and ideas concerning the development of his estates or of Elba ranch are imported from outside and synchronized with the local knowledge system.

3. *John Fru Ndi*

Ni[4] John Fru Ndi, chairman of the main opposition party in Cameroon, Social Democratic Front (SDF), hails from Baba 2 village in Santa subdivision of the North West region. His educational path after the Baforchu Basel Mission and Santa Native Authority schools took him across the borders into Nigeria, where his training at the Zairian Flying School was terminated prematurely due to the Biafra war in July 1967. He returned home and got engaged in Ebibi Magazine, trying to promote a reading culture by making good literature available to the general public. This enterprise later developed into Ebibi Bookshop. He became a renowned bookshop owner, and a major supplier of books to most of the schools in the region. As stipulated by the party's constitution, he had to give up his bookshop in the early 90s when he took up leadership of the SDF. He regretted this very much. In the October 1992 presidential elections he stood as the main challenger of President Biya and is widely believed to have won this rigged election. The SDF under his leadership has become the biggest opposition party in parliament, but CPDM continues to hold a majority of seats. Although his party boycotted the 2007 presidential elections, among other things for lack of transparency, the party has taken part in subsequent elections, and John Fru Ndi maintains his position as the strongest opposition leader.

Defying all odds in 1990 to establish an opposition party in the then one-party state system, John Fru Ndi gave birth to the multi-party system in Cameroon. A farmer, he owns over 200 hectares of farm land in the North West region of the country, which is believed to be the stronghold of the SDF party he is heading. The biggest farm estate is in Ngoh near Befang,

---

[4] *Ni* is a term of respect when addressing an older person.

where he is engaged in agro-pastoral farming. His farm is situated some 23km from the divisional headquarters of Wum, in Menchum division of the North West region. Among his smaller farms, which mostly have food crops like colocasia, plantains and maize, are the farms in Obang, lower Bafut, the farm of Bambui, a so-called 'memorial farm' in honour of his late wife, and the farms in his home village of Baba 2. The produce of these farms are for subsistence and commercial purposes. John Fru Ndi is widely known for his generosity. He sells the farm's surpluses and cash crops at the local markets. The Ngoh farm estate has fruit trees such as lemon, lime, oranges, shallots, pears, mangoes. In addition to food crops, the farm has a herd of over 200 cows. These cows are crossbred so as to get the highest possible milk production of high quality. Much of the produce is donated to orphans and under-privileged children. To ensure the quality and quantity of milk, there are hectares of land with bracaria, guatemala and sunflower to improve the feed of these animals. Growing up with his grandmother on the farm, he started acquiring cows from an early age. He used the farming proceeds to acquire more animals and start large-scale agro-pastoral activities. Like Hon. Yoyo and Dan Pullo, he has commercial houses, one of which came under public scrutiny when he rented part of it out to the France lottery company, PMUC. Since the SDF party at that time was against French investments and French goods in Cameroon, there was a public outcry when PMUC appeared to use one of Ni John Fru Ndi's buildings along the commercial avenue of Bamenda. People felt betrayed and wanted to know why Fru Ndi allowed such a company to occupy his business premises. Other houses he owns are in Baba 2 village and in Ntarikum, where he owns an entire compound, popularly known as presidency. The compound not only accommodates family members, but also SDF party supporters and sympathisers. (Wasaloko 2009; Konings 2004).

The Three Land Acquisition Biographies Compared

The three men described are political and public figures. They are all thought to have used their positions in society and their political powers to gain access to large tracts of land. Typically, the three have acquired vast terrains of land outside their home villages, where they are engaged in food and cash crop farming and cattle rearing. In all three cases, the acquisitions include land that was before considered private, family or community land or property. This type of land acquisition politics has caused great resentment in some parts of the country, especially among people who have lost all means of livelihood as a result of these acquisitions. The case of Tole inhabitants and tea workers in the South West region, discussed above, is illustrative.

In addition to sharing the asset of political connections, Honourable Yoyo, El Hadji Dan Pullo and Ni John Fru Ndi developed skills of accumulating wealth by starting with little investments in livestock and later on in houses and tracts of land. As a result of these first investments at home, they acquired the label of 'belonging' in their grassfield communities, qualifying them as mature, responsible and independent men, who were ready to start up their own families (Ndjio, 2009 and Nyamnjoh, 2002). All of them continued in the family tradition of rearing animals, and aimed at doing it on a large scale. Their educational background/travel experiences, financial viability and their socio-political ties became instrumental in how they acquired these vast terrains, and since then have owned and managed them.

El Hadji Dan Pullo is probably the most extreme example of how the politics of 'belonging' can take shape. An economic magnate, a member of the central committee of the CPDM party, a big financial donor to the ruling party and a personal friend of the president, he uses his political and financial capital to create 'belonging'. One vivid example of Dan Pullo's politics is his participation in the creation of the ethnically inspired Mbororo Social and Cultural Development Association, MBOSCUDA, which he left for a less ethnically pronounced association when he considered the association a threat to his political and business ambitions. He created a rival association, the Socio-Cultural Association for Livestock Breeding and Development in Cameroon (SODELCO), for his own political gain. Although these associations cannot be a guarantee for belonging—since they are highly politicised bodies—they helped him in being allocated vast stretches of land by the government.

The politics of 'belonging' is played out less in the inner political circles in the case of Ni John Fru Ndi and Honourable Yoyo. In their positions of SDF party chairman and divisional parliamentarian respectively, they have not the same access to them as Dan Pullo. Their political positions are basically dependent on their interpersonal relations with the people at the grassroots. Different from Dan Pullo, these two men bring out the importance of urban-rural connectivity (Geschiere and Gugler 1998; Nyamnjoh and Rowlands 1998).

Thanks to the mobility through education, trade/business and professions the three men have been able to make their way up on the social-political ladder. During different stages in their lives they made huge investments to become political leaders. Their positions influenced their access to more land whether directly or indirectly. As politicians, their investments became open for public scrutiny and a source for political slander across political boundaries. The expansionist activities of El Hadji Dan Pullo in particular led to major resistance of the local people, who felt discriminated in favour of 'foreigners' who were granted their cultivated patches of community fields. Indeed, the three men might well be qualified 'foreigners'; apart from the Ndawara tea estate with huge investments on home soil, most of the hectares of land acquired by the three men is outside their home areas.

In the context of 'belonging', El Hadji Dan Pullo's mixed—Kom/Fulani—parentage is an additional complicating factor.[5] For the majority of the people of Boyo division, the Kom, he is considered an outsider, because he has openly declared himself a Fulani. In the eyes of the Fulani, however, he is not 'pure' because he is of mixed parentage. He is therefore given the paradoxical position of being labelled in both communities as a 'foreigner' and welcomed as a true son of the soil. Due to the tense relation between SODELCO and MBOSCUDA and the claims of dispossession by his own ethnic group members from a land commonly used for grazing, security around and on this property is crucial. This may also explain the presence of a police post on this estate, which, as was argued before, is an unusual phenomenon at this level. In view of his highly politicised identity, Dan Pullo's police post may be considered a demonstration of power and connection to the president.

From the perspective of their home communities, the 'sons of the soil' can benefit them in different ways. One is that the men owe community service to the people. Being generally considered 'foreigners' who belong, they can be asked by individuals of the community for assistance for health care or education. As was seen in the biography of Honourable Yoyo in the context of the land acquisitions, the 'foreigner-belonging' status is further consolidated during special social events, where food and drinks are provided free of charge. These manifestations of generosity are not only expressions of a cultural system, but are also inspired by religious persuasions. In the case of Dan Pullo, generosity is abundantly shown during

[5] See Nyamnjoh and Rowlands 1998; Geschiere and Nyamnjoh 1998 on the creation and workings of associations in Cameroon when it comes to politics of belonging.

Ramadan and Id, while in Fru Ndi's and Yoyo's case Christmas is a time of great generosity.

Lastly, these men offer livelihoods. Indeed, as was pointed out before, employment recruitment is mostly done locally by the three men. In addition to local employment possibilities, their projects stimulate local capacity building; smaller farmers benefit from improved plant varieties and animal breeds, produced on their estates/ranches. Also, unlike common practices before and big multi-national company practices nowadays, products from the farms of these three large-scale land owners are not grown for international markets. Most often their produce is sold to local traders.

Of the three men, Dan Pullo has been applauded most for his diverse investments. His use of newly acquired knowledge in the form of a private television network for creating job opportunities, mainly for the youths of this area, was highly acclaimed by public and state officials.

Conclusion

In this chapter the theme of 'belonging' has been placed in the context of present-day large-scale land acquisitions by political elite from the Western Highlands of Cameroon. This is a relatively new phenomenon, which is facilitated by a land tenure system that is incoherent and mediated by government institutions. The discussion has demonstrated that highly mobile and educated rich men construct notions (of legitimization) of land ownership that are 'foreign' to their society's practices and ideologies. One marked deviating notion is the acquisition of land outside their home areas. Apart from the Ndawara tea estate with huge investments on home soil, the vast majority of acquired tracts of land of the three men are elsewhere. This unusual situation raises questions concerning the relationship between the land acquisition and socio-cultural practices of belonging.

Nonetheless, although the acquisitions create social tensions, the three men discussed above consider themselves 'sons of the soil', stimulating economic, social and educational programmes in their home areas. Their connection to 'home' comes out also in their largely opting for producing for the local rather than the export market. On a personal level, bonds between the men and their communities are strengthened through social events, hosted by them and to which they are invited, participate and/or partake in.

From the local community perspective, it can be concluded that 'belonging' has acquired a new—if paradoxical—dimension, which is 'foreigner'. The above land acquisition biographies have demonstrated that this is not an unproblematic fusion; large groups of 'home' people could be seen to stand up against their 'benefactors'. Considering the different perceptions of 'belonging' between the land-owning political elite and the local communities, it seems safe to conclude that the position of 'belonging' is one precariously held by large-scale land owners in their home areas. Although these land transactions are legitimised by the government in the name of the development and modernisation of the agricultural sector, they can easily lead to major outbreaks of resistance among the 'home' communities if the land owners do not continuously re-negotiate their bonds of belonging with 'home'.

Bibliography

Adams, B. 2006. Tole Tea Estate Crisis: Who Is Fooling Who? http://www.postnewsline.com/2006/07/tole_tea_estate.html#tp.

AfDB. 2009. Cameroon: diagnostic study for modernization of the lands and survey sector. http://www.afdb.org/fileadmin/uploads/afdb/Documents/Project-and-Operations/Cameroon_Etude%20sur%20le%20cadastre_english_001.pdf (accessed 05 September 2011).

Anon. 2008. Northwest Fons Bless Baba Danpullo http://www.postnewsline.com/2008/10/northwest-fons.html#tp.

Barten, J. 2008. Families in Movement: Transformation of the family in urban Mali, with focus on intercontinental mobility, Msc Thesis Wageningen University.

De Bruijn M. and Van Dijk H. 2003. "Changing Population Mobility in West Africa. Fulbe Pastorialists in Central and South Mali.", *African Affairs* 102 (407): 285–307.

Eko, L. 2003. IMF and World Bank-Sponsored Sordid Fraud—CDC Privatization Fraud: A View from the Ground. http://ambazonia.indymedia.org/en//2003/01/165.shtml.

Englund, H. 2002. "The Village in the City, the City in the Village: Migrants in Lilongwe." *Journal of Southern African Studies* 28 (1): 137–154 Special Issue: Malawi.

Fai, C. 2006. After assassination of Fon: Uncertainty in Kedjom-Keku http://www.thefarmersvoice.org/9.php?subaction=showfull&id=1141960375&archive=&start_from=&ucat=9&.

Fonjong, L.N. 2004. "Changing Fortunes of Government Policies and its Implications on the On the Application of Agricultural Innovations in Cameroon." *Nordic Journal of African Studies* 13 (1): 13–29.

Geschiere, P. and Gugler, J. 1998. "Introduction: The Urban-Rural Connection: Changing Issues of Belonging and Identification." *Journal of International African Institute* 68 (3): 309–319.

Geschiere, P. and Nyamnjoh, F. 1998. "Witchcraft as an Issue in the "Politics of Belonging": Democratization and Urban Migrants' Involvement with the Home Village", *African Studies Review* 41 (3): 69–91.

Geschiere, P. and Jackson, S. 2006. "Autochthony and the Crisis of Citizenship: Democratization, Decentralization, and the Politics of Belonging.", *African Studies Review* 49 (2): 1–7.

GOC. 1974. Ordonnance No. 74–1 du juillet 1974 fixant le regime foncier. http://camerounforet.com/fr/system/files/18_93_99.pdf (accessed 05 September 2011).

——. 1974. Ordonnance No. 74–2 du juillet 1974 fixant le regime domanial. http://camerounforet.com/system/files/18_93_99.pdf (accessed 05 September 2011).

Gugler, J. 2002. "The Son of the Hawk Does Not Remain Abroad: The Urban-Rural Connection in Africa." *African Studies Review* 45 (1): 21–41.

Halle, N. 2006. Ntumfor Nico Halle speaks on vital issues: Murder of the Fon of Babanki, Santa tea crisis, homosexual imbroglio rocking the nation, issue of Government Delegates http://starheadlines.blogspot.com/2006/03/ntumfor-nico-halle-speaks-on-vital.html.

Hebinck, P. and Lent, P. (eds). 2007. *Livelihoods and Landscapes: The People of Guquka and Koloni and their Resources.* Leiden, Brill.

Konings, P. 2008. "Privatisation and Labour Militancy: The case of Cameroon's Tea Estates." *Journal of Contemporary African Studies* 26 (1): 51–70.

——. 2004. "Opposition and social-democratic Change in Africa: The Social Democratic Front in Cameroon.". *Commonwealth & Comparative Politics* 42 (3): 289–31.

Mbunwe, C. 2006. Why Dethroned Babanki Fon Was Murdered http://www.postnewsline.com/2006/01/why_dethroned_b.html#tp.

Monga, Y. 2000. "Au village: Space, Culture, and Politics in Cameroon." *Cahiers d'Études Africaines* 40 (160): 723–749.

Nana, W. and Mbom, F. 2006. Danpullo, Striking Workers Boycott Crisis Meeting http://www.postnewsline.com/2006/08/danpullo_striki.html#tp.

Ndjio, B. 2009. "Migration, Architecture, and the Transformation of the Landscape in the Bamileke Grassfields of West Cameroon." *African Diaspora* 2: 73–100.

Nyamnjoh, F. 2002. "'A Child is One Person's only in the Womb': Domestication, Agency and Subjectivity in the Cameroonian Grassfields." in Postcolonial Subjectivities in Africa, edited by R. Werbner, 111–138. London: Zed Books.

——. 2005. "Images of Nyongo Amongst Bamenda Grassfielders in White-man Kontri", *Citizen Studies* 9 (3): 241–269.

Nyamnjoh, F. and Rowlands, M. 1998. "Elite Associations and the Politics of Belonging in Cameroon." *Journal of International African Institute* 68 (3): 320–337.

Pelican, M. 2008. "Mbororo Claims to Regional Citizenship and Minority Status in North-West Cameroon'" *The Journal of the International African Institute* 78 (4): 540–560.

USAID. 2011. Land Tenure and Property Rights Portal-Cameroon Country Profile http://usaidlandtenure.net/usaidltprproducts/country-profiles/cameroon (accessed 05 September 2011).

Vubo, Y.E. 2003. "Levels of Historical Awareness: The Development of Identity and Ethnicity in Cameroon." *Cahiers d'Études Africaines* 43 (171): 591–628.

Vubo, Y.E. and Ngwa, A.G. 2001. "Changing Intercommunity Relations and the Politics of Identity in the Northern Mezam Area.", *Cahiers d'Études Africaines* 41 (161): 163–190.

Wamey, P. 2005. Villagers Protests CTE Extension Plan http://www.postnewsline.com/2005/04/strongvillagers_1.html#tp.

Wasaloko, K.W. 2009. Ni John Fru Ndi: I am Also a Farmer. *Summit Magazine.* http://www.summitmagazine.net/2009/11/summit-09-ni-john-fru-ndi-i-am-also-a-farmer.html.

ANCESTORS AND TITLE DEEDS: RURAL TRANSFORMATION IN 20TH CENTURY SOUTH AFRICA AND THE CONSOLIDATION OF ETHNIC-BASED IDENTITIES

Gitte Postel

Introduction

By the end of the 20th century, an infinite series of conquests, land reforms, and land deals had left 90% of South Africa's productive land in the hands of 50.000 white farmers (Bradstock 2005). Their land ownership, legally and often financially supported by the state, implied that most South Africans had involuntarily lost their access to land. This slow, prolonged and painful process continues even today: after Apartheid ended in 1994 there are more stories to be told of African farm dwellers who have been forced to leave the land on which they lived and worked, than there are success stories of land redistribution under the new laws of land reform (Bradstock 2005; see also Andrews et al., elsewhere in this volume).

In South Africa large-scale FLAs started at a time when they were not yet the topic of international debate and much earlier than in most African countries. Throughout South African history these land deals and the disputes that came along with them were no different from other land deals or land disputes in that they all reflect contestations between different cultural paradigms. This was the case with conflicts over grazing rights between San hunters and Xhosa pastoralists as much as with territorial conflicts between Zulu warriors and *Voortrekkers* or labour disputes between landlords and their tenants. Still, white farmers' views on land rights in late nineteenth century Transvaal shared more resemblance with those of their black tenants and neighbours than with the views of white farmers in late nineteenth century Cape Colony or in late 20th century Transvaal. Even if they were at one time the foreigners who were given title deeds by the government, at this point they can be seen as part of the local community. When in the 1910s and 1920s the national government applied new legislation, advocating increased implementation of private property and new FLAs, this led to a major rural transformation.

After the second Boer War, the Cape Colony, British Natal, Transvaal and Orange Free State were unified into the Union of South Africa (1910).

Formally a dominion of the British Crown, but in effect an independent state, the disputes over land use that now arose were often more a result of national perspectives contesting with local ones than of cultural-ethnic differences. The Union government inherited two devastated Afrikaner Republics with a feudal, paternalistic agricultural system, and aspired to make the fertile region prosper. One of the tools was the Natives Land Act (1913), meant to turn black independent farmers into wage labourers to create a powerless, flexible and cheap work force for industries, mines and modernised agriculture. Promoting FLAs was another. The uneducated white landowners and tenants without any liquid capital and the (often more educated and wealthy) black tenants without any legal rights who made up the majority of the local community, had common interests and were initially equally ill-disposed towards the new laws. Many local farmers were forced to leave while their land was allocated to cash-rich 'foreigners', coming from either Britain or the Western Cape. Under influence of policy makers, ideologists and circumstances black and white farmers came to be polar opposites in increasingly inter-ethnic conflicts. Moreover, in the nationalist discourses of ethnically based land rights, the farmer became a central metaphor for what was perceived as the inherited responsibility for and right to control over South Africa's territory, while cultural "traditions were continuously reinvented to back conflicting claims of different social groups" (Cotula, Toulmin and Hesse 2004, 2).

Traditions, however, can only thrive when they convincingly suggest continuity. Like history, fiction is a powerful tool to lend continuity to traditions and to interpret reality. In the first half of the 20th century, Afrikaner historians and novelists worked together to create a past and present that fitted the political plans of the emerging Nationalist party and as such also accompanied the state's legitimation and dispute resolution regulations around FLAs. Afrikaner literature helped to legitimize changes in land rights and agricultural practices and sweeten the pill for those who lost their livelihood in the process, by rewriting history and thus re-interpreting reality. The following discussion explores the links between literature and political propaganda, to find out which contribution 20th century literature made to the nationalist programme of re-writing traditional claims to the land. To be able to do so we need to consider the genre that was initially targeted to propagandise the state's policy on land, the *plaasroman* or farm novel, in juxtaposition with the historical events that could have shaped them, as well as literary productions from the African majority of the South African population. Additionally, we may find that by taking a chronological perspective the genre shows differences in tone and contents over time, slowly revealing the conflicts and internal ideological and historical contradictions it had meant to conceal. The following sections present first a historical description of the developments in the state's land tenure and labour policies of the first three decades of the 20th century and uses the description as a backdrop to discuss the Afrikaner genre of the farm novel and African (oral) literature written in the 20th century. Apart from highlighting themes of propaganda in Afrikaner literature and counter discourse in African (oral) literature, the discussion explores literary representations of realities that were ignored or denied by the state, such as South Africa's history of local farmers losing (access to) land, and of contesting land claims and their accompanying cultural paradigms.

National Policy Versus Local Realities

More than a history of stealing, conquering or buying land, land dispossession in South Africa has been a process of gradually undermining black independent agricultural production. Of course one of the main initial drivers behind the process was the establishment of colonial governments in the Western and Eastern Cape and later in the Northern Republics, giving out title deeds only to farmers from European descent. However, the state's engagement with FLAs and land reforms after the Anglo Boer War and the subsequent formation of the Union of South Africa in 1910 have in due course affected many local farmers more profoundly, At least in the Northern parts of South Africa, this was the time when not only the phases 1 to 4 of state engagement with FLAs took place (preparing and executing land deals) but also phases 5 and 6: mediation, legitimation and dispute regulation.[1]

In the 19th century, what is now South Africa consisted of two British Colonies (Natal and the Cape Colony) and two Afrikaner Republics (Transvaal and Orange Free State). Especially in the Cape Colony the British had successfully used their military power and thorough administration to make the territory legible and turn African farmers into a cheap labour force for white commercial farming, mining, and industry.[2] By contrast, the Afrikaner Republics were hardly industrialised nor were they

[1] See the Introduction in this volume.

[2] 'Legibility' as a concept (J. Scott: *Seeing Like a State*, 1998) is explained in this volume's Introduction.

in any way legible. Policy and reality were miles apart. All the land was officially white: owned by land companies, mission stations, the Crown, absent landlords and white families. The law prescribed that black people could only live there as servants; no more than five black families were allowed to stay on a white man's farm. In reality, however,

> the ... coercive equipment was so lacking, the rule so tenuous, the value of land so low for so long, and the forms of African resistance so varied, that Africans occupied, tilled and grazed nominally white lands in enormous numbers; their ability to subsist was for a considerable period not dramatically altered (Bundy 1988, 198/9).

After the discovery of diamonds and gold had led to a European rush in late 19th century Transvaal, many black farming communities benefited from the booming food market in the new, rapidly growing towns. Furthermore, from 1850 onward, large numbers of individual black farming families migrated to the Transvaal or Orange Free State to take land on lease from land companies and white farmers in order to be able to build a future for themselves. The old African systems did not give much opportunity for personal advancement. Inheritance and land allocation was organised through lineages, in a way which prevented individual accumulation of wealth or land (Bundy 1988). White landowners in these days had an abundance of land, but lacked money, manpower, oxen, seed and skills to make it profitable, so they readily rented out their land to black tenants with their know-how and large social networks. Black tenants were preferred over white tenants. The land owners themselves often did not do any actual farming, they could easily live of their tenants' rent. (Keegan 1988)

Migration had always been a common feature in black society. Droughts, warfare or bad government had made people move; a successful chief had followers from everywhere (Ross 1999). Most of the time, immigrants were accepted as a full member of the new community, which implied that the chief would allocate them land like everybody else. Access to land would grant civic status and the right to participate in the community (Dolny & Klug 1992). The chief administrated and distributed the land, but did not own it; once

> a tribal member had asked for land and had been given it, the control of the chief ended ... By implication, allocated land was the tribeman's—... because the link between the land and the individual tribesman was stronger than the link between the land and the chief (Letsoalo 1987).

So when black families and homesteads took their cattle and moved away from overcrowded Lesotho or the barren stretches of land reserved for black occupation and settled in the Highveld, entering into crop-sharing arrangements with white farmers, this did not immediately conflict with earlier experiences. African and European farmers may have had a different understanding of the relationship to the land, but in practice the two systems were very alike: the white landowner allocated land that was officially his, and collected rent from the people who farmed it, whereas an African chief distributed land that belonged to the community and was often paid taxes for community services. In fact, many Afrikaners, especially those in remote areas, had become rather African in their ways. In 1970, Shula Marks already stated that

> In the 19th century, both African and Afrikaner communities were small scale, closely-knit communities, based on subsistence agriculture, with wealth and prestige concentrated on cattle.... [B]oth tended to fragment easily and were prone to break up under dominant leaders along lines of kinship.... For both, literacy meant the Bible and in both, the elite in the late nineteenth century was dominated by churchmen, later by lawyers and teachers.... For both, the problems of resistance and collaboration when confronted by the greater imperial power of Britain, rural impoverishment, the adaption to an industrial environment and the growth of nationalism... are the major themes of their 20th century history (Marks 1970, 439).

Another important parallel is that both societies were strongly patriarchal in their organisation, based on extended families. Membership of these families did not depend on blood relatedness; they were foremost economic units. Like their black colleagues, white patriarchs created extended families by offering gifts and use of land to 'kinsmen'. Black tenants thus became part of the white patriarch's family, entering a social structure which in some ways looked similar to the one they left behind, but differed in some aspects. Afrikaner household heads, for instance, tended to be more authoritarian than black patriarchs, a difference which often led to conflicts in labour relations and sometimes to violent repression (Ross 1995). Still, the relationship between landlord and tenant was not necessarily very hierarchical. If conflicts did arise, tenants moved on, just as they had done with an unjust chief. In these years, commercial black farming communities were often so successful, that they were able to buy a farm or a Crown estate. A new class of black, independent, wealthy and respected farmers had come into being. In 1904, after the second Boer War, of the 900,000 Africans who lived in the Transvaal, 130,000 farmed their own land, 618,000 leased land and only 50,000 were in service of a white farmer, despite official policy (Bundy 1988; Keegan 1988; Van Onselen 1997).

The first decades of the 20th century were a time of major social changes in rural society. The Boer War had devastated the rural economy in the old republics; farm houses were burnt down, families had been decimated, cattle had died, fields were destroyed. Black tenants had returned to Lesotho or appropriated deserted farms. White tenants and non-commercial farmers were often forced to leave the farm and find work in the city. For those who remained more changes were impending. The national government strove for incorporation of the new Union of South Africa into the global economy and for unity in their white electorate. In the first decade of its existence, the Union government's main goal was to promote the emergence of a white, capitalist agriculture in the former Boer Republics. Although the Union Land Bank was established to help farmers pay off their debts, the Land Settlement Act simultaneously provided for large-scale state purchase of land for subsidised settlement of new—often British—commercial farmers (Keegan 1991). Furthermore, since the Transvaal Labour Commission had concluded that the black farmers' success "would not only withhold labour from industry, but also bring them into competition with white agricultural producers" (Transvaal Labour Commission 1903–4), new laws were designed to break the economic independence of black farmers and make them into wage labourers. The 1913 Native Land Act stripped black farmers of any official right to buy land in "white" territory, which made up 87% of South Africa's surface area. More sweeping, however, were the restrictions of existing tenancy arrangements. In the nineteenth century tenants had leased land by paying in cash, kind, or labour. Labour tenancy was least preferred by the tenants; it meant doing certain tasks for the landlord, using their own cattle and tools. The Land Act forbade all tenancy except labour tenancy, which now implied a labour contract for three to six months a year, and being paid for that labour by cash or crop and the use of cattle, equipment and land of the landlord. To stress the importance of the new legislation, Louis Botha, the Union's first president, organised information gatherings where he himself was present, "influencing," as a black Free State tenant recounted,

> [white farmers] by saying that if they kept on allowing us to plough and practise pastoral farming on our own, it would not be long before we took those farms away from them. (Keegan 1988, 21)

Changing from share cropping to labour tenancy greatly undermined the tenants' legal status with respect to labour relations and access to land. Their customary claim on the land had become meaningless. Unlike share cropping, labour tenancy fell within the Master and Servant Act, which prescribed adverse power relations. The tenants' productivity diminished substantially, unable as they were to work their own land when it was most needed (Bernstein 1996; Bundy 1988; Ditlhake 1997). In the end, the only beneficiaries of the new land and labour laws were those white farmers who could afford to modernise their farms. Or, as often was the case: only those who were strong enough to survive, abided by the new laws. As local farmers mostly lacked both liquid capital and agricultural and organisational skills to keep their farms viable without the resourcefulness of their tenants, many illegal tenancy arrangements continued to exist. Still, over the years, roles were adapted, loyalties changed, arrangements shifted and the relationship between black and white farmers deteriorated profoundly. The new laws had led to social unrest, violence, and to heightened fears: white landlords feared violent uprisings of black workers and tenants feared violent repression and intimidation from their landlords, against which authorities hardly took any active measures (Murray 1989).

In the 1920s another series of new labour laws led to large-scale uprisings by black and white workers in Natal, the Orange Free State and the Transvaal. In the Eastern Cape, where farm workers were already highly proletarised and hard to organise, the uprisings mainly took place in the cities, but elsewhere the countryside was also greatly upset. What started with local sabotage (cattle poisoning, crop burning, boycotting farm stores) ended in nationally organised protests against, amongst other things, the eviction of tenants, under the flag of the Industrial and Commercial Workers Union of Africa (ICU). By 1928 the ICU claimed to have close to 200,000 African, 15,000 coloured and 250 white, most rural members. Expectations were high: "it was generally believed the ICU was struggling to regain the lands of the ancestors, who would give strength to the movement" (Ross 1999, 92). These actions in turn infuriated white farmers, who felt not only threatened, but also betrayed. As Van Onselen (1997, 207) put it:

> With the established racial order in the countryside being challenged by smart talking city folk from the outside, and time-honoured social practices on the farm being questioned by previously loyal quasi-kin from the inside, white anger was fuelled almost as much by a sense of treachery and betrayal as it was by feelings of insecurity and vulnerability.

ICU members were intimidated, molested and sometimes killed by both vigilantes and police. In 1932, after the rebellion had died down due to lack of success and internal differences, the Native Service Contract Bill was adopted which extended the landlord's powers over his servants, even legalizing whipping. (See also Bradford 1987; Crais 2002; Murray 1989; Schirmer 1997). More tenants left or were evicted. More bankruptcies hit white land owners and more land was sold to new, often foreign settlers, who were heedless of customary rights and practises and had no scruples about employing the modern techniques, methods and labour regulations. The already densely populated black reserves now became severely overcrowded. As had happened decades earlier in the Eastern Cape, most black men and women were forced to become migrant labourers, either finding work in the cities or the mines, or eventually accepting bad conditions as (seasonal) labourers on commercial white farms. In 1979 labour tenancy was abolished too; any form of tenancy has since been officially (though not effectively) non-existent. In 1993 South Africa had 1.5 million farm workers; almost half of them were employed only in season (Department of Land Affairs 1997). Labour shortages, however, would always remain a big issue in white South African agriculture.

All in all, black farmers have been crucial in the history of (white) farming, especially in the productive Northern parts of South Africa. Here black semi-independent farmers had been the key to white farmers' success in the 19th century and in the first decades of the 20th century; their departure had led, more often than not, to their bankruptcies. Since then, as in the (former) Cape Colony, it had been cheap black labour that had been indispensable for the viability of white farms.[3] When the British colonial government after a century of warfare had confiscated the whole of the Eastern Cape, new laws made sure the African subjects entered colonial society not as farmers but as labourers, not only for economic reasons, but also "to destroy all possibility that they might again pose a military threat" (Bouch 1997, 8). As early as 1880 English wool farmers in the Cape Colony were producing for an international market, using black seasonal labour on a broad scale. Within a few decades, the amount of black tenants had been reduced from 40,000 to 7,000 (Bouch 1997). When in 1913 the Land Act for the whole of South Africa was implemented, its main objective (segregation leading to a safe form of proletarisation of black South Africans) had already been accomplished in the Eastern Cape.

[3] New labour laws and agricultural policies have proved this: especially in the dry Eastern Cape a lot of farmers cannot cope financially when confronted with compulsory minimum wages, forty-hour working weeks and the loss of state subsidies. (See also Andrews et al. in this volume).

Nationalist (Counter)Discourses and Landownership

Afrikaners and Africans were both severely affected by the 1913 land reforms and subsequent labour laws. The big difference between them was that Afrikaners were in every respect citizens of the Union of South Africa and were given the opportunity to fight their way back, while Africans were more and more legally restricted to make a living in South Africa, or represent themselves in any way. Both Africans and Afrikaners, however, bemoaned the loss of their lives as independent farmers. At the same time, the ancestor based link to the land became for both the core of their nationalist discourses. This is nowhere as visible as in the genre of the farm novel, which has maintained a more or less significant place within white South African literature since the 1920s. Between 1920 and 1940, the Afrikaans novel was concerned almost exclusively with the farm. The Afrikaner intelligentsia knew that the technical and economical transformation from a pre-industrial to industrial society had to be accompanied by a social transformation. Education was therefore seen as crucial. Language, literature and culture were effectively used to "build the nation from words". (Hofmeyr 1987; Devarenne 2009; Keegan 1991)

Farm novels dealt with the economic crisis, growing class differences, and the rapid social transformation of the 1920s and 1930s, which provided the well-known themes of hardship and ruin, love for the land and responsibility towards family members and neighbours. Yet for more than half a century, the influence black farmers had on white rural life has been almost completely left out of these stories of melancholy and hardship; their contributions in the way of labour and agricultural expertise, their social organisation, even the anger and fear they had caused have been largely ignored by white writers. Literary reception often failed to recognise this. When *Laat Vrugte*, one of the early Afrikaans farm novels, was reissued in 1987, Elize Botha still called it "a recreation of those days long gone, when farming was the most important part of Afrikaans society" (Botha 1987, *my translation*), and even in 1998, Heilna du Plooy still writes of the "realistic representation" and "state of reality" of this novel (Du Plooy 1998, 655, *my translation*). JM Coetzee (1988, 91) was one of the first to recognise that the fictional farm was "contradictive" and "elusive", and in fact "placed outside history".

One of the major reasons behind the antinomy of the fictional farm was the fact that it had to help create a nationwide Afrikaner identity. The National Party needed the support of both the rich, idealistic, Afrikaans speaking commercial farmers and industrialists of the Western Cape and the poor, embittered Afrikaans speaking workers (often ex-farmers) in the former Republics, who had to compete with black workers. Before, these two groups had felt hardly related and had little in common besides their language. If writers wanted all Afrikaans speaking South African readers to identify with the protagonist of the farm novels, labour and property had to be ideologically united, even when labour and property had never coincided in real life. The fictional hard working white farmer and his inherited family farm were metaphors for a shared identity and history, a solid past on which the Afrikaner people could build its future. Labour, as a concept, tied the Afrikaans family to the land, it created a sense of belonging and legitimised its presence. The black tenant as an intermediary did not fit the image; at most a few black servants, lazy yet obedient, made their appearances in the farm novels, acting as a foil for white men's authority and vigour.

At the same time the farm novel was a tool to give expression to the Northern Afrikaner's feelings of loss and turn them into something positive and conciliatory. The bemoaned destruction of the old way of life in fact shows the downside of the successful FLA policy initiated by the (Afrikaner) president Botha—the policy that had turned the backward heartland of South Africa into a promising area of commercial agriculture. In the farm novels, however, the British are held responsible; not the government who imposed the land laws, not even the black tenants who had turned against their landlords. The British, instigating the Boer war and purchasing the bankrupt farms afterwards, were the bad guys. This way the recent developments could be added to the long history of Afrikaner struggle against the British, dating from the early 19th century. They may have chased us from the Cape and won the war and taken our farms, was the message, but we Afrikaners will always be 'farmers' (*Boere*); looking after each other and finding new grounds. The fictional farm also reflected, certainly in the years when the National Party was gaining power, the ideal of Afrikaner rule in a larger perspective. The farmer was the perfect example of how an Afrikaner president would look after his fellow Afrikaners in his 'own' land and would keep the black population in place. Thus, even before the independent African farmer had actually disappeared from white South Africa, he had disappeared from formal and creative discourses, both as a friend and a foe. He metaphorically belonged to the African wilderness that was supposed to be either tamed or erased by white civilisation.[4]

---

[4] It may be called ironic that where in earlier times black people's farm (and other) dwellings often were kept out of sight because they distorted this idea of a tamed Africa-free

Although black farmers were thus not only erased from the domains of legal landownership and independent farming, but also from history and other representations of reality, in other domains they remained visible enough. Being given fewer and fewer official and legal opportunities to farm and thus be part of a community, black South Africans found other ways to mark their space, express their identity, and resist hegemonic control. Lacking official means of protest, black farmers started using white man's land as grazing land for their own livestock (at night if necessary), stealing chickens and vegetables, hunting white farmers' game, cutting down fences, or working slowly for a boss. Other forms of resistance could be found at a more symbolic level. In a way, Apartheid stimulated the preservation of certain traditions and belief systems in black South Africa. One of the domains that remained important, regardless of or thanks to Apartheid, was the spiritual domain of the ancestors. Because they were untouchable by colonial rule African ancestors could, as Chidester (1992, 13) argues,

> discount the white colonial presence in South Africa.... Identified with the homestead, the land, and a specific locality, the ancestors might have become even more crucial as a spiritual anchor that tied people to places that were being threatened and destabilized by European colonial encroachment.

Graves of the ancestors became what Colson (1997) called 'land shrines'; simple monuments offering an alternative for official history writing and legal land rights. At their graves the ancestors were honoured who had once conquered and developed the land now inhabited. They represented the continuity of human life and offered, just as in earlier days, a home and a past, i.e. a territory in both space and time, to people from various origins and bloodlines. Therefore, notwithstanding the unsettling South African reality of absence of land rights, migration labour and the constant threat of evictions, the ancestors would provide a sense of stability to black communities, even more because their existence was ignored in any official way. Christianity in South Africa was widespread, but with most people it had not ousted older traditions. Going to church did not prevent people from performing ancestral rituals at home, or from believing that God was the same as Unkulunkulu (Berglund 1976; Chidester 1992). Thus, for the vast majority of black South Africans, both Christians

---

civilization, in modern South African game farms, as Andrews et al. show elsewhere in this volume, they are being removed because their presence distort the idea of pure wilderness.

and non-Christians, the ancestor discourse was increasingly perceived as a domain in which white people had no access, which provided an alternative 'map' and an alternative past, safe from white people's manipulation (Crais 2002).

Connected to the ancestor discourse is the discourse of witchcraft. Beliefs in witchcraft have been said to originate from "a deep suspicion of power" (Laburthe-Tolra 1977, 1080). At the same time, according to Geschiere (1995, 212), it

> expresses the frightening realization that aggression threatens from within... the very space where complete solidarity and trust should reign without fail. But this discourse also expresses the effort to maintain relations despite this terrible threat—after all,... 'one must learn to live with one's sorcerer'.

In the course of the 20th century, witchcraft became increasingly associated with bureaucracy, capital and large-scale land ownership, whether black or white. The unbalance between man and earth, the parched and exhausted soil in the reserves and around the homesteads, the spread of diseases amongst people and cattle, and the migrant worker's loneliness and poverty were ascribed to evil powers which had brought chaos to the world. Landowners were often associated with witchcraft and suspected of having evil powers, although they were not often directly accused of witchcraft. The stereotypical witch was someone within the community who envied another's success, which made white capitalist landowners unlikely witches. Still, possessing the same attributes as witches, they were seen as metaphorical 'witches' (e.g. witchlike masters who had turned their workers into zombies),[5] or witches' familiars. Because of their wealth, they were also potential victims of witchcraft. Either way, they were vulnerable within the discourse of witchcraft; they could be cursed by witches, combated by witch-doctors, or, although it did not happen often, attacked by angry neighbours. (Comaroff & Comaroff 1999; 2004; Crais 2002; Niehaus 2001)

Another domain where the bond between the African and his land still existed, was in narratives. As was the case in Afrikaner farm novels, loss of land and the need to re-establish a continuous relationship with it was reflected as part of a nationalist discourse in black literature; the Afrikaner National Party originated in the same era as the ANC. African writers, too,

---

[5] Zombies are people who have died but are resurrected by witches, or they have been drugged and hypnotised by them.

tried to find a grip in the past. For both Africans and Afrikaners, struggling with the early 20th century present, a grip on the past was a grip on the land, not through title deeds, but through the presence of the ancestors. The economic and physical reality of land was connected to "the metaphysical concept that man was linked to his ancestors through the belief in the concept of continuity, the living, the dead and the unborn" and in which "history speaks through the rewriting of the land and its names" (Adewoye 1989, XIII; Gunner 1996, 123).

Shortly after the Natives Land Act had been implemented in 1913, Sol Plaatje wrote his highly successful book *Native Life in South Africa* (1916), starting with the sentence, "Awaking on Friday morning, June 20, 1913, the South African native found himself, not actually a slave, but a pariah in the land of his birth" (Plaatje 2006, 21). He presented the book in London and Canada, hoping one of the overseas governments would see the injustice of the Land Act and intervene. Although the public sympathised, his campaign had no effect. While still in London, Plaatje wrote the first black South African novel, *Mhudi, an epic of South African Native life a hundred years ago*, in which he painted a picture of the pre-colonial past that reflected on political issues of his time. As Chennells (1997, 47) summed up *Mhudi*'s message:

> The pre-colonial order may have lacked breadth of vision but it gave people an opportunity to live in harmony with the land, whereas the Act of Union had by 1920 revealed itself as creating for blacks a metaphorical wilderness where they are alienated from their past, from whites and from the land itself.

Mhudi was only published in 1930, after drastic editing.

Because of the difficulty in getting work published in English, some black writers preferred publishing in their mother tongue, even though it often meant being less widely read. In the 1920s Nontsizi Mgqwetho published numerous poems in a Xhosa newspaper. Her work has only recently been reviewed by literary critics and translated into English. She focussed on land issues, politics and the role of the poet:

> Today you are a stranger in Africa
> You go about clutching at straws:
> Groom your shield, the land of your fathers
> Is now the playground of strangers.
> (Brown 2006, 42)

The choice of language and its aesthetic consequences became a political issue when in 1938 BW Vilakazi publicly attacked his colleague HIE Dhlomo for writing in English instead of Zulu (Atwell 2002). Even so, both their work showed, according to Liz Gunner (1996, 121), the same "intent on a process of reclamation through culture" and concern with "loss of land, nation, history". In the following fragment, Vilakazi (1973, 101/127) shows how the land lends inspiration to the poet and therefore meaning to history:

> ... Give me, I pray, a place like this—
> O you spirits of my fathers!—
> When I, one day, shall have the power
> To glean the wisdom of the Zulus
> And write about it in my books....

After the 1940s, black written literature dealing with land issues became scarce. Black writers increasingly encountered problems in getting their work published, and those who persevered turned their focus to the cities. There might also have been a reluctance to write about land, as Antjie Krog pointed out, remembering her days as a township school teacher in the 1980s. One day, she recounts, she asked her students to look out of the window to the fields outside, and write about what they saw. After a few minutes one of the students threw down his pen and said, "Why should *we* write about *your* land?" (Krog 2006, XVI).

The lack of written literature however, did not imply silence. As Liz Gunner (2004, 4) wrote: "The need for societies to have memory banks that act as mirrors and as a form of working archive led in many instances to the extensive use of oral poetry to formalize memory of the past, and to make the past comprehensible and accessible." Unlike written literature, oral literature was independent, could not be censored and had no language problems. Furthermore, like the ancestor discourse, it was 'invisible'—if only because it was not recognised as literature—and inaccessible, often incomprehensible, for white people. Left in peace, oral literature remained a thriving medium which was continually renewed, embodying an identity rooted in time and space. In the townships and the mines new genres of migrants' songs came into being, in which people's identities were linked to places of origin and stories of eviction or migration. (Barber 1999; Brown 1999, 2006; Coplan 1987; James 1999; Gunner 1996; Van Vuuren 1996)

Some oral narratives offer quite explicit comments on the farm workers' reality, often in the form of satirical allegories. In the early 1980s, Hewitt (1985, 30) recorded Kalahari Bushmen telling

> humorous stories about a jackal trickster who works as a gardener for a foolish, brutal, white farmer and whose efforts are largely aimed at outwitting his employer.

Another example can be found in the many stories about zombies that have circulated in Africa, especially since colonial times.[6] In these stories, zombies often take the form of a witch's non-resisting, harshly treated slaves, working hard, mostly as farm labourers. They can never return home, they have forgotten about their past and have no other desire than eating porridge. Their tongues are cut out: which means that they lack the ability to express themselves, to criticise or to complain. As such they symbolise the effects of social disruption, homelessness and loss of identity. As the witch's helpers, they are a danger to the community, as migrant labourers they explain the high levels of unemployment at the countryside. (Comaroff 1999; Niehaus 2001)

All these forms of indirect resistance to hegemonic control can be interpreted as what Deleuze and Guattari (1988) called 'nomadism'. Nomadism is "any activity that transgresses contemporary social codes through dissolution of cultural and territorial boundaries" (Young 1994, 24). Ignoring territorial boundaries and notions of ownership, creating alternative territorial perceptions by building land shrines or performing ancestor rituals, fighting power blocks by means which are culturally and epistemologically not recognised by the people in power, and 'writing' back in a non-existent literary genre can all be seen as forms of nomadism. Not surprisingly, for a long time these nomadic activities were almost non-existent in any official record. Only recently have researchers shown interest in them, and they often had to leave the 'beaten tracks' to find their data.

Nomadic Appearances in Farm Novels

Interestingly, in white literature one may not find many black farmers, but one or more of the forms of nomadic resistance just mentioned can often be deduced from within the text. Like white farmers and politicians, farm novels' protagonists claimed their exclusive rights to the land (one of the premises of Apartheid) on the grounds that they had worked and loved the land for generations and that their ancestors were buried there (Coetzee 1988; Coetzee 2000). Of course, many (former) black tenants and farm workers could (and among themselves did) make exactly the same claims, even if it was only in the 1990s that these claims could be more overtly ventured. Before that, one had to read between the lines to

[6] See note 5.

find references to black farmers and their protest against land and labour laws in South African literature. Still, they are there. Even in the most traditional *plaasromans*, the version of reality the writer so meticulously tries to display is at some point inconsistent and, more often than not, another version of reality is hinted at. This often happens when somebody in the novel dies or comes close to death, in these unsettling moments when constructions of reality are being shaken. Nomadic forms of black resistance could be kept out of sight in superficial constructions of daily life, but death has the habit of giving glimpses of what lies beneath the surface: the hidden and ignored aspects of a multifaceted reality.

In literature of the 1920s and 1930s, some South African English writers avoided the metaphorical complications of death by burying their white characters in marginal, uncommon places, or omitting the burial completely from the text (Postel 2008). When not buried or buried high on a mountain in a grave made of solid rock, the dead are taken out of both the social and natural cycle of life and death. Thus, readers would not so easily be reminded of the fact that the remains of the dead all decompose into the same soil, bearing witness to a multi-cultural history and present. But in Afrikaans farm novels, graves were specifically part of the cyclic continuity of rural order and could therefore not be marginalised; the farmer's duty was to link the individual to nature and lineage: to "transport the subject into the mythic time of the ancestors" (Coetzee 1988, 99). In *Laat vrugte* (1939) Van den Heever almost reveals how little white this mythic time really is. Farmer Sybrand alienates his (extended) family from him by letting profit prevail over solidarity. His wife dies, his son leaves him. Even a passing group of farm labourers cannot be bothered to stay and work for him, which suddenly infuriates him—one of the very few references to changing labour relations. When at the end of his now lonely life he suffers a severe stroke, he suddenly becomes aware of a terrifying, omnipresent chaos:

> Everything that had always been far apart and separated by reason, has now appeared unto him as so close together that life itself, the dark movement caused by the conversion of space and time, completely overwhelms him.... More and more he is sinking into the abyss where life lies undivided, a big, terrible oneness; but he cannot tell his secret to a living soul because he cannot speak; the secret is safe now. (Van den Heever 1987, 212; *my translation*)

It is not more than a hint; eventually preference is given to the construction of a reality conformable to the Afrikaner Nationalist ideology of his time. The son returns and buries the father; the continuity of social structures is guaranteed.

A decade later, Herman Charles Bosman seems to be mocking these constructions by magnifying a similar moment of existential agony and leaving it unresolved. In the story "Unto dust", first published in the 1940s, Oom Schalk Lourens has had unsettling nightmares. In his dreams it had seemed to him

> that the whole world was a burial ground. I thought it was the earth itself that was a graveyard, and not just those little fenced-in bits of land dotted with tombstones, in the shade of a western-province oaktree or by the side of a Transvaal koppie (Bosman 1974, 13).

When Oom Schalk tells his friend Stoffel about his dream, the latter tells him a story to reassure him. This story is a *mise-en-abyme*: a story within a story within a story, all mirroring, mimicking and mocking each other, just as they are mirroring and commenting on certain developments in the 1940s. At the centre of all these stories is Hans' grave, in which, accidentally, the bones of a black and a white man have been mixed. Knowing that ancestors and their graves tend to symbolise the continuity of collective or individual land rights, this grave questions, at the very least, the very foundation of that continuity. Our fenced-in white people's graveyards, Bosman seems to be saying to his readers, are as superficial and cosmetic as Malan's Apartheid plans.

Much as secret and/or sacred spaces in South Africa offered ground for an independent black cultural identity, they also represented an uncanny, indistinct threat to the people in power. Not surprisingly then, in literature the invisible *other* starts haunting the protagonists (and the reader) in non-human forms. They do not only point to the existence of an alternative, suppressed reality, but also to the possibility of that reality becoming the ground for a new socio-political order. In the 1970s writers like Nadine Gordimer (*The conservationist*, 1974), Anna Louw (*Kroniek van perdepoort*, 1975) and JM Coetzee (*In the heart of the country*, 1977) would put the competing ancestors at the heart of their farm novels. Even then, one has to read between the lines. Black farmers are present here, more than in earlier decades, but on the surface they seem to have accepted the status quo. References to resistance are only found at a subconscious or metaphorical level. In *The Conservationist* several events indicate forms of nomadism; some people are ignoring the farmer's fences and signs and take shortcuts over his farm, others are living at the farm without the farmer's knowledge or consent. Scarier for the farmer, however, are the fires that scorch his fields (even though they might be nothing more than regular bushfires) and the presence of a black man's body which he knows lies buried in these fields, and which at some point floats to the surface due to torrential rains. Both fire and body can be interpreted in many ways; they are metaphors in several discourses, including the discourses of resistance: the fire of purifying rituals performed to diminish the evil powers of capitalism, and the black ancestor rising from the grave to take revenge or demand justice. Eventually these metaphorical or ritual forms of resistance turn out to be more powerful than any rebellious act could be, powerful enough to chase the farmer from the farm. (Postel 2007)

In later farm novels more horror stories are told. In Etienne van Heerden's *Toorberg* (1986) the anger that has been suppressed for centuries is transformed and released as a force of nature. Here too purifying rituals take place, not performed by humans but by Mother Earth herself, when underground water rises to the surface with such force that the farmer's ancestors' coffins are all washed away. It is only in 1993, one year before the National Party transferred power to the ANC, that Eben Venter in *Foxtrot van die Vleiseters* shifted the focus from uncanny representations of invisible people's wrath to disturbed human beings in a complicated reality. His novel can be read as Van den Heever's *Laat vrugte* rewritten; the mutual pain and uncertainties caused by strained interracial relations that were still hidden in *Laat vrugte* are in *Foxtrot van die vleiseters* a central theme. The farmer is evicting farmworkers' families after their lifelong service because he does not know what benefits they will try to gain from pending political changes—reflecting a real trend in the early 1990s. The farmworker's daughter Buziwe takes revenge by telling the farmer's son a story that shows the raw nature of interracial relations, while feeding old, colonial fears. According to an old local legend, a white woman once went for a walk and was attacked by jackals; when they found her, all that was left of her legs were the bones. Buziwe, however, reveals a version of the story which serves as a counter-memory of the history of early land dispossession. The truth, she says, is that the woman was ambushed by Bushmen, who were hiding in the hills and were so hungry that they ate her legs. Through this small, embedded, oral narrative Venter shows the reader a frightening passage to an invisible world of counter narratives and everything they stand for, turning the ignored black inhabitant with retroactive effect into an undeniable presence.

Conclusion

In the first half of the 20th century, the South African state implemented land reforms which were meant to improve the legibility of the region, integrate the white community, restrict the (economical) freedom of black farmers, and adapt the agricultural industry to make it internationally competitive. These reforms, abolishing most current tenure systems, and facilitating land deals with foreign investors who did not only contribute capital, but were also more prone to abide by the new laws and ignore customary rights of tenants, brought about a more profound rural transformation than the colonisation process and the introduction of individual landownership had done almost a century earlier. Both white and black farmers lost title deeds of and access to land, tenants were evicted, new crops were introduced, farms expanded, land use changed, labour relations were transformed. These and following events were dramatic for so many people that they led to violent strikes and rural uprisings, to which the government responded with regulations that again favoured whites over blacks, thus deepening racial differences. In a bid to mollify the white part of the population to its land and labour 'project', the state had involved Afrikaner authors of history and literature. As could be seen above, in the Afrikaner farm novel the white farmer was staged as a son of the soil, and on that score entitled to the ownership of land. Indeed, the white farmer of the past became a metaphor for ethnic superiority and political power for the future. In this respect, Afrikaner literature can be argued to have boosted the state's land and labour policy of the first half of the 20th century. However, as the discussion of later farm novels has demonstrated, the literary assertion of traditional white ownership of land and supremacy over the African population gradually crumbles. Thus, we may conclude that the farm novel as a genre has found its origin in a politically engineered discourse of the continuity of land use and agricultural labour relations in which the legacy and supremacy of the Afrikaner Boer and the white foreigner's individual ownership of large tracts of land were imagined traditions. At the same time, however, conflicts between black and white farmers, partly provoked or at least deepened by national land policy in the first decades of the 20th century, continuously kept inspiring South African writers and story tellers, even when the subject was categorically denied and ignored by politicians and historians. Thus, from its initial propagandistic status the farm novel grew into a genre that revealed a more complex reality, where defined oppositions with regard to traditions and land rights, oppositions between white and black, and local and foreign, were problematized.

Black South African literature and other black cultural discourses have undoubtedly influenced the farm novel over time. For black South Africans, loss of access to land was the main cause for their socio-economic and existential vulnerability, which was consolidated by their marginalisation in space, and in official and mainstream legal, political and literary discourses. In parallel discourses they however kept finding ways to mark space and express political aspirations, and here too land rights became a basic condition or a metaphor for cultural identity, power and autonomy. Like the acute and still unresolved problems land reforms have caused for black South Africans, these counter-discourses have been largely ignored by those in power in the 20th century. Yet they have become more and more visible in white writing of the same era. Transgressing cultural and social boundaries, these surfacing counter-narratives also represented the increasingly nomadic forms of black farmers' resistance to hegemonic control, and they proved to have been pointers to future land claims under the post-Apartheid government.

Acknowledgements

Research for this paper was funded by the National Research Foundation (NRF), South Africa.

Bibliography

Adewoye, Sam A. 1989. *The Concept of Land in the African Novel.* Ibadan: Evans Brothers.

Atwell, David. 2002. "Modernizing Tradition/ Traditionalizing Modernity. Reflections on the Dhlomo-Vilakazi Dispute." *Research in African Literatures* 33.1: 94–119.

Barber, Karin. 1999. "Obscurity and Exegesis in African Oral Praise Poetry." In *Oral Literature and Performance in Southern Africa*, edited by Duncan Brown, 27–49. Oxford: James Curry.

Berglund, Axel-Ivar. 1976. *Zulu Thought Patterns and Symbolism.* London: C. Hurst & Co.

Bernstein, Henry. 1996. "South Africa's Agrarian Question: Extreme and Exceptional?" *The Journal of Peasant Studies* 23.2&3: 1–52.

Bosman, Herman Charles. 1974. "Unto Dust." In *Unto Dust*, edited by Lionel Abrahams, 13–17. Cape Town: Human & Rousseau.

Botha, Elize, 1987. "Inleiding" In *Laat vrugte*, C.M. van den Heever. Pretoria, Van Schaik.

Bouch, Richard. 1997. "Eastern Cape Wool Farmers: Production and Control in Cathcart, 1920–1940." In *White Farms, Black Labor. The State and Agrarian Change in Southern Africa 1910–1950*, edited by Allan H. Jeeves and Jonathan Crush, 94–113. Portsmouth/ Pietermaritzburg/ Oxford: Heinemann/ University of Natal Press/ James Curry.

Bradford, Helen. 1987. *A Taste of Freedom: The ICU in Rural South Africa, 1924–1930.* New Haven: Yale University Press.

Bradstock, Alastair. 2005. "Changing livelihoods and land reform: evidence from the Northern Cape Province of South Africa." *World Development* 33.11: 1979–1992.

Brown, Duncan. 1999. Introduction to *Oral Literature and Performance in Southern Africa*, edited by Duncan Brown, 1–17. Oxford: James Curry.

——. 2006. *To Speak of this Land: Identity and Belonging in South Africa and Beyond.* Scottsville: University of Kwazulu Natal Press.

Bundy, Colin. 1988. *The Rise and Fall of the South African Peasantry.* Cape Town/ Johannesburg/ London: David Philip/ James Curry.

Chennells, Anthony. 1997. "Plotting South African History: Narrative in Sol Plaatje's 'Mhudi'." *English in Africa* 24.1: 37–58.

Chidester, David. 1992. *Religions of South Africa.* London/New York: Routledge.

Coetzee, Ampie. 2000. *'n Hele Os vir 'n Ou Broodmes. Grond en die Plaasnarratief sedert 1595.* Pretoria/ Kaapstad: Van Schaik/ Human & Rousseau.

Coetzee, John M. 1988. *White Writing. On the Culture of Letters in South Africa.* New Haven/ London: Yale University Press.

Colson, Elizabeth. 1997. "Places of Power and Shrines of the Land." *Paideuma. Mitteilungen zur Kulturkunde* 43: 47–58.

Comaroff, Jean, and John L. Comaroff. 1999. "Alien-nation: Zombies, Immigrants and Millennial Capitalism." *Codesria Bulletin* 3 & 4: 17–28.

——. 2004. "Policing Culture, Cultural Policing: Law and Social Order in Postcolonial South Africa." *Law & Social Inquiry* 29.3: 513–545.

Coplan, David. 1987. "Eloquent Knowledge: Lesotho Migrants' Songs and the Anthropology of Experience." *American Ethnologist* 14.3: 413–433.

Cotula, Lorenzo, Camilla Toulmin, and Ced Hesse. 2004. *Land Tenure and Administration in Africa. Lessons of Experiences and Emerging issues.* London: International Institute for Environment and Development.

Crais, Clifton. 2002. *The Politics of Evil: Magic, State Power, and the Political Imagination in South Africa.* Cambridge: Cambridge University Press.

Deleuze, Gilles, and Felix Guattari. 1988. *A Thousand Plateaus: Capitalism en Schizophrenia.* London: Athlone.

Department of Land Affairs. 1997. *White Paper on South African Land policy.* Department of Land Affairs, Pretoria.

Devarenne, Nicole. 2009. "Nationalism and the Farm Novel in South Africa, 1883–2004." *Journal of Southern Afrian Studies* 35.3: 627–642.

Ditlhake, Abie. 1997. "Labor Tenancy and the Politics of Land Reform in South Africa." In *No more tears. Struggles for land in Mpumalanga, South Africa,* edited by R. Levin and D. Weiner. Trenton: Africa World Press.

Dolny, Helena & Heinz Klug. 1992. "Land Reform: Legal Support and Economic Regulation." *South African Review* 6: 322–337.

Du Plooy, Heilna. 1998. "C.M. van den Heever (1902–1957)" In *Perspektief en Profiel. 'n Afrikaanse Literatuurgeskiedenis. Deel 2,* edited by H. van Coller. Pretoria, J.L. van Schaik. 653–664.

Geschiere, Peter. 1995. *The Modernity of Witchcraft. Politics and the Occult in Postcolonial Africa.* Charlottesville/London: University Press of Virginia.

Gunner, Liz. 1996. "Names and the Land. Poetry of Belonging and Unbelonging, a Comparative Approach." In *Text, Theory, Space. Land, Literature and History in South Africa and Australia,* edited by Kate Darian-Smith, Liz Gunner and Sarah Nutall. London/NY: Routledge.

——. 2004. "Africa and Orality." In *The Cambridge History of African and Caribbean Literature,* edited by F. Abiola Irele and Simon Gikandi. Cambridge, CUP.

Hewitt, R.L. 1985. "The oral Literature of the San and Related People." In *Literatures in African Languages. Theoretical Issues and Sample Surveys,* edited by B.W. Andrzejewski, S. Pilaszewicz and W. Tyloch. Warschau/Cambridge: Wiedza Powszechna State Publishing House/ Cambridge University Press.

Hofmeyr, Isabel. 1987. "Building a Nation from Words: Afrikaans Language, Literature and Ethnic Identity, 1902–1924." In *The Politics of Race, Class, and Nationalism in Twentieth-Century South Africa,* edited by Shula Marks and Stanley Trapido, 95–123. London / New York: Longman.

James, Deborah. 1999. *Songs of the women migrants.* Edinburgh, Edinburgh University Press.

Keegan, Tim. 1988. *Facing the Storm. Portraits of Black Lives in Rural South Africa.* London/ Athens: Zed books ltd./Ohio Universiy Press.

——. 1991. The Making of the Rural Economy. In *Studies in the Economic History of South Africa. Volume Two: South Africa, Lesotho and Swaziland,* edited by Konczacki, Z.A.; Parpart, Jane L.; Shaw, Timothy M. Krog, Antjie. 2006. "From //Kabbo to Zapiro: A Foreword." In *To Speak of this Land. Identity and Belonging in South Africa and Beyond,* edited by Duncan Brown, VIII–XX. Scottsville: University of KwaZulu-Natal Press.

Laburthe-Tolra, Philippe. 1977. *Minlaaba, Histoire et Societé Traditionelle chez les Beti du Sud Cameroun.* Paris: Champion.

Letsoalo, Essy M. 1987. *Land Reform. A Black Perspective.* Johannesburg: Skotaville.

Marks, Shula. 1970. "Review: African and Afrikaner history." *Journal of African History* 11.3: 435–447.

Murray, Martin J. 1989. " 'The Natives are Always Stealing': White Vigilantes and 'the Reign of Terror' in the Orange Free State, 1918–24." *Journal of African History* 30: 107–123.

Niehaus, Isak. 2001. *Witchcraft, Power and Politics. Exploring the Occult in the South African Lowveld.* London: Pluto Press.

Plaatje, Sol. 2006. *Native Life in South Africa. Before and Since the European War and the Boer Rebellion.* Hard Press.

Postel, Gitte. 2007. "The Diviner's Task. Confinement and Transformation through Myth and Ritual in Gordimer's 'The Conservationist'." *Research in African Literatures* 38.4: 47–60.

——. 2008. "The Unsettling Side of Death. Post-colonial Irony in Bosman's 'Unto Dust'." *Safundi. The Journal of South African and American Studies* 9.2: 193–205.

Ross, Robert. 1999. *A Concise History of South Africa.* Cambridge: Cambridge University Press.

——. 1995. "Paternalism, Patriarchy and Afrikaans." *South African Historical Journal* 32: 34–47.

Schirmer, Stefan. "Land, legislation and Labor Tenants: Resistance in Lydenburg, 1938." In *White Farms, black Labor. The state and Agrarian Change in Southern Africa, 1910–1950,* Alan H. Jeeves & Jonathan Crush (eds). Portsmouth/ Pietrmaritzburg/Oxford, Heinemann/University of Natal Press/ James Currey, 1997: 46–60.

Transvaal Labour Commission. 1903–4. *Reports of the Transvaal Labour Commission.* London: British Parliament.

Van den Heever, C.M. 1987. *Laat Vrugte.* Pretoria: J.L. Van Schaik.

Van Onselen, Charles. 1997. "Paternalism and Violence on the Maize Farms of the South-Western Transvaal, 1900–1950." In *White Farms, Black Labor. The State and Agrarian Change in Southern Africa, 1910–1950,* edited by Alan H. Jeeves and Jonathan Crush, 192–314. Portsmouth/ Pietermaritzburg/ Oxford: Heinemann/ University of Natal Press/ James Currey.

Van Vuuren, Helize. 1996. "Orality in the Margins of Literary History: Prolegomena to a Study of Interaction between Bushmen Orality and Afrikaans Literature." In *Rethinking South African Literary History,* edited by J.A. Smtih, A. Van Wyk and J.-P. Wade. Durban: Y Press.

Venter, Eben. 1993. *Foxtrot van die Vleiseters.* Cape Town: Tafelberg.

Vilakazi, B.W. 1973. *Zulu Horizons. Translations of Inkondlo kaZulu and Amal'ezulu.* Edited by D. McK. Malcolm, J. Mandlenkosi Sikakana and Florence Louise Friedman (trans.). Johannesburg: University of Witwatersrand Press.

Young, Robert. 1994. "Colonialism and the Desiring-Machine." In *Liminal Postmodernisms: the Postmodern, the (Post-)Colonial, and the (Post-)Feminist,* edited by Theo D'haen and Hans Bertens, 11–34. Amsterdam: Atlanta.

COMPETING RHETORIC IN THE CONTEXT OF FOREIGN LAND ACQUISITIONS: THE CASE OF 'NEW NIGERIA'

Akachi Odoemene

Introduction

As one of the countries in Africa which has been and probably will continue to be targeted for large scale land-grabbing by foreign investors (Liversage, 2010: 3), Nigeria offers an interesting example of government-supported foreign land acquisitions (FLAs). Over the last years white Zimbabwean farmers in particular have been attracted by the government to set up their large-scale farms in different parts of Nigeria. Unlike the economic 'surge' of the last half century, triggered off by the finding of oil in the country, this new government strategy seeks to modernise and improve agricultural practices and productions. In this respect the Nigerian case resembles those of other African countries which lease out land to foreign farming investors. However, while in many other African countries foreign land acquisitions are couched in secrecy because of highly controversial land appropriations, the Nigerian government seems to have opted for a different strategy to prevent local resistance, openly and emphatically supporting this new development.

The following discussion explores the government rhetoric and the public response that has accompanied the State's latest agricultural reform, focusing on the metaphor of the 'New Nigeria'. The trope was introduced by the then president Olusegun Obasanjo when the first white Zimbabwean farmers came to Nigeria. The metaphor has been a key strategic element in the government's rhetoric of its agricultural programme, and has stirred quite some counter rhetoric. Therefore, the discussion focuses specifically on the use of it in government and public (anti)rhetoric, and does not include other rhetorical tropes that accompany the coming of the white Zimbabwean farmers to Nigeria, such as neo-colonialism.

The discussion is held against the background of pertinent topics in the "Vision 2020", a policy plan launched by the Nigerian Government on 15 October 2009. The document contains a "Seven Point Agenda", which lists as focal policy areas, among others, land reform, food security and agricultural development. Politically charged as they are, these three areas can be expected to become even more hotly debated in the context of the current large-scale foreign land acquisitions in Nigeria. Paradoxically, the Nigerian government seems to think that with the introduction of the "New Nigeria" metaphor the sting is taken out of the debate. In the following discussion the themes of land reform, food security and agricultural development are approached from a historical perspective. In fact, this historical contextualisation is a necessary preliminary to gaining insight into some salient political strategies implicit in the government's use of the rhetorical trope, "New Nigeria", in the context of FLAs.

Once the historical dimensions have been laid out, the concept is analysed in its contemporary rhetorical manifestations. The government's rhetoric on and their reception of the Zimbabwean farmers have evoked a great number of public reactions, ranging from the Zimbabwean farmers themselves to journalists, politicians, and subsistence farmers affected by the Zimbabwean farms. The discussion presents samples from magazine articles and personal interviews reflecting these views. In this way the discussion aims to demonstrate that the government rhetoric of the 'New Nigeria' directs the public debate away from the encounter between white Zimbabwean farmers and local farmers as a result of granted land leases, to a much more positive vision, that of a 'New Nigeria' which is the result of 'magical' intervention.

Nigerian Land Reform in Its Historical Context: Land Tenure, Rights, Access and Use

Land lies at the heart of the social, economic and political life in Nigeria, as it remains a major factor in the country's well-being, not only because of its economic values, but also because of the social recognition and status it confers on its owner or owners. However, a lack of clarity regarding land rights causes land tenure to be a bitterly contested issue. This is predominantly due to the various transformations which different communities in Nigeria have undergone in terms of land tenure systems. The three different periods of the country's national development—the precolonial, the colonial and the post-colonial—have all left their traces on the character of land rights, use and access in the country.

Prior to colonialism, security of tenure in most of what eventually became Nigeria depended on collective and communal holding by the male members of a society. Also, there were (and still are) strong traditional beliefs of cultural ties between people, especially among indigenous groups, and the land of their birth or land of their forefathers (ancestral land). Ordinarily, membership of such indigenous groups confers (indigenes) 'autochthonous rights' of ownership over the ancestral lands. Society-specific customary laws provided the means through which individuals or groups, differentiated by ethnicity, class, and gender, negotiated access to and control of such lands (Korieh, 2010).

Under colonial rule, two broad categories of land tenure systems prevailed (Meek, 1957). In Northern Nigeria, all hitherto customarily-held lands were placed under the control of and subject to the disposition of the colonial Governor, who was empowered to grant rights of occupancy for definite or indefinite terms, to impose conditions and to charge a rent. In contradistinction, the system in southern Nigeria recognised land ownership by lineages or extended families, although the colonial authorities reserved exclusive rights over lands which had been expressly acquired for public purposes as Crown land (Mabogunje, 2010: 3). The only control imposed by law on the lineages and other local land holders was an obligation to seek the consent of government when rights were being conveyed to aliens.

In post-colonial Nigeria, land became a key political, social and cultural asset and consequently a common focus of political manipulation (Toulmin, 2002; Turner, 2004). The reworking of customary land law by the male-dominated Nigerian government privileged not only male rights, but also the interests of wealthier men. One such instance is the introduction of the highly controversial Land Use law enacted by the military head of state, Olusegun Obasanjo (1976–1979). Promulgated in 1978 as "Decree 6" and annexed to the 1979 Constitution as an "Act" on the eve of the military junta's hand-over of political power to elected civilians (Ako, 2009: 293–4), the Land Use legislation is perhaps the most controversial law in Nigeria. It was ostensibly designed to nationalise landholding in the country, purportedly due to the increasing difficulty experienced by private and government institutions to acquire land for development. Combined with changes in Local Government powers, the Act shifted the balance of power significantly against the local inhabitants, essentially making the federal government the owner of all lands which it held in trust and administered for the use and common benefit of all Nigerians.

In contradistinction, private persons were only entitled to a leasehold interest through a right of occupancy. Furthermore, it removed from local chiefs and traditional leaders their power to allocate 'unused' lands and vested such authority in the governor of a state and the chairman of a local government area (Blench, 2003: 4). Thus, the land tenure reform did not seek to redistribute land, but rather facilitated an abrogation and stripping of the customary (or "autochthonous") rights of ownership of communal (and ancestral) lands. In fact, the law made the procedure for obtaining and developing land become excessively bureaucratised, obstructive, and riddled with corruption (Nwaka, 2005). For instance, Francis (1984: 5–28) revealed that groups of elite, who had access to the state structure, managed to benefit disproportionately from the Act by consciously manipulating the allocations committee. Additionally, by virtue of this Act, most Nigerian cities and towns have become land speculators' paradise. The activities of these speculators have driven up the economic value of land beyond the reach of local populations. In the rural areas government functionaries, under the guise of the Act, have dispossessed illiterate natives of their lands.

These illegal land acquisitions have led to protests by thousands of Nigerian citizens unduly dispossessed by this process. They demand the Act to be either amended in a substantial way or be expunged from the constitution (Mabogunje, 2010). In some cases, even after government invoked its 'right of eminent domain' to compulsorily acquire and pay compensation for land for public purposes, owners of land have refused to vacate their land, and instead challenge such actions by the government in law courts. Presently, although the Act remains in force despite severe criticism regarding its impact on land tenure, rights, access and use generally, it is noteworthy that a Land Use (Amendment) Bill, which seeks to review the exclusive powers of government in relation to the alienation/parting of possession with property, is currently under discussion by the country's National Assembly.

Food Security and Agricultural Development in a Historical Context

In contrast to its present position as one of the largest net and massive food importers in the world, Nigeria once depended solely on agriculture as its main source of foreign exchange.[1] From the pre-colonial times up to the early post-colonial era Nigeria experienced a period that could well be described as the 'golden era' of agricultural production. Especially since

[1] Import of agricultural products is presently estimated at 3 billion Naira (approximately $20 million USD) annually (Ajayeoba, 2011; Bakare, 2009) and in 2010 the import bill for rice alone, one of the country's main staple foods, was $1billion (Anon., 2011).

the late colonial period when agriculture accounted for 60–70% of total exports, Nigeria depended heavily on agricultural production to support its economy. For instance, average annual growth rates of 3–4% were achieved for agricultural and food crops. Government revenues depended heavily on agricultural export taxes, and both the current account and fiscal balances depended to some extent on agriculture. Although this was attained through complete reliance on small scale farming and farmers (Auta and Dafwang, 2010: 138), general development activities were undertaken to modernise the agricultural sector (Adekanye et al., 2009: 6; Piñeiro, 2007).

At the time of independence (1960), Nigeria was self-sufficient in agricultural production and food, and was actually a net food exporter, with minimal imports of processed food for the elite (Daramola et al., 2007). At the time experiments with new agricultural activities such as "farm settlements" and "nuclear plantations" in Western and Eastern Nigeria respectively were highly successful. Modelled after the Israeli *Kibutz* system, they relied on public institutions and universities, such as the Agricultural Development Boards and Agricultural Research Institutes. In fact, they were acclaimed nationally and internationally as revolutionalising the agricultural production in the component regions of the Nigerian state (Olayiede and Olatunbosun, 1972; FAO, 1966). Not until the Nigerian civil war period (1967–70), did the country witness its first 'food shocks'.

By the first half of the 1970s Nigeria began to experience chronic food deficits, or what Sano (1983) has termed 'food crisis'. Failure on the part of consecutive Nigerian governments to implement country-wide agricultural innovations to improve productivity that included the local peasants, resulted in the fall of total annual food production in the country (Mustapha, 2010; Hans-Otto, 1983: 23). The immediate cause of the agricultural crisis, however, was the 'launching' of crude oil into the Nigerian economy and the eventual over-dependence of its economy on oil revenue. Since the oil wealth was not invested in agriculture, but rather in commerce, construction and manufacturing, the result was a dramatic neglect of the agricultural sector (Daramola et al., 2007). The drop in food production led to heavy increases of food imports, so much so that by the end of the 1970s the level of food imports was about 15 times higher than at the beginning of the decade (Ogen, 2007). Between 1970 and 1974, for instance, agricultural exports as a percentage of total exports fell from about 43% to slightly over 7% (Daramola et al., 2007).

The extent of this shift in governmental priorities and their implications for a food crisis were only partly recognised in the Third National

Development Plan (1975–1980), where agriculture was allocated a meagre 5% of the total expenditure in the plan, while mining and quarrying under primary production i.e., investment in crude oil production, received 8.2% of the total investments (FRN, 1975: 84). The effects of this development on agricultural exports were equally notable. From the mid-1970s to the mid-1980s, the average annual growth rate of agricultural exports declined by 17%. By 1996 agriculture accounted for only 2% of exports. At present, agricultural exports are negligible and represent about 0.2% of total exports.[2] Nevertheless, an estimated 60% of Nigerians are employed in the rural sector (Daramola et al., 2007).

Another factor with a serious impact on agricultural and food production was the rural—urban migration, including in particular youths, teenagers and young unmarried adults, who diversify into a number of trading and non-agricultural service activities (Bryceson, 2002: 733; Mustapha, 1999; Yunusa, 1999). This migratory trend was particularly notable in the years following the end of the civil war (1967–1970). Impacting heavily on food production and sustainability, the consistent rural—urban migration not only strangulated the agricultural and food sector, it equally caused an increase in food imports.

Since the 1970s many development programmes have been instituted as corrective measures aiming at re-stimulating and reviving agricultural development and food production in Nigeria.[3] Most of these programmes were largely ill-conceived, prepared and implemented. Indeed, their high number underlines a lack of continuity, coordination and direction. The additional high-level corruption, caused most, if not all, to become a failure (Korieh, 2010; Joseph, 1978: 232; Forrest, 1977: 77–80).

---

[2] This economic phenomenon, as witnessed in Nigeria, is popularly referred to as 'Dutch disease' after events that occurred in the Netherlands during the 1970s following the discovery of natural gas under the North Sea. It can be triggered by sudden large inflows of foreign currency and is often associated with exports of a natural resource (typically oil or natural gas). "Dutch disease" weakens the economy when the sectors that are crowded out are vital to the country (World Bank, 2006).

[3] Among them are: the River Basin Development Authorities (RBDAS) of 1976, the Operation Feed the Nation (OFN) of 1977, the Green Revolution Programme (GRP) of 1980, the National Accelerated Food Production Project (NAFPP) of 1972; the Directorate for Food, Road and Rural Infrastructure (DFRRI) of 1986; National Agricultural Land Development Authority (NALDA) of 1992; National Accelerated Industrial Crops Production Programme (NAICPP) of 1996; Agriculture Development Programme (ADP); National Seed Service Programme (NSS); the establishment of the Federal Agriculture Coordinating Unit (FACU), Agriculture Credit Guarantee Scheme (ACGS), the Nigerian Agricultural Corporative and Rural Development Bank (NACRDB) and the contentious #200bn Commercial Agricultural Credit Scheme of 2009.

In recent years, Federal and State Governments of Nigeria have experimented with the agricultural components of the New Partnership for African Development (NEPAD), and the National Economic Empowerment Development Strategy (NEEDS) (GoN, 2004). While agricultural exports have strengthened since 2000, performance is still far below the economy's potential (Daramola et al., 2007). Agricultural holdings are small and scattered, and farming is still carried out with simple tools. Large-scale agriculture is not common. Not until the coming to power of the Obasanjo administration have far-reaching reforms been embarked on. One highly controversial reform measure is the "New Nigeria" programme which involves the invitation of foreigners, particularly white Zimbabweans (whom he called the "New Nigerians"), to come and invest in the country's agricultural sector (Daramola et al., 2007).

Rhetoric of the "New Nigeria" and the "New Nigerians"

1. *Background*

From 2000 some hundreds of white Zimbabwean commercial farmers who had been affected by the country's controversial land redistribution policy migrated to different other parts of the world in order to restart their agricultural businesses. In April 2004, Dr. Bukola Saraki, the Governor of Kwara State in the western part of Nigeria's Middle Belt region, took steps to bring some of the farmers to the country, citing Nigeria being in dire need of their expertise. This unprecedented move received presidential support from Chief Olusegun Obasanjo, a farmer himself. The claimed intention in wooing the white farmers was essentially to use their expertise for jump-starting Nigeria's moribund agricultural sector, and transform it into a commercial and mechanised one. By this, Saraki hoped his state "will be the backbone for Nigeria's agricultural drive" (Borzello, 2005).

Of the 3,500 evicted white Zimbabwean farmers, fifteen arrived in Nigeria in 2005 to evaluate and begin the task of commercial and mechanised farming in the country. They were settled at Shonga, a one-million resident semi-urban area located about 110 kilometres (68 miles) north of Ilorin, the Kwara State capital. Soon after, they organised themselves into a farmers union, the Kwa-Zimbo Enterprises Limited (now known as Shonga Farm Holdings Nigeria Limited). From this platform they began to relate with both the government and the people and indigenes of Shongaland. From among the latter, the farmers recruited farm workers and helps. The terms of the Memorandum of Understanding (MOU) between the Kwara State government and the Zimbabwean farmers "committed the State government to the provision of a series of services essential for the development of the commercial farms. Crucially, it committed the government to provide land" (Mustapha, 2010).

2. *Samples of Government Rhetoric*

Kwara State's Permanent Secretary of Lands and Housing Ministry, Mrs. Tayo Alao, affirmed the state's readiness to providing far reaching support to the Zimbabwean farmers, noting that the state "will do anything in our [sic] power to make this project a success" (Hofstter, 2004: 15). To this the then President Obasanjo added during the reception of a courtesy visit of the Zimbabwean farmers to the Presidential State House: "There's no need to worry about land, you'll get a "C of O"[4] of up to 99 years leasehold. The question of farmland is no problem here."[5] In fulfilment of this promise, the government invoked the provisions of the Land Use Act which vested it with the sole right to determine what, where and when any landed property could be given out and to whom. It initially allocated almost 200,000 hectares of choice agricultural land of the indigenous farmers, right next to the River Niger in Shongaland to the Zimbabwean farmers. This was not only almost twice as much as the white farmers had asked for, the government also promised to give more should the need arise (Hofstter, 2004).

The government's rhetoric concerning the first coming of the Zimbabwean farmers suggests that the "New Nigeria" contains unexplored and fertile land in abundance. Additionally, it implies that the farmers are attracted for their expertise, which is expected to be a solid support for overdue improvements in the country's agricultural sector. The grand gesture of the Kwara government to give the "New Nigerians" as much land as they need may be explained from the high expectations concerning their abilities—and the implicit government's own historically demonstrated lack of abilities. However, there is more political interest involved, for Kwara government has committed itself to the "New Nigeria" rhetoric in

[4] "C of O" is a Nigerian common parlance for the "Certificate of Occupancy," which is a legal document issued by the government for any land acquisition, irrespective of any circumstance. It embodies the land acquirer's rights of claim on the said land.

[5] "Nigeria Welcomes White Farmers," *Zimbabwe Crisis Reports*. http://allafrica.com/stories/200502231026.html (accessed July 25, 2010).

which Zimbabwean farmers play a key role. Should their agenda fail, the image of the "New Nigeria" will suffer a dramatic blow. Already discontent Nigerians will have good reason to highlight the failed promise of a "New Nigeria" project, which may trigger mass demonstrations and outbreaks of violence, not uncommon phenomena in Nigerian society.

3. *Samples from Zimbabwean Farmers' Rhetoric*

Citing some of the assistance they received from the government, one of the early Zimbabwean farmer settlers, Graham Hatty, noted that:

> In order to show us that they were serious, the Kwara State government paid for the whole trip. We went around the country and met the president, the vice president, bank managers and entrepreneurs. They really made sure that we knew what was behind what they wanted us to do.... They provided the land and the finance...We also received a lower interest rate and we only have to start paying back our loans after five years, when we will be more established (Maritz, 2008).

In the same vein, Graham's wife, Judy Hatty, further revealed the kind of treatment they got while in Aso Rock Villa, Nigeria's Presidential State House. She commented: "We were welcomed with open arms and treated like Hollywood film stars by President Obasanjo, who told us: 'You are the best farmers in Africa. Don't leave Africa. Africa needs you'."[6]

From the two passages it is clear that the government of Kwara State and the Nigerian president have great interest in the Zimbabwean agricultural scheme. Zimbabwean Graham Hatty concludes from the involvement of high-level players as well as from the special financial benefits granted to the Zimbabwean farmers that the government is serious about its business intentions. His wife's reaction reveals the social status attributed to the newcomers by the government, welcoming the Zimbabweans as people of public fame and with qualities of a saviour. Thus, a picture emerges of the foreign farmers that coincides with the message of hope which the image of the "New Nigeria" entails. Underlining a new beginning in Nigerian (agricultural) history—or rather the clean break with the past—is the 'pioneer status' which the government grants the Zimbabwean farmers. Obviously, this status is primarily given to the farmers for the financial benefits it includes, exempting the newcomers from

[6] Judy Hatty, quoted in "Nigeria Welcomes White Farmers." *Zimbabwe Crisis Reports* (Tuesday, March 23, 2010). http://allafrica.com/stories/200502231026.html (accessed May 10, 2010).

the burden of taxes and duties. It is also a clever rhetorical device in the promotion of a "New Nigeria", highly suggestive of a 'virgin' situation, in which the Zimbabweans are the first to set up farming.

4. *Nigerian Farmers' Rhetoric on "New Nigeria"*

Since the New Nigerians' first coming, some farming successes are said to have been recorded. Reports argue that the government of Kwara State is already making gains from the Zimbabwean farmers' project: the large-scale farming has increased food supply, brought new skills to local farmers and encouraged the awakening of new agricultural industries. Professor Mohammed Yisa, the State's Commissioner for Agriculture, confirmed that an additional 15 commercial farms had been developed with the already existing 13 at Shonga and about 3,000 people had found jobs on the farms (Bakare, 2009). Another interesting account of the transformative nature of these farmers' 'presence' was presented in the *Christian Science Monitor*, a U.S. based newspaper. It published an article entitled: "White Zimbabweans Bring Change to Nigeria" (2 May 2010), which heavily relies on the perspective of a former subsistence farmer, who is currently employed by one of the Zimbabweans. The Nigerian is full of praise, having secured a wage job, a cell phone and a motorbike, in addition to having learned new farming skills (*CSM*, 2010).

Supporters of the white farmers' project have argued that the cell phone networks which were put up to support the commercial farmers have benefited the neighbouring community as well, and so will the national electricity grid when it arrives in the area. In fact, an impressed Nigerian, who is a former subsistent farmer turned farm manager, was quoted as saying: "If there were at least 20 white Zimbabwean farmers in each state, Nigeria would become one of the richest countries in the world and we would not even depend on our oil."[7]

Although the above individuals are voicing reactions that are in line with the government's rhetoric of a new Nigeria with its implicit promise of a better life for Nigerians, the majority of Nigerian farmers do not seem to be convinced by this promise of a brighter future. One farmer summarises the situation as follows:

[7] "White Zimbabwean farmers highlight Nigeria's agricultural failures" (March 24, 2008). http://zimreview.wordpress.com/2008/03/24/white-zimbabwean-farmers-highlight-nigerias-agricultural-failures/ (accessed May 18, 2010).

> One would have thought that when promises of 'technology transfer' are made, such would naturally include visits and seminars for the local farmers by these experts, the dissemination of improved crops and *new* production techniques, giving of advice and counselling to local farmers, and the diffusion of *new* knowledge into the local communities' production system. On the contrary, we have not witnessed any of these. Instead, what we have seen is the forceful confiscation of our lands for the *new people*. (Abdulkareem Olukoshi, 2011: PC) (italics added)

Olukoshi's recurrent use of the word 'new' echoes the government's rhetoric of a 'New Nigeria'. In fact, the farmer cleverly uses the central persuasive element of the government's rhetoric to dismantle its hollow promise. This play on the word 'new' becomes poignant in the phrase "new people". Instead of the usual word 'foreigners', Olukoshi suggests with "new people" a novel species of human being endowed with new characteristics. This image recalls the earlier description of the President's first reception of the Zimbabweans by Zimbabwean farmer's wife, as super-human beings.

Playing on the same 'new' characteristics of the 'New Nigerian', Mr. Olaseinde Makanjuola, the leader of the United Small and Medium Scale Farmers' Associations of Nigeria (USMEFAN), uses it to criticise the government's agricultural policies:

> It is a known fact that the same governments that neglected their own farmers, provided these 'magical' farmers with all imaginable forms of support: credit guarantees, hundreds of hectares of farmland practically for free, access to fertilisers and other inputs, newly tarred roads from their farms; freedom to repatriate earnings, etc., Beyond this, the new farmers have had an inexhaustible supply of cheap labour whose conditions of work cannot be scrutinised by any media or reporter and who have not been allowed to form or join unions to protect their interests from [the] farmers (GRAIN, 2011).

Makanjuola presents an image of the Zimbabwean farmer as 'magical', suggesting a 'miraculous' ability to produce high agricultural yields. In addition, he has a miraculous and never-ending supply of cheap labour as well as a miraculous protective shield. Implicit in this picture of the white Zimbabwean farmer as a magician is that of a popular folktale figure, the trickster, who manages to make use of people's ignorance and naiveté to play tricks on them, in which they lose out and the trickster gets away with his tricks.

This double identity of magician/trickster is also suggested in the following description of the Zimbabwean farmers. Mustapha (2010: 1) notes that the torrents of accounts concerning the farmers' activities in Nigeria have been suggestive of "a massive agricultural transformation driven by the ingenuity of foreign farmers, and without financial and other support schemes from Nigerian governments." In the following description the trickster qualities of the 'New Nigerian' are thrown in even stronger relief. Making great rhetorical use of the word 'free', Francis Ishola (2010: PC), a public affairs analyst, presents a very convincing new 'trickster' tale:

> Are these "foreign investors" not going to invest their own money? The state is giving them "free" land—land stolen from local communities who need it to sustain themselves. They will enjoy "free" money from the world bank and "free" fertilizer, labour, seeds, etc paid for by the loans and taxes imposed on the people. They will sell their products outside the country and get "investment concessions" calculated to ensure they suffer no tax, interest or environmental costs. Haba! [*Exclamation*] What kind of business is this?[8]

In addition to presenting a powerful picture of the unusual benefits that the Zimbabwean farmers have managed to procure, thanks to their 'tricks', the description portrays the Nigerian government and the World Bank as the 'fools', being fooled out of their money and land by the 'new Nigerian'.

From the above it has become clear that the image of the new Nigerian as a trickster/magician is pervasive in public anti-'New Nigeria' rhetoric. Interestingly, it is a well-known figure which is part of a narrative tradition that is familiar to most Nigerians.[9] As a result, the trickster—and its entailed qualities—is a very powerful metaphor for the white Zimbabwean farmer in Nigeria in the anti-'New Nigeria' rhetoric.

---

[8] The Zimbabwean farmers had easy access to financial support. They were promised a $500,000 USD loan by the Federal Government. Besides, Governor Saraki also promised to help facilitate bank loans for the new farmers, and invest about #300 million—#400 million Naira ($2 million–$2.7 million at the time) in irrigation, electricity, roads and housing to make the farmers comfortable (Borzello, 2005). In 2006, the Kwa-Zimbo Enterprises Ltd. took a #650 million Naira loan from the Nigerian Agricultural Cooperative and Rural Development Bank Ltd backed by an ISPO (Irrevocable Standing Payment Order) of the Federal Ministry of Finance authorising deduction of the State Government's statutory allocation in the event of the client's inability to liquidate the loan (Okulaja, 2010).

[9] The notion and figure of a notable trickster, the Tortoise, is very pervasive in Nigerian traditional folktales. In these folktales, the Tortoise—*Mbe* (Igbo) or *Ijapa* (Yoruba)—is often presented as full of cunning and wisdom, malicious, selfish, not really evil or irredeemably wicked, but just 'naughty' and greedy. Though physically weak and slow, the tortoise is very patient, seemingly vulnerable but quick-witted and endowed with special intelligence which it sometimes misuses by playing on the intelligence of others—human beings and animals alike. It should be noted that in some tales he may be caught and exposed, yet somehow he manages to survive and in the end makes fun of those who attempted to expose it.

Conclusion

The metaphor of the 'New Nigeria' has been demonstrated to be used by the Nigerian government as an instrument to persuade ordinary Nigerians into accepting an unprecedented government strategy for boosting Nigeria's agricultural production, while instilling in the Zimbabwean farmers a sense of belonging and of safety. Evoking a space that is new and common to Nigerians and white Zimbabweans, the 'New Nigeria' metaphor brushes over differences between the two groups. Yet, the government's metaphor includes for each group different messages, it was shown. It suggests to the white Zimbabweans that they are the people that are needed in a 'New Nigeria', while at the same time it intends to include a message of hope of a better future to the 'old' Nigerians.

In addition to suggesting a new space, 'New Nigeria' could also be seen to suggest a 'new time' in government rhetoric, cleverly brushing away 'time past' in which white Zimbabwean farmers may have been regarded suspiciously in Nigeria due to historical experiences, both of the British colonial regime and white (minority) regimes elsewhere on the African continent. The portrayal of the white Zimbabwean farmer as being able to perform agricultural magic and endowed with saviour like qualities for the welfare of Nigerians is another indication of this 'new time'. Lastly, the government seems to want to convey to the 'old Nigerians' that there is 'a new beginning', a clean break from failed past government agricultural policies.

However, the impact of the 'new Nigeria' on the local reality appears to be very different from the government's rhetoric. The "Vision 2020" themes of 'land reform', 'food security' and 'agricultural development' in the 'New Nigeria' appear to be based on previous frameworks. For instance, the widely criticised Land Use Act of 1979, in which the government is conferred authority over all lands, including customarily held ones, is used as the basis for the development of an agricultural 'New Nigeria'. As a result, access to previously used land is denied to many local farmers, which leads to food and social insecurity. Therefore it may be concluded that the metaphor is fundamentally charged with human rights abuses. The anti-rhetoric of farmers and political analysts could be seen to cleverly capture these abuses by portraying the white Zimbabwean farmers as the African folktale figure of the trickster in opposition to the government's image of the Zimbabweans as magicians/saviours.

The government seems to be aware of the local negative evaluations of their new line of agricultural policies. Governor Saraki used strong language in defence of the Zimbabwean farmers' presence, declaring that the 'new Nigeria' implied guarantees for the white farmers that "*their land* will not, never ever, be repossessed in the future",[10] as has been the case where they originally came from. How true and strong the government's 'New Nigeria' programme will prove to be, only time will tell.

Personal Communication

Abdulkareem Olukoshi, (Mr.), 48 years, Male, Nigerian. Farmer and Agricultural Extension Service worker, Ilorin, Nigeria. Interviewed on Friday, 19 August 2011.

Francis Ishola, (Mr.), 51 years, Male, Nigerian. Public Affairs Analyst, Ibadan, Nigeria; Interviewed on Tuesday, 18 May 2010.

Bibliography

Adekanye, T.O., Otitolaiye, J.O. and Opaluwa, H.I. "Food and Agricultural Production in Nigeria: Some Empirical Considerations for Engendering Economic Policy for Africa," paper presented at the IAFFE Conference on Feminist Economics, Boston, Massachusetts, USA; June 26–28, 2009.

Ajayeoba, Ayodeji. "Concerning Food Security in Nigeria," *West Africa Insight*, a publication of the Centre for Democracy and Development (December 2010). http://westafricainsight.org/articles/PDF/81 (accessed May 12, 2011).

Ako, Rhuks T. "Nigeria's Land Use Act: An Anti-Thesis to Environmental Justice." *Journal of African Law*, vol. 53, no. 2 (2009).

Anon. "Food Security in Nigeria," (April 2011). http://uk.oneworld.net/guides/nigeria/food_security?gclid=CPW2ipHC4KgCFcRtfAodiC-WuQ (accessed May 9, 2011).

Auta, S.J. and Dafwang, I.I. "The Agricultural Development Projects (ADPs) in Nigeria: Status and Policy Implications." *Research Journal of Agriculture and Biological Sciences*, vol. 6, no. 2 (2010).

Bakare, Muritala. "Nigeria's Agricultural Success Story and Ex-Zimbabwean Farmers: Nigeria's Shonga is the New Harare." *Afrik News* (Thursday, Nov. 26, 2009). http://www.afrik-news.com/article16541.html (accessed May 30, 2010).

Blench, Roger. "The Transformation of Conflict between Pastoralists and Cultivators in Nigeria" (2003). http://www.rogerblench.info/Conflict/Herder-farmer%20conflict%20in%20Nigeria.pdf (accessed Aug. 5, 2010).

Borzello, Anna. "Zimbabwe Farmers Mark New Territory." *BBC News* (Wednesday, Feb. 9 2005, 10:29 GMT). http://news.bbc.co.uk/2/hi/africa/4247993.stm (accessed June 12, 2010).

Bryceson, Deborah Fahy. "The Scramble in Africa: Reorienting Rural Livelihoods." *World Development*, vol. 30, no. 5, (2002).

Burke, Kenneth. *A Rhetoric of Motives*. Berkeley: University of California Press, 1969.

Christian Science Monitor (*CSM*) Newspaper, (2 May 2010).

Daramola, A., S. Ehui, E. Ukeje and J. McIntire. 2007. "Agricultural Export Potential in Nigeria," www.csae.ox.ac.uk/books/epopn/AgriculturalexportpotentialinNigeria.pdf (accessed Aug. 20, 2011).

[10] "White Farmers in Nigeria: Like Play, Like Play". http://nigeriavillagesquare.com/forum/main-square/19-white-farmers-nigeria-like-play-like-play-2.html (accessed Feb. 13, 2010).

Ebeku, K. "Oil and the Niger Delta people: The injustice of the Land Use Act", CEPMLP Internet Journal 9, Centre for Energy, Petroleum and Mineral Law and Policy, University of Dundee (2001). Available at: http://www.dundee.ac.uk/cepmlp/journal/html/vol9/vol9-14.html (accessed Aug. 20, 2011).

Food and Agriculture Organization of the United Nations (FAO). *Agricultural Development in Nigeria, 1965–80*. Rome: FAO, 1966.

Forrest, T. "The Economic Context of Operation Feed the Nation." *Savanna*, vol. 6, no. 1 (June 1977).

Francis, P. "For the Use and Common Benefit of all Nigerians: Consequences of the 1978 Land Nationalization" *Africa: Journal of the International African Institute*, vol. 54, no. 3 (1984).

Federal Republic of Nigeria (FRN). *Third National Development Plan, 1975–80* (Vol. I–II). Lagos: The Federal Ministry of Economic Development, 1975.

Government of Nigeria (GoN). *Meeting Every Body's NEEDS: National Economic Empowerment and Development Strategy*. Abuja: National Planning Commission, 2004.

GRAIN. "Nigerian farmer leader talks about resistance to land grabs" An interview with Olaseinde Makanjuola Arigbede of the United Small and Medium scale Farmers' Associations of Nigeria (USMEFAN) (Aug. 11, 2011). http://www.grain.org/bulletin_board/entries/4340-nigerian-farmer-leader-talks-about-resistance-to-land-grabs (accessed Aug. 21, 2011).

Hofstter, Stephan. "Zimbabwean Farmers Get 200,000 Land Hectares in Kwara," *This Day* Newspaper (Lagos) (May 5, 2004).

Joseph, Richard. "Affluence and Underdevelopment: The Nigerian Experience." *Journal of Modern African Studies*, vol. 16, no. 2 (June 1978).

Korieh, Chima J. *The Land Has Changed: History, Society and Gender in Colonial Eastern Nigeria*. Calgary, Alberta: University of Calgary Press, 2010.

Liversage, Harold. "Responding to 'land grabbing' and promoting responsible investment in Agriculture," IFAD Occasional Paper no. 2 (December). Rome: International Fund for Agricultural Development, 2010.

Mabogunje, Akin L. "Land Refor in Nigeria: Progress, Problems and Prospects," proceedings of them Annual Bank Conference on Land Policy and Administration, Washington DC; April 26–27, 2010.

Maritz, Jaco. "Farming in Nigeria: First hand insight from one of the Zim farmers" (Thursday, January 10, 2008). http://www.tradeinvestafrica.com/feature_articles/913950.htm (accessed Aug. 31, 2011).

Meek, C.K. *Land Tenure and Administration in Nigeria and the Cameroons*. London: HMSO, 1957.

Mustapha, Abdul Raufu. "Zimbabwean Farmers and Nigerian Agriculture." *West Africa Insight*, a publication of the Centre for Democracy and Development (December 2010). http://www.westafricainsight.org/articles/PDF/85 (accessed May 12, 2011).

Mustapha, Abdul Raufu. "Cocoa farming and income diversification in South-western Nigeria," Working Paper, vol. 42. Kano: Center for Documentation and Research and Leiden: African Studies Center, 1999.

Nwaka, Geoffrey I. "The Urban Informal Sector in Nigeria." *Global Urban Development Magazine*, vol. 1, no. 1, (May 2005).

Ogen, Olukoya. "The Agricultural Sector and Nigeria's Development: Comparative Perspectives from the Brazilian Agro-Industrial Economy, 1960–1995." *Nebula*, vol. 4, no. 1, (March 2007).

Okulaja, Ayo. "Zimbabwean farmers' debt puts bank at risk" (Tuesday, March 23, 2010). http://234next.com/csp/cms/sites/Next/News/National/5466423-146/story.csp (accessed May 19, 2010).

Olayiede, Olajuwon S. and Dupe Olatunbosun. *Trends and Prospects of Nigeria's Agricultural Exports*. Ibadan: NISER, 1972.

Piñeiro, Martín. "Agricultural Technology Transfer to Developing Countries and the Public Sector," Science and Development Network (SciDev.Net) (Jan. 2007). http://www

.scidev.net/en/policy-briefs/agricultural-technology-transfer-to-developing-cou.html (accessed Aug. 26, 2011).

Sano, Hans-Otto. *The Political Economy of Food in Nigeria, 1960–1982: A Discussion on Peasant, State and World Economy* (Research Report No. 65). Uppsala: Nordiska Afrikainstitutet, 1983.

Strecker, Ivo and Stephen Tyler (eds.) *Culture and Rhetoric: Studies in Rhetoric and Culture*, (vol. 1) Oxford: Berghahn, 2009.

Toulmin, Camilla. "Negotiating Access to Land in West Africa. Who is Losing Out?," paper presented at the African Studies Association UK Biennial Conference, Birmingham; Sept. 9–11, 2002.

Turner, M. "Political Ecology and the Moral Dimensions of 'Resource Conflicts': the Case of Farmer-Herder Conflicts in the Sahel." *Political Geography*, vol. 23 (2004).

World Bank. "Nigeria: Competitiveness and Growth," a report jointly prepared with DfID, Africa Region, Report No. 36483-NG (Sept. 20, 2006). Abuja: World Bank.

Yunusa, M.B. "Not farms alone: A study of rural livelihoods in the middle belt of Nigeria," Working Paper, vol. 38. Kano and Leiden: Center for Documentation and Research and African Studies Center, 1999.

'KEEPING THIS LAND SAFE': STAKEHOLDER CONCEPTUALISATIONS OF PROTECTION IN THE CONTEXT OF A MIJIKENDA (KENYA) WORLD HERITAGE SITE

Froukje Krijtenburg

Introduction

The following discussion presents a case-study of the inscription of ten Mijikenda *kayas* (sacred places) as cultural landscape on the World Heritage list, in a context of growing pressure on land by domestic and foreign agro-industrial and mining explorations as well as tourism industrial expansions in the Coast Province of Kenya. In Mijikenda cosmology, the *kayas* take an essential place, as they are considered the abodes of the spirits of Mijikenda ancestors and constitute the essence of Mijikenda identity. Characteristically, they are forested areas with a central clearing and are situated on hill tops. Each *kaya* is looked after by a group of *kaya* elders, whose main duty is to keep *kaya* traditions alive and the physical contours of the forest intact for the well-being of the living Mijikenda—a collective of nine ethnic subgroups with distinct languages—and the ancestor spirits.[1] Thus, the inscription in 2008 of ten *kayas*, comprising 1,500 hectares of sacred Mijikenda land, could be described as a major victory of local 'sacred land' discourse over national and international discourses of 'land for development'. Indeed, the nomination dossier argues that Mijikenda traditional leaders and officials from the National Museums of Kenya started the nomination process specifically for the protection of Mijikenda sacred land against dispossession and/or destruction by domestic or foreign investors (NMK 2008, 76).

No doubt, the action of the National Museums and the Mijikenda *kaya* elders is timely; the coastal region of Kenya—the home of Mijikenda sacred land—has been earmarked in government policy documents for the exploration of large-scale foreign and domestic agricultural and mining projects (Government of Kenya 2008). Yet, we may ask, how effective is the World Heritage inscription as an instrument of protection against

[1] The nine Mijikenda ethnic subgroups are the Digo, Rabai, Ribe, Duruma, Kambe, Chonyi, Giryama, Jibana and Kauma.

the destruction of Mijikenda *kayas*? As the world has seen for instance in the context of Mali in June and July 2012, World Heritage sites were destroyed while the World Heritage Committee was powerless. Events like those in Mali make clear that the World Heritage Committee depends on the particular country's government and population to support a site as having "universal value". In the case of the Mijikenda *kayas* this is a complex situation, as in contemporary Kenyan history Mijikenda *kayas* have been used for political ends.[2] However, the National Museums of Kenya seem to have found a persuasive argument for keeping Mijikenda sacred land safe from political tampering with their strong emphasis on the benefits of the 'conservation' activities of *kaya* elders with respect to the *kayas*. In fact, this particular perspective echoes observations made by a team of researchers from Oxford in the eighties of the twentieth century. They had qualified *kayas* forests as "relics of a coastal woodland", which had been preserved thanks to the taboos and traditions that *kaya* elders had kept alive (Willis 2009, 237). In addition to being able to depoliticize *kayas* through a discourse of 'conservation', the National Museums of Kenya have been able to mediate the authenticity of *kaya* practices and the integrity of the physical dimensions of ten *kayas* to the international forum of the World Heritage Committee.

Granted that the National Museums of Kenya have played a pivotal role in the inscription process of the *kayas*, the inscription is the product of three different stakeholder discourses. And it is this product, the status of World Heritage cultural landscape, that should be able to provide the necessary safeguards for the protection of land that Mijikenda consider sacred. Now the central question is, does this product do what it is meant to do from the perspective of those who experience the impact of the newly acquired status of *kaya* land, i.e. the local people? This seems a relevant issue considering the high demand of land for commercial exploitation in Kenya's Coast Province. Answers to this question are not easy to give considering the complex and politicised land situation in Kenya. In fact, it requires a study that goes beyond the scope of this chapter. However, we can start by finding out how Mijikenda conceptualisations

[2] For instance, the Minister for Local Governement, the Mijikenda Karisa Maitha was annointed at *Kaya Fungo*, the day after President Kibaki's inititiation in 2002, in a bid to assert his authoirty over the coastal peoples of Swahili, Arabs and Mijikenda (Willis 2009, 235). Mazrui (ca. 1997) argues that *kaya Bombo* was used for rituals of 'immunity' among Mijikenda youths ahead of the Likoni clashes in 1997, which were instigated by senior policitans, i.a. Karisa Maitha, and were intended to expel people from central and western Kenya from the coastal region.

of 'site cultural and natural conservation' (a phrase taken from the nomination dossier (NMK 2008, 15)) of Mijikenda sacred land relate to those of the World Heritage Committee and the National Museums of Kenya , the other two stakeholders involved in the inscription of ten Mijikenda *kayas* as World Heritage site.

In view of this, the following discussion explores stakeholders' oral and written articulations of conceptualisations of 'site cultural and natural conservation' in the context of the inscription on the World Heritage list of Mijikenda *kayas*, to find out to what extent these conceptualisations and their practical implications match and diverge. A first hint of divergence in stakeholder perceptions is perhaps already the inscription of ten out of a total number of 47–60 *kayas* on the World Heritage list. Although the exact number of *kayas* is a matter of debate among Mijikenda, scholars and National Museums of Kenya, the selection of ten *kayas* raises the question of what exactly is 'kept safe' for Mijikenda people. Furthermore, we may ask whether this is what *kaya* elders, or Mijikenda people for that matter, wanted to agree to when they gave their 'free, prior and informed consent' to the inscription of the ten *kayas* on "the agency's [i.e. WHC's] safeguarding list" (Institut de Recherche pour le Développement 2011).

Observations made during my ethnographic and semantic fieldwork between 1998 and 2010 into conceptualisations of 'land' in the context of ideologies of peace and conflict among the Mijikenda—particularly the Giryama—constitute the basis for the present exploration. In this context, Mijikenda oral histories as well as a contemporary account seem to be particularly relevant as representations of Mijikenda conceptualisations of 'land' and 'protection'. Documents that were produced by NMK and WHC during the inscription process have been a major source of information for reflecting on these two stakeholder discursive articulations of 'land' and 'protection' in the context of the ten inscribed *kayas* (World Heritage Convention 2008; National Museums of Kenya 2008). Focal themes in the analysis of stakeholder representations of 'land' and 'protection' are questions such as who protects the land, for who, why and how. In the discussion the western ideologically charged term 'conservation' has been replaced by the more neutral phrase 'keeping safe' to refer to a shared stakeholder objective relating to Mijikenda *kaya* land. 'This land' highlights stakeholders' joint efforts to 'keep safe' a geographically defined 'site'.

From the above it may be concluded that the analysis is embedded within the reality of the Mijikenda experience of land explorations by domestic and foreign companies. The discussion begins with an introduction of the current land issues in Kenya and the role of the State in them. It focuses in particular on Kenya's coastal region where the Mijikenda *kayas* can be found. The second section introduces the conceptual framework for analysis. It presents 'land access' and its pertaining aspects as a thematic focus to interpret stakeholder concepualisations of 'keeping this land safe'. The analysis is preceded by an introduction of the stakeholders and their motivations for inscribing ten Mijikenda *kayas* on the World Heritage list.

Land Issues

Like in other sub-Saharan African countries, Kenya has seen legal and illegal transfers of large swaths of sparsely populated land into the hands of foreign investors in the wake of the World Bank promotion of foreign investment in agricultural land in capital poorer and land rich countries (see also Chapter 1, this volume). However, this is not a new experience for the people of Kenya, who have been faced in varying degrees since colonial times with displacement and re-settlement for large-scale agricultural projects. The historically ingrained phenomenon of illegal land awards to those who are close to Kenya's political elite has a strong ethnic component, as Kenya's political parties can be roughly divided along lines of ethnicity. Therefore, it is generally expected that those who belong with the ethnic group of the ruling President are favoured above others. This has led to widespread distrust of the state being a trustworthy partner in safeguarding the land against 'foreign' dispossession, and has additionally sharpened ethnic boundaries (O'Brien 2011, 4; Southall 2005). In fact, historical land injustices have been used by politicians as a successful instrument for electoral gain over the last decades, causing eruptions of violence between ethnic groups in the run-up or during general elections (Human Rights Watch 2002, 21ff; Mazrui ca. 1997).[3] Not until 2003, when president Mwai Kibaki came under severe political pressure to look into these extravagant land appropriations and their beneficiaries, was the Commission of Inquiry into the Illegal/Irregular Allocation of Public Land established, commonly known as the Ndung'u Commission after its chairperson Paul Ndung'u (Southall 2005). The commission published a report

[3] The most serious ethnic clashes occurred after the 2007 general elections between Luo/Kalenjin and Gikuyu.

with shocking findings on the extent and beneficiaries of illegal large-scale land acquisitions. However, its set of recommendations to redress historical injustices "thus far has had limited impact on the phenomenon of land-grabbing" in Kenya, as a report commissioned by the International Land Commission argues (O'Brien 2011: 1).

With the adoption of the new Constitution in 2010, Kenyans have acquired a new—and more equitable—legal framework of land tenure. Land reform bills aim to create equivalent legal frameworks for 'ownership' across the three different categories in which land in Kenya is divided (*Public* land, *Private* Land and *Community* Land), as well as a land governance institution that is independent (Constitution of Kenya, chapter 5). However, so far no such laws have been enforced, nor have the members of the National Land Commission, the land governance institution, been officially appointed. As a result of this transitional situation, both legal and illegal acquisitions of large tracts of land have remained a feature of Kenyan society until this day.

Under the old Constitution there were also three categories of land ownership. *Government* land comprises land that is used for the 'public interest' (e.g. infrastructure, town and country planning, schools, health clinics); *Trust* land is owned by a community, but held in trust by a county council on behalf of its citizens; *Private* land is registered according to a law, and a title deed has been issued for it. Most of the large-scale land acquisitions have occurred on Government land (under the new constitution called Public Land) and Trust land (now called Community land). Most communities in the coastal region, where the present discussion is set, live on land that falls into this latter category (Beja 2012).

While large parts of Kenya came under private ownership in the ninety sixties and seventies of the last century, the coastal region had until the new Constitution in 2010, a land ownership regime that was the result of British colonial arrangements with the coast's formal owner, the Sultan of Zanzibar. In return for granting the coast the status of British protectorate in 1895, the Sultan demanded that his subjects kept their titles to land for time immemorial (cf. Goldsmith 2011, 11). Practically, this meant that Arab and Swahili populations kept title deeds over urban and plantation land along the coast, while all other land was turned into property of the Crown, and therefore belonged to the government (Goldsmith 2011, 9; Salim 1973, 119ff). This arrangement has led to an unequal land situation for coastal ethnic groups such as the Mijikenda. On one hand, some have lived for several generations as 'squatters' on land that is owned by absentee landlords, the grandchildren of Arab families who owned big plantations on the coast.[4] On the other hand, most other parts of coastal land is under the custody of county councils (Trust land) or the government (Government land) and has therefore been a major object of land appropriation by Kenya's elite since Kenya's independence in 1963. These land acquisitions by 'foreigners'—people from other parts of Kenya are referred to as *wat'u wa bara* (people of the mainland) by the indigenous coastal population—have been considered locally a cause of impoverishment, land dispossession, and a source of conflict (Human Rights Watch 2002, 24ff; Goldsmith 2011, 13ff).

Over the last four years, the issue of land has been compounded in the coastal region by the Kenyan government's Vision 2030 (Government of Kenya 2008), a document that contains the government's long-term blueprint for the development of Kenya into a middle-income economy. Specifically targeting the coastal region in a bid to tap its under-utilized economic potential, the coastal hinterland as well as the less densely populated coastal land north of the town of Malindi, have been targeted by the government for exploration. Thus, 16,000 ha of fertile land in the delta of the river Tana, north of Malindi, has been earmarked for sugar cane plantations (Smalley and Corbera 2012). The project not only jeopardizes the area's rich biodiversity; by pushing Orma and Wardei pastoralists off grounds that they traditionally use for grazing their cattle during the dry season, it additionally exacerbates land scarcity and may lead to an increase of conflicts between pastoralist Orma/Wardei/Somali and agricultural Pokomo in the area (Gemson and Mojtehedzadeh 2012).[5]

While the sugar cane project is expected to be run by a Kenyan sugar company, other large-scale land acquisitions were made by foreign investors with local subsidiaries, such as the Canadian company of Bedford Biofuels (126,000 ha) and the Italian Nuove Iniziative Industriali Srl (initially 50,000 ha) for *jatropha curcas* plantations. At present, however, the Italian company is barred from operation by the National Environment Management Authority, as the jatropha project would destroy indigenous woodland. Bedford Biofuels has met some serious opposition from NGOs

[4] Recently a court case initiated by 'squatters' on land in Takaungu against the Arab Mazrui family was concluded in favour of the Mazrui family on the basis of historical legal ownership (Standard team October 2, 2012).

[5] Ahead of the operations, which seem to be impeded by major lack of funds, Wardei pastoralists were evicted from the area in 2011.

as well as the Ministry of Environment, as a result of which BB may pull out of its Kenyan activities (Gemson and Mojtehedzadeh 2012).

While the northern part of the coast is characterised by large-scale agricultural projects, the southern part hosts major extraction activities, e.g. titanium mining by Base Titanium Ltd (a Kenyan subsidiary of Australian Base Resources Ltd), with serious threats to the natural and cultural landscape of the area.

In reaction to the general experience of socio-economic neglect of the coastal region by the central government and the highly skewered land ownership situation in favour of foreign investors, Kenyan elites, Swahili and Arabs, other coastal groups have been vocal at regular intervals about their rights to land. In fact, the recent popularity of the coastal political group of Mombasa Republican Council (MRC) is closely related to this general discontent among the coast' s indigenous population. In spite of being banned in 2008 by the central government for its arguable incitement to violence, the MRC has enjoyed major support among the local population with its ringing slogan of "Pwani si Kenya" (the coast is not Kenya) and its agenda of secession from the rest of Kenya (Goldsmith 2011: 4).

Within this generally shared view of and activist stand on coastal land as owned by the coastal peoples, the Mijikenda, and in particular their *kaya* elders, have taken a distinct line of action. Over the last roughly fifteen years, *kaya* elders have been public mediators of a discourse that aims at branding large parts of the coastal hinterland, roughly between the Tanzanian border in the south and beyond the coastal tourist town of Malindi in the north, as Mijikenda ancestral land because of the approx. 47–60 *kayas* that are scattered across its surface (Willis 2009: 237; Githitho n.d.). Connecting with national leaders, state agencies and international communities, the traditional Mijikenda leaders have created a wide and powerful platform for their discourse. Their latest and formidable alliance with UNESCO's World Heritage Committee (since 2008) seems to go a long way to boosting Mijikenda 'land' discourse.

Conceptual Framework of Analysis

As was explained above, the Mijikenda reality of land 'ownership' has been one of customary rights. Although the formal legal framework was—until the introduction of the new Constitution in 2010—that of Trust land, as explained above, Mijikenda discourse on *kaya* land can be assumed to relate more readily to the socio-cultural reality of access to land than to land as property. Definitions of land 'ownership' will therefore include implicit entailments such as *which* land can be accessed, *by whom* is access granted and *to whom, how* and *when.*[6]

Similarly, partner and stakeholder in the inscription of the ten Mijikenda *kayas* on the World Heritage list, UNESCO respects 'access to land' as a valid claim to land. Indeed, it explicitly endorses the legal status of customary law and customary management systems in the context of cultural landscapes (Mitchell 2009, 4). Since the ten Mijikenda *kayas* have been inscribed under this label, the descriptions by all three stakeholders in reference to Mijikenda *kayas* are analysed through the lens of land access. Apart from offering a comparative framework of analysis, this lens facilitates the exploration of its constituting conceptual dimensions, such as the *who, which, how* and *when* elements presented above. Teasing out these dimensions, we will be able to find differences and compatibilities in stakeholder conceptualisations of 'keeping this land safe'.

Ribot and Peluso (2003, 160) define an analysis of access as "the process of identifying and mapping the mechanisms by which access is gained, maintained, and controlled." Access analysis holds that "beliefs, ideological controls and discursive practices, as well as negotiated systems of meaning" are effective mechanisms for securing and maintaining resource access (Ribot and Peluso 2003, 168). Captured under the heading of *access to knowledge* by Ribot and Peluso (2003), and distinguishable from seven additional examples of 'access' mechanisms (see pp. 165–172), these discursive and ideological factors are particularly relevant to the present focus on verbal articulations of 'keeping this land safe'.[7]

Practically, this implies that the following analysis of stakeholder discourse instances highlights stakeholder understandings of 'this land' and 'keeping safe' through the lens of land access and its previously mentioned aspects. The analysis is made through a 'close reading',[8] which implies a detailed interpretation of statements that refer to meanings and practices of 'keeping this land safe'.

---

[6] Seven of the inscribed *kayas* are National Monuments, three are Forest Reserves.

[7] Other mechanisms can be found in Ribot and Peluso (2003) pp. 165–172.

[8] 'Close reading' is practiced in literary criticism to refer to an interpretative process that is confined to brief passages of text and is characteristically careful and detailed. This practice of analysing literary tetxts was pioneered by I.A. Richards in 1929.

Alliance Partners: Mijikenda *Kaya* Elders, National Museums of Kenya and World Heritage Committee

I. *Mijikenda, kaya Elders and kayas*

Present-day Mijikenda are generally familiar with the historical narrative of their first beginnings. However, they appear to differ widely among themselves on the ways they relate to the spiritual legacy that is associated with *kayas* and *kaya* elders. Living their lives in the socio-economic margins of Kenya, most Mijikenda depend on the produce of the land they cultivate and use for cattle grazing. In fact, widespread poverty and unemployment actually seem to be determining factors in Mijikenda relations to the phenomenon of *kaya* and its belief system. For instance, the gangs that rallied at *kaya Bombo* and *kaya Waa* in advance of the Likoni clashes in 1997 have been argued to consist of Mijikenda youths who were uneducated and unemployed (Mazrui ca. 1997). Others, in an attempt to make a living for themselves, have been found to cut indigenous trees, harvest sand or make bricks in the immediate surroundings of *kayas*. These actions are considered within the Mijikenda belief system a major threat to the spiritual integrity of *kayas* (NMK 2008). Generally, Mijikenda relations to *kayas* are driven by pragmatic considerations. A survey done among 400 Mijikenda men, women and children in 1998 demonstrates that women are six times as likely as men to say that *kayas* have no value. Younger people (especially members of revivalist Christian churches) tend to be ignorant of and openly hostile to the belief systems represented by the *kayas* (Nyamweru 2012: 280). One explanation for this explicit rejection among Christian Mijikenda youths might be that the rituals performed at *kayas* include in their eyes 'heathen' practices, such as ritual killings of cows, goats and/or chickens for the well-being of Mijikenda land.

Traditionally, *kaya* elders are the keepers of Mijikenda well-being. Their authority extends from conducting ceremonies and solving conflicts among Mijikenda to being the political leaders of the Mijikenda. According to traditional Mijikenda beliefs, *kaya* elders operate as mediators between the living and the ancestors, some of whose spirits live in *kaya* trees (Parkin 1991; McIntosh 2009a). In 1998 Jimbi Katana, then head of the department of Immobile Heritage of the National Museums of Kenya (NMK) Mombasa, introduced me to one of the most prominent *kaya* elders of his time, the late Simba Wanje wa Kagujo. An octogenarian, he had spent a good many years in and near *kaya Giryama* (also known as *kaya Fungo*) and had learned to regard the Kenyan administration with healthy distrust considering their professed intentions to uplift Mijikenda society. When we met for the first time, he explained that his fears for the state had made him refuse to talk to the NMK representatives in 1990. At the time, NMK aimed to register all Mijikenda *kayas* as national monuments. Simba Wanje's attitude changed when he found out that the NMK official involved was a fellow Giryama, namely Jimbi Katana. He trusted that Jimbi Katana could keep *kayas* safe against destruction (as illustrated in the analysis of Simba Wanje's narrative below). However, he remained skeptical about *kayas*' continued existence, he said, because *kaya* elders had been greatly ignored by the general Mijikenda public. Moreover, the general disrespect among younger Mijikenda for their own traditions made him argue that matters would get worse and would finally lead to the destruction of Mijikenda culture.

Since the late 1990s the scene has dramatically changed. Simba Wanje's pessimistic view on the deteriorating status of *kaya* elders has been replaced by a general sense of self-confidence among the *kaya* guardians, as their public communications indicate (Nation Team 2012; McIntosh 2009b; Beja 2008). In fact, Mijikenda *kayas* have proven a perfect platform for *kaya* elders—including Simba Wanje during the last years of his life—to engage with high level politicians and foreign officials (McIntosh 2009b). As a result of ceremonies at *kaya Giryama*, which included, for instance, president Mwai Kibaki and the then US ambassador in Kenya, Michael Rannenberger, *kaya* elders have been given extensive national media coverage. Although some of the ceremonies have caused major resentment and competition among *kaya* elders from other *kayas*, *kaya* elders at other times speak out unanimously, as was the case when they strongly disapproved of Mombasa Republican Council members disrupting a mock election in the coastal tourist town of Malindi (McIntosh 2009b; Nation Team 2012). In spite of—or more probably thanks to—the contestations among themselves the guardians of *kayas* have enhanced public awareness of Mijikenda identity as well as awareness among Mijikenda of *kayas* as the core of their cultural identity and a resource for political voice (McIntosh 2009a, 36).

Before acquiring their status as sacred places in the course of the 19th century, *kayas* were settlements. Thus, each of the nine Mijikenda subgroups built and lived in a *kaya* when they first settled in Kenya's coastal region, as is narrated also in the Mijikenda oral history discussed below. When *kayas* became too small for the growing populations, people gradually moved out. Ever since their designation as sacred places, *kayas* have been closely associated with assertions of Mijikenda identity (Brantley

1981; McIntosh 2009b). The following narratives, featuring *kaya Giryama*, can therefore be assumed to belong within this tradition.

As was indicated in the introduction, *kayas* have a similar design and spatiality and are characteristically located on elevated land. Of the ten inscribed *kayas* only *kaya Giryama* is situated in a less fertile and flat area. Typically, a few huts can be found in the central clearing, one of which is used as temporary living quarters by two or more *kaya* elders. Furthermore, strict rules apply to entering a *kaya*; being barefoot and dressed in traditional clothes are among them. Since the time Mijikenda people considered *kayas* the abode of ancestors and therefore a sacred place, there has been a taboo on cutting trees in *kayas*. That is why, until today, many *kayas* have indigenous forests of great biodiversity. In fact, the survival of indigenous forests thanks to local communities' restrictions on their use has been the core argument for WHC to label the ten Mijikenda *kayas* as cultural landscape of "Outstanding Universal Value" (UNESCO 2008, 190).

The eleven *kayas* that feature in the nomination dossier for inscription on the World Heritage List—and of which *kaya Kinondo* was not inscribed—represent eight of the nine Mijikenda subgroups. Only *kaya Chonyi* is missing on the list. Its exclusion is probably the result of a set of criteria that NMK has used to assess whether a *kaya*'s lay-out was authentic and thus viable for inscription (cf. NMK 2008, 16). In fact, the list of nominated sites includes five out of the six *kayas* consistently associated among Mijikenda with the very beginnings of Mijikenda settlement, namely *kaya Giryama, kaya Jibana, kaya Kambe, kaya Ribe* and *kaya Kinondo* (*kaya Chonyi* is missing). The other six *kayas* of the nomination list—three Rabai *kayas*, two Duruma *kayas* and *kaya Kauma*—were set up later, but are closely associated with the first *kayas*.

In keeping with the senior historical position of the eleven, they are revered as the most authentic *kayas* and therefore attributed a central role in promoting Mijikenda well-being. Thus, although Mijikenda have 35–49 other *kayas*, these eleven *kayas* are tantamount to being the core of Mijikenda identity, with at present, Willis (2009, 236) argues, *kaya Giryama* as *primus inter pares*.

II. *National Museums of Kenya*

In the 1980s a team of ethno-botanists from Oxford University reported for the first time on the *kaya* forests, qualifying them at the same time as threatened ecosystems. Moreover, they pointed out the key role *kaya* elders played in the conservation of the indigenous forests. Until then, the

National Museums of Kenya, with a remit embracing both human culture and natural history, had not been concerned about the fate of Mijikenda *kayas* (Willis 2009, 237). However, the ethno-botanical report triggered them into becoming the main state driver in a process to protect the spiritual and biophysical properties of *kayas*. Apart from initiating a procedure to formally declare Mijikenda *kayas* national monuments or forest reserves, NMK supported *kaya* elders in their efforts to reduce the rate of extraction of forest resources (see discussion of *kaya* elders above; Nyamweru 2012, 279–80; Willis 2009, 237). Since then, NMK has been instrumental in "giving the elders access to a wide forum including regional meetings, and for a few, trips to biodiversity conferences and workshops in Nairobi" (Nyamweru 2012, 280). Until now, NMK and its partner organisation the Coastal Forest Conservation Unit (CFCU) have listed "40 of 47 (sic)" *kayas* as national monuments or forest reserves (Githitho n.d., 31).[9] In 2006, it started up a nomination process for the inscription of eleven Mijikenda *kayas* as a World Heritage site. Their selection of eleven *kayas* has largely been motivated by considerations of the authenticity and—to a lesser extent—the integrity of a *kaya* and *kaya* practices as well as the active roles of *kaya* elders in keeping *kaya* traditions alive and the physical contours of a *kaya* intact. Thus, they arrived at a list of eleven *kayas*. It seems that NMK included *kaya Kinondo*, which had been affected by sand extraction, because of its authenticity and the active involvement of Digo community members in profiling the *kaya* as a symbol of Mijikenda culture as well as in preserving its biodiversity.

III. *UNESCO's World Heritage Committee*

During the 32nd session of the UNESCO World Heritage Convention in 2008 the World Heritage Committee "... inscribed the Sacred Mijikenda Kaya Forests, Kenya, with the exception of Kaya Kinondo" as cultural landscape for their "outstanding universal value" (UNESCO 2008, 190). Thus, it was decided that ten *kayas* met the essential conditions of authenticity and/or integrity and an adequate protection and management system to ensure the safeguarding of the property (UNESCO 2011: paragraph 78). The rejection of *Kaya Kinondo* was made on the grounds that human activities

---

[9] Willis (2009: 238) describes how NMK inventorisation of *kayas* for conservation led to an explosive growth of the number of *kayas*.

had corrupted the integrity of its forest.[10] Following the positive evaluation of the other ten *kayas*, WHC set out guidelines for the protection of the ten *kayas* in line with its general policy and accompanying discourse for the conservation of cultural landscapes.

The Analysis

As was explained above, the following discussion explores stakeholders' discursive articulations of 'keeping this land safe'. In line with local valuations of land ownership in terms of access to land, the analysis is guided by a thematic focus on salient aspects of access to land, such as *which* land can be accessed, *by whom* is access granted and *to whom*, *how* and *when*. The following narrative presents a picture of Mijikenda understandings of types of land access. In doing so, it paints a picture of the essential connection between Mijikenda understandings of land ownership and 'keeping this land safe'. The story relates the migration of the Mijikenda to the coastal area of Kenya.

I. *Mijikenda Narratives on (Kaya) Land*

A. *Historical Narrative of the Beginnings of the Mijikenda*

The historical 'truth' of the Mijikenda narrative on their beginnings has been contested by several scholars over the last few decades (Willis 1993; McIntosh 2009a; Walsh 1995). Walsh even argues that the "[history] merely provides a narrative thread on which to attach a number of significant cultural statements" (1995, 4), thus discounting any historical reality. Regardless of the 'truth' value, this chapter is concerned with what Walsh describes as the core tenets of *kaya*: 'significant cultural statements' relating to *who* has (control over) and access to *kaya* land, *when, why and how*.

The text is a Giryama version of the history of 'the beginning of the Mijikenda' (*Chaho cha Midzichenda*). Although the story may not be exactly the same among Mijikenda nor known to the same extent, Mijikenda in general argue that they have a shared origin and that their place

[10] In the meantime it has developed into an ecotourism community project, where visitors are familiarised with the cultural and botanical significance of the *kaya* (Nyamweru 2012).

of origin is Shingwaya (or Shungwaya). The history below was recorded by the Kilifi Bible and Literacy Bureau in 2002 during a group story-telling session of 20 Giryama elders (*Midzichenda* 2002).[11]

The narrative starts in 'the land of Abyssinia'. There, the two founding couples of the Mijikenda get killed in a war. Their children flee to a place that is called 'the land of Zaire'.

> *There they stayed without any trouble from war or hunger. Because Zaire was a foreign land, Ye* [male] *thought it was not a bad idea to marry his relatives* [Mbodze and Matsezi] *to become his wives. Well, they gave birth to children who were called the children of Mbodze and Matsezi. People continued to live there, intermarried and gave birth to children within their clan. These people were farming and setting traps. When many years had passed, the clan had increased and their land started to become small. Thus, Ye and the people of his clan considered that it was better to start breaking up and look for land that would be enough for them.*

The passage is about a period of Mijikenda history when the Mijikenda live on land that they do not consider theirs. This is obvious from the—anachronistic—names of Abyssinia and Zaire. The phrase *kwakula Zaire were ni ujenini* ('because Zaire was a foreign country') underlines the 'foreign' status of the Mijikenda. Interestingly, the Giryama word *ujenini*, translated in English as 'foreign country' for lack of a more equivalent phrase, literally means 'in visitorship'. This word is a first indication that control of access to land is one of different Mijikenda categories of access to land, and that each category has a distinct set of norms and values.

The 'visitor' status, for instance, makes Ye decide to marry his female relatives rather than a Zairian lady. In this way, he indicates that he does not mean to make a claim to the land that has been granted to his people. Moreover, he shows that he is aware of the temporary status of the Mijikenda in terms of access to land. Another Mijikenda normative expectation going with 'in visitorship' is brought out in Ye's decision to move out of Zaire when his people threaten to become too many for the land granted to them by their host. Implied in this act is a visitor's moral obligation to abide by Mijikenda 'visitorship' norms.

The journey continues for some years until Ye and his people arrive in the land of the Oromo, called Shingwaya.

[11] For convenience, I have translated Giryama texts in English and used only the English version.

> *When they stayed in the land of the Oromo,*[12] *the Oromo taught them their traditions...... One of the customs of the Oromo was that should one of [Ye's] male offspring marry a wife, on the day of the wedding this foreign lady must sleep with an Oromo man, they make the way, on the second day she can sleep with her husband. The Oromo young man would come and stab his spear in the door to show that he entered inside the house until the time he would come out and take his spear to go home.*

This paragraph makes clear that the Mijikenda stayed on the land of the Oromo under different conditions to those in Zaire. Rather than living in a separate cultural space, the Mijikenda are forced to submit themselves to the traditions of the Oromo, and even allow Oromo men the right to initiate their newly-wed Mijikenda women into married life. The Giryama word for the land of the Oromo is telling: *tsi'ngwa* (lit. land taken). Clearly, the Mijikenda consider themselves squatters on the land, deprived of the right to live according to their own value system by the Oromo, who enforce their values on the Mijikenda.

The story continues by telling that as soon as a Mijikenda couple got married, an Oromo man showed up at their door. However, he did not go far, as he and others who followed his action were killed by Mijikenda men. As an Oromo reaction would be forthcoming, the Mijikenda decided to move elsewhere. However, since the migration to the land of the Oromo, the Mijikenda population had grown dramatically. Therefore Ye decides to appoint a number of leaders for the journey. They are six men, who are ordered to carry a *ngiryama* ('witness'), a clay pot containing a concoction of leaves, roots and herbs from Shingwaya, the place they leave behind. Appropriately called 'witness', the pot is the symbol of Mijikenda shared identity and is carried as a safeguard against strife and animosity among the migrants.

At a river crossing, a carrier accidentally drops the *ngiryam*a (witness) into the river. The pot breaks to pieces and the concoction that it holds flows into the river. This marks the end of the journey of the Mijikenda as a single people.

> *Now those who were with the person who had dropped the ngiryama, they spread about on one side next to Weruni, from Godhoma to Galana, on the other side neighbouring the Langulo. They were called the Giryama. Well the breaking of the ngiryama brought the existence of kaya. Kaya is a village and*

[12] In the original Giryama version the name 'Galla' is used in reference to the ethnic group which is nowadays called 'Oromo'. Since 'Galla' is experienced as pejorative, it has been replaced in the English version.

> *a village with all the traditions of the clan. When the ngiryama got dropped, it broke completely. The medicine that was in it went with the water, but the shards of the pot were shared and the Mijikenda made kayas.*[13]

From this passage it is clear that the shards of *ngiryama* are the essential basis for the nine Mijikenda groups, thus indicating a category of 'land access' conceptualisation that is fundamentally different from the two described before. Because of the shards, the link between the new land and Mijikenda identity has been physically established, providing the Mijikenda with an ontological motivation for their control over land under a Mijikenda-Giryama regime of norms and values.

This argument gains strength with the construction of *kaya* that follows upon the burial of the pot shard. The word *kaya* literally means 'home', a living place that includes physical and emotional associations of 'one's own'. The building of the *kaya*, the 'first home', thus symbolises the essence of Mijikenda-Giryama society.

In the passage above, as an addition to the ontological arguments for the present-day extent of the Mijikenda settlement, a matter-of-fact geographical description of the present-day Giryama area is given. This seems to have to do with Giryama elders' eagerness to demarcate the area of 'their' ethnic subgroup, as the areas of settlement of the other groups are not presented in similar detail. More interesting here, the newly-found land is described as 'neighbouring' rather than 'in' the country of a specific ethnic group. Thus the narrative strongly suggests that the land accessed by the Giryama was an empty place, which could be argued to be a logical and essential pre-condition for a shard of the *ngiryama* to be able to infuse the soil with Mijikenda-Giryamaness.

Concluding, the narrative of the beginnings of the Mijikenda demonstrates that control over land access in the Mijikenda perception is framed by norms and values that have been part of the history of this land from the time that the first ancestors settled there. The image of the *ngiryama* being buried in the land on which the Mijikenda finally settle, physically underscores the ontological connection between the Mijikenda people and *kaya* land. In fact, the narrative suggests that this connection extends beyond the boundaries of *kaya*, indicating a geographical area that coincides with the present-day Giryama area of settlement. Implic-

[13] Only the matrilocal Duruma refused to build a *kaya* (home) according to Mijikenda history.

itly, therefore, this land is also under the symbolic power of *ngiryama* and by extension under the authority of *kaya* elders. However, this argument needs further substantiation. The following passage from the life-story of the late *kaya* elder, Simba Wanje wa Kagujo, sheds some more light on the relationship between *kaya Giryama*, land outside its boundaries and the authority of *kaya* elders.

B. *A kaya Elder Statement on 'Keeping this Land Safe'*

The following passage has been selected from a much longer story which Simba Wanje wa Kagujo told a local audience of approx. 20 people, the NMK official Jimbi Katana and me in the year 2000. The story highlights some personal and political events that happened during Simba Wanje's adult life. The passage below recollects an earlier meeting with Jimbi Katana, to whom Simba Wanje addresses these words:

> When you came the other day, you said: "People are going completely crazy. It is better we seek the clouds, so that the land will be quiet (at peace)." You had followed the footsteps of our elders. (...) Because he who brings rain is fighting for the land. (...) Now if Jimbi had not been here, we would already have big problems. But when Jimbi came here, he said: "The land is destroyed. The children will be more and more like that [i.e. thiefs]." Jimbi gave his money, it went there where there is rain. (translation mine)

Framing the NMK official's actions within traditional *kaya* elders' discourse and thus showing Jimbi Katana's ability to change Mijikenda society for the better, Simba Wanje at the same time makes a fundamental statement on the relations between *kaya*, land and the Mijikenda. Unraveling the seemingly disconnected remarks and their implied references, we can gain a first insight into the general meaning dimensions of this statement.

Simba Wanje's main argument is that the communities in the area were rapidly losing Giryama norms and values by the time Jimbi Katana first came ("people were going crazy"). It appears that Katana's suggestion to seek clouds that can produce rain is a meaningful reaction within the Mijikenda framework. In the statement that Simba quotes as being expressed by Katana, a link is established between the vitality of the Mijikenda value system and the vitality of the soil. Simba argues that a person, such as Jimbi Katana—who operates within the tradition of the elders (i.e. the *kaya* elders)—can revitalize both the soil and the moral soundness of people living on that land.

What had actually happened during his earlier visit at Simba Wanje's compound, the NMK official told me, was that he had given the *kaya* elders money, which they had used to send someone to find herbs in Tanzania for a rain-making ritual in *kaya Giryama*. This addition to Simba Wanje's narrative highlights the pivotal role that *kaya* has in keeping Mijikenda society and the land on which they live 'at peace' (a term used by Simba Wanje in the passage above). Also implied is *kaya* elders' evaluation of moral degradation as an existential threat to Mijikenda society. The conflation of drought in the land and moral degradation implicit in Simba Wanje's argument is illustrative of the existential repercussions attributed to moral degradation. The connection is mediated by the ancestor spirits. Although not expressed in the passage above, drought and other social disasters, such as disease, are attributed by *kaya* elders to the anger of the ancestor spirits, who are considered the eternal judges of the moral soundness of the living (Parkin 1991).

Therefore, we may conclude that adherence to Mijikenda norms and values is an essential pre-condition for living a good life. Conversely, if morality is low, *kaya* and *kaya* elders are indispensable tools in restoring the well-being of the land, in terms of soil and people. In view of the social disasters that come with wide-spread moral degradation, it is not surprising that *kaya* is considered an essential resource for the Mijikenda's continued existence. As Simba Wanje expresses it in his life story: "Even here, in our homesteads, it is truly this *kaya* which is our food".

From this conclusion follows another relating to Mijikenda perceptions of *kaya* and the land that belongs with it. If Mijikenda norms and values can only be vital in a context where land is infused with Mijikenda identity and its adherent value system, the two must be essentially connected. In fact, this observation is not only continuous with the mediating function of *kaya* in restoring the vitality of the land (soil and people), it is also consistent with the Mijikenda metaphoric rendering of the beginning of Mijikenda land and society in the narrative of the beginnings of the Mijikenda. The impregnation of the soil with Mijikenda identity as a result of burying *ngiryama* (witness) in its centre vividly illustrates the same essential intertwining of land and culture. This implies that not only *kayas* but the entire geographical area in which Mijikenda have traditionally lived is infused with Mijikenda identity. The practical implications of this argument are that *kaya* cannot exist without Mijikenda living on the land near it, nor can land outside it be productive without a *kaya* that is intrinsically connected with Mijikenda society.

C. *Statements on Access to Land in the Two Mijikenda Narratives*
Having argued that the two narratives are a complex but continuous statement on Mijikenda perceptions of the ontological dimensions of *kaya* land, we can draw some general conclusions on Mijikenda narrative statements relating to the thematic focus of this analysis, i.e. *which* land can be accessed, *by whom* is access granted and *to whom, how* and *when.*

While the first narrative specifically highlights *kaya* as a living place of the Mijikenda, we could argue in the light of the analysis of the *kaya* elder's narrative that *kaya* is the ultimate resource for Mijikenda continued access to land outside it. Thus, land outside *kaya* is granted access to those whose ancestors buried *ngiryama* in *kaya. Kaya* elders are indispensable for maintaining access for the Mijikenda, not only physically by controlling access to *kaya* but also spiritually by mediating between the ancestor spirits and the living in *kaya* when relations have been disturbed. As a result, they are the authorities that control access not only to *kayas* but to all (Mijikenda) land. *Kaya* elders can give access to those whose ancestors buried *ngiryama,* because this enables them to tap into the vitality of the land. On the grounds of the narrative also visitors, who observe the Mijikenda terms of visitorship, can be given (temporary) access to the land.

II. *National Museums of Kenya and World Heritage Committee Statements on 'Keeping this Land Safe'*

The official documents that were used in the nomination process and the inscription of the ten Mijikenda *kayas* are explored below for their particular perspectives on access to land. A major part of the texts concerns valuations of the historical and ontological dimensions of *kayas.* This section, however, explores NMK and WHC manifestations of the thematic focus of *who* controls access to *which* land, *who* can access land, *why* and *when* in the context of the ten Mijikenda *kayas.* As was argued before, both stakeholders use 'authenticity' and 'integrity' of the nominated object as essential preliminaries for inscription on the World Heritage list. Thus, their perceptions of the different dimensions of access to land are guided by these normative evaluations.[14]

---

[14] The concepts 'authenticity' and 'integrity' are used in UNESCO's 'Operational Guidelines' etc. (2011) without being explicitly defined. A multiplicity of interpretations of the two terms is the result cf. Martin and Piatti (2009, 27ff). NMK's distinction between the two is that 'authenticity' refers to *kaya* practices, 'integrity' to physical aspects of a *kaya* (NMK 2008).

A. *National Museums of Kenya*
The nomination dossier (NMK 2008) prepared by the National Museums of Kenya in cooperation with *Institut de Recherche pour le Développement* (IRD 2011), cites different reasons why the authenticity and integrity of Mijikenda *kayas* are under major threat. The document argues that local infringements on their integrity in the form of cultivation practices and logging activities are a result of widespread poverty in the area and a "gradual decline in knowledge and respect for traditional values" (NMK 2008, 77). Cited major non-local hazards are foreign and domestic large-scale commercial developments in the form of mining operations and tourism related industries (p. 76).

In the nomination dossier, present and projected measures of protection against similar incursions on *kaya* land are indicated. The NMK states that the status of a *kaya* as a national monument or a forest reserve "has the effect of backing up the protective rules and measures of the *kaya* elders with the legal recognition and protection afforded by the Museums and Heritage law or the forest law" (NMK 2008, 79). With respect to the physical security of *kaya* sites, one of the projected NMK plans is "clearly defining the *kaya* forest site boundaries, using visible and culturally recognized methods" (NMK 2008: Annex 5, 10). Formulating its goals with a keen eye to locally salient definitions of the circumference of a *kaya* and to Mijikenda perceptions of authentic practices in them, NMK presents *kaya* as a place with boundaries. *Kaya* elders and the local communities are considered the rightful overall authority over access to *kaya* land: "They [i.e. the local people] are the true owners and NMK and other agencies are merely facilitators and guarantors" (NMK 2008: Annex 5, 15). Therefore consultations with *kaya* elders and communities are considered essential "...in all activities concerning site cultural and natural conservation of the Kaya forests" (15). While NMK qualifies its own contribution to 'keeping safe' *kayas* as "the foremost authority in presentation and interpretation and well placed to communicate this precious heritage to a national and foreign audience" (9), its activities fall under the governance of the local communities, which have, as NMK argues, "the right...to protect the sanctity of their Kayas (13)". In sum, NMK activities respect Mijikenda perceptions of *kaya* as a resource, of the authorities who grant access to it and the communities who access it. However, there is no sign that NMK makes an intrinsic connection between *kaya* and the land that is outside it. Thus, the authority of *kaya* elders is implicitly constrained to the physical area of the ten *kayas*.

B. *World Heritage Committee*

In the list of recommendations included in the World Heritage Committee's inscription decision, WHC's concern about the reality and the nature of the threats indicated by NMK to *kayas'* integrity and authenticity is translated in a clear line of action. WHC requests the State Party (i.e. National Museums of Kenya) to "identify the settings of the Kayas and put in place Buffer Zones with protection from major developmental threats, particularly mining extraction and building construction, and other appropriate measures to protect the wider settings" (UNESCO 2008, 191).[15]

The term 'buffer zone' is used in UNESCO's Operational Guidelines to indicate "an area surrounding the nominated property ... to give an added layer of protection to the property" (UNESCO 2011, 26). Thus by adding a buffer zone, WHC connects a demarcated zone of a different status to the inscribed zone. Generally considered to entail potential problems in its application (Martin and Piatti 2009, 23 ff), in the case of *kayas* the extra zone of protection could imply that large-scale developments, such as mining, could take place on the edges of these buffer zones. Another possible implication of implementing a buffer zone is that three formally and conceptually bounded areas are introduced, the inscribed zone under the authority of *kaya* elders, the buffer zone under the authority of NMK, and the area that lies beyond the buffer zone under (local) government authority. This situation could easily cause friction among the agencies in charge over the three types of land. Moreover, the clear conceptual break between the inscribed zone and the buffer zone could discourage interaction between *kaya* and Mijikenda people. In view of these possible implications, it may not be coincidental that although the concept of 'buffer zone' is mentioned in NMK's nomination dossier, it is not adopted as a protective measure (NMK 2008, 9, 78). In fact, NMK cursorily refers to "customary laws/taboos and practices regulating the communal lands immediately outside the forest" (9). Whether this was a point overlooked by WHC or a reason to advise buffer zones around *kayas*, WHC's advice clearly diverges from local practices as well as from the state party's statement on the immediate zone around *kayas*.

---

15 WHC's decision to turn down the application for inscription of *Kaya Kinondo* on the grounds of being affected by logging and sand extraction activities bears evidence of this concern as well as of the reality of commercial threats to *kaya* land.

With respect to who has control over access to *kayas*, WHC appears to coincide with NMK statements on future management. In its list of recommendations it advises the State Party (i.e. NMK) "to enter into agreements with Kaya Elders to establish them as the guardians of the Kayas" (UNESCO 2008, 191). Here WHC demonstrates that it intends to conform with the Mijikenda framework of governance relating to *kayas*. No mention is made of the local communities as 'true owners of *kayas*', a phrase used in the NMK nomination dossier (see above).

In sum, the WHC decision and the recommendations included in it suggest that authenticity and integrity demand that *kaya* is a clearly demarcated place under control of *kaya* elders. Although mention is made in the WHC decision of *kayas* as 'focal points for Mijikenda religious beliefs and practices' and a 'defining characteristic of Mijikenda identity', no explicit reference is made to the status of local people in the context of access to *kayas* (World Heritage Committee 2008, 190).

Conclusion

The above discussion has explored stakeholder conceptualisations of 'keeping this land safe' in the context of ten Mijikenda *kayas*, which became World Heritage in 2008. It was set against the wider background of high pressure on Kenya's coastal land as a result of large-scale agricultural, tourism and mining activities in the area, to throw into greater relief the efforts of Mijikenda leadership in partnership with NMK to protect Mijikenda sacred places against destruction. With a thematic focus on *who* has access to *which* land, *who* grants access, *when* and *how*, it was shown that stakeholder perceptions diverge significantly on the size of land that comes in for being kept safe and what 'keeping safe' entails. The narrowest interpretation of the size of land can be found with WHC. Emphatically stating that *kaya* forests should be mapped and buffer zones put into place, WHC expects to be able to preserve Mijikenda *kaya* practices as well as the biodiversity of the *kayas* by drawing clear boundaries around them. Considering WHC's implicit creation of three types of areas with three different protective regimes and three different authorities managing them, it may be concluded that WHC's conceptualisation of 'keeping this land safe' is a far cry from Mijikenda conceptualisations and practices. Rather than linking ten out of the eleven prominent *kayas* to Mijikenda communities at large, WHC has secluded *kaya* forests from the outside world and *kaya* elders as their guardians with them. Although

NMK, the Kenyan State party that is expected to implement WHC directives, takes a view on demarcating the boundaries of *kayas* that is more in line with Mijikenda traditional practices of keeping the *kayas* safe, it does not understand *kayas* to be an intrinsic part of a wider geographical area. Thus, WHC and NMK conceptualisations of *kayas* diverge from Mijikenda understandings of the inscribed *kayas* as intrinsically connected with the land on which Mijikenda have lived since a distant past. Consequently, Simba Wanje's statement on the role of *kaya* elders as guardians of the vitality of Mijikenda land does not resound in the discourses of the other two stakeholders.

All this implies that Mijikenda discourse on 'land' as including *kaya* as well as land around it is excluded from the WHC framework, and that the inscription of ten Mijikenda *kayas* on the World Heritage list may lead to estrangement between the stakeholders and withdrawal of *kayas* from the World Heritage list. Alternatively, it may cause estrangement between *kaya* elders and Mijikenda communities if *kaya* elders continue to support the inscription of the ten *kayas* and its practical implications. Mijikenda people, and particularly women and youths, could be seen to entertain already relationships with *kayas* that indicate a gradual moving away from the cultural heritage that *kayas* are expressive of. A more distinct separation between *kaya* and *kaya* elders from the outside world will not be beneficial to enhancing the bond between ordinary Mijikenda and their *kayas*.

Considering these observations within the broader context of domestic and foreign large-scale land acquisitions in Kenya's coastal region, it becomes clear that the World Heritage framework does not offer Mijikenda a viable instrument to 'keep this land safe'. Moreover, although it was argued that the eleven nominated *kayas* constitute the core of Mijikenda identity, separating ten listed *kayas* from the other approx. 47–60 *kayas* through a formal framework, could have negative repercussions on the status and continued existence of these others. With the current heightened interest of the State in exploiting large tracts of coastal land for agricultural and mining projects—the present mining activities near *kaya Kinondo* are an example—this does not seem an unlikely development. Thus, the alliance with the World Heritage committee has probably not brought the Mijikenda *kaya* elders nor the Mijikenda communities what they had hoped for.

Considering the World Heritage nomination process from the local perspective, the discussion has demonstrated that local discourse on *kayas* has been a major mechanism in mobilising an alliance that is viewed by the alliance partners as empowering local sovereignty. Whether the implicit restrictions placed on local practices will be sustainable within the World Heritage framework or whether they will force the Mijikenda to break away from their allies and find more suitable ones remains to be seen. Viewed in this light, the inscription of ten Mijikenda *kayas* on the World Heritage list may be qualified as one of several strategies of local actors to boost local land 'ownership' discourse. In fact, Goldsmith's remark on the Mombasa Republican Council' s dealings makes it clear that the *kaya* elders' alliance with the World Heritage Committee is expressive of a much more general trend, where local actors join forces with supra-national organisations to "reclaim degrees of sovereignty from below" (Goldsmith 2011: 5).

Meanwhile, the Mijikenda *kaya* elders seem to capitalise on the increase of political prestige that the WHC alliance has brought them in Kenya's public domain.[16]

Bibliography

Anon. 2002. *Kimidzichenda*. Published by the Department of Adult Education: Nairobi.

——. 2010. *Laws of Kenya: The Constitution of Kenya, 2010*. http://www.kenyaembassy.com/pdfs/The%20Constitution%20of%20Kenya.pdf (accessed November 2012).

Beja, Patrick. 2008. "Mission that compelled US envoy to go barefoot." *The Standard*, September 24.

——. 2012. "Coast Land Problem a Disaster in Waiting." *The Standard*, October 2.

Brantley, Cynthia. 1981. *The Giriama and Colonial Resistance in Kenya, 1900–1920*. Berkeley: University of California Press.

FIAN. 2010. Land Grabbing in Kenya and Mozambique: A Report on Two Research Missions—and a Human Rights Analysis of Land Grabbing. http://www.fian.org/resources/documents/others/land-grabbing-in-kenya-and-mozambique/pdf (accessed July 2012).

Gemson, Sara-Christine and Sara Mojtehedzadeh. 2012. "Trouble Simmering In Tana over 'Annexed Land'." *Daily Nation*, December 3.

Githitho, Anthony A. n.d. The Sacred Mijikenda Kaya Forests of Coastal Kenya and Biodiversity Conservation. Presentations of Case-Studies of Africa and Latin America. http://sacredland.org/PDFs/Mijikenda_Kaya.pdf.

Goldsmith, Paul. 2011. The Mombasa Republican Council: Conflict Assessment: Threats and Opportunities for Engagement. http://www.kecosce.org/downloads/MRC_Conflict_Assessment_Threats_and_Opportunities_for_Engagement.pdf (accessed Nov 2012).

Government of Kenya. 2008. Vision 2030. http://www.vision2030.go.ke (accessed November 2012).

Human Rights Watch. 2002. Playing with Fire: Weapons Proliferation, Political Violence and Human Rights in Kenya. http://www.hrw.org/reports/2002/kenya (accessed Nov 2012).

[16] Nipashe 7.00 pm news on 11 November 2012 showed *kaya* elders talking with Charity Ngilu, a senior politician, on land issues in the coastal region.

Institut de Recherche pour le Développement. 2011. Kenya Sacred Sites listed by UNESCO. http://en.ird.fr/the-media-library/videos-on-line-canal-ird/kenya-sacred-sites-listed-by-unesco (accessed July 2012).

Martin, Oliver and Giovanna Piatti eds. 2009. World heritage and Buffer Zones: International Expert Meeting on World Heritage and Buffer Zones. Davos, Switzerland, 11–14 March 2008 http://whc.unesco.org/en/series/25/ (accessed July 2012).

Mazrui, Alamin M. ca. 1997. *Kayas of Deprivation, Kayas of Blood: Violence, Ethnicity and the State in Coastal Kenya.* Nairobi: Kenya Human Rights Commission.

McIntosh, Janet. 2009a. *The Edge of Islam: Power, Personhood and Ethnoreligious Boundaries on the Kenya Coast.* Durham: Duke University Press.

——. 2009b. Elders and 'Frauds': Commodified Expertise and Politicized Authenticity among Mijikenda. Africa 79 (1): 35–51.

Mitchell, Nora and Mechtild Rössler and Pierre-Marie Tricaud. 2009. World Heritage Cultural Landscapes: A Handbook for Conservation and Management. http://whc.unesco.org/documents/publi_wh_papers_26_en.pdf.

National Museums of Kenya. 2008. Nomination Dossier for the Inscription on the World Heritage List: the Sacred Mijikenda Kaya Forests (Kenya) http://whc.unesco.org/uploads/nominations/1231rev.pdf (accessed August 2012).

O'Brien, Erin. 2011. Irregular and illegal land acquisition by Kenya's elites: Trends, processes, and impacts of Kenya's land-grabbing phenomenon. http://www.landcoalition.org/publications/irregular-and-illegal-landacquisition-kenya's-elites-trends-processes-and-impacts (accessed July 2012).

Parkin, David. 1991. *Sacred Void: Spatial Images of Work and Ritual among the Giryama of Kenya.* Cambridge: Cambridge University Press.

Ribot, Jesse and Nancy Lee Peluso. 2003. A Theory of Access. *Rural Sociology* 68 (2): 153–181.

Salim, A.I. 1973. *Swahili-Speaking Peoples of Kenya's Coast 1895–1965.* Nairobi: East African Publishing House.

Smalley, Rebecca and Esteve, Corbera. 2012. Large-Scale Land Deals From Inside Out: Findings from Kenya's Tana Delta. *The Journal of Peasant Studies* 39: 3–4, 1039–1075.

Southall, Roger. 2005. Ndung'u Report: Land and Graft in Kenya. *Review of African Political Economy* 103: 142–51.

Spear, Thomas T. 1978. *The Kaya Complex: A History of Mijikenda Peoples of the Kenya Coast to 1900.* Nairobi: Kenya Literature Bureau.

Standard Team. 2012. "Coast Residents Clutching at Straws." *The Standard,* October 2.

UNESCO. 2011. Operational guidelines for the Implementation of the World Heritage Convention. http://whc.unesco.org/archive/opguide11-en.pdf (accessed December 2012).

Walsh, Martin. 1992. Mijikenda Origins: A Review of the Evidence. *Transafrican Journal of History* 21: 1–18.

Willis, Justin. 2009. The King of the Mijikenda, and Other Stories about the Kaya, Heritage, Politics and Histories in Multi-Party Kenya. In *Recasting the Past: History Writing and Political Work in Modern Africa,* edited by Derek R. Peterson and Giacomo Macola, 233–250. Athens, OH: Ohio University Press.

——. 1993. *Mombasa, the Swahili and the Making of the Mijikenda.* Oxford: Clarendon Press.

World Heritage Committee. 2008. UNESCO Convention concerning the protection of the world cultural and natural heritage. 2008. "World Heritage Committee 32nd Session. Quebec City, Canada 2–10 July 2008 Decision: 32 COM 8B.50." http://whc.unesco.org/archive/2008/whc08-32com-24reve.pdf (accessed December 2012).

INDEX